EVANGELICALS AND DEMOCRACY IN AMERICA

Contents

About the Authors

Steven Brint is professor of sociology at the University of California, Riverside, director of the Colleges & Universities 2000 study, and associate dean of the College of Humanities, Arts, and Social Sciences.

Jean Reith Schroedel is dean of the School of Politics and Economics at Claremont Graduate University.

Seth Abrutyn is graduate student at the University of California, Riverside.

Wayne E. Baker is professor of management and organizations and professor of sociology at the University of Michigan. He is also faculty associate at the Institute for Social Research and holds the Jack D. Sparks Whirlpool Corporation Research Professorship.

Connie J. Boudens is professor of psychology at Trent University in Peterborough, Ontario, Canada.

Kimberly H. Conger is assistant professor in the political science department at Iowa State University.

Andrew Greeley is professor of sociology at the University of Arizona and research associate with the National Opinion Research Center (NORC) at the University of Chicago.

Peter Dobkin Hall is senior research fellow at the Hauser Center for Nonprofit Organizations at Harvard University.

Michael Hout is professor of sociology and demography at the University of California, Berkeley.

Julie Ingersoll is associate professor of religious studies at the University of North Florida.

Nathaniel Klemp is assistant professor of political science at Pepperdine University.

D. Michael Lindsay is assistant professor of sociology and associate director of the Center on Race, Religion and Urban Life at Rice University. He is also Rice Scholar at the James A. Baker III Institute for Public Policy.

Stephen Macedo is Laurance S. Rockefeller Professor of Politics at the University Center for Human Values at Princeton University.

Pippa Norris is McGuire Lecturer in Comparative Politics at the John F. Kennedy School of Government at Harvard University.

Clyde Wilcox is professor in the Government Department at Georgetown University.

Rhys H. Williams is professor and chair of sociology, and director of the McNamara Center for the Social Study of Religion, at Loyola University, Chicago.

Introduction

JEAN REITH SCHROEDEL AND STEVEN BRINT

FROM THE beginning, Americans have held disparate views on the role religion should play in public life. On the one hand, many colonial governments were established under biblical covenants, where God was called upon to witness the creation of the governing body, whose aim was to further Christianity as well as to establish the common good (Lutz 1988).[1] This vision of America as the new Israel, one with the mission to redeem, not only its own people, but perhaps also—serving as a model—the rest of humanity, is an enduring Puritan legacy.[2] On the other hand, the country's founding document, the U.S. Constitution, is secular, completely lacking in references to the Deity. And rather than establish a state church as existed in much of Europe, the First Amendment, at least according to some observers, establishes a "wall of separation between church and state"—a phrase first used by Thomas Jefferson in his famous letter to the Danbury Baptist Association. Jefferson, during his presidency, also discontinued Washington's and Adams's practice of declaring national days of prayer and fasting.

Two hundred years later, Americans remain divided over whether religious belief and practices should be publicly embraced or a private matter best left to the individual conscience. People often hold internally inconsistent views, welcoming the efforts of religious leaders to promote causes we support, but denouncing their actions on behalf of policies we abhor. Public opinion polls also find that more than two-thirds of respondents characterize the United States as a Christian nation but only one-third believe that the Bible rather than the will of the American people should determine the country's law (Pew Research Center 2006, 5). Taken together, these survey results suggest that though Americans revere the nation's Christian heritage, most are not willing to allow any particular biblical "truth" to override the collective wisdom of the American people. Yet that one of every three Americans would favor biblically based law cannot be dismissed as irrelevant.

1

There is an inherent tension between the idea that the United States is a Christian nation and a pluralist democracy that includes people of all faiths, as well as those with no religious beliefs. Finding a balance between these two can be challenging. Consider, for example, the ways that Pastor Rick Warren's invocation at the Barack Obama's inauguration tried to satisfy these competing imperatives. First, simply by giving the invocation, Warren reaffirmed the nation's religious heritage. There is no intrinsic reason why a government transition needs to be marked by prayer, yet it has always been done. This particular invocation, however, broke new ground. In five short minutes, Warren managed to evoke all three of the world's great monotheistic religions, starting with the words, "Hear, O Israel, the Lord is our God, the Lord is One" from Jewish prayer and then moving on to praise God as the "compassionate and merciful," language drawn from the Koran and regularly recited during Muslim prayers. Yet ultimately, by praying Jesus's name and concluding with the Lord's Prayer, Warren left himself open to the criticism that the invocation was too Christian.

The title to this volume, *Evangelicals and Democracy in America: Religion and Politics*, the second of the series, was chosen because evangelicals have been at the forefront of American democracy. In fact, some would argue that our democratic freedoms, as enshrined in the nation's founding documents, are a reflection of evangelical Christianity's assertion of inviolable individual rights. But is it possible for a Christian nation to maintain a democratic public sphere that encourages dialogue and respect across diverse religious and political boundaries? These chapters focus on political topics: religious conservatives and partisan politics, the mobilizing rhetoric of evangelicals, and the cycles and evolution of the evangelical movement. What are the causes and consequences of their political mobilization? In what ways have evangelicals strengthened pluralist democracy in the United States? What challenges, if any, do they pose to democratic practices in a diverse polity?

The companion first volume, *Evangelicals and Democracy in America: Religion and Society*, examines the sources of evangelicals' growing prominence and activism in American society, the relations between evangelicals and other groups in American society, and the influence of evangelicals on America's social institutions. Over the past thirty years, evangelicals have entered the halls of power and nearly every sphere of American life has been touched by their mobilization. What has their impact been on public education? How has the media responded to pressures to clean up the content of their programs? These are just a few of the questions explored in volume 1.

We believe that there are compelling reasons to focus on evangelicals.[3] First, American history and development cannot be understood separately from the influence of evangelical Protestantism. Not only have their beliefs, most notably the idea that the United States has a covenant with God, shaped the nation's identity, evangelicals have also been at the forefront of nearly all movements for social change, both on the Left and on the Right. We argue that the Christian Right is simply the most recent manifestation of the evangelical impulse for social change.

Second, the Christian Right's emergence as a major political force within the Republican Party has fundamentally altered the political landscape. Not only have large numbers of white evangelicals shifted their political allegiance from the Democratic Party to the Republican Party, many have also become party activists. That a similar movement has not occurred among doctrinally conservative members of the historically African American churches is a reminder of the continuing salience of race in the American polity. As Clyde Wilcox notes in the concluding chapter of this volume, it would have been inconceivable three decades ago for major party presidential candidates to be denouncing evolution in a primary debate.[4] Yet today they all feel they must clearly establish their religious bona fides.

Third, the Christian Right has transformed the nation's political discourse, particularly with respect to moral values. They have been very successful in defining a particular group of traditional and pro-family values as synonymous with moral values more generally and in bringing a set of specific policy issues to the forefront while ignoring others. Moreover, how and why has Christian identity come to be associated with supporting a narrow set of issues? Why has the phrase *moral values* come to conjure up images of protesters outside abortion clinics and opponents of gay marriage rather than of taking steps to decrease one's carbon footprint? Why does poverty, which is mentioned more than 2,000 times in the Bible, have less political salience among evangelicals than homosexuality, which is mentioned only a couple times?

Yet because only about one in four Americans identify as evangelicals, evangelicals need to work cooperatively with like-minded groups in the pursuing their political aims. John Green uses the term *traditionalist alliance* to describe this broader coalition of religious traditionalists (see volume 1, chapter 4). Although the core of the traditionalist alliance is evangelical, most notably Baptist, it also encompasses other conservative Protestant denominations—Missouri and Wisconsin Synod Lutherans, Presbyterian Churches of America, holiness churches, and Pentecostals—as well as traditionalist elements within mainline Protestant denominations, conservative Catholics, Mormons, and conservative Jews. In this volume, we consider the role of evangelicals in building the traditionalist alliance as well as the difficulties inherent in maintaining such a diverse political coalition. We also consider their relations with groups outside this alliance.

The Privileged Position of Evangelical
Protestants amidst Religious Diversity

Any celebration of a common Christian heritage must be juxtaposed against the religious diversity that has characterized the nation since its inception. There are several early and interrelated causes for the diversity. First, the country was settled by people with different religious backgrounds. Moreover, the dispersal of colonial settlements across a large geographical area provided opportunities for disparate patterns of belief to become established. Given this history, it is not surprising that the Founding Fathers enshrined religious liberty in the First Amendment to the Constitution, thereby creating the conditions for religious diversity to flourish in the long term.

Geographical patterns of religious belief in colonial America were clear. Although the Dutch established Reform congregations and the Swedes established Lutheran congregations in their colonies, the predominant religious influences were English, with the biggest split between the Puritans in New England and Anglicans in the South. The New England Calvinists tended to view themselves as New Hebrews with a mission to create a new Zion. At least in part because of their ties with the Church of England, the Anglicans developed a less distinctly American character, which reduced their impact after the Revolutionary War. The mid-Atlantic region was primarily Calvinist, of which the less strict Presbyterians were the most numerous. Baptists, Mennonites, and even Quakers were also accepted in the region. The Catholic Church established early roots in colonial America as well.

By the early eighteenth century, the establishment churches had become staid and overly formal, leaving the populace largely disconnected from their faith. The Great Awakenings of the 1720s through the 1740s, a series of jeremiad-oriented revivals, were populist expressions of a pent-up desire to regain the religious purity and fervor of the early settlers (Morone 2003, 40).[5] End Time speculation was rampant, with many revivalist ministers preaching that the Millennium foretold by John in Revelations was approaching and that the Kingdom of God was eminent (Boyer 1992, 70). As the colonists moved closer toward revolution and separation from England, revivalist preachers, such as Jonathan Edwards, speculated that America might become the center of Christ's kingdom during his thousand-year rule (Boyer 1992, 72).[6]

The Great Awakenings transformed the religious landscape, giving rise to new denominations, most notably Methodists, and greatly increasing the influence of Baptists, and lessening that of the Congregationalists, the old establishment denomination in New England. The rapidly growing sects were clearly evangelical with salvation based on one's personal relationship with God. For example, in 1740 there were only three Baptist congregations in Connecticut and eleven in Massa-chusetts, but thirty years later thirty-six in the former and thirty in the latter, and thirty years later still, by the turn into the nineteenth century, 312 across all of New England (Morone 2003, 110).

The Second Great Awakening, another series of revivals in the late eighteenth and early nineteenth centuries, accelerated the trend toward diversity and made evangelicals the dominant force in the religious landscape.[7] By 1800, that landscape had become even more fragmented, with the Baptists, Congregationalists, Methodists, Lutherans, Presbyte-rians, and Episcopalians comprising the largest denominations. It was during this period that the Mormon prophet, Joseph Smith, received his revelations from the angel Moroni in the infamous burned-over district of western New York.[8] Smaller denominations included German Re-formed, Dutch Reformed, Quaker, Moravian, and Mennonite, as well as Roman Catholic churches (Handy 1984, 25).

As evident from this accounting, the dominant ethos was Protestant. Moreover, the two great periods of revivalism gave the nation a strongly evangelical flavor. The historian Mark Noll estimated that evangelical Protestant denominations accounted for 85 percent of all U.S. churches in 1860 (2002, 170). Although the evangelical spirit as manifested in the First and Second Great Awakenings was a direct offshoot of New En-gland Puritanism, it contradicted basic Calvinist doctrines. Arminian-ism, the belief that salvation is made possible by Christ's suffering and salvation is available to all who accept Jesus as their personal savior, supplanted the Calvinist belief in predestination.

According to Robert Handy, the religious mainstream in the nine-teenth century was comprised of large and medium-sized evangelical Protestant denominations[9] and an evangelical wing of Episcopalians; nearly all of whom shared the dream that "some day the civilization of the country would be fully Christian" (1984, ix–x). Unlike their counter-parts today, most Protestants then were postmillennialists, who believed that the Second Coming would only occur after society was fully Chris-tianized.[10] Much of the popular support in antebellum America for Man-ifest Destiny, the belief that the United States destined to stretch from the Atlantic Ocean to the Pacific Ocean, was derived from evangelicals, who believed it would help spread the gospel throughout the world. Again, America was to serve as a "light of the world," a redeemer nation.[11]

During the Civil War, both sides believed they were fighting for a Christian America. Northern clergy stressed the evils of slavery and the need for national redemption,[12] and Southern ministers held that slav-ery was in keeping with God's plan for humanity and benefited both master and slave. Although few former Confederates recanted their be-liefs about slavery, they did accept their loss on the battlefield as being divinely mandated.[13] In the postbellum era, white Northerners and white Southerners both returned to the mission of creating a Christian civilization, both domestically and globally. Presbyterians, Lutherans, Episcopalians, Baptists, and Methodists were deeply engaged in missionary work by the end of the century (see Ammerman, volume 1, chapter 2).

During the early part of the twentieth century, nearly all evangelical denominations underwent fundamentalist-modernist conflicts (Marsden 1980). The modernists tried to reconcile biblical truths with scientific developments, such as evolution, and fundamentalists emphasized a literal reading of the Bible. Following the 1925 Scopes trial, many theologically conservative evangelicals largely withdrew from the public sphere,[14] but others tried to find a way to reach an accommodation with modern society. The former became identified as fundamentalists, and the latter as neo-evangelicals. All of these splits, as well as a pervasive sense that traditional religious beliefs and practices could not address the changing needs of modern society, led some to argue that the era of Protestant hegemony ended during the 1930s, though the nation's elite was still overwhelming Protestant (Handy 1984).[15] What followed was an era during which the cultural forms of Protestant Christianity continued to be invoked, but increasingly the United States was increasingly characterized by the tripart framing of Protestant, Catholic, and Jew.

During the 1960s and 1970s, all forms of evangelical Protestantism experienced an upsurge in membership. The political and cultural turmoil of the period left many people searching for answers that the mainline churches seemed unable to provide. Evangelical churches, with their emphasis on biblical inerrancy and the importance of personal morality, provided many with the clear guidance they sought. During this period, the distinctions between fundamentalists and neo-evangelicals became less important. Many also were attracted to the more enthusiastic and experiential forms of religious expression characteristic of Pentecostalism and charismatic worship, which resulted in their becoming a bigger part of the evangelical Protestant mix (Watson 1999, 14–16).

To a large extent, the liberal-conservative divide that occurred 100 years ago continues to shape contemporary divisions among Protestants. Although some denominations, such as Southern Baptists and Assemblies of God, are overwhelmingly conservative, many mainline denominations also have conservative elements, albeit in smaller numbers. One of the major differences, which has become increasingly important, is that many liberal Protestants have begun to question whether salvation requires the acceptance of Jesus Christ as one's personal savior. In other words, can a Hindu or a Muslim lead a godly life? Moreover, what role, if any, should non-Christians occupy in American public life? This shift moves liberal Protestants even further away from their more conservative evangelical brethren.

The level of religious diversity in the United States skyrocketed after the 1965 Immigration and Nationalization Act eliminated the European bias in the immigration system, resulting in "radical pluralism as the cardinal mark of religion in America" (Cherry 1998, 8).[16] The religious map of the United States, which used to encompass three variants (Protestant, Catholic, and Jew), now is comprised of eight: Catholics, Jews, other world religions,[17] mainline Protestants, African American churches, white conservative Protestants, homegrown American religions and finally, the nones, who do not "find any religious tradition to their liking" (see volume 1, chapter 2). Although the far fewer Americans identify themselves as nonreligious, the most recent Pew survey found that the percentage of respondents indicating no religious affiliation (16 percent) is significantly higher than it was a few decades earlier (2008, 19). Probably no image conveys the shift in the nation's public religious landscape as much as the image of Siraj Wahaj, a Muslim imam, giving the opening prayer in the U.S. House of Representatives on June 25, 1991 (Eck 2001, 31).[18]

Evangelicals as an Embattled Group

A few months after Imam Wahaj's prayer, the tension between an explicitly Christian national identity and pluralism erupted at a meeting of the Republican Governors Association, when Mississippi Governor Kirk Fordice stated unequivocally, "the United States is a Christian nation." When rebuked by South Carolina Governor Carroll Campbell, who said that the nation's value base comes from its Judeo-Christian heritage, Fordice reiterated his view that the United States is a Christian nation. When pressed to include Judeo as part of the nation's foundation, Fordice responded, "If I wanted to do that I would have done that" (Richard Berke, "With a Crackle, Religion Enters G.O.P. Meeting," *New York Times*, November 18, 1992). In 2004, the Texas Republican Party followed suit, adopting a convention plank that declared the "United States of America is a Christian nation" (Cathy Young, "GOP's 'Christian Nation,'" *Boston Globe*, July 12, 2004) and in 2006 a Missouri House Committee approved a "Christian nation" resolution as well (Bennet Kelley, "The Christian Nation Movement and the Alabama Ban," *Huffington Post*, April 18, 2006). In the 2008 presidential campaign, John McCain reignited the controversy by stating that "the Constitution established the United States of America as a Christian nation," but later issued a clarification stating that it was founded on "Judeo-Christian values."[19]

The acrimonious exchanges over whether the United States is an explicitly Christian nation are not simply an outgrowth of the changing religious demographics, but are at least as much a reflection of evangelical Protestant concerns that they are an embattled group. Evangelicals became increasingly aware of a cultural disjuncture with the rest of society during the 1960s and early 1970s. Handy considered the early 1960s to be the point where even the "Protestant quasi-establishment" became a "thing of the past" (1984, 194). The Supreme Court's 1962 Engel v. Vitale ruling, which held that a New York State Board of Regents approved prayer could not be given in public schools because it constituted an establishment of religion, was the first of a series of court decisions that undercut traditional religious prerogatives.[20] Subsequent Supreme Court decisions, most notably Roe v. Wade, 410 U.S. 113 (1973), which legalized abortion, helped solidify evangelicals' sense of being under attack

The 1976 election of a born-again Christian, Jimmy Carter, raised hopes that the country was going to regain its moral footing. However, when "one of their own" consistently took positions diametrically opposed to those held by most evangelicals—such as abortion, school prayer, busing, gay rights, and the Equal Rights Amendment—it generated enormous anger. The proverbial straw that broke the camel's back was the Carter administration's support for an Internal Revenue Service policy that threatened to remove the tax exempt charitable status of Bob Jones University, which allowed unmarried African Americans to enroll, but refused admission to those who advocated interracial marriage or dating.[21] Ralph Reed wrote that evangelicals considered the attack on Bob Jones University to be "nothing less than a declaration of war on their schools, their churches and their children" (1996, 105; for more on the impact of Supreme Court decisions on mobilizing rank and file evangelicals to become political active in conservative political organizations and the Republican Party, see volume 1, chapter 11, and chapter 11, this volume).

The Politicization of Evangelical Discontent

In the 1960s and 1970s, evangelicals came to believe that their way of life was under direct attack and channeled their discontent into the Christian Right and through that into the Republican Party.[22] Matthew Moen described the contemporary Christian Right as going through four developmental stages (1994, 1996). During the first, from 1978 to 1984, the movement experienced tremendous growth, in terms of both the numbers of individual identifying with the movement and the creation of influential organizations, such as the Christian Voice and the Moral Majority.[23] Movement leaders forged close ties with the Republican Party during the 1980 election. President Ronald Reagan's speech to a meeting of one of these new groups, the Religious Roundtable, was heralded by Ralph Reed as the "coming out party" for religious conservatives (1996, 112).[24] The strident rhetoric that helped mobilize the evangelical base, however, alienated many other people.

In the second stage, in 1985 and 1986, the movement was forced to retrench as the direct mail donor base grew weary of the constant appeals. Nearly all groups lowered their public profile and some actually ceased operating. Although the Moral Majority did not shut down its operations until 1988, it had ceased to be a significant political force by the mid-1980s. Its harsh rhetoric made it unpopular even among its core target group, white evangelicals (Jelen 1999, 165). At this juncture, many observers predicted that the movement would wither away.

In the third stage, from 1987 to 1995, the movement got a new burst of energy with Pat Robertson's 1988 presidential campaign, which mobilized many Pentecostals. The primary characteristic of the period, however, was its emphasis on institution building. The leadership reassessed their sources of funding, established links with other religiously conservative elements (conservative Catholics, Mormons, and conservative Jews), embraced rights-based rhetoric rather than explicitly Christian jeremiads, and intensified their grassroots political activism. The Christian Coalition, established in 1989, is known for its very sophisticated get-out-the-vote operation. Its voting guides have been distributed to millions of churchgoers.[25]

Beginning in 1995, the movement entered into fourth stage of working even more closely with the Republican Party, which had built of a well-organized network of supporters affiliated with evangelical churches. These efforts paid off in 2000 and 2004, when white evangelicals gave Bush 68 percent and 78 percent of their votes. In the 2004 election, evangelical Christians comprised more than one-third of all Bush votes (Pew Research Center 2004). Leaders have become more willing to compromise on social issues and emphasize returning political authority to the states, where they expect to have a greater ability to enact their reform agenda.

Challenge for a Democratic Polity

Arguably, there has never been another point in American history at which the level of interest in the interplay between religion and politics has been greater than it is today. The growth of the Christian Right over the past thirty years has reignited academic interest in the interplay between religion and democratic politics. Although the extremist rhetoric of some Christian Right figures generates tremendous media attention, these comments cannot be taken as representing the views of evangelicals as a group. According to a recent public opinion poll, only 11 percent of respondents identify with the "religious right political movement," and even more significant, only one in five self-identified white evangelicals consider themselves part of it (Pew Research Center 2006, 10).

Rather than viewing the high level of religiosity as likely to dissipate as the country follows the modernization path forged by European countries, scholars have come to realize that secularization is not necessarily a concomitant of the modernization process.[26] According to the most recent Pew survey, 56 percent of Americans say that religion is very important in their lives, and another 26 percent indicate that it is at least somewhat important (Pew Forum on Religion & Public Life 2008, 22). But it is also worth noting that the number of Americans identifying as secular has increased, though their proportion of the population remains quite small. Interestingly, this may become more significant in the future in that younger Americans are more likely to indicate they are not affiliated with any religious tradition (2008, 29).

The increasing significance of religious conservatives in the Republican Party is unprecedented in the American context. Unlike European countries, which have long had political parties whose social base is a particular religion, the major parties in the United States have been an aggregation of diverse social interests. Although definitely an exaggeration, the heightened role of the Christian Right led Representative Christopher Shays (R-CT) to claim that "this Republican Party of Lincoln has become a party of theocracy" (Adam Nagourney, "G.O.P. Right is Splintered on Schiavo Intervention," *New York Times*, March 23, 2005).

Yet it is not simply Republicans who are trying to mobilize evangelicals. The Democratic Party, which Nixon labeled the party of acid, amnesty, and abortion, has sought to overcome its so-called God gap by reaching out to evangelicals. The extent of the party problem was evident in a recent survey (Pew Research Center 2006), which showed that only 26 percent of respondents believed that the Democratic Party is friendly to religion. From the beginning of the 2008 presidential campaign, Democrats aggressively courted the evangelical electorate. Throughout the primary, Hillary Clinton spoke about the importance of prayer in her life. In both the primary season and then during the general election, Obama spoke about his faith a forum organized by Rick Warren at his Saddleback Church in Orange County, California. Campaign operatives handed out a twelve-page booklet chronicling Obama's "Christian journey" to the 2,200 people attending the event (Shailagh Murray and Perry Bacon Jr., "Key Constituency is at Play at Candidates' Faith Forum," *New York Times*, August 17, 2008, A01).

Overview of Chapters

To develop as broad a perspective as possible on these topics, we assembled a group of leading scholars from different academic disciplines. As might be expected in a volume written by scholars trained in sociology, political science, religion, psychology, and history, the methods range from aggregate data analysis to archival research to close textual analysis. The various analytical lenses provide insights and raise questions that might be overlooked in an edited volume that reflects the issues and approaches predominate in a single discipline. As is evident in what follows, the authors do not always agree, but we think that is part of what makes this volume an intriguing exercise.

This volume is divided into three sections. Part I covers Christian conservatives and partisan politics, part II is titled Discourses of Mobilization and Public Reason, and part III discusses the cycles and evolution of a movement. Although each section focuses on different elements that are important in terms of understanding the impact of evangelicals on democracy in the United States, there are obvious connections between the sections. For example, if one wants to understand the current position of evangelicals in the Republican Party, it is useful to not only understand voting and party identification trends covered in part I, but also the types of appeals that have been most successful, which are covered in part II, and how those appeals play out in different contexts, which is covered in part III.

The chapters in part I bring different analytical lens to bear on questions related to party identification and voting patterns. The authors focus on evangelical Protestants but recognize that they are most fruitfully understood in comparison with other groups. Because no nation exists in a vacuum, we begin with a chapter that places the United States within a comparative politics framework. Subsequent chapters consider the extent to which partisanship is a function of the interaction between religious identification and other factors, most notably race and class. They also delve into the meaning of the term *values*, a concept that has gained prominence in recent elections.

In chapter 1, Pippa Norris reconsiders the question of American exceptionalism, not with respect to the absence of socialism, but in terms of an American religiosity gap. As noted earlier, the United States has a much higher proportion of religious believers than any other country at a comparable level of economic development. Although this appears to be prima facie evidence of American exceptionalism, Norris provides cross-national data to show that the American case is more mixed.

A key question is whether recent increases in self-identified secular Americans is an indication that the United States is simply a laggard in following the European countries. Norris suggests several possible reasons why religion has greater salience in the United States than in comparable nations.

In chapter 2, Michael Hout and Andrew Greeley use time series data to examine trends in voting and party identification. As expected, they find a trend toward Republican Party identification and voting among nearly all religious groups. Their data, however, indicate that the relationship is mediated by the continuing salience of race and a widening class cleavage among evangelicals. In other words, conservative Protestants are far from the monolithic bloc presented in many popular accounts. Hout and Greeley found no evidence that the Christian Right persuades low- and moderate-income evangelicals into voting against their economic interests.

Although the term values is regularly invoked as an explanation for particular patterns of partisanship and voting, its meaning is generally left vague. In chapter 3, Wayne Baker and Connie Boudens make a major contribution to our understanding of the term by mapping out the conceptual elements it encompasses and how the different configurations can result in systematic differences in party identification and voting. Like Hout and Greeley, Baker and Boudens find that race often trumps values in determining partisanship.

Chapter 4 explores the paradox of why white evangelical Protestants, many of whom hold moderate to liberal views on a wide range of issues, have become a key constituency of the Republican Party. Steven Brint and Seth Abrutyn argue that the explanation lies in the Republican Party's successful construction of a system of moral values politics. They treat moral values politics as an organizational and rhetorical structure that links the white evangelical social base, local social movement activists, leaders of national Christian Right organizations, and the national Republican Party. This party-movement-church electoral system highlights issues of cultural difference from secular elites and downplays areas where the white evangelical base supports positions closer to those favored by the Democratic Party. Brint and Abrutyn argue that three primary commitments—religiosity, gender role traditionalism, and moral absolutism—underlie white evangelical support for the Republican Party.

The chapters in part II focus on the mobilizing rhetoric and ideological frameworks that Christian Right leaders have used to activate their base and reach out to other members of the traditionalist alliance. Again, we begin with an historical chapter that helps provide a context for understanding contemporary events. The other two chapters in this section directly address the question of whether democracy is enhanced or threatened by this movement, and reach rather different conclusions.

In chapter 5, Rhys Williams provides an overview of how evangelicals going back to the early Calvinist settlers have divided "the social and moral world into Manichean dualisms." Not only does Williams show how this creation of sharp boundaries between us and them has been a consistent theme across time, he also argues that it is an essential element of the evangelical subculture. He shows that the primary objects of moral concern have shifted over time from Quakers to immigrant Catholics and Jews to Communists and now to atheists, agnostics, and secular elites. Immigration, international politics, and the politics of lifestyle have all played into the history of constructing these groups as moral others. Although the process is a potent way to mobilize the faithful, Williams posits that it may undercut democratic practices, because those defined as moral others are also often considered less than fully American or even un-American.

Julie Ingersoll argues in chapter 6 that Reconstructionism, a small Calvinist offshoot, has played an extremely important role in creating the underlying metaphor of the contemporary Christian Right. Reconstructionists are called that because they advocate reconstructing society to bring it into accordance with Old Testament law. Although self-identified Reconstructionists are relatively few in number, Ingersoll uses close textual analysis of core writings by Rousas John Rushdoony to argue that their themes have become an integral part of the more mainstream discourse of conservative Protestants. Ingersoll shows that Rushdoony first articulated many of the Christian Right attacks on contemporary culture, as well as the idea of the traditional family as a bulwark for cultural renewal. In this highly provocative essay, Ingersoll makes a strong argument that Reconstructionists should not simply be dismissed as a fringe group.

In chapter 7, recognizing that the Christian Right has become an "increasingly powerful voice in American democracy," Nathaniel Klemp and Stephen Macedo nonetheless argue that it largely adheres to the norms of public reason. By this they mean that the Christian Right activists and leaders attempt to appeal to a broader audience by marshalling reason and evidence that supports their position. The authors draw on a broad range of original documents as well as on interviews with Christian Right leaders and activists and their political opponents.

Klemp and Macedo find evidence that leaders rely on a two-tiered rhetorical strategy that uses one type of rhetorical argument among adherents and a very different type among the broader public. Klemp and Macedo conclude that, over time, major Christian Right leaders have come to embrace something akin to public reason, as might be expected by any group seeking to pursue its ends in a pluralist democracy.

The chapters in part III provide new ways of thinking about the development of the Christian Right as a political movement. Each conceptualizes evangelical Protestant cycles of political activism in starkly different terms. Here too we open with a historical chapter that puts contemporary developments in a broader context, leaving subsequent chapters to highlight disparate aspects of the modern Christian Right's relationships with other sectors of the population. A clear subtext in each chapter, however, is the question of whether the political mobilization of evangelicals is a boon or bane to democracy.

In chapter 8, the historian Peter Dobkin Hall traces the roots of the Christian Right's involvement in public life back to the antebellum era. He draws on archival materials to show that early nineteenth-century churches faced disestablishment from any ties to state governments and were "forced to compete for adherents in the religious marketplace" (chapter 8, this volume, 250). He argues that these fundamental facts established the parameters within which religious bodies have struggled to find successful strategies of engagement in the public sphere.

Hall analyzes the tension between sectarianism and ecumenicalism among evangelicals, focusing on three episodes of pan-Protestant mobilization: the leadership of Lyman Beecher in the 1840s, of Dwight Moody in the early 1900s, and of the neo-evangelicals of the 1980s and 1990s. Hall finds that every time evangelicals have developed a reform-oriented social movement, they have shown a propensity to fragment on the shoals of sectarianism. Although the current movement has shown more staying power, reaching out to conservative Catholics, Mormons, and Jews, Hall suggests that this incarnation also may shatter.

In chapter 9, Kimberly Conger also explores evangelical political cycles, but limits herself to the past several decades. She argues that the relationship between the Christian Right and state Republican parties can be explained in terms of cycles of conflict and accommodation, primarily driven by how important the movement is to the achievement of the party's electoral aims. The electoral imperative will make working with Christian Right activists more or less attractive to state party leaders, depending on the policy context and the makeup of internal party coalitions.

Conger draws on data from two national surveys and interviews with more than 100 party leaders, activists, commentators, and political observers. In states where the party was weak and needed the grassroots activists and funds that the movement could provide, leaders were open to integrating Christian Right activists into the organization. But in states where the party was strong, leaders were much more likely to rebuff overtures. Changes in the policy context, however, can lead to shifts in the cycle. Case studies from a cross-section of states—Arizona, Georgia, Indiana, Massachusetts, Minnesota, and Missouri—provide a feel for the actual give-and-take that occurs as state Republican parties and Christian Right activists learn to work together.

The construction of boundaries also figures prominently in Michael Lindsay's chapter 10. Lindsay argues that elastic orthodoxy—a concept he defines as the ability of evangelicals to hold firm to a set of core beliefs while being flexible enough that they can ally with people who do not share all of their convictions—is a key strength of the contemporary Christian Right. According to Lindsay, the elasticity of these boundaries allows the contemporary movement to overcome, at least for a time, the sectarianism that Hall identified as undermining previous periods of ecumenicalism, but without undermining the strength of their identity as evangelicals.

Lindsay conducted interviews with evangelical leaders from government, the media, religion, business, higher education, and the social sector. Because politics entails building relations with others, Lindsay asked his respondents questions designed to uncover how they identified members of their own subculture, allies from outside that subculture, and opponents. He discovered that identifying a devil was key to unifying religiously disparate groups, but that on a practical level the bases of support for the traditionalist alliance varied depending on the groups involved.

In chapter 11, which concludes this volume, Clyde Wilcox uses metaphors to encapsulate three alternative frameworks—two conventional, albeit competing, narratives and a radically different narrative—for understanding the relationship between the Christian Right and the Republican Party. The first conventional account describes the Christian Right as a "barbarian army invading the citadel of the Republican Party politics, overrunning moderates and taking control." Among Christian Right activists, the invading army is doing God's will in redeeming America through the Republican Party. Their opponents, however, tend to envision the invading army in jack boots. The second conventional narrative uses the metaphor of seduction. In this story, the Christian Right is a creation of the Republican Party and evangelical voters are seduced into supporting the Republican Party, but get little in recompense. In this narrative, the Republican Party is the driving force behind the creation of the nexus of Christian Right organizations, which serve simply as a mechanism for partisan mobilization.

Wilcox finds each narrative lacking and proposes an alternative narrative derived from evolutionary biology. He argues that the metaphor of coevolution more fully captures the relationship. By thinking of the GOP and Christian Right as "overlapping subspecies with diverse population characteristics," Wilcox is able to trace how the relationship has changed each of the parties over time. He discovers that, as in nature, some members are advantaged and others are disadvantaged through the interaction. Wilcox concludes by showing how the coevolution of the Christian Right and the GOP has affected the Democratic Party's ecological niche. We believe that the dynamism inherent in this metaphor is an appropriate way to end the volume.

We believe that the two volumes in this series realize our hope for a deeper, more balanced, and better integrated portrait of the evangelical movement and the traditionalist alliance than has so far been available.[27] The volumes combine a sophisticated view of religious doctrines and organizations with a sharp sense of the distinctiveness of the American context, and an awareness of the dependence of religious actors on well supported secular institutions and the broader political coalitions in their environment.

These volumes are the product of a conference held in New York in April 2007 at the Russell Sage Foundation. We thank the Foundation for its generous support of the conference. We also thank the Center for Ideas and Society at the University of California, Riverside, for providing funds for a research assistant to help with conference organizing.

Notes

1. Puritan leader John Winthrop evoked this sentiment in his depiction of their settlement: "We shall be as a city on a hill, the eyes of all people are upon us" (Winthrop 1603/1931, 294–95).
2. See, for example, the Jonathan Edwards sermon "The Latter-Day Glory is Probably to Begin in America," where he prophesizes that "God has made as it were two world here below, two great habitable continents, far separated one from the other: The latter is as it were now but newly created; it has been, till of late, wholly the possession of Satan, the church of God having never been in it, as it has been in the other continent, from the beginning of the world. This new world is probably now discovered, that the new and most glorious state of God's church on earth might commence there; that God might in it begin a new world in a spiritual respect, when he creates the new heavens and new earth" (1830/1998, 55).
3. There is some ambiguity about the meaning of the term *evangelical* because often times it is used without being defined. In this context, we use the term to refer to a specific subset of Protestants who share a distinctive set of beliefs, experiences and practices. Lyman Kellstedt and Corwin Smidt distinguished evangelicals from other Protestants on the basis of four core beliefs: the Bible is the literal word of God; salvation is possible only through personal acceptance of Jesus as savior; personal experience of Jesus as savior often occurs through the born-again experience, an intense event of spiritual renewal marking their life from that point on; and the obligation to witness one's beliefs to others (1991).
4. Moreover, in 2008, the Republicans nominated, as their vice presidential candidate, Sarah Palin, who supports the teaching of creation science in the public schools.

5. David Gutterman explained that American history has been punctuated by these periods of religious enthusiasm, that he labels the "great jeremiad," where religious leaders in prophetic mode call upon the nation to repent of its sins and warn that it is on the verge of incurring the Almighty's wrath, while offering hope if the people return to righteousness (2005, 9).

6. Although concerned with repentance, most of the preaching also emphasized that America was especially loved by God and would prosper during the thousand years following Satan's being cast into the bottomless pit. This era would be capped by Christ's return. An alternative and much smaller vein of apocalyptic thought held that humanity had to suffer through a millennium period of darkness and travail, although some posited that the righteous may be saved prior to the final conflagration (Boyer 1992, 75).

7. Peter Dobkin Hall's chapter in this volume includes an in-depth discussion of the impact of Lyman Beecher, one of the great populist preachers of the Second Great Awakening, on mid-nineteenth-century America (see chapter 8).

8. The covenant theme is particularly strong in Mormon theology, which holds that America is the new promised land and that Christopher Columbus's discovery of the New World was divinely inspired.

9. The Baptists, Methodists, and Presbyterians were the largest evangelical Protestant denominations in the nineteenth century. The medium and smaller denominations, which shared the vision of a Christian America, included Congregationalists, Disciples of Christ, and United Brethren (Handy 1984, ix).

10. Most Protestants today are pre- rather than postmillennialists. Rather than believing that Christ's resurrection ushered in the Kingdom of God, premillennialists believe that life on Earth will get worse until Christ's Second Coming, when He establishes the Kingdom of God on Earth. There are many positions about what exactly will occur before Christ's return. Some evangelicals believe there will be the Rapture, where believers are saved just before the worst events on Earth, and others that all must endure the worst while waiting.

11. African Americans developed a strong counternarrative that identifies blacks as the chosen people—a people held in bondage just as the ancient Jews were held in bondage during their sojourn in Egypt. Rather than being a city of a hill, America in this narrative is the oppressor (Gutterman 2005; Moses 1998, 131).

12. In his second inaugural address, Abraham Lincoln suggested that the nation's suffering during the Civil War is penance for the sin of slavery, and that it might continue until "every drop of blood drawn with the last shall be paid another drawn with the sword so still it must be said that the judgments of the Lord are true and righteous" (http://www2.scholastic.com/browse/article.jsp/id=4692).

13. For more on the biblical justifications for slavery and the ways that Southern whites tried to find a biblical explanation for their defeat in the Civil War, see Stephen Haynes (2002).

14. Even though the Scopes court upheld Tennessee's antievolution law, many

evangelicals felt that the best way to protect their way of life and practice their faith was to withdraw from the public sphere. Because most of them had adopted the more pessimistic premillennialist view that there was little that could be done to prevent massive suffering during the time of tribulation, believers needed to focus on individual redemption (Boyer 1992, 104–5).

15.   Digby Baltzell in his 1964 study of intersecting business and political power relations in the United States still identifies the nation's elite as overwhelmingly Protestant.

16.   The Pluralism Project at Harvard University has identified listings for 5,000 worship centers for non-Judeo-Christian religious traditions (Eck cited in chapter 2, volume 1).

17.   According to the American Religious Identification Survey, the number of Muslims in the United States doubled between 1990 and 2001, from 527,000 to 1,104,000. Buddhists increased during the same period from 401,000 to 1,082,000, and Hindus from 227,000 to 766,000 (Kosmin, Mayer, and Keysar 2001).

18.   However, when the opening invocation in 2001 was offered by a Hindu priest, the action was denounced by the Family Research Council as "one more indication that our nation is drifting from its Judeo-Christian roots" (Koff, cited in Eck 2001, 25).

19.   Alexander Mooney, Sareena Dalla, and Scott Anderson, "Groups Criticize McCain for Calling U.S. 'Christian Nation,'" *CNN Politics*, October 1, 2007, http://www.cnn.com/2007/POLITICS/10/01/mccain.christian.nation/index.html.

20.   Engel v. Vitale, 370 U.S. 421 (1962). The requirement that Pennsylvania schools read ten Bible verses a day was ruled invalid the following year in Abington Township School District v. Schempp, 374 U.S. 203 (1963). Because the Bible verses generally were taken from Protestant rather than Catholic translations, this decision was applauded by some faith groups, but those who were displaced saw it as a secular attack on the Christian character of the nation.

21.   Bob Jones University contested the removal of their tax exempt status, but in 1974 the Supreme Court ruled that to receive tax exempt status an institution "must serve a public purpose and not be contrary to established public policy" (Bob Jones University v. United States 416 U.S. 725).

22.   It would be misreading history to characterize any period as devoid of evangelical political activism. However, there was a definite diminution of efforts in the aftermath of the Scopes trial, when many evangelicals were convinced they should put their energies into creating their own parallel institutions rather than contest in the public arena. Fundamentalists created their own Bible-centered schools and colleges, Bible summer camps, Bible study groups, and Christian radio programming. At the same time, neo-evangelicals continued to be publicly engaged. Both the founding of the National Association of Evangelicals in 1942 and the Billy Graham revivals of the 1940s and 1950s were expressions of an outwardly looking populist orientation among evangelical Protestants. Throughout the cold

war era, evangelical leaders, such as Billy James Hargis and Carl McIntyre, were active in anti-Communist crusades, but they had only limited success in mobilizing their base.

23. In early 1979, several West Coast antigay, antipornography and pro-family groups merged to create Christian Voice, the first national Christian Right organization. By the mid-1980s, Christian Voice had a mailing list of 150,000 people and claimed to have support from thirty-seven denominations; the most important being independent Baptist, Bible, and Assembly of God churches. The Moral Majority, which was founded in mid-1979, drew its support from independent Baptist churches and small fundamentalist sects, predominantly in the South and Southwest. Within a couple years, the Moral Majority claimed to have a membership of 300,000 (Moore 1999, 211).

24. The membership of the Religious Roundtable is primarily comprised of Southern Baptist, Presbyterian, and Methodist ministers. The organization tries to educate its members about moral and family issues. They also run workshops to teach ministers how to mobilize their membership to support conservative causes (Moore 1999, 212).

25. By the mid-1990s, the Christian Coalition had a membership of 1,700,000 and had become the most influential Christian Right group (Moore 1999, 212).

26. Starting with Max Weber (1930), scholars have posited that economic modernization leads to secularization (see, for example, Swatos and Christiano 2001). The basic argument is that economic development requires a more highly educated workforce, which in turns leads to a greater belief in science and rational explanations for phenomena, all of which undercuts support for a religious world view. More recent research identifies possible reasons—most notably high levels of insecurity—that explain why countries such as the United States and Austria have not followed the dominant pattern of secularization (Almond, Appleby, and Sivan 2003; Norris and Inglehart 2004; chapter 1, this volume).

27. Supplemental materials available at: https://www.russellsage.org/publi cations/evangelicalTimelines.

References

Almond, Gabriel, R. Scott Appleby, and Emmanuel Sivan. 2003. *Strong Religion*. Chicago: University of Chicago Press.

Baltzell, E. Digby. 1964. *The Protestant Establishment: Aristocracy and Caste in America*. New Haven, Conn.: Yale University Press.

Boyer, Paul. 1992. *When Time Shall Be No More: Prophecy Belief in Modern American Culture*. Cambridge, Mass.: Harvard University Press.

Cherry, Conrad. 1998. *God's New Israel: Religious Interpretations of American Destiny*. Chapel Hill: University of North Carolina Press.

Eck, Diana L. 2001. *A New Religious America*. New York: HarperCollins.

Edwards, Jonathan. 1830/1998. "The Latter-Day Glory is Probably to Begin in America." Reprinted in *God's New Israel: Religious Interpretations of American Destiny*, edited by Conrad Cherry. Chapel Hill: University of North Carolina Press.

Gutterman, David S. 2005. *Prophetic Politics: Christian Social Movements and American Democracy*. Ithaca, N.Y.: Cornell University Press.

Handy, Robert T. 1984. *A Christian America: Protestant Hopes and Historical Realities*, 2nd ed. New York: Oxford University Press.

Haynes, Stephen R. 2002. *Noah's Curse: The Biblical Justification of American Slavery*. New York: Oxford University Press.

Jelen, Ted G. 1999. "Moral Majority." In *Encyclopedia of Religion in American Politics*, edited by Jeffrey D. Schultz, John G. West, and Iain Maclean. Phoenix, Ariz.: Oryx Press.

Kellstedt, Lyman A., and Corwin W. Smidt. 1991. "Measuring Fundamentalism: An Analysis of Different Operational Strategies." In *Religion and the Cultural Wars: Dispatches from the Front*, edited by John C. Green, James Guth, Corwin Smidt, and Lyman Kellstedt. Boulder, Colo.: Rowman & Littlefield.

Kosmin, Barry A., Egon Mayer, and Ariela Keysar. 2001. *American Religious Identification Survey*. New York: City University of New York.

Lutz, Donald S. 1988. *The Origins of American Constitutionalism*. Baton Rouge: Louisiana State University Press.

Marsden, George M. 1980. *Fundamentalism and American Culture*. New York: Oxford University Press.

Moen, Matthew C. 1994. "From Revolution to Evolution: The Changing Nature of the Christian Right." *Sociology of Religion* 55(3): 345–58.

———. 1996. "The Evolving Politics of the Christian Right." *PS: Political Science and Politics* 39(3): 461–64.

Moore, William V. 1999. "Religious Right." In *Encyclopedia of Religion in American Politics*, edited by Jeffrey D. Schultz, John G. West, and Iain Maclean. Phoenix, Ariz.: Oryx Press.

Morone, James A. 2003. *Hellfire Nation: The Politics of Sin in American History*. New Haven, Conn.: Yale University Press.

Moses, Wilson Jeremiah. 1998. *Afrotopia: The Roots of African American Popular History*. Cambridge: Cambridge University Press.

Noll, Mark A. 2002. *America's God, From Jonathan Edwards to Abraham Lincoln*. New York: Oxford University Press.

Norris, Pippa, and Ronald Inglehart. 2004. *Sacred and Secular*. Cambridge: Cambridge University Press.

Pew Forum on Religion & Public Life. 2008. "U.S. Religious Landscape Survey." Washington, D.C.: Pew Research Center. http://religions.pewforum.org/pdf/report2religious-landscape-study.

Pew Research Center. 2004. "Religion and the Presidential Vote: Bush Gains Broad Based." December 4, 2004. Washington D. C.: Pew Research Center for the People and the Press. http://peoplepress.org/commentary/display.php3?analysisid=103.

———. 2006. "Many Americans Uneasy with Mix of Religion and Politics." August 24, 2006. Washington D. C.: Pew Research Center for the People and the Press. http://people-press.org/reports/pdf/287.pdf.

Reed, Ralph. 1996. *Active Faith: How Christians are Changing the Soul of American Politics*. New York: The Free Press.

Swatos, William H. and Kevin J. Christiano. 2001. "Secularization Theory: The Course of a Concept." *Sociology of Religion* 60(30): 209–28.

Watson, Justin. 1999. *The Christian Coalition: Dreams of Restoration, Demands for Recognition*. New York: St. Martin's Press.

Weber, Max. 1930. *The Protestant Ethic and the Spirit of Capitalism*. New York: Scribner.

Winthrop, John. 1630/1931. "A Modell of Christian Charity." *Winthrop Papers*, vol. II. Boston: Massachusetts Historical Society.

PART I

CHRISTIAN CONSERVATIVES AND PARTISAN POLITICS

Chapter 1

A Global Perspective: U.S. Exceptionalism (Again?)

Pippa Norris

S INCE AT least the mid-twentieth century, Protestants have been part of the bedrock Republican voting base. In the early 1990s, the American party system experienced an important long-term realignment, however: as the religious population shifted toward the Republicans, secularists shifted toward the Democrats. Is this religiosity gap, which evidence from the NES suggests has persisted in subsequent elections, another example of American exceptionalism, reflecting particular characteristics of U.S. society, politics, and history (Lipset 1997)? Alternatively, might it reflect broader developments with the heightened political salience of religion, which is also evident in other societies? To examine these issues, I analyze in this chapter the impact of religiosity on political ideology and voting behavior in cross-national perspective. After setting out Lipset and Rokkan's classical theoretical framework for understanding processes of party-religious alignment, I consider cross-national survey evidence from the Comparative Study of Electoral Systems (CSES) and the World Values Survey (WVS). My analysis compares the strength of religious participation, religious values, and types of religious faith with Left-Right ideological orientations and voting support for religious parties. The results suggest two major findings. First, religious participation is consistently associated with more right-wing ideological orientations in many postindustrial and industrial societies, not just in the United States. At the same time, support for religious parties exemplified by the Christian Democrats has gradually eroded in many postindustrial societies, which is a pattern consistent with broader processes of secularization evident in these nations

(Broughton and Napel 2000). In this regard, the United States remains an outlier among affluent nations in the strength of religiosity and the powerful role it plays in shaping contemporary patterns of party politics and electoral behavior.

The emergence and persistence of the religiosity gap in American voting behavior during the early 1990s is a well-known phenomenon. According to the series of American National Election Studies (ANES) surveys, with just two exceptions (1986 and 1988), in every presidential and congressional election from 1952 to 2004, Protestants were significantly more likely to identify with the Republican Party, even after controlling for other structural factors such as age, education, marital status, race, region, and gender. The 2008 exit polls confirm the persistence of this pattern, with Protestants giving a 9-point edge to McCain over Obama. What changed, however, is that the strength of religiosity (monitored by the self-reported frequency of attending church at least weekly) emerged as a consistently significant predictor of party identification in 1992, as indicated by a series of regression models using the same set of standard controls. This pattern has persisted in every subsequent American presidential and congressional contest for more than two decades (see tables 1.1 and 1.2). Starting in the early 1990s, the Republicans captured and held on to the support of the most religious sectors of American society. By contrast, during the same period, atheists and the unaffiliated, defined as those who report attending church just a few times a year or never, proved more likely to vote Democrat.

In the 2000 presidential election, for example, the strength of religiosity was by far the strongest predictor of who voted for George W. Bush and for Al Gore, which dwarfed the explanatory power of social class, occupation, or region. Marked contrasts were evident between Bush supporters—strong among middle-aged, married voters with children who lived in the rural South and Midwest and came from a religious background—and Gore voters—who included single, college-educated professionals who lived in cities or urban areas on both coasts and rarely attended church (Norris 2000a). The religiosity gap was also evident in the 2004 contest, in which observers commonly noted sharp divisions between Democrats and Republicans over controversial social issues where the public is sharply polarized, exemplified by the legitimacy of gay marriage, stem cell research, the role of prayer in schools, sexual liberalization, the availability of divorce and abortion rights, and other family values. The religiosity gap in voting choice persisted in the 2008 presidential contest. During the spring primary season, controversies about religious issues were often featured in popular commentary, exemplified by the brouhaha over the remarks of the Reverend Wright, Senator Barack Obama's pastor, as well as Obama's off-the-cuff remarks about bitter voters turning to religion. In the end, according to the CNN

Table 1.1 Religiosity and Partisan Identification, U.S. Elections

Year	Protestant Identification				Strength of Religiosity				Total Model Adjusted R^2
	B	SE	Beta	Sig.	B	SE	Beta	Sig.	
1970	1.117	.212	.246	***	.133	.111	.031	N/S	.109
1972	1.101	.211	.248	***	−.083	.092	−.018	N/S	.086
1974	.923	.305	.201	***	.333	.121	.070	**	.095
1976	.877	.214	.207	***	.115	.097	.025	N/S	.112
1978	1.089	.202	.254	***	−.030	.102	−.006	N/S	.084
1980	.958	.235	.219	***	.298	.123	.061	**	.076
1982	.623	.286	.137	*	.148	.128	.031	N/S	.111
1984	.841	.224	.189	***	.161	.108	.032	N/S	.077
1986	.447	.247	.099	N/S	.041	.104	.008	N/S	.118
1988	.414	.285	.091	N/S	.074	.111	.015	N/S	.093
1990	.470	.100	.108	***	.160	.109	.033	N/S	.076
1992	.661	.087	.155	***	.270	.094	.057	**	.105
1994	.807	.103	.186	***	.330	.111	.069	**	.129
1996	.736	.103	.169	***	.568	.115	.116	***	.137
1998	.439	.122	.103	***	.308	.137	.061	*	.116
2000	.391	.101	.092	***	.479	.112	.100	***	.118
2002	.336	.111	.077	***	.336	.111	.077	***	.134
2004	.666	.123	.157	***	.240	.138	.048	*	.151

Source: Author's compilation based on American National Election Study 1970 to 2004.

Note: The OLS regression models monitor the impact of Protestant identities and the strength of religiosity (measured by at least weekly self-reported church attendance) on partisan identification. Partisan identification is measured on a 7-point scale. "Generally speaking, do you usually think of yourself as a Republican, a Democrat, an Independent, or what?" (If Republican or Democrat) "Would you call yourself a strong (Republican/Democrat) or a not very strong (Republican/Democrat)?" (If Independent, Other [1966 and later; or No Preference] "Do you think of yourself as closer to the Republican or Democratic party? Coded from 1 (strong Democrat) to 7 (strong Republican). The models control for other religious identities (Catholic and Atheist), age (years), education, gender, region (political south versus nonsouth), marital status (married), and race (white, black, other). *** $p < .000$; ** $p < .01$; * $p < .05$; N/S not significant.

Table 1.2   U.S. Church Attendance, 1970 to 2004

	'70	'72	'74	'76	'78	'80	'82	'84	'86	'88	'90	'92	'94	'96	'98	'00	'02	'04
Every week	38	26	25	25	25	25	28	24	27	25	27	27	28	25	24	25	25	23
Almost every week	—	11	12	12	11	12	12	11	11	11	11	11	11	12	13	11	12	12
Once or twice a month	16	12	12	14	12	11	13	14	13	14	14	14	13	16	14	16	18	15
A few times a year	30	32	31	29	30	29	27	29	28	28	16	15	16	18	15	16	13	15
Never	12	14	13	13	14	14	11	14	12	12	33	34	33	30	33	33	32	35
No religious preference	5	4	7	6	9	9	9	8	8	9	—	—	—	—	—	—	—	—
N	1,475	2,677	2,480	2,827	2,271	1,589	1,397	2,225	2,144	2,024	1,963	2,475	1,769	1,703	1,271	1,789	1,498	1,204

Source: Author's compilation based on American National Election Study 1970 to 2004.
Note: 1970 to 1988: (If any religious preference) "Would you say you/do you go to (church/synagogue) every week, almost every week, once or twice a month, a few times a year, or never?" 1990 and later: "Lots of things come up that keep people from attending religious services even if they want to. Thinking about your life these days, do you ever attend religious services, apart from occasional weddings, baptisms, or funerals?" (If Yes) "Do you go to religious services every week, almost every week, once or twice a month, a few times a year, or never?"

2008 exit polls, among those regularly attending church at least weekly, 55 percent voted for McCain versus 43 percent for Obama (CNN 2008). The exit poll data suggest that the size of the religiosity gap shrank substantially from 2004 to 2008, from 22 to 12 points. Nevertheless, President Obama's explicit emphasis on his personal faith, and his attempt to reach out to some moderate evangelicals during the campaign, did not eradicate this long-standing pattern.

The American religiosity gap is all the more striking given the conspicuous absence of similar patterns in at least some comparable postindustrial societies, such as Britain. Anglo American party politics often display similar cycles, such as the predominance of liberal-left politics during the early 1960s, and the Thatcher-Reagan market conservatism rolling back the state during the 1980s. As leaders, both President George W. Bush and Prime Minister Tony Blair displayed strong personal religious convictions. Nevertheless, moral value issues did not feature in the 2005 British general election. Here, party support was predicted largely by attitudes toward valance or consensual apple pie issues, with parties battling over managerial competency on issues such as the economy (Whiteley et al. 2005). The "most important issue" question suggested that, during the 2005 campaign, the British public was concerned primarily about health care, taxes and services, education, crime, the economy, immigration, terrorism, Europe, and Iraq, in that order (Norris and Wlezien 2005). The only minor role that religious identities played was a modest vote swing from Labour to the antiwar, Liberal Democrats in seats with a high proportion of Muslim residents, which was probably a reaction against Britain's intervention in Iraq. At the turn into the nineteenth century, religion was one of the most fundamental cleavages in British party politics, dividing high church Tories from disestablishment Liberals. Today, outside of Northern Ireland, the long-term process of secularization has neutralized the importance of religious identities within the British electorate.

Therefore, is the religiosity gap in the United States yet another example of American exceptionalism, reflecting particular characteristics of U.S. society, politics, and history, as Seymour Lipset suggested (1997)? Or does it reflect broader developments also evident in other societies? To examine these issues, we need to analyze the impact of religiosity on voting behavior and ideological orientations in cross-national perspective. As in the United States, the more religious populations in many developed nations are generally more conservative. Nevertheless, religious parties have gradually lost voting support in many postindustrial nations, which is consistent with broader processes of secularization evident in such nations (Broughton and Napel 2000). The United States, therefore, remains an outlier among affluent nations in the strength of religiosity and the powerful role it plays in shaping contemporary patterns of electoral behavior.

Structural Theories of Partisan Alignment

The seminal cross-national theories of voting behavior that Seymour Lipset and Stein Rokkan developed during the 1960s emphasized that social identities formed the basic building blocks of party support in western Europe (1967). For Lipset and Rokkan, European nation-states had been stamped by social processes decades earlier: the divide that emerged with urbanization between the national capital and the rural regions at the periphery of power, the growth of manufacturing industry that fueled the class struggle between workers and labor unions against property owners and capitalists, and the religious schism that split Christendom between Catholics and Protestants, as well as the rift between practicing churchgoers and others who were only nominally Christian in their beliefs and practices. These traditional social cleavages remained politically salient for several reasons. First, they reflected major ideological fissions in party politics. Divisions over social class mirrored the basic schism between the socialist and community Left, which favored a strong role for the state with redistributive welfare policies and interventionist economic management, and the pro-market Right, which advocated the rule of laissez-faire economics and a more limited role for government. Moreover, the religious division in party politics reflected heated moral debates concerning the role of women, marriage, and the family. The differences between the core and periphery concerned how far governance in the nation-state should be centralized with parliaments in London, Madrid, and Paris, or how far decision-making powers should be devolved to the regions and localities with their own identities, languages, and national minorities.

Lipset and Rokkan argued that organizational linkages gradually strengthened over the years as the party systems in place when the working class gained the franchise gradually froze. Stable patterns of party competition in the 1950s and 1960s continued to be based on the most salient primary cleavages and social cues dividing each society in the early twentieth century, exemplified by the role of social class in Britain, religion in France, and language in Belgium (Butler and Stokes 1974; Lewis-Beck and Skalaban 1992; Mughan 1983). The electoral systems in western Europe, when the mass franchise was first expanded, played a vital role in stabilizing party competition by reinforcing the legitimacy of those parties and social groups that had achieved parliamentary representation. Challenger parties, threatening to disturb the partisan status quo, faced formidable hurdles in the electoral thresholds needed to convert votes into seats and—an even more difficult hurdle—

competing against the established party loyalties and party machines that had been built up by the existing major Parliamentary parties. Thus, patterned and predictable interactions in the party competition for government became settled features of the electoral landscape throughout most established democracies. Lipset and Rokkan's structural theory became the established sociological orthodoxy for understanding voting behavior and party competition in western Europe and in other established democracies such as Australia and Canada. In the United States, Angus Campbell and his colleagues presented a similar social psychological model that gave central importance to the concept of partisan identification, but also emphasized that this orientation was deeply rooted in structural divisions within American society, above all those of socioeconomic status, race, religion, and region (Campbell et al. 1960; Brooks and Manza 1997a, 1997b).

Why did religious cleavages remain important in industrial societies? A large part of the explanation for Lipset and Rokkan rested on the way that the dominant churches in western Europe succeeded in creating organizational networks, including strong links with Christian Democratic and other religious parties, just as trade unions had mobilized workers into supporting socialist, social democratic, and communist parties. The church was linked with parties on the Right that represented conservative economic policies and traditional moral values—initially concerning marriage and the family, and later including gender equality, sexual liberalization, and gay rights. In the United States, born-again fundamentalist Protestant churches became closely linked to the Republican Party, especially in the South. During the early 1980s, the Christian Right in America mobilized vigorously around conservative policies, such as the Right to Life movement advocating limiting or banning abortion, policies favoring prayer in school and later against legal recognition of homosexual marriage (Wilcox 1992; Leege and Kellstedt 1993). Elsewhere, the role of religion in party politics has developed within varying contexts. In Ireland, Poland, and Italy, for example, the Catholic Church has taken conservative positions on issues such as divorce and reproductive rights, but in Poland it has also become associated with nationalist opposition to the Soviet Union (Borowik 2002). In Latin American societies, it has often sided with liberal movements and actively defended human rights in opposition to repressive states and authoritarian regimes (Jelen and Wilcox 2002).

The structural theory, however, needs to be qualified, as many other factors also shape long-term patterns of party competition and electoral behavior. The mass basis of electoral politics and party competition can also be affected by such factors as the impact of World War II or the end of the cold war, the influence of major electoral reforms on party fortunes, or significant expansions of the electorate (Bartolini and Mair

1990). Important shifts in the mass base of American parties, for example, were triggered by the diverse coalition assembled by Franklin Delano Roosevelt during the Great Depression, the postwar loss of yellow-dog Democratic hegemony in the South, and the emergence of the modern gender gap in the early 1980s (Clubb, Flanigan, and Zingale 1990). Nevertheless, until at least the mid-1960s, party systems in many established democracies seemed to exhibit a rock-like stability, characterized by glacial evolution rather than radical discontinuities.

For most religious parties in western Europe, the two decades after World War II were a period of unparalleled electoral success; in both Italy and West Germany, the Christian Democrats became the dominant parties. Throughout Catholic Europe, including Belgium and Austria, Christian Democratic counterparts became the largest or next largest parties (Madeley 1991; Hanley 1996; Warner 2000; Keslman and Buttigieg 2003). In postwar Britain, however, class was the dominant cleavage, reinforced by older religious divisions between high-church Tories in England and low-church Liberals in the periphery (Butler and Stokes 1974; Franklin, Mackie, and Valen 1992). Cleavages between Protestant and Catholic communities deeply divided the electoral and party politics of Northern Ireland (Mitchell, O'Leary, and Evans 2001). In Latin America, Christian Democrat parties have played a major role. Religion has also been viewed as a fundamental political cleavage in party politics throughout the Middle East, South Asia, and Southeast Asia, but until recently little cross-national survey data have been available to analyze systematic patterns of party competition and electoral support in these countries (Moyser 1991; Mainwaring and Scully 2003).

Theories of Partisan Dealignment

From the mid-1970s onward, a consensus developed in the electoral behavior literature, suggesting that the traditional linkages between social groups and party support had weakened. Scholars found that structural factors such as class, age, gender, and religion remained important predictors of voting choice, and there is little agreement among observers about the precise reasons for this phenomenon (Crewe, Alt, and Sarlvik 1977; Nie, Verba, and Petrocik 1976; Crewe and Denver 1985; Franklin, Mackie, and Valen 1992; Dalton, Flanagan, and Beck 1984; Manza and Brooks 1999; Clark and Lipset 2001). Various observers have attributed trends in partisan dealignment in established democracies to a variety of complex developments in postindustrial societies. The most important of these developments are: secularization, which tends to erode religious identities; intergenerational value change, which leads to new issues that cut across established party divides; social and geographic mobility, which weaken community social networks; television broadcasting, which replaces older channels of political communications through partisan newspapers, personal discussion, and party campaign organizations; growing multiculturalism in the wake of migration, which was generating social divides based on racial and ethnic identities; and the increased complexity of newer issues on the policy agenda, such as globalization, environmentalism, sexuality, and international terrorism, that do not comfortably fit into older patterns of party competition (Dalton, Flanagan, and Beck 1984). As a result, identities based on religious identities no longer seem as capable of generating unwavering and habitual party loyalty in many postindustrial societies as they were in the postwar era, which opens the way for new types of parties to challenge the status quo.

Electoral developments seemed to confirm these observations in many countries. New parties not based on the traditional social anchors of class and religion started to gain electoral momentum and Parliamentary representation. These new parties ranged from ethnonationalist parties in Canada, Spain, and the United Kingdom to Green parties in Germany, France, Sweden, and elsewhere, to the anti-immigrant radical Right such as the National Front in Britain and France, and a range of diverse protest parties advocating cross-cutting moral and economic issues in Denmark, Italy, and the Netherlands (Daalder and Mair 1985; Pederson 1979; Kitschelt 1995; Norris 2005). In recent years, the decline of the Christian Democratic parties and the center-right in Europe seems to have opened the way for electoral breakthrough by diverse new parties with a populist anti-immigrant, antimulticultural campaign message. Recent examples include Jean-Marie Le Pen, leader of the National Front, who was able to supplant the Socialist candidate as the second strongest vote-winner in France's 2002 presidential election. Such parties garnered other prominent successes as well. That Joerg Haider's far-right Freedom Party won more than 25 percent of the vote in the 1999 Austrian general election is worthy of note, as is the dramatic rise of the neopopulist List Pim Fortuyn in the May 2002 elections in the Netherlands and the assassination of its leader, Pim Fortuyn. The surge in support for Vlaams Blok, who won 20 percent of the vote in Flanders in the May 2003 Belgian general election, is also remarkable. The most successful radical right parties have been largely secular in orientation and appeal, and focus on economic populism and anti-immigrant rhetoric in an effort to tap into growing frustration with center-right parties rather than the moral issues that have resonated for Christian conservatism in the United States (Norris 2005).

If the ballast of traditional religious identities no longer ties voters to established parties, there will likely be growing volatility in electoral behavior and in party competition, opening the door for more split-ticket voting across different electoral levels, facilitating the sudden rise of protest politics, and creating more vote-switching within and across the left-right blocks of party families. Moreover, this process should boost the political impact of short-term events during election campaigns and heighten the importance of short-term party strategies, the appeal of candidates and party leaders, and the impact of political communications, opinion polls, and the news media (Norris 2000b).

Evidence of Partisan Dealignment

Has secularization, though, actually eroded support for religious parties throughout postindustrial societies as a whole? Some light can be thrown on these questions from the analysis of data drawn from the Comparative Study of Electoral Systems (CSES), which is examined in more detail elsewhere (Norris 2003). This survey includes a range of established and newer democracies, as well as agrarian, industrial, and postindustrial societies classified according to the United Nations Development Programme's Human Development Index (UNDP 1999). Data from the World Values Survey, which provides a broader range of nations, world religions, and types of society, supplemented the CSES survey data.

There are many ways of classifying political parties and party families according to their ideological orientation, and none are perfect. One difficulty is the way that individual parties within party families can differ depending on where they are, for example, the British Labour Party under Blair moved sharply center-left in the mid-1990s relative to the French Socialists under Lionel Jospin and the more traditional welfare state policies they defended. It is often most difficult to classify personalist parties, which represent changeable leadership factions more than any continuous record of programmatic policies. Classifying parties as belonging to the Left or the Right is relatively straightforward among established democracies, but becomes much more difficult when comparing the many parties in newer transitional and consolidating democracies. To ensure that the results remained robust, this study used two approaches to classification.

First, party support among the electorate was compared using the CSES dataset based on expressed voting intentions among respondents. Political parties were classified on a 10-point left-right scale, where votes for each party family were recoded on a single ideological scale ranging from left (low) to right (high) as follows: Communist, Ecology, Socialist, Social Democrat, Left Liberal, Liberal, Christian Democrat, Right Liberal, Conservative, and Nationalist-Religious. The continuous scale was used in the ordinary least squares regression analysis models, and then dichotomized into right-wing and left-wing blocks to simplify the presentation of the descriptive statistics.

To supplement this approach, and to check whether the results remain consistent regardless of coding decisions, the study also used the CSES data to compare ideological orientations among the electorate based on where respondents placed themselves on a simple 10-point left-right ideological scale. Respondents were asked how they would place their political views on a general left-right scale. Many public opinion researchers have questioned whether ordinary citizens can understand and apply abstract political concepts like Left and Right. Early electoral research argued that during the 1950s few Americans understood the meaning of the terms; only half received a passing score in their recognition of liberal and conservative (Converse 1964). A contrasting view offers a more positive perspective on the use of the left-right dimension among contemporary publics (Inglehart 1976; Fuchs and Klingmann 1989; Knutsen 1999). This approach accepts that most citizens do not have a sophisticated philosophical understanding of ideological concepts such as socialism or liberalism that are embedded in the terms Left and Right. Instead, the left-right framework provides a source of political identity that helps orient the individual to politics. Empirical research demonstrates that left-right attitudes in western democracies typically summarize individuals' positions on the issues that are most important to them (Knutsen 1995). It remains to be seen whether these concepts travel well to orient voters in other continents.

The results of the CSES scale proved to be well balanced with minimal skew, and showed a normal distribution in all three types of society. We also found low nonresponse rates in most societies; even less-educated respondents in poorer societies could place themselves on this scale. The continuous scale was used for the multivariate analysis, and for descriptive comparisons, the 10-point ideological orientation scale was also dichotomized into left and right categories for ease of presentation. This scale consistently proved a strong predictor of voting choice in those countries where we could unambiguously place the political parties on a right-left scale. Two major findings are evident.

First, as shown in figure 1.1, the results based on voting intentions for parties on the Right demonstrate that among different structural identities, religiosity remains more strongly and more consistently related to voting choice today than any of the various indicators of socioeconomic status. In the pooled model used in the CSES study, which compared thirty-seven presidential and parliamentary elections from the mid- to the late 1990s in thirty-two nations, almost three-quarters (70 percent) of the most religious, defined as the 15 percent who reported attending religious services at least once per week, voted for parties of the Right. By contrast, among the most secular or unaffiliated, defined as the 39 percent who never attended religious services, fewer than half (45 percent) voted for the Right.

Figure 1.1   The Social Characteristics of Right-Wing Voters, CSES

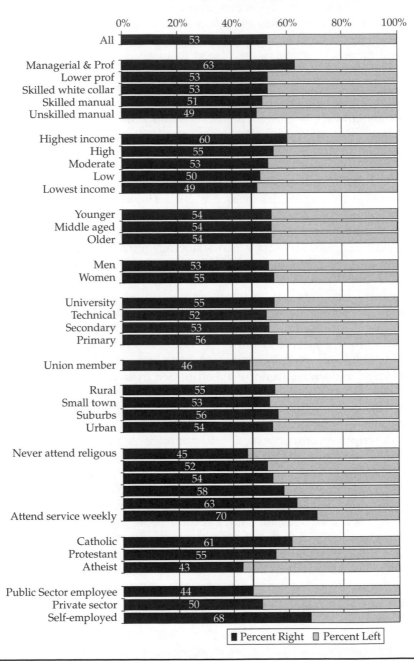

Source: Author's compilation based on Comparative Study of Electoral Systems, Module 1 1996 to 2002. Pooled sample.
Notes: Left-Right Vote: Party vote in legislative elections for the lower house classified on a 10-point scale ranging from communist (1) to Nationalist (10) dichotomized into right-wing and left-wing blocks.

Table 1.3   Baseline Models Predicting Right-Wing Voting Support, Pooled Legislative Elections

	Model A				Model B				Coding
	B	S.E.	Beta	Sig.	B	S.E.	Beta	Sig.	
Social Structure									
Age	-.008	.001	-.05	***	-.006	.001	-.04	***	A2001 Years old
Sex (male)	.226	.035	.05	***	.112	.032	.02	***	A2002 Male=1/Female=0
Education	.040	.018	.02	*	.047	.017	.02	**	A2003 Highest level of education of respondent. Primary 1, secondary 2, postsecondary technical 3, university 4.
Income	.113	.014	.06	***	.081	.012	.05	***	A2012 5-point scale of household income from lowest to highest quintile.
Union member	-.609	.040	-.11	***	-.374	.036	-.07	***	A2005 Respondent is union member 1, else 0
Linguistic majority	.362	.036	.08	***	.224	.033	.05	***	A2018 Language usually spoken at home. Linguistic majority 1, else 0
Religiosity	.311	.010	.24	***	.189	.009	.15	***	A2015 6-point strength of religiosity scale from never attend religious service (1) to attend at least weekly (6).
Ideology									
Left-right ideology					.409	.006	.43	***	A3031 Position respondents placed themselves on the 10-point scale from left (0) to right (10).
Constant	4.6								
Adjusted R^2	.074				.248				

Source: Author's compilation based on Comparative Study of Electoral Systems, Module 1 1996 to 2002.

Notes: The figures represent the results of OLS multiple regression analysis models including unstandardized beta coefficients (B), standardized error (S.E.), standardized beta coefficients (Beta) and their significance (P).

Voting Choice: For the dependent measure, votes for each party family are recoded using a 10-point scale ranging from left (low) to right (high) as follows: (1) Communist, (2) Ecology, (3) Socialist, (4) Social Democrat, (5) Left liberal, (6) Liberal, (7) Christian Democrat, (8) Right liberal, (9) Conservative, and (10) 'Nationalist/Religious.' A positive coefficient indicates support for parties on the right. The pooled sample of legislative elections includes 28 nations and 17,794 respondents. Data was weighted by A104_1 to ensure that the size of the sample is equal per nation.

*** $p < .001$; ** $p < .01$; * $p < .05$

The substantial 25-point mean religiosity gap proved far stronger than that produced by any of the alternative indicators of socioeconomic status, such as education, social class, or income. The results continued to prove significant in multivariate models using the pooled CSES sample in twenty-eight nations, where again religiosity is a better predictor of right-wing voting than any other social variable (table 1.3). Across all elections in the CSES, Catholic voters were significantly more likely to vote for parties of the Right than Protestants were, and atheists were the most likely of all groups to vote for the parties of the Left. Religiosity was particularly strongly related to voting choice in Israel, the Netherlands, and Belgium—all countries where religious divisions have long been regarded as some of the most critical components of cleavage politics, but this was also true in such ex-communist countries as Hungary and the Czech Republic.

Left-Right Orientations and Religion

The CSES provides evidence from thirty-two nations, including established and newer democracies and both industrial and postindustrial societies. The WVS covers a considerably wider range of nations, covering low-income societies, nonindustrial societies, Muslim and other cultural regions, as well as industrial and postindustrial societies (Norris and Inglehart 2004). Does the evidence from this broader range of variation show similar patterns? In particular, does it confirm the finding that the relative influence of religious participation, values, and identities is greater than that of social class? And what is the linkage between religiosity and voter choice in relatively agrarian societies? Replication is important to confirm the initial results suggested in the analysis of the CSES dataset. For the WVS analysis, an ideological left-right 10-point self-placement scale was used, which is similar to that included in the CSES. Table 1.4 presents the proportion placing themselves on the right half of the scale (those placing themselves at points 6 through 10), analyzed by type of society and by individual religious faith in the WVS dataset.

The descriptive results, with no social controls applied, confirm that religious participation was associated with right ideological self-placement. Across all nations, 53 percent of those who attended services of worship at least weekly, placed themselves on the right; only 41 percent of those who did not attend this frequently, placed themselves on the right, generating a 12-point religious gap. This difference was relatively strong in postindustrial and industrial societies, but relatively weak in agrarian societies. The individual's self-described level of religiosity shows a similar pattern (not surprisingly, given the strong link that we have found between religious values and participation): 50 percent of

Table 1.4   Percent Support for the Right by Society and Religiosity

	Agrarian	Industrial	Postindustrial	All	Coef.	Sig.
Religious participation						
Attend church at least						
weekly	48	54	55	53		
Do not attend weekly	46	40	40	41	.112	***
Religious values						
Religion 'very important'	48	51	52	50		
Religion not 'very						
important'	45	40	40	40	.115	***
Religious faith						
None	52	37	32	36	.094	***
Catholic	46	49	45	47	.047	***
Protestant	47	50	48	48	.028	***
Orthodox	35	39	39	38	.033	***
Jewish	42	43	39	41	.007	**
Muslim	48	42	38	46	.033	***
Hindu	48	50	45	48	.015	***
Buddhist	76	63	63	64	.043	***
ALL	47	44	44	45	.049	***

Source: Author's compilation based on World Values Survey pooled, 1981 to 2001.
Notes: Left-right self-placement: Q: *"In political matters, people talk of 'the left' and 'the right.' How would you place your views on this scale generally speaking?"* Left (1) Right (10). The scale is dichotomized for this table into Left (1-5) and Right (6-10). The figures represent the proportion that is Right in each category, with the remainder categorized as Left.
Religious participation: *"Do you attend religious services several times a week, once a week, a few times during the year, once a year or less, or never?"* The percentage that reported attending religious services *'several times a week'* or *'once a week.'*
Religious values: Q10 *"How important is religion in your life? Very important, rather important, not very important, not at all important?"*
The significance of the mean difference on the left-right scale is measured by the Eta coefficient using ANOVA.
*** $p < .001$; ** $p < .01$; * $p < .05$

those who believed that religion was very important placed themselves on the right, versus 40 percent of those who viewed it as less important. This religious gap was again in a consistent direction across all types of societies, though again, it was largest in postindustrial societies. Figure 1.2 confirms that the relationship between religious values (measured by the 10-point "importance of God scale") and left-right self-placement shows a similar relationship. In all three types of societies, rising levels of religiosity go with rising levels of political support for the Right (with minor fluctuations in the trend line).

The contrasts by type of individual religious faith were also striking: only 33 percent of those who said they did not belong to any faith placed themselves on the right of the ideological spectrum, and fully 66

Figure 1.2   Religious Values and Left-Right Self-Placement

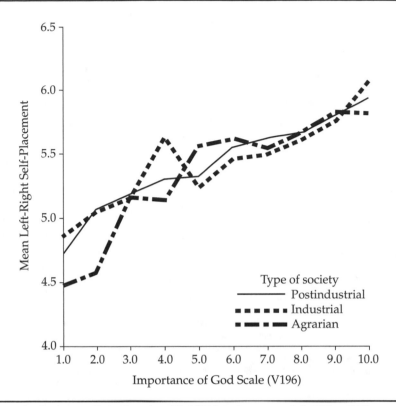

Source: Author's compilation based on World Values Survey pooled, 1981 to 2005.

percent placed themselves on the left. This pattern was clearest in post-industrial societies, and was not evident in agrarian societies. Jews were also more likely to place themselves on the left than average, and Protestants, Hindus, and Buddhists were relatively likely to place themselves on the right. The Orthodox tended to place themselves on the left, but this is linked with the fact that the Orthodox tend to be concentrated in ex-communist societies, where left ideological affiliations are relatively widespread.

It seems likely that certain social characteristics that help to predict religiosity, such as age, could also be associated with more right orientations. Multivariate analysis can help us sort out the impact of such variables. Table 1.5 presents a model with the full battery of developmental and social controls where the dependent variable is the 10-point scale of left-right ideological orientations. In industrial and postindustrial soci-

Table 1.5 Explaining Right Orientations, Pooled Model All Nations

	Agrarian				Industrial				Postindustrial			
	B	St. Err.	Beta	Sig	B	St. Err.	Beta	Sig	B	St. Err.	Beta	Sig
Developmental controls												
Level of human development (100-point scale)	-1.08	.235	-.05	***	-2.45	.548	-.04	***	2.43	1.74	.01	N/S
Level of political development	-.074	.021	-.04	***	.025	.014	.01	N/S	.977	.091	.10	***
Social controls												
Gender (Male=1)	.179	.051	.03	***	.120	.029	.03	***	.199	.028	.05	***
Age (years)	.003	.002	.01	N/S	-.003	.001	-.02	***	.006	.001	.05	***
Education (3 categories low to hi)	-.103	.040	-.03	**	-.212	.022	-.07	***	-.085	.022	-.07	***
Income (10 categories low to hi)	.007	.010	.01	N/S	.005	.006	.01	N/S	.055	.006	.08	***
Class (4-point scale)	-.053	.023	-.02	*	-.098	.014	-.05	***	-.147	.015	-.08	***

(Table continues on p. 41.)

Table 1.5   (Continued)

Religious participation and type of faith	Agrarian				Industrial				Postindustrial			
	B	St. Err.	Beta	Sig	B	St. Err.	Beta	Sig	B	St. Err.	Beta	Sig
Religious participation	-.051	.015	-.04	***	.171	.008	.15	***	.151	.008	.15	***
Protestant	.476	.098	.08	***	.393	.075	.04	***	.281	.077	.07	***
Catholic	.537	.107	.06	***	.321	.057	.07	***	.120	.081	.03	N/S
Orthodox	-.531	.172	-.03	***	.302	.081	.03	***	-3.71	.891	-.03	***
Muslim	.697	.096	.12	N/S	.035	.075	.01	N/S	-.242	.258	-.01	N/S
Jewish	.295	.285	.01	***	-.202	.332	-.01	N/S	-.670	.199	-.03	***
Hindu	.513	.114	.06	***	.331	.926	.01	N/S	.528	.464	.01	N/S
Buddhist	2.46	.302	.08	***	.631	.127	.03	***	.731	.133	.05	***
None/Atheist	1.04	.122	.09	***	.196	.052	.04	***	-.089	.082	-.02	N/S
(Constant)	6.54				7.23				-4.06			
Adjusted R^2	.025				.034				.067			

Source: Author's compilation based on World Values Survey pooled, 1981 to 2001.

Note: The table presents the results of an ordinary least squares regression model where ideological orientation on the 10-point left-right scale is the dependent variable, with left=1, and right=10. The figures represent the unstandardized beta (B), the standard error (s.e.), the standardized Beta, and the significance of the coefficient (Sig).

Religious participation: Q185 "Apart from weddings, funerals, and christenings, about how often do you attend religious services these days? More than once a week, once a week, once a month, only on special hold days, once a year, less often, never or practically never."

Religious faith: 'Do you belong to a religious denomination' If yes, 'Which one?' If 'No' coded None/atheist (0). Measured at individual level.

*** $p < .001$;   ** $p < .01$; * $p < .05$; N/S not significant eties, the results show that religious participation remains a significant positive predictor of right orientations even after entering controls for levels of human and democratic development and the traditional social factors associated with ideological orientations including gender, age, education, income, and social class. Indeed, in these societies, religious participation emerges as the single strongest predictor of right ideology and shows far more impact than any of the social class indicators. Across the different types of faith, the pattern is mixed, which suggests a relation to the political role of the church, temple, or mosque. In all industrial and postindustrial societies, though, Protestants consistently emerge as more likely to place themselves on the right than the average respondent. In agrarian societies, by contrast, religious participation is associated with left self-placement.

To examine this pattern further we need to examine the results within each nation and within each wave of the survey to see whether secularization has generated religious dealignment and a weakening of the religious-ideological relationship over the last twenty years. Table 1.6 displays the simple correlations, without any controls, between religious values and right orientations in each country and period. The results show two main patterns. First, the significance of the correlations demonstrates the consistency of the underlying relationships: those who regard religion as important to their lives are more right in orientation in almost all nations and at different periods. The exception is Nigeria, where the impact of religious values consistently proves insignificant. In large part, this reflects a lack of variation in religious values: almost all Nigerians consider religion to be very important.

Religion continues to be a relatively strong predictor of an individual's ideological positions. However, we find indications that this relationship has weakened over time, as dealignment theory suggests. The summary change symbol in the right-hand column represents the shift in the correlation coefficient across each available wave of the survey: a negative polarity (-) indicates that the strength of the relationship between religious values and right ideological self-placement has weakened over time, from the first to the last available observation. Table 1.6 shows that among the twenty postindustrial societies, this relationship has weakened in fifteen nations and grown stronger in only five (one of which is the United States). In industrial societies, we find a broadly similar pattern in which the correlations have weakened in eleven nations and grown stronger in only six. Last, in the few agrarian societies where comparison is possible over time, South Africa shows a complicated picture, in large part because of the ceiling effect already noted for Nigeria (almost everyone is religious), whereas India and Bangladesh both show increasingly strong links between religious values and right orientations over time.

Table 1.6   Correlations between Religious Values and Right Orientations

	Early 1980s	Early 1990s	Mid-1990s	2000	Chg
Postindustrial					
Australia	.179***		.113***		—
Austria		.098***		.163***	+
Belgium	.391***	.266***		.173**	—
Britain	.205***	.111***		.152***	—
Canada	.148***	.102***		.065**	—
Denmark	.263***	.154***		.095**	—
Finland	.203***	.139***	.149***	.208***	+
France	.322***	.281***		.200***	—
Germany, East		.306***	.187***	.219***	—
Germany, West	.267***	.224***	.185***	.220***	—
Iceland	.137***	.091***		.087**	—
Ireland	.244***	.298***		.267***	+
Italy	.325***	.288***		.227***	—
Japan	.097***	.111***	.136***	.128***	+
Netherlands	.346***	.384***		.164***	—
Norway	.158***	.126***	.064*		—
Spain	.434***	.342***		.360***	—
Sweden	.151***	.112***	.048N/S	.034N/S	—
Switzerland		.188***	.132**		—
United States	.157***	.220***	.176***	.172***	+
Industrial					
Argentina	.270***	.221***	.233***	.165**	—
Brazil		.094***	.081**		—
Bulgaria		.258***	.154***	.154***	—
Chile		.182***	.077*	.065*	—
Croatia			.277***	.194***	—
Czech Rep			.188***	.144***	—
Hungary		.204***	.158***	.167***	—
Latvia			.096**	.129***	+
Mexico	.160***	.245***	.090***	.068*	—
Poland		.140**	***	.221***	+
Portugal		.210***		.136***	—
Russia		.068*	.065*	.036N/S	—
Serbia			.082**	.066N/S	—
Slovakia			.162***	.221***	+
Slovenia		.178***	.252***	.313***	+
Turkey		.313***		.314***	+
Ukraine			.132***	.192***	+
Agrarian					
South Africa	.234***	.109***	.013N/S	.003N/S	—
Nigeria		.032N/S	.014N/S	−.013N/S	
India		.157***	.368***		+
Bangladesh			.062*	.183***	+

Source: Author's compilation based on World Values Survey, 1981 to 2001.
Note: The coefficients represent simple correlations between *religious values* (measured by the 10-point 'importance of God' scale) and *Right orientations* (measured by the 10-point left-right ideology scale when 1 = left and 10 = right), without any prior controls.
Chg represents change in the strength of the correlation coefficient from the earliest data point to the latest data point, where − = weaker and + = stronger.

These results suggest that religion has by no means disappeared as a factor predicting ideological positions. This is especially true in countries such as Spain, Ireland, Italy, France, and Belgium, as well as in Slovenia, Turkey, and Croatia, where the correlations between religion and ideological self-placement are still moderately strong in the latest wave. However, less there are indicators that during the last twenty years this relationship has been gradually weakening as an ideological cue in most industrial and postindustrial countries, as predicted by secularization theory. This does not seem to be happening in the few agrarian societies for which we have time-series data.

Voting Support for Religious Parties

We have examined the relationship between religion and ideological placement on the left-right scale, but what about absolute level of support for religious parties? Let us compare the electoral strength of religious parties during the postwar era, as measured by their share of the vote cast in national elections in sixteen postindustrial societies from 1945 to 1994. In the second edition of the *Political Data Handbook OECD Countries*, Jan-Erik Lane, David McKay, and Kenneth Newton classified parties as religious and monitored their share of the vote.

The results in table 1.7 and figure 1.3 illustrate the trends, showing a decline in support for religious parties during the last half century, especially in Catholic Europe. The decline is sharpest in Belgium, France, and Italy (as well as a shorter-term trend in Portugal), and more modest in Luxembourg and Austria. By contrast, Ireland shows a slight strengthening of this relationship. Most countries in Protestant Europe, as well as in Shinto Japan and Orthodox Greece, show a pattern of weak but stable support. The only traditionally Protestant country showing a sharp decline is the Netherlands. In some European countries, religious parties have virtually ceased to exist, which probably reflects the broader erosion of religious participation and adherence to religious values evident in the region (Norris and Inglehart 2004).

Conclusion and Discussion

In earlier stages of history, religious identities provided a cue that oriented electors toward political parties, as well as toward their ideological positions. Differences between Protestants and Catholics in western Europe functioned as a cognitive shortcut, like social class, which linked voters to parties; these linkages often persisted throughout an individual's lifetime. In recent decades, however, as secularization has progressively weakened religious identities, the political impact of denominational differences can be expected to prove less important in party and

Figure 1.3   Electoral Strength of Religious Parties in National Elections, 1945 to 1994

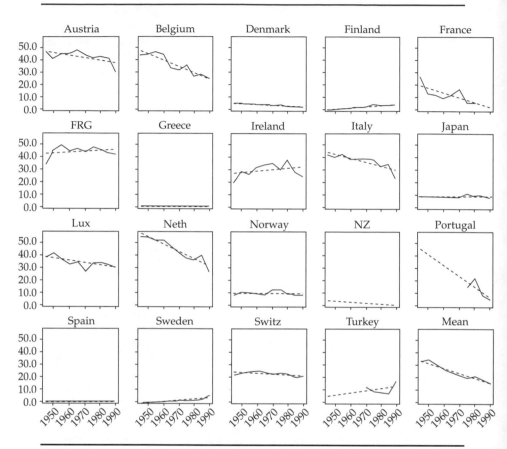

Source: Author's compilation based on data from Lane, McKay, and Newton 1997.

electoral politics. As a result, parties that once had strong organizational links to the Catholic Church, notably the Christian Democrats in West Germany, Italy, and Austria, have become more secular in their electoral appeals, moving toward bridging strategies that enable them to win support from many diverse social groups.

The pattern documented in this chapter at both the individual and the macro level is broadly consistent with these expectations. Two findings are evident. First, in postindustrial nations, religious participation and religious values continue to predict ideological orientations and voting support for right-wing parties. For example, among those who place themselves on the right there is a 15 percent gap between those

Table 1.7 Electoral Strength of Religious Parties in National Elections

Nation	1945 to 1949	1950 to 1954	1955 to 1959	1960 to 1964	1965 to 1969	1970 to 1974	1975 to 1979	1980 to 1984	1985 to 1989	1990 to 1994
Catholic cultures										
Austria	46.9	41.3	45.1	45.4	48.3	43.9	42.4	43.0	41.3	29.9
Belgium	44.2	44.9	46.5	44.4	33.3	31.3	36.1	26.4	28.4	24.5
France	26.4	12.5	11.2	8.9	11.5	16.2	5.3	5.2		
Ireland	19.8	28.9	26.6	32.0	34.1	35.1	30.5	37.7	28.2	24.5
Italy	41.9	40.1	42.4	38.2	39.0	38.7	38.5	32.9	34.3	22.7
Luxembourg	39.2	42.4	36.9	33.3	35.3	27.9	34.5	34.9	32.4	30.3
Portugal						14.3	22.3	8.0	4.4	
Protestant cultures										
Finland			0.2	0.8	0.4	1.8	4.1	3.0	2.6	3.0
Norway	8.2	10.5	10.2	9.6	8.8	12.3	12.4	9.4	8.4	7.9
Germany, West	34.1	46.0	50.2	45.3	46.9	44.9	48.6	46.7	44.3	42.7
Netherlands	55.4	54.7	52.5	52.2	47.4	41.9	37.8	36.7	40.5	27.0
Switzerland	22.1	23.5	24.5	25.0	23.7	22.8	23.4	22.5	20.0	20.5
Sweden						1.8	1.4	1.9	2.7	5.6
Denmark				0.9	1.5	3.0	3.8	2.5	2.2	2.1
Other religious cultures										
Japan					8.2	8.5	10.4	9.6	9.4	8.1
Turkey						11.9	8.6		7.2	16.9
Mean	32.4	33.7	30.1	26.4	24.2	21.3	19.4	20.8	18.0	15.1

Source: Author's compilation based on Lane, McKay, and Newton (1997) for 1945 to 1994 data and *Elections around the world.* Available at: http://www.electionworld.org/election/

Notes: Religious parties: For the classification of parties in each country, see table 7.3 in the source handbook. No religious parties with more than 1 percent of the vote were identified in Spain, Greece, Iceland, United Kingdom, Canada, the United States, or Australia. The table lists the percentage share of valid votes cast for religious parties in national elections. The percentage includes the CDU/CSU, ÖVP and DC.

who do and those who do not attend church regularly. This gap remains significant even after applying the standard battery of societal and individual controls. The gap occurs in many postindustrial societies, which suggests a general pattern at work in people's ideological orientations.

Nevertheless, at the same time, the relationship between religiosity and right-oriented political orientations appears to have weakened over the last twenty years in most industrial and postindustrial societies, with a few exceptions, such as the United States and Austria. In an important sense, the bottom-line test lies in the votes actually cast in national elections. The study documents how, during the past fifty years, support for religious parties has fallen in most postindustrial nations, especially in Catholic Europe. This trend almost perfectly reflects patterns of regular churchgoing in Europe: in both cases, religion starts from a far higher base, and then falls more sharply in Catholic than in Protestant European countries. Secularization appears to have started in Protestant Europe well before survey evidence was available, which suggests that at the start of the postwar era these countries already had less active religious behavior and less support for religious parties than Catholic countries. Consequently, during the past half century, secularization has affected Catholic Europe most strongly, so that these countries are now approaching, but not yet attaining, the low levels of religiosity found in northern Europe. The reasons Protestant Europe saw an earlier erosion of religiosity than Catholic Europe can be attributed to a variety of factors, such as industrialization, higher standards of living, and the growth of a welfare state, all undermining the role of the church. In developing countries, no substantial body of time-series data is available to analyze trends. The limited evidence that is available, however, indicates that these trends are not evident there: no worldwide decline of religiosity or of the role of religion in politics. That is, secularization appears to be a phenomenon characteristic of industrial and postindustrial society.

Evidence presented elsewhere suggests that secularization has generally swept through most affluent nations, in politics as well as in society, though the pace of change and its effects differ from one place to another (Norris and Inglehart 2004). In the United States, as well, the proportion of the unaffiliated and the secular appears to have risen since the 1970s (Hout and Fischer 2002). The massive emigration from Hispanic countries has partly masked this trend because those countries tend to have relatively traditional worldviews (and high fertility rates). Nevertheless, the United States does remain an outlier among comparable postindustrial societies, as is clear with the emergence of the religious cleavages in electoral politics since the early 1990s. Reported churchgoing in American public opinion polls is substantially exaggerated compared with estimates based on congregational head-counts (Hadaway and Marler 2005).

Nevertheless, the proportion of Americans who report that they are regular weekly churchgoers (40 percent), according to opinion polls, also remains far higher than in most comparable European societies.

Many reasons can be advanced to account for the strength of religiosity in the United States compared with other postindustrial societies. In the Fundamentalism Project, Gabriel Almond and his coauthors sought to explain this phenomenon by distinctive characteristics commonly observed in America, such as social and geographic mobility, large-scale migration, and economic insecurity (Appleby, Almond, and Sivan 2003). Other possible explanations include status politics, lifestyle politics, and demographic shifts among Christian whites toward more homogeneous exurban communities. Religious market theory emphasizes supply-side factors, suggesting that exceptionally strong competition in America among a wide variety of denominations promotes and mobilizes active congregations, though the evidence supporting this claim is marred by several important flaws (Finke and Stark 1992).

A more plausible explanation suggests that the strength of religiosity in society lies in patterns of existential insecurity, which encompass a wide range of phenomenon arising from a sense of external threat (Norris and Inglehart 2004). In this regard, virtually all major traditional religious cultures provide reassurance that, even though the individual cannot understand or predict what lies ahead, a higher power will ensure that things work out. Both religion and secular ideologies assure people that the universe follows a plan, which guarantees that if one follows the rules, everything will turn out well, in this world or the next. The rains will come, life will prosper, and—for those believing in an afterlife—the good will be rewarded and death will not end contact with loved ones. This belief reduces stress and uncertainty, enabling people to shut out terrifying anxieties and to focus on coping with immediate problems. Without such a belief system, extreme stress and pain tend to produce withdrawal reactions. Under conditions of insecurity, people have a powerful need to see authority as both strong and benevolent—even in the face of evidence to the contrary. The theory is not mechanically deterministic: perceptions of threats can generate increased fears even in affluent societies, as exemplified by the events of 9/11 and their aftermath in the United States, as well as by the 2007–2010 global economic recession. The insecurity thesis predicts that people in poorer societies and more vulnerable sectors of affluent societies will usually regard religion as far more important than more those of affluent nations and states with generous welfare safety nets and with deeper reservoirs of household savings, private insurance, and investments. A sense of social and individual security is expected to lead toward predictable probabilistic variations in religious values, reflecting the vital importance of religion in people's lives. At the same time, however, residual religious beliefs, ritualistic practices, and religious institutions will continue to bear a strong imprint stamped by each specific type of faith.

One central prediction is that the salience of religious values will tend to be strongest in the least developed societies, as demonstrated elsewhere (Norris and Inglehart 2004). Low-income countries are most vulnerable to life-threatening sociotropic threats from sudden natural and man-made disasters such as floods, famines, and social instability, and the appeal of religious values is strongest in these circumsdtances (Zaidise, Canetti-Nisim, and Pedahzur 2007).

But even among relatively affluent postindustrial societies, the thesis can also help explain variations in religiosity, including contrasts between the relatively secular smaller welfare states such as Sweden and Japan, and more religious nations, such as Italy, Ireland, and the United States. There is not room in this brief conclusion to provide thorough support for this claim from the cross-national evidence, discussed elsewhere, but several indicators from the American data can be observed. A detailed examination of income, religiosity, and voting behavior in the United States noted the link between income and religiosity: "The percent of people who say they are born-again Christians is much higher among the poor than the rich, especially outside the South. Similarly lower-income people are much more likely to pray daily and to consider religion to be very important to their lives" (Gelman 2008, 81–93; Pew Forum on Religion & Public Life 2008).

Previously we did not have direct evidence of security values. In the latest wave of the World Values Survey (2005–2007), however, respondents were for the first time asked directly about the importance of security values, using a 6-point scale. The results of the U.S. analysis in table 1.8 and figure 1.4 demonstrate that, as theorized, those Americans who gave a high priority to the importance of living securely were also significantly more likely to regard religion as important. This pattern persisted even after controlling for other characteristics commonly associated with religiosity, including age and gender (with older Americans and women more religious), income and education (confirming that the poor and less educated Americans were also more religious). Indeed, a comparison of the standardized beta coefficients showed that security values proved the strongest predictor of religiosity. Moreover, the relationship proved robust: when replicated, similar regression models (not shown here) confirmed that security values were significantly linked to many other indicators of American religiosity, from the frequency of church attendance to how often people thought about the meaning of life and the importance that children should learn religious faith.

Cross-national macro-level comparisons further confirm the relationship. As illustrated in figure 1.5, among the Organisation for Economic Cooperation and Development (OECD) postindustrial nations, the

Table 1.8   Link Between Religiosity and Security, United States, 2005 to 2007

	Unstandardized Coefficients		Standardized Coefficients	
	B	S. E.	Beta	Sig.
Important to live securely	.283	.038	.146	.000
Age	.020	.003	.131	.000
Female	.692	.105	.130	.000
Income scale	−.075	.024	−.065	.002
Education scale	−.076	.030	−.053	.011
(Constant)	6.593	.290		.000
Adjusted R²	.076			

Source: Author's compilation based on World Values Survey 2005 to 2007, United States sample only (N. 2458)

Note: The dependent variable is religious values (measured by the importance of God 10-point scale). The Schwartz value scale was used to measure security values: *"Now I will briefly describe some people. Using this card, would you please indicate for each description whether that person is very much like you, like you, somewhat like you, not like you, or not at all like you? Living in secure surroundings is important to this person; to avoid anything that might be dangerous."*

United States was relatively high in the priority given both to security and to religiosity, located close to Poland, Mexico, and Turkey, each with far lower per capita GDP. By contrast, affluent Norway, Sweden, and Japan gave far less. Well-known structural factors in each society can help explain these underlying perceptual contrasts. According to OECD social indicators, for example, among the thirty member states in 2004–2005, the United States ranked highest in the prison population rate (738 prisoners per 100,000 versus 68 in Norway) and third highest in per capita GDP ($34,681 in current PPP, or purchasing power parity). It also ranked twenty-third lowest in life expectancy and twenty-fifth lowest in both public social spending as a percentage of GDP and unemployment benefits (OECD 2007).

These characteristics can help explain general patterns of American religiosity. The broad popularity of religion in American society provides fertile grounds for linking groups with voting behavior. The more specific explanation, which has been evident over successive contests since the early 1990s, rests on the organizational linkages that developed a decade earlier between certain wings of the Republican Party and the leadership of the Christian conservative movement. This alignment built on historic links, where, according to the ANES, Protestants have been one of the bedrock foundations of the Republican Party base since at least the mid-twentieth century. As Lipset and Rokkan suggested,

Figure 1.4   Religiosity and Security Values, United States, 2005 to 2007

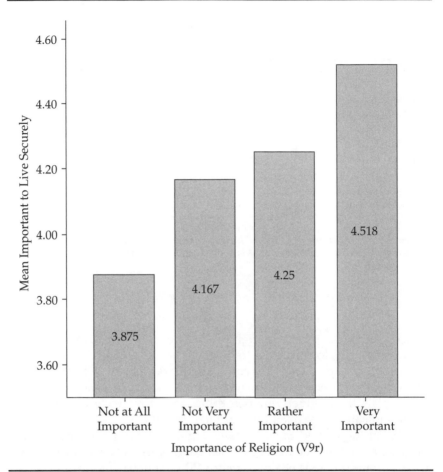

Source: Author's compilation based on World Values Survey 2005 to 2007, United States sample only (N=2458).
Note: The Schwartz value 6-point scale was used to measure security values: "Now I will briefly describe some people. Using this card, would you please indicate for each description whether that person is very much like you, like you, somewhat like you, not like you, or not at all like you? Living in secure surroundings is important to this person; to avoid anything that might be dangerous."

linkages between parties and core social cleavages first emerge because they reflect basic ideological fissures in party politics and then freeze into durable alignments over successive elections (1967). In this regard, religiosity in American society, despite some secularization, and stronger organizational links between the Religious Right and the Re-

Figure 1.5   Religiosity and Security Values, OECD Nations, 2005 to 2007

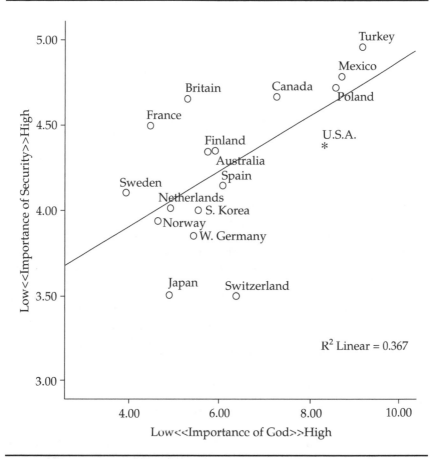

Source: Author's compilation based on World Values Survey 2005 to 2007, OECD nations only (N = 22,763)
Note: The Schwartz value 6-point scale was used to measure security values: "Now I will briefly describe some people. Using this card, would you please indicate for each description whether that person is very much like you, like you, somewhat like you, not like you, or not at all like you? Living in secure surroundings is important to this person; to avoid anything that might be dangerous."

publican leadership, help explain patterns of party competition and the religious gap among the electorate.

References

Appleby, R. Scott, Gabriel Almond, and Emmanuel Sivan. 2003. *Strong Religion*. Chicago: University of Chicago Press.

Bartolini, Stephano, and Peter Mair. 1990. *Identity, Competition, and Electoral Availability: The Stabilization of European Electorates, 1885–1985.* Cambridge: Cambridge University Press.

Borowik, Irena. 2002. "The Roman Catholic Church in the Process of Democratic Transformation: The Case of Poland." *Social Compass* 49(2): 239–52.

Brooks, Clem, and Jeff Manza. 1997a. "Social Cleavages and Political Alignments: U.S. Presidential Elections, 1960 to 1992." *American Sociological Review* 62(6): 937–46.

———. 1997b. "The Religious Factor in U.S. Presidential Elections, 1960–1992." *American Journal of Sociology* 103(1): 38–81.

Broughton, David, and Hans-Martien ten Napel, eds. 2000. *Religion and Mass Electoral Behavior in Europe.* London: Routledge.

Butler, Daid, and Donald Stokes. 1974. *Political Change in Britain*, 2nd ed. London: Macmillan.

Campbell, Angus, Philip Converse, Warren E. Miller, and Donald E. Stokes. 1960. *The American Voter.* New York: John Wiley & Sons.

Clark, Terry Nichols, and Seymour Martin Lipset. Eds. 2001. *The Breakdown of Class Politics.* Baltimore, Md.: The Johns Hopkins University Press.

Clubb, Jerome M., William H. Flanigan, and Nancy H. Zingale. 1990. *Partisan Realignment: Voters, Parties and Government in American History.* Boulder, Colo.: Westview Press.

CNN. "Exit Polls." CNN Election Center 2008. Available at: http://www.cnn.com/ELECTION/2008/results/polls.main/ (accessed March 15, 2009).

Converse, Philip. 1964. "The Nature of Belief Systems in Mass Publics." In *Ideology and Discontent*, edited by David Apter. New York: Free Press.

Crewe, Ivor, Jim Alt, and Bo Sarlvik. 1977. "Partisan Dealignment in Britain 1964–1974." *British Journal of Political Science* 7(2): 129–90.

Crewe, Ivor, and David Denver, eds. 1985. *Electoral Change in Western Democracies: Patterns and Sources of Electoral Volatility.* New York: St. Martin's Press.

Daalder, Hans, and Peter Mair, eds. 1985. *Western European Party Systems.* London: Sage Publications.

Dalton, Russell J., Scott Flanagan, and Paul Allen Beck, eds. 1984. *Electoral Change in Advanced Industrial Democracies: Realignment or Dealignment?* Princeton, N.J.: Princeton University Press.

Finke, Roger, and Rodney Stark. 1992. *The Churching of America, 1776–1990: Winners and Losers in Our Religious Economy.* New Brunswick, N.J.: Rutgers University Press.

Franklin, Mark N., Tom Mackie, and Henry Valen. 1992. *Electoral Change: Responses to Evolving Social and Attitudinal Structures in Western Countries.* Cambridge: Cambridge University Press.

Fuchs, Dieter, and Hans-Dieter Klingmann. 1989. "The Left-Right Schema." In *Continuities in Political Action*, edited by M. Kent Jennings and Jan von Deth. Berlin: de Gruyter

Gelman, Andrew. 2008. *Red State/Blue State/Rich State/Poor State: Why Americans Vote the Way They Do.* Princeton, N.J.: Princeton University Press.

Hadaway, C. Kirk, and Penny Long Marler. 2005. "How Many Americans Attend Worship Each Week? An Alternative Approach to Measurement." *Journal for the Scientific Study of Religion* 44(3): 307–22.

Hanley, David, ed. 1996. *Christian Democracy in Europe: A Comparative Perspective.* New York: Pinter.

Hout, Michael, and Claude S. Fischer. 2002. "Why More Americans Have No Religious Preference: Politics and Generations." *American Sociological Review* 67(2): 165–90.

Jelen, Ted Gerard, and Clyde Wilcox, eds. 2002. *Religion and Politics in Comparative Perspective.* New York: Cambridge University Press.

Keslman, Thomas, and Joseph A. Buttigieg, eds. 2003. *European Christian Democracy: Historical Legacies and Comparative Perspectives.* Notre Dame, Ind.: University of Notre Dame Press.

Kitschelt, Herbert, ed. 1995. *The Radical Right in Western Europe.* Ann Arbor: University of Michigan Press.

Knutsen, Oddbjørn. 1995. "Left-Right Materialist Value Orientation." In *The Impact of Values*, edited by Jan Van Deth and Elinor Scarbrough. New York: Oxford University Press.

———. 1999. "Left-Right Party Polarization Among the Mass Publics." In *Challenges to Representative Democracy*, edited by Hanne Marthe Narud and Toril Aalberg. Bergen, Norway: Fagbokforlaget.

Leege, David C., and Lyman A. Kellstedt, eds. 1993. *Rediscovering the Religious Factor in American Politics.* New York: M. E. Sharpe.

Lewis-Beck, Michael, and Andrew Skalaban. 1992. "France." In *Electoral Change: Responses to Evolving Social and Attitudinal Structures in Western Countries*, edited by Mark Franklin, Tom Mackie, and Henry Valen. Cambridge: Cambridge University Press.

Lipset, Seymour Martin. 1997. *American Exceptionalism: A Double-Edged Sword.* New York: W. W. Norton.

Lipset, Seymour Martin, and Stein Rokkan. 1967. *Party Systems and Voter Alignments.* New York: Free Press.

Madeley, John. 1991. "Politics and religion in Western Europe." In *Politics and Religion in the Modern World*, edited by George Moyser. London: Routledge.

Mainwaring, Scott, and Timothy R. Scully, eds. 2003. *Christian Democracy in Latin America: Electoral Competition and Regime Conflicts.* Stanford, Calif.: Stanford University Press.

Manza, Jeff, and Clem Brooks. 1999. *Social Cleavages and Political Change: Voter Alignments and U.S. Party Coalitions.* New York: Oxford University Press

Mitchell, Paul, Brendan O'Leary, and Geoffrey Evans. 2001. "Northern Ireland: Flanking Extremists Bite the Moderates and Emerge in their Clothes." *Parliamentary Affairs* 54(4): 725–42.

Moyser, George, ed. 1991. *Politics and Religion in the Modern World.* London: Routledge.

Mughan, Anthony. 1983. "Accommodation or Diffusion in the Management of Ethnic Conflict in Belgium." *Political Studies* 31(3)(September): 431–51.

Nie, Norman, Sidney Verba, and John Petrocik. 1976. *The Changing American Voter.* Cambridge, Mass.: Harvard University Press.

Norris, Pippa. 2000a. "US Campaign 2000: Of Pregnant Chads, Butterfly Ballots and Partisan Vitriol." *Government and Opposition* 36(1): 3–26.

———. 2000b. *A Vicious Circle? Political Communications in Post-Industrial Democracies.* Cambridge: Cambridge University Press.

————. 2003. *Electoral Engineering*. New York: Cambridge University Press.

————. 2005. *Radical Right*. Cambridge: Cambridge University Press.

Norris, Pippa, and Ronald Inglehart. 2004. *Sacred and Secular*. Cambridge: Cambridge University Press.

Norris, Pippa, and Christopher Wlezien. 2005. "'Introduction' and 'Conclusion.'" In *Britain Votes 2005*, edited by Pippa Norris and Christopher Wlezien. Oxford: Oxford University Press.

Organisation of Economic and Social Development (OECD). February 2007. *Selection of OECD Social Indicators*. Paris: Organisation of Economic and Social Development. Available at: http://www.oecd.org/els/social/indicators/SAG.

Pederson, Morgens N. 1979. "The Dynamics of European Party Systems: Changing Patterns of Electoral Volatility." *European Journal of Political Research* 7(1): 1–26.

Pew Forum on Religion & Public Life. 2008. *US Religious Landscape Survey*. Washington, D.C.: Pew Research Center. Available at: http://pewforum.org/.

United Nations Development Programme (UNDP). 1999. *Human Development Report*. New York: UNDP/Oxford University Press.

Warner, Carolyn M. 2000. *Confessions of an Interest Group: The Catholic Church and Political Parties in Europe*. Princeton, N.J.: Princeton University Press.

Whiteley, Paul, Marianne C. Stewart, David Sanders, and Harold D. Clarke. 2005. "The Issue Agenda and Voting in 2005." In *Britain Votes 2005*, edited by Pippa Norris and Christopher Wlezien. Oxford: Oxford University Press.

Wilcox, Clyde. 1992. *God's Warriors: The Christian Right in Twentieth Century America*. Baltimore, Md.: The Johns Hopkins University Press.

Zaidise, Eran, Daphna Canetti-Nisim, and Ami Pedahzur. 2007. "Politics of God or Politics of Man? The Role of Religion and Deprivation in Predicting support for Political Violence in Israel." *Political Studies* 55(3): 499–521.

Chapter 2

Interests, Values, and Party Identification between 1972 and 2006

MICHAEL HOUT AND ANDREW GREELEY

CONSERVATIVE PROTESTANTS developed political clout just as two other major political trends emerged in the United States. The South realigned with the Republicans and party loyalty once again dictated the outcome of presidential elections. The conventional wisdom emphasizes values as the common thread in religious and regional realignment. Voters with strong religious identities and those in red states have distinct values that guide their political choices. They supposedly look past their personal and family concerns to express those values in voting and they identify with the party they vote with most of the time. By this reckoning, the Republican Party has grown since the 1980s and the Democrat Party has waned because Republican candidates have articulated the concerns of values voters better than Democrats have. The values thesis misses the role of growing inequality and partisanship based on pocketbook issues like tax rates and social spending. The either-or nature of the public discussion in electronic media and mass market nonfiction books more or less requires a one-cause explanation. So, if values shape political trends, class issues must be beside the point. But in real life there are many paths to the voting booth. Some voters get there by consulting their values, but others go the way their family budgets (or stock portfolios) tell them to go. Income matters as well as values.

Interests and values affect politics independently. The influence of one does not preclude the influence of the other. Let us suppose for the moment that society is composed of two value groups—traditional and progressive—and two economic classes—affluent and poor. The traditional group and the affluent class tend to identify with the Republican Party and the progressive group and the poor class with the Democrats. Among voters who find their value group and economic class in agreement—traditional affluent people and progressive poor people—politics is straightforward. For the others—traditional poor people and progressive affluent people—political signals are mixed. In the aggregate, we would expect strong majorities of the consistent combinations but close to even splits among those whose values contradict interests. That is, pretty much, what the evidence shows. In recent years, 70 percent of affluent abortion opponents, for example, identified with the Republican Party (versus 30 percent of the entire electorate), and 47 percent of poor abortion supporters identified with the Democratic Party (versus 34 percent).[1]

We focus in this chapter on voters' party identification (for voting results, see Greeley and Hout 2006). Party identification is an important factor in the political changes of the last thirty years because people have tended more and more to vote along party lines.

We present evidence that trends that were important for voters in general were stronger among conservative Protestants. We find that both interests and values played significant roles in the growing Republican identification of conservative Protestants. Family income and attitudes about the economy, taxes, and government regulation sway the party preferences of conservative Protestants just as much as church attendance and attitudes about abortion and homosexuality.

Data and Statistics

The General Social Survey (GSS) began in 1972 as an annual survey of American adults covering a broad list of social and cultural issues. Since 1977 it has been a full-probability sample of households with a randomly selected adult from each; in the early years quotas were used for all (1972) or half (1973–1976) of the sample. Interviews are conducted face to face. English was the only language until 2006, when a Spanish version was added. In 1994 the design was changed from annual to biennial.[2] The annual survey had target sizes of roughly 1,500 interviews—funding sometimes dictated smaller targets—and the new biennial design calls for 2,800 to 3,000 interviews. Response rates remain high, well over 70 percent throughout the history of the project (see Davis, Smith, and Marsden 2006).

Every respondent in every year was asked whether they voted in most recent presidential election, their vote choices if they did vote, and which political party they identify with (see Davis, Smith, and Marsden

2006). Everyone was also asked, "What is your religious preference? Would that be Protestant, Catholic, Jewish, no religion at all, or some other religion?" Protestants were asked, "Which specific denomination do you identify with?" We coded the specific denominations into three categories: conservative, African American, and mainline. Our schema is based on Tom Smith's (1990) with modifications in response to a critique by Brian Steensland his colleagues (1999), but we do not follow either schema exactly (see Greeley and Hout 2006, 6–9).

Other key variables in our analysis include two standard demographic items—gender and region—that were coded by the interviewer without asking the respondent, and age, racial ancestry, marital status, education, and family income that were asked of everyone. Church attendance was also asked of all respondents. Abortion attitudes and specific questions about social spending, taxes, and the economy were asked of a random two-thirds of respondents (not the same two-thirds so only one-third of each year's sample answered all the questions of interest).

We process the data as little as possible for the analyses reported here and we rely more on figures with smoothed time lines than on tables of statistics to make our points. However, we have done extensive multivariate modeling of the data and certify that all the results we discuss in the text stand up to the statistical scrutiny of the multivariate analyses. In particular, all the differences over time and among religions that we discuss are statistically significant, except on occasion when we expected a significant difference and remark on the lack of one.

We use locally estimated (loess) regression to smooth time lines (Cleveland 1979; Cleveland and Devlin 1988). Loess regression is a more reliable alternative to the moving averages often used in smoothing time series. At each point in the time series, loess calls for fitting a low degree polynomial to a subset of the data near the point to be estimated. The technique uses weighted least squares to obtain coefficients for the polynomial regression, giving more weight to points near the point of interest and less weight to points further away. The smoothed data point is the predicted value for that year from the loess regression. The details of the regression differ for each data point in the time series. The number of data points in each regression (that is, the degree of the polynomial) and the exact weights used are options that make each fit different. We used 80 percent of the data in most figures; for small groups we occasionally used 99 percent of the data. We do not display lines based on fewer than 200 cases. We used tricube weights—the default in Stata—for each smoothing exercise.

Throughout the analysis we restrict the sample to those twenty-five years old and older. We do so because many of the relationships we are most interested in—religious and political identification—are very much in flux during young adulthood. Some people craft their identities in adolescence and make lifelong commitments at young ages. Others wait. We drop the youngest respondents to remove this element of changeability from the data.

We also restrict our attention to voters, people who said that they voted in the most recent presidential election. Nonvoters are worthy of study in their own right but our focus throughout is on the electorate.

Partisanship and Voting

Political party identification invokes a personal attachment a voter might have to a political party. The GSS question is, "Generally speaking, do you usually think of yourself as a Republican, Democrat, Independent, or what?" Independents were asked whether they lean to the Republicans or Democrats. In the classic formulation of *The American Voter*, party identification informed all political choices, especially the choice between candidates in a partisan election (Campbell et al. 1960). Voters were capable of the occasional crossover as when, in 1952 and 1956, Catholic Democrats voted for Eisenhower because Stevenson was divorced.

The data series that *The American Voter* authors created—the American National Election Studies (ANES)—soon compiled evidence against the classic theory. In 1964, northern Republicans abandoned Goldwater and handed Johnson a landslide as many southern Democrats went the other way in a losing cause, prompting Kevin Phillips to craft former Vice President Nixon's so-called southern strategy (1969). That strategy worked in the South and elsewhere as crossover votes from Democrats handed Nixon a narrow victory over Humphrey and Wallace in 1968 and more than 60 percent of the vote against McGovern in 1972. Democrats voting for Republicans led to serious questions about the classic theory (Niemi and Weisberg 1976) and questions about the future of the two-party system itself (Wattenberg 1996).

Since the 1972 election, party identification has become a good predictor again, each subsequent election proving more partisan than 1972 (Bartels 2000). Political scientists continue to debate the underlying causes of the rising predictive validity of party identification (Fiorina 2002), but two trends are clear. First, voters defected from the major parties between 1964 and 1976 but not since (identification may have increased in the mid-1990s), and nonvoters continued to defect until 1992. Second, voters loyally chose the candidate from their own party more in the 2000 and 2004 elections than in any previous elections in the ANES time series (that is, since 1952).

Republican loyalty has seldom been the issue. More than 85 percent of Republicans have voted for the Republican presidential candidate in all but the two elections when Ross Perot ran. Democratic disloyalty changed the outcome of several elections. In 1968 former Governor George Wallace siphoned Democrats' votes from Vice President Hubert Humphrey. In 1972 Nixon got more than 30 percent of Democrats' votes; Reagan did almost that well in 1984. Democratic loyalty increased to near-Republican levels from 1988 to 2004.

In the 2004 election, 95 percent of Republicans voted for incumbent President Bush and 88 percent of Democrats voted for Senator Kerry. The increased loyalty of Democrats raised Bartels's partisan voting index from a low of .92 in 1972 to 1.28 in 2000 and 1.26 in 2004 (2000, 39). A simpler calculation—the difference between Republicans and Democrats in the percentage voting for the Republican candidate—rose from 58 percentage points in 1972 to 83 in 2004.

Religion, Crossover Voting, and Partisan Realignment

The four largest religious groups in the United States—conservative Protestants, mainline Protestants, Catholics, and people with no religion—all voted in ways consistent with the national trend toward increased partisanship; the smaller groups—African American Protestants and Jews—were distinct in different ways. Figure 2.1 shows the details. Each point shows the percentage voting for the Republican candidate; the solid lines show trends for Republicans and Democrats (independents are not shown); the dashed lines show the difference between parties. Conservative Protestant Republicans supported the Republican candidate consistently; the percentages range from highs in 1984 and 2004 of 98 percent to a low in 1996 of 75 percent.[3] Conservative Protestant Democrats, on the other hand, became far more loyal over time. In the 1972 election, half voted for Nixon, one-third voted for Reagan in 1984 and Bush in 1988, but only one-fifth voted for the younger Bush in 2000 and 2004. The difference between conservative Protestant Republicans and Democrats grew from 46 percentage points in 1972 to 80 in 2004.

Mainline Protestant Republicans and Democrats were hardly distinguishable from their conservative Protestant counterparts in any of these elections. Catholics, though very similar, differed in some elections. Catholic Democrats did not vote quite as strongly for Nixon in 1972 or Reagan in 1984, and Catholic Republicans supported both Clinton and Perot significantly more than conservative Protestants did in 1992. Voters with no religion were not significantly different from Catholic voters in any of elections until this decade; Democrats with no religion voted more consistently with Gore and Kerry than Catholic Democrats did.

Figure 2.1   Republican Party Vote and the Difference Between Republicans and Democrats by Election Year, Party Identification, and Religion

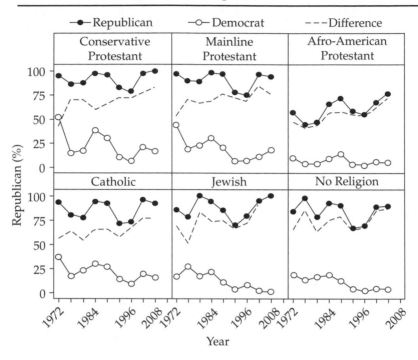

Source: Authors' compilation based on General Social Surveys, 1973 to 2006.
Note: Independents not shown.

African American Protestant Democrats were significantly more loyal than Democrats from other religions in the Nixon and Reagan eras. It was African American Protestant Republicans who defected during those elections; half backed McGovern in 1972 and one-third voted for Carter in 1980 and again for Mondale in 1984. Jewish Democrats and Republicans voted more strongly for McGovern in 1972 than conservative Protestants did. Twenty percent of Jewish Republicans voted for Clinton in 1992, making them significantly different than both conservative Protestants and Catholics in that election.

Crossover votes can be either a one-time occurrence reflecting a particular candidate's special appeal or, if repeated, the harbinger of change to come. The available evidence strongly supports the harbinger hypothesis. Some GSSs asked not only about the most recent presidential election but also about the one before that. From those data, we note that

79 percent of the Democrats who voted for Nixon in 1968 also voted for him in 1972; similarly, 80 percent of the Democrats who voted for Reagan in 1980 voted for him again in 1984. In contrast, only 17 percent of the Democrats who voted for Bush in 1988 voted for him again in 1992. The dramatic drop-off in persistent crossover voting is attributable to the drop-off in Democratic identification. From 1972 to 1988 Democrats decreased from 51 to 39 percent of voters; between 1980 and 1988 Republican identification rose from 27 to 37 percent of voters.

Figure 2.2 shows how, over time, Republican identification converged on Republican voting in five of the six religion groups, all but African American Protestants for whom Republican voting and identification were equally rare events. Nearly half of conservative Protestants (48 percent) identified with the Republicans by 2008; only 29 percent did in 1972. Their identification climbed toward their long-term average of 59 percent voting Republican. Similarly, Catholics came to identify more with the Republican Party over time, catching up with their evenly divided voting tendencies (only in 1980 did the Catholic vote not go to the winner). Mainline Protestants did not change their identification but nonetheless closed the gap between voting and identification as their voting pattern fell from a stronger to a weaker Republican tendency close to their roughly 40 percent Republican identification. About 10 percent of Jewish voters adopted a Republican identification in the late 1970s and early 1980s, but did not change their preferences after that. Meanwhile, the Jewish vote became more and more strongly Democratic as time went by. The pattern for voters with no religion resembles that of Jews, though in each year the nonreligious voters were more Republican than the Jews were. African American Protestants—the most Democratic segment of the electorate—changed neither their identifications nor their votes.

Our analysis of the partisanship trends accords well with most scholarly conclusions about religion and politics (for example, Layman 2001), but an alternative exists. Some scholars and journalists see the political divisions among religions less in denominational terms and more as the divide between active and inactive believers or, more trenchantly, as the value conflict between believers and secular Americans (Hunter 1992; Norris and Inglehart 2004). If this idea, call it the religiosity hypothesis, is correct, then active members of all denominations should identify mostly as Republican to the same extent, and the trends in partisanship ought to be attributable to a growing association between attending services and favoring Republicans. Our denominational hypothesis implies the converse: identification should reflect the changing relationship between denomination and party we showed in figure 2.2. To test these competing views, we use multivariate models that include attendance at religious services and dummy variables for each denomination, fit for

Figure 2.2   Republican Party Vote and Party Identification by Year and Religion

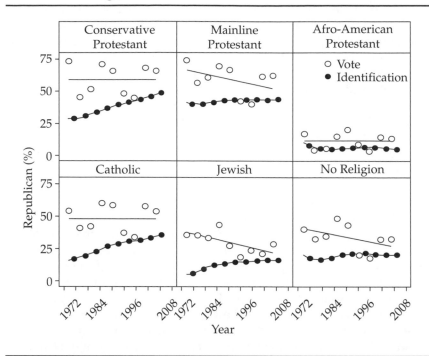

Source: Authors' compilation based on General Social Surveys, 1972 to 2006.
Note: Vote data smoothed by linear (OLS) regression; identification data smoothed by locally estimated (loess) regression.

different periods. The religiosity hypothesis implies that the association between attendance and party identification rose over time and between denomination and party identification fell, perhaps to zero, over time. The denominational hypothesis implies the converse—steady or declining attendance coefficients and strong trends within denominations (strong trends show up as statistically significant interactions between denomination and time).

We experimented with several periods. The simplest one that preserved the key results divided the GSS time series into three political eras: the Nixon-Carter era of 1972–1980, the Reagan-Bush era of 1982–1991, and the Clinton-Bush era of 1993–2006. We also experimented with how to specify the attendance relationship and found that the simplest—using the scores in the GSS data file[4]—worked best. Although we know of no explicit discussion of the subject among proponents of the religiosity hypothesis, it made sense to assume that attendance affects only people with a religious preference, so we constrained the effect of attendance to be zero for people who prefer no religion. Previous research on voting showed that attendance intensified African American Protestants' Democratic tendencies (Greeley and Hout 2006, chapter 4), so we introduced an interaction effect for that group. Because of our special interest in conservative Protestants, we also included an interaction between conservative Protestant and attendance. We also tried three statistical models: ordered logit regression, stereotype ordered logit regression, and multinomial logit regression (for a discussion of the models, see Clogg and Shihadeh 1994). The ordered logit model is most parsimonious, but its key assumption failed statistical tests.[5]

We present the results for multinomial logistic regressions in each of the three political eras in table 2.1.

The regression results support the denomination hypothesis and imply a substantial revision to the attendance hypothesis. Denominational differences in party identification dwarf differences between members of denominations who attend frequently or infrequently. By 2006, 51 percent of conservative and 49 percent of mainline Protestants who attended church services weekly were Republicans. That kind of close outcome is precisely what the attendance hypothesis predicts. But the devout of the other denominations were not nearly that Republican. Among people attending weekly, 37 percent of Catholics, 24 percent of Jews, 24 percent of people of other religions, and 5 percent of African American Protestants were Republicans. That was a ten-to-one range of differences. If we dismiss African American Protestants as somehow exceptional, then the ratio was two to one, and if we focus on the three biggest denominations we still see that conservative and mainline Protestants were still 1.35 times more Republican than Catholics—among the devout. Among those who never attend services, partisan differences were smaller, mainly because attendance mattered more for conservative Protestants than others. Among the nonattenders, mainline Protestants were most Republican (36 percent), followed by conservative Protestants (31 percent) and Catholics (26 percent).

Conservative Protestants increased their Republican identification even more than could be predicted by their combination of above-average church attendance and greater attendance gradient. In the Nixon-Carter era, conservative Protestants who did not attend services were as Republican as voters with no religion; those who attended weekly were only about 10 percentage points more Republican. Churchgoing conservative Protestants became more Republican in the Reagan-Bush era and then emerged in the Clinton-Bush era as the most Republican. Conservative Protestants who did not attend church frequently also became more Republican in the Clinton-Bush years. Conversely, African American Protestants who attended services remained as loyally Democratic

Table 2.1   Coefficients for Log-Odds on Republican Party Identification by Denomination, Attendance at Religious Services, and Political Era

Attendance Coefficient	1972 to 1980	1982 to 1991	1993 to 2006
Conservative Protestant	.068*	.111*	.101*
	(.026)	(.019)	(.015)
Mainline Protestant	.069*	.020	.072*
	(.015)	(.013)	(.011)
Afro-American Protestant	.064	−.033	−.105
	(.082)	(.083)	(.070)
Catholic	.069*	.020	.072*
	(.015)	(.013)	(.011)
Jewish	.069*	.020	.072*
	(.015)	(.013)	(.011)
Other religion	.069*	.020	.072*
	(.015)	(.013)	(.011)
No religion	.000	.000	.000
	—	—	—
Constants			
Conservative Protestant	−.783*	−.415*	−.106
	(.172)	(.134)	(.095)
Mainline Protestant	−.074	.436*	.162
	(.115)	(.102)	(.073)
Afro-American Protestant	−2.915*	−2.400*	−2.041*
	(.477)	(.476)	(.377)
Catholic	−1.460*	−.450*	−.415*
	(.133)	(.111)	(.078)
Jewish	−2.519*	−.1.277*	−1.367*
	(.315)	(.207)	(.161)
Other religion	−.775*	−.709*	−.890*
	(.329)	(.271)	(.158)
No religion	−.952*	−.392*	−.631*
	(.180)	(.147)	(.084)
Year dummies	Yes	Yes	Yes
Observations	7,034	9,134	13,637

Source: Authors' calculations based on General Social Survey, 1972 to 2006.
Note: Standard errors in parentheses.
* $p < .05$.

as ever and those who did not attend drifted ever so slightly toward the Republicans. In summary, churchgoing mainline Protestants, Catholics, Jews, and voters with other religions were somewhat more Republican than their coreligionists who did not attend, but attendance differences did not account for the divergent partisan trends among denominations.

Returning to the main point, then, we conclude that the rise of partisan voting in recent years largely reflects the adjustment of political identities to conform to voting patterns—not the other way around. The American electorate was in a state of disequilibrium in the late 1960s and throughout the 1970s. From 1972 to 1985, equilibrium was more or less restored as some voters changed parties so that their political identities came to mesh with how they had been voting. Conservative Protestants emerged from this process of finding a new equilibrium as the most Republican religious constituency. That is, their identification with the Republican Party caught and surpassed that of the mainline Protestants. Catholics moved as sharply to the right as conservative Protestants did. But they did so from a stronger Democratic starting point, so they ended up just about evenly divided, with 35 percent identifying with each party and 30 percent as independent. In contrast, the conservative Protestants split 48 percent Republican to 29 percent Democrat (23 percent independent). Attendance at services intensified the diverging trends for conservative and African American Protestants but the denominational trends are not proxies for the emergence of a religious-secular divide.

Conservative Protestants or Southerners?

In addition to the rise of conservative Protestants within the Republican Party, the other noteworthy trend of the late twentieth century was the realignment of the South. For a hundred years, the party of Lincoln was anathema to southern whites. But when the national Democratic Party started talking about a progressive civil rights agenda, southern whites started to vote for third-party and Republican presidential candidates.

The political realignment of the South was no accident. Kevin Phillips pored over detailed election returns from throughout the twentieth century, up to the 1964 election, to uncover weaknesses in the Democrats' "solid South" (1969). As early as 1948, Senator Strom Thurmond—a Democrat running as the "Dixiecrat"—won four deep-South states and one electoral vote from Tennessee. In 1960, Democratic candidates for Alabama's Electoral College delegation who were not pledged to Senator John F. Kennedy outpolled those who were pledged to Kennedy. In 1964, Goldwater polled strong throughout the South and won the four states Thurmond had won in 1948 as well as Georgia. Phillips reasoned that a Republican candidate who combined an appeal to these deep-South white voters with traditionally Republican states of the Northeast and Midwest plus California could win. In 1968, Nixon won even though former Alabama Governor George C. Wallace won his home state plus Arkansas, Louisiana, Mississippi, Georgia, and one vote from North Carolina. Nonetheless, the by-then long-running weakness of the Democratic presidential candidates in the South put the once-solid

South into political play for the next several elections. Recent elections have made the South solid once again, now as solidly Republican as it once was solidly Democratic. Eventually those votes—and votes for Republicans like Senators Jesse Helms and Trent Lott—led to a reassessment of party identification, sparking a trend toward Republican identification in the South. In line with this voting shift, Republican identification increased throughout the South.

The question for us is whether the political realignment of the South explains the Republican surge among conservative Protestants. Conservative Protestants are prevalent in the South; 38 percent of southern voters and 41 percent of southern white voters are conservative Protestants and 50 percent of conservative Protestant voters are southerners.[6] If the regional hypothesis is true, then Republican identification should rise for southerners of all religions but not for others.

The results in figure 2.3 show clearly that the regional hypothesis is wrong. Conservative Protestants outside the South—in the Midwest and Mountain states in particular (details not shown)—moved to the Republicans before those living in the South did. Conservative Protestants realigned their party identifications late relative to conservative Protestants elsewhere and even to mainline Protestants and Catholics in the South. By 2000, conservative Protestants in the South were as closely identified with the Republican Party as conservative Protestants elsewhere, but in 1986, at the height of the Reagan era, the southerners were 14 percentage points behind conservative Protestants in other states. Only among traditionally Republican mainline Protestants did southerners move to the Republican Party and coreligionists elsewhere not change. That hardly counts as support for the regional hypothesis because the mainline Protestants outside the South were such strong Republicans to begin with. For Catholics, the regional difference was insignificant from 1972 to 1986; then, as Catholics outside the South quit adopting a Republican identity, southern Catholics continued to become more so. Southern black Protestants and Jews did not increase their Republican identification, and the modest increase in Republican identification among voters with no religion is not statistically significant.

The cohort succession hypothesis suggests that demographic turnover could explain the trend to Republican identification. Glenn Firebaugh and Kenneth Davis (1988) showed that antiblack prejudice abated in the South when the Old Guard segregationists passed away and were replaced by a less-prejudiced generation. A similar demographic changing of the guard could spark a national trend to more Republican identification. As the cohorts that first became eligible to vote at the height of the New Deal era pass away, the younger cohorts entering the electorate might be more open to Republican appeals. The cohort succession hypothesis is mainly relevant for conservative Protestants

Figure 2.3   Republican Party Identification by Year, Region, and Religion

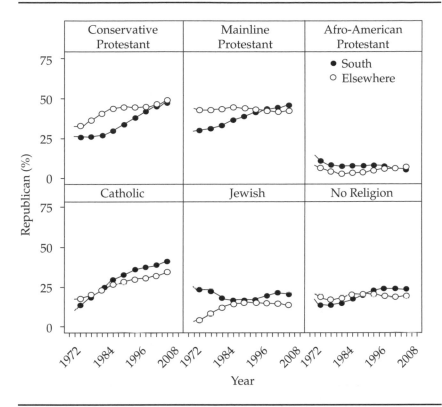

Source: Authors' compilation based on General Social Surveys, 1972 to 2006.
Note: Data smoothed by locally estimated (loess) regression.

and Catholics—the two religions with rapidly growing Republican identification. This is important because if the cohort succession hypothesis is correct, then we should stop focusing on trends over time and switch our attention to differences among cohorts.

Figure 2.4 shows Republican identification for five cohorts defined by years of birth from 1900 to 1974; these people became eligible to vote between 1921 and 1992. If cohort succession was an important part of political change, then Republican trends within cohorts should be insignificant. If the hypothesis was true, all or most of the change over time would be reflected in differences among the cohorts; the oldest two cohorts would be significantly less Republican than the middle or younger cohorts; and the 1960–1974 cohort ought to be the most Republican. The data clearly contradict the first expectation. Conservative Protestants

Figure 2.4   Republican Party Identification by Year, Cohort, and Religion

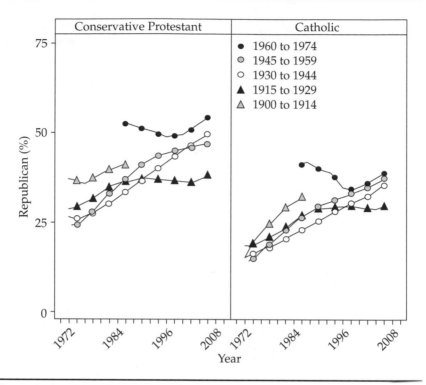

Source: Authors' compilation based on General Social Surveys, 1972 to 2006.
Note: Data smoothed by locally estimated (loess) regression.

and Catholics born between 1930 and 1944 and between 1945 and 1959 became substantially more Republican between 1972 and 1992. The oldest cohort was more Republican than the three that came after it. Thus we are correct in focusing on change over time.

The Abortion Issue

We turn to substantive issues—first the values issues of abortion and homosexuality, and then family income and economic interests. In the political context dominated by ten-second sound bites, abortion attitudes have come to summarize candidates' family values. We prefer not to voice an opinion on whether this tendency to reduce discussion is lamentable or efficient and simply note that attitudes regarding abortion emerged as effective partisan predictors in the late 1980s (Miller and Shanks 1996) and were the key marker of the culture wars (DiMaggio,

Bryson, and Evans 1996; Hout 1999). Most of this research investigated abortion attitudes and their correlation with voting. Here we explore the connection between abortion attitudes and party identification.

The main hypothesis is that abortion attitudes intensified the partisan split as abortion opponents in all religions moved toward Republican identification over time and abortion supporters in those religions moved toward the Democrats. Because the number of opponents roughly equals the number of supporters, the upshot of the polarizing trends was the polarized, stand-off electorate of the 2000 and 2004 elections.

The GSS measures abortion attitudes via the Rossi scale, Alice Rossi's six items that ask whether a pregnant woman ought to be able to get a legal abortion under six conditions: her pregnancy endangers her health; she became pregnant when she was raped; it is likely that the baby, if born, will have serious birth defects; she is poor; she is unmarried and does not want to marry the father; and she has children already and wants no more. The items conform to most of the requirements of a Gutman scale, that is, most of the information is captured by the sum of favorable responses (Clogg and Sawyer 1981). We reduced that to three categories: voters who opposed all or all but one item; voters who favored two, three, or four items; and voters who favored five or all six items. In recent years, 20 percent of voters favored keeping abortion legal in none or one of the conditions, 43 percent favored legal abortion in two, three, or four conditions, and 37 percent favored it in five or all six conditions. Conservative Protestants, Catholics, and African American Protestants oppose abortion significantly more than other voters, as shown in table 2.2.

Figure 2.5 shows the association between partisan trends and abor-

Table 2.2   Support for Legal Abortion by Religion: Voters Twenty-Five Years Old and Over

	Favor Legal Abortion Under:				
Current religion	0 or 1 conditions	2 – 4 conditions	5 or 6 conditions	Total	(N)
Conservative Protestant	29	49	22	100	(614)
Afro-American Protestant	22	57	21	100	(130)
Mainline Protestant	16	44	40	100	(610)
Catholic	24	46	30	100	(555)
Jewish	6	15	79	100	(38)
Other religion	7	36	57	100	(60)
No religion	4	24	72	100	(278)
Total	20	43	37	100	(2,286)

Source: Authors' compilation based on General Social Survey, 2002 to 2006.
Note: Association statistically significant ($p < .05$).

Figure 2.5   Republican Party Identification by Year, Abortion Attitude, and Religion

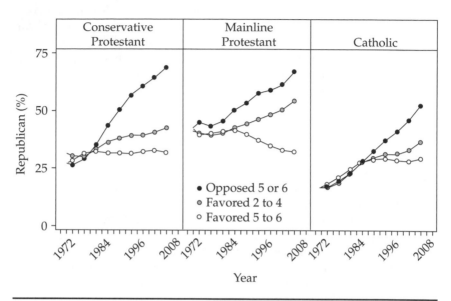

Source: Authors' compilation based on General Social Surveys, 1972 to 2006.
Note: Data smoothed by locally estimated (loess) regression.

tion attitudes for the three largest groups. The conventional wisdom is indeed correct for these three groups. Conservative Protestant and Catholic abortion opponents (29 and 24 percent of the groups, respectively) dramatically increased their identification with the Republican Party over time; the 22 percent and 30 percent of these two groups who support abortion rights did not change their party identification. Mainline Protestants did not show much change in party identification in the aggregate, but figure 2.5 shows how abortion opponents and supporters diverged. Mainline abortion opponents became more Republican and mainline abortion supporters became more Democratic. So, although the denomination looked static in the aggregate, its members did take different paths depending on their views about abortion.

African American Protestants challenge the conventional wisdom. They strongly oppose abortion—as much as any group—but continue to identify with the Democrats. Obviously, for African American voters, other issues are more politically salient than abortion. For most American voters, though, abortion rights were both salient and, over time, divisive.

Class Issues and (Unspoken) Economic Interests

The crude version of the values argument supposes that when lower-income conservative Protestants and Catholics vote their values, they overlook their own economic interests. Popular books like Thomas Franks's *What's the Matter with Kansas?* argue that if low-income socially conservative voters would only give weight to those interests they would never abandon the Democrats (2004). The growing inequality literature counters with the observation that income mattered more for voting in the 1990s and the 2000 election than it had in the 1970s and probably before (Brooks and Brady 1999; Bartels 2005, 2008).

General Social Survey (GSS) data show that conservative Protestants actually give a higher than average and growing weight to economic self-interest (see figure 2.6). True to that view, low-income conservative Protestants—those whose family incomes fell below $32,000 a year—did not shift toward the Republicans. From 1972 to 2006, just under one-third of them (32 percent) identified with the Republicans. Middle-income conservative Protestant moved to Republican identification in the 1980s and early 1990s, but stopped sometime in the Clinton years and never resumed. Only relatively affluent conservative Protestants—those from families that made more than $75,000 a year—moved sharply and persistently toward the Republican Party. Their GOP identification rose from 32 percent in the early 1970s to 65 percent in the most recent data.[7]

Among mainline Protestants the income-party relationship reflects a different, somewhat milder dynamic. Before 1984, income was not consistently related to party identification among mainline Protestants. But low-income mainline Protestants (about 20 percent of the denomination's voters in recent years) moved away from the Republicans throughout the period of observation, and their middle-income counterparts (about 44 percent of the mainline) moved toward the Republicans between 1976 and 1982.

With red-state versus blue-state rhetoric competing with religious rhetoric for airtime, it is imperative to note that, in our multivariate analyses, neither region nor religion can override the class divide evident in these calculations. The net effect of family income—controlling for a wide variety of sociodemographic factors and several key political opinions, including abortion attitudes—is statistically significant in recent decades. The importance of income is statistically and politically significant whether we look at adults in general or conservative Protestants in particular.

Table 2.3 confirms the independence of class voting and its particular salience for conservative Protestants. We regressed party identification on income, abortion attitudes, gender, racial ancestry, region, marital

Table 2.3 Associations of Income and Abortion Attitude with Political Party Identification, by Political Era

Independent variable	1972 to 1980	1982 to 1991	1993 to 2006
Family income (ratio scale)			
Conservative Protestant	.056	.377*	.480*
	(.083)	(.088)	(.084)
Mainline Protestant	.309*	.453*	.421*
	(.065)	(.076)	(.080)
Catholic	.381*	.384*	.517*
	(.094)	(.090)	(.092)
Support for legal abortion			
Conservative Protestant	.003	−.101*	−.290*
	(.031)	(.028)	(.028)
Mainline Protestant	−.008	−.038	−.260*
	(.026)	(.027)	(.030)
Catholic	−.003	.007	−.136*
	(.031)	(.029)	(.030)

Source: Authors' calculations based on General Social Survey, 1972 to 2006.
Note: All regressions also include controls for gender, racial ancestry, region, marital status, birth cohort, and year.
* $p < .05$.

Figure 2.6 Republican Party Identification by Year, Family Income, and Religion

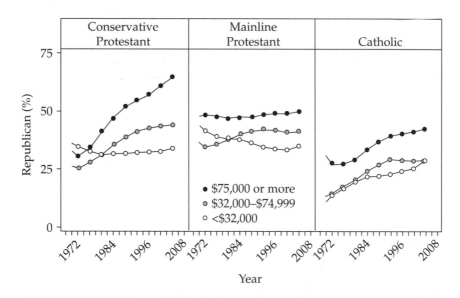

Source: Authors' compilation based on General Social Surveys, 1972 to 2006.
Note: Data smoothed by locally estimated (loess) regression.

status, birth cohort, and year using multinomial logistic regression (we only report the Republican versus Democrat contrast because it is the relevant one). We performed separate regressions for each denomination and each of three periods corresponding to major political eras. Income substantially divided the political identities of all three groups. The 95 percent confidence intervals of the three income coefficients for the current era overlap, indicating that the difference is not statistically significant. It was not that way back in the pre-Reagan period. Then income did not matter at all for conservative Protestants' political identities and significantly less (in a one-tailed test) for Catholics.

To calibrate the relative effects of abortion attitudes and family incomes on party identification we can ask about the marginal effects of attitudes and incomes for conservative Protestants for a person with a baseline probability of identifying as Republican of 40 percent. We have to be specific like this because the multinomial logit model is nonlinear. Moving one point closer to a pro-life, antiabortion stance would move such a person—all else being equal—to a probability of identifying as Republican of 59 percent. A 50 percent increase in family income—from $20,000 to $30,000, $30,000 to $45,000, or whatever—would have a slightly smaller effect, raising the probability of being Republican to 53 percent. Considering that income inequality rose substantially between 1972 and 2006, we can say that income was almost as polarizing as abortion in the last quarter of the twentieth century.

A skeptic might ask whether it is fair to consider income differences in party identification as evidence of class politics when class is so seldom raised as a political issue. Might the incomes differences in party identification merely indicate some odd, unanticipated connection that has little to do with class interests? After all, the affluent have different lifestyles and preferences than the middle class and the poor.

To answer these questions, we investigated some issues that could connect the class gap in voting to a class-based political agenda. Spending priorities help set a class-based political agenda. Democrats Clinton, Gore, Kerry, and Obama proposed national health plans aimed at lower-income voters who lack health coverage; Republicans opposed those proposals. Poor people routinely rate fighting crime and drugs as the leading social problems where they live, and support increased spending for government attempts to solve those problems.[8]

To see whether these class-related spending issues explain the statistical correlation between income and party, we formed an index that gives each person a point for thinking that the government does not spend enough on improving the nation's health, solving problems of the big cities, and fighting crime.[9] Conservative Protestants were more likely to support increased spending for health and solving the problems in big cities in the recent years than in the 1970s. In the Nixon-

Carter era (1972–1980), 59 percent of conservative Protestants thought that the government spent too little on health care; in the current decade, 70 percent think so. Support for increased spending to solve cities' problems rose from a low of 29 percent among conservative Protestants in the late 1970s to 42 percent in 2006.

Throughout the last thirty years, roughly two-thirds of conservative Protestants have felt that the government in Washington is spending too little to fight crime. And differences among them predicted well which conservative Protestants became Republicans. The more of these liberal issues the person supported, the less likely she or he was to switch to the Republicans. Table 2.4 summarizes these trends. Surprisingly, though, these three items together explain only 4 percent of the baseline effect of family income on Republican versus Democratic identification in the current decade.[10]

We extended the analysis to include subjective social class, membership in unions, confidence in union leaders, and support for the government taking a role in reducing income disparities (not shown). Adding this list of variables to our multivariate model cut the sample in half, reducing the precision of our results.[11] Again we found that each variable discriminated Republicans from Democrats, but collectively they failed to reduce the income coefficient much below its initial value.

Thus, we can say not only that conservative Protestants respond to their class interests by increasing their identification with the Republicans as their income rises, but also that they respond to specific spending and organizational issues associated with class. The surprise in all these results is the independence of income. Its effect is robust even after class-based political issues are included in statistical models. This robust income effect and the relevance of other class-based issues contradict the notion that conservative Protestants check their self-interest outside the voting booth. Contrary to the conventional wisdom, conservative Protestants are more—not less—divided by class issues than other large social groups are. The class divisions were not there before the increase in income inequality during the 1980s. They emerged during the Reagan era and persist in the current decade.

Conclusions

We live and write in partisan times. Elections are close. All the cleavages are mobilized. Any one of them could make the difference in a tight election. Practically everything that predicted which Americans were Republicans and which were Democrats in the 1970s predicts more accurately in the current era. Religion and moral values became more salient in American politics alongside a growing class divide in partisan prefer-

Table 2.4   Associations of Income and Spending Priorities with Political Party Identification, by Religion

Independent variable	Conservative Protestant	Mainline Protestant	Catholic
Family income (ratio scale)	0.447*	0.626*	0.727*
	(0.174)	(0.152)	(0.171)
More spending on health	0.544*	0.788*	0.729*
	(0.187)	(0.172)	(0.197)
More spending on cities	−0.110	0.509*	0.471*
	(0.147)	(0.142)	(0.165)
More spending to fight crime	0.403*	−0.086	0.064
	(0.186)	(0.170)	(0.188)
Support for legal abortion	−0.340*	−0.341*	−0.135**
	(0.052)	(0.052)	(0.048)

Source: Authors' calculations based on General Social Survey, 1972 to 2006.
Note: All regressions also include controls for gender, racial ancestry, region, marital status, birth cohort, and year.
* $p < .05$.

ences, a new gender gap, and a persistent difference between central cities and their suburbs.

Voters weigh their values and their economic interests in deciding to identify as Republican, Democrat, or independent. The conventional wisdom that income is irrelevant just because abortion is an important election issue is wrong. The research reported here and similar work by other scholars (for example, Manza and Brooks 1999; Bartels 2008) shows that partisan cleavages accumulate; they do not cancel out.

America's religious cleavage, in particular, did not blunt the economic cleavage in recent decades. The impact of family income on partisanship increased over the past three decades. As it did, it followed the rising class voting trends from the 1970s to 2000.

From these strong and growing class cleavages, we conclude that values voting is not a form of false consciousness; voters do not forget their material interests when they vote their values or vice versa. Both mattered in the Reagan-Bush era of the 1980s, and both matter more now. The strongest evidence on that point is the contrast between conservative Protestant voters from relatively affluent families with incomes of $75,000 or more per year and relatively poor families with incomes below $32,000 per year. Affluent conservative Protestants abandoned the Democrats and shifted to the Republicans over the course of the 1980s and 1990s; only 29 percent were Republicans in the early 1970s and more than 60 percent were Republican today. Low-income conservative Protestants are as loyal to the Democrats as ever; conservative

Protestants with family incomes under $32,000 a year were 30 percent Republican in the early 1970s and again in 2006.

In the popular imagination and public discussion, of course, religion eclipses economic differences. The sense that President George W. Bush won reelection because he was better on religion has not gone away even though his popularity has waned. In 2007, Democratic hopefuls Clinton, Obama, and Edwards sat down with the Reverend Jim Wallis for a discussion of religion, values, and liberal social policy; after clinching the nomination, Obama announced his intention to expand the role of churches in social spending. As we said in *The Truth About Conservative Christians*, we suspect that religion remains the story of recent elections because it suits both religious and secular interests. Some religious activists want to further the influence of their brand of religion on important decisions like Supreme Court nominations. Tales of religious intolerance help liberal fundraisers, too. If they succeed in portraying the opposition as a credible menace, they can rally their base.

Ironically, by exaggerating how strange the other side is, demagogues on both sides can rest assured that they will run afoul of very few real people. If you insult a real opponent you have to face his answer; if you insult a mythical opponent you get the floor all to yourself. Is that fairness for the values voter? Probably not. Does it fit well in the 24-hour news and talk format? You bet.

Real religious cleavages exist; it is not all hype. Where do they come from and how do they persist? Conservative and mainline Protestants differ on abortion and homosexuality. Protestants who agree on these issues, regardless of denomination, are equally likely to identify with the Republicans. But the surprise is that, despite their differences on abortion and homosexuality, conservative and mainline Protestants end up at the same political destination. When all is said and done, 45 percent of both Protestant groups identify with the Republicans. Turning to the differences between Protestant denominations and other religious groups in the United States, we can find no single issue or cluster of issues that explains those differences. History and culture meld into politics in mysterious ways. One way is outsider status. African American Protestants, Catholics, Jews, people of small minority religions, and people who prefer no religion all feel an outsider status that finds validation in the Democrats' tendency to stand for the excluded. Even when they have similar opinions on social issues and the same family income, Catholics and non-Christians are less likely than either conservative or mainline Protestants to identify with the Republican Party.

Conservative Protestants feel embattled too, as Christian Smith pointed out in *American Evangelicalism: Embattled and Thriving* (1998). But conservative Protestants' embattlement is not an outsider's sympathy for other outsiders. Its spark rises from entitlement. The conservative Protestant leadership talks like people who feel they are outside by mistake (for example, Lindsay 2008, 74). They are certain of their place at the heart of America just as they are certain of their faith in God. The name the Reverend Jerry Falwell used to launch his political movement—Moral Majority—captures this sensibility. From the point of view of conservative Protestant leadership, their movement differs from what is going on with outsider groups because the others are neither as American nor as close to God. To some evangelical leaders, conservative Protestants deserve more say, and others can wait to speak.

The sure and absolute faith of conservative Protestants makes them this way. In *Christian America?* Smith reported that 77 percent of conservative Protestants and 87 percent of self-identified evangelicals thought of the United States as a nation founded on Christian principles, and a majority agreed that "Christian morality should be the law of the land even though all Americans are not Christians" (2000, 200). Only 25 percent of other Americans, including mainline Protestants, agreed with that statement.

Moral values got the headlines in 2004. But the religious cleavage is less about the relevance of values than about which values ought to be relevant (Baker 2005). Conservative Protestants, like any large aggregation of Americans, are a mixed lot thrown together by one common factor—their religious affiliation. But that commonality makes them more similar than a random assortment of Americans would be. In addition, what they have in common has made them closer to Republicans than to Democrats in recent years.

The contribution of this chapter has been to highlight the important differences among conservative Protestants. Above all they are more deeply divided on class and class issues than any other similarly large group in American society. In the 1990s, Bill Clinton got more votes from conservative Protestants with below-average incomes than either George H. W. Bush or Bob Dole did. To repeat Clinton's success in future elections, Democrats need to appeal to the economic needs of those conservative Protestants who share the values announced by their leaders but who identify with politicians who advance their families' interests.

Notes

1. These and almost all statistics in this paper come from the General Social Survey (GSS), a biennial survey of social and cultural trends. These particular calculations pertain to voters twenty-five to seventy-four years old who were interviewed in 2002, 2004, or 2006. We provide more data details later in the paper.
2. Funding cuts led to the cancellation of the 1979, 1981, and 1992 surveys, but the design always called for an annual survey.

3. Mostly conservative Protestant Republicans who did not vote for Senator Dole in 1996 voted for Ross Perot; only 5 percent voted for incumbent President Clinton.
4. The GSS data file reports a score of 0 if those who said they attended "never," 1 for "less than once a year," and 8 for "more than once a week."
5. Technically, the ordered logit regression model requires that the four logits implied by the model all have the same coefficients for the substantive variables, that is, that the four equations have common slopes but different intercepts. Tests reject that assumption. The stereotype ordered regression model allows the slopes to be different across equation but requires that the differences be proportional, for example, if the attendance effect is half the size in one equation compared with another the denominational differences come out to be half the size too. That model fits the data well if we allow specify two dimensions in the party identification responses—one for the partisan dimension of interest (ordered from Democrat to independent to Republican) and one for intensity (independent to leaning to partisan). All this statistical complexity distracts from the substantive discussion without changing our substantive conclusions, so we present the multinomial logistic regression results for the key contrast between Republican and Democratic identification.
6. These are recent statistics from the 2002–2006 GSSs.
7. All these income figures and all income figures in this chapter are adjusted for inflation using the Consumer Price Index research series. We use 2005 as the base year so these incomes reflect 2005 prices.
8. Our analysis of the 2002–2006 GSSs show that 63 percent of voters from families with incomes below $32,000 per year thought the government spent too little fighting crime, versus 51 percent of voters from families that made over $75,000 per year. Switching to the question about drug spending, we got an identical 63 percent to 51 percent margin of difference between low- and high-income voters.
9. The index fails to meet statistical criteria for a proper scale, so we entered these items separately in the multivariate analyses.
10. There is no income effect to explain in the early years.
11. The GSS design calls for asking each respondent only a subset—roughly two-thirds —of the (rather long) list of questions. This increases the number of variables measured while keeping the length of the interview to less than ninety minutes. But it means that the number of cases in a multivariate analysis can shrink quickly if the questions of interest are parts of different subsets of questions.

References

Baker, Wayne. 2005. *America's Crisis of Values*. Princeton, N.J.: Princeton University Press.

Bartels, Larry M., 2000. "Partisanship and Voting Behavior, 1952–1996." *American Journal of Political Science* 44(1): 35–50.

———. 2005. "Partisan Politics and the U.S. Income Distribution." Social Inequality Working Paper. New York: Russell Sage Foundation.

———. 2008. *Unequal Democracy: Political Economy of the New Gilded Age*. New York: Russell Sage Foundation.

Brooks, Clem, and David Brady. 1999. "Income, Economic Voting, and Long-Term Political Change in the U.S., 1952–1996." *Social Forces* 77(4): 1339–374.

Campbell, Angus, Phillip Converse, Warren Miller, and Donald Stokes. 1960. *The American Voter*. Chicago: University of Chicago Press.

Cleveland, William S. 1979. "Robust Locally Weighted Regression and Smoothing Scatterplots." *Journal of the American Statistical Association* 74(368): 829–36.

Cleveland, William S., and Susan J. Devlin. 1988. "LocallyWeighted Regression: An Approach to Regression Analysis by Local Fitting." *Journal of the American Statistical Association* 83(403): 596–610.

Clogg, Clifford C., and Darwin O. Sawyer. 1981. "A Comparison of Alternative Models for Analyzing the Scalability of Response Patterns." *Sociological Methodology* 12(1981): 240–80.

Clogg, Clifford C., and Edward S. Shihadeh. 1994. *Statistical Models for Ordinal Variables*. Thousand Oaks, Calif: Sage Publications.

Davis, James A., Tom W. Smith, and Peter V. Marsden. 2006. *General Social Survey Cumulative Codebook, 1972–2006*. Storrs, Conn.: Roper Center for Public Opinion Research.

DiMaggio, Paul, Bethany Bryson, and John H. Evans. 1996. "Have American's Social Attitudes Become More Polarized?" *American Journal of Sociology* 102(3): 690–755.

Fiorina, Morris P. 2002. "Parties and Partisanship: A Forty-Year Retrospective." *Political Behavior* 24(2): 93–115.

Firebaugh, Glenn, and Kenneth E. Davis. 1988. "Trends in Antiblack Prejudice, 1972–1984: Region and Cohort Effects." *American Journal of Sociology* 94(2): 251–72.

Frank, Thomas. 2004. *What's the Matter with Kansas?* New York: Metropolitan Books.

General Social Survey. Cumulative data file. Produced by the National Opinion Research Center. Available at: http://www.norc.org/GSS+Website/Download (accessed April 20, 2009).

Greeley, Andrew, and Michael Hout. 2006. *The Truth about Conservative Christians*. Chicago: University of Chicago Press.

Hout, Michael. 1999. "The Terms of the Debate: Abortion Politics in the United States, 1972–1996." *Gender Issues* 17(1): 3–34.

Hunter, James D. 1992. *Culture War: The Struggle to Define America*. New York: Basic Books.

Layman, Geoffrey. 2001. *The Great Divide: Religious and Cultural Conflict in the American Political Party System*. New York: Columbia University Press.

Lindsay, D. Michael. 2008. "Evangelicals in the Power Elite: Elite Cohesion Advancing a Movement." *American Sociological Review* 73(1): 60–82.

Manza, Jeff, and Clem Brooks. 1999. *Social Cleavages and Political Change*. Oxford: Oxford University Press.

Miller, Warren E., and J. Merrill Shanks. 1996. *The New American Voter*. Cambridge, Mass.: Harvard University Press.

Niemi, Richard G., and Herbert F. Weisberg. 1976. *Controversies in American Voting Behavior*. San Francisco: W. H. Freeman.

Norris, Pippa, and Ronald F. Inglehart. 2004. *Sacred and Secular: Re-Examining the Secularization Thesis*. Cambridge: Cambridge University Press.

Phillips, Kevin. 1969. *The Emerging Republican Majority*. New Rochelle, N.Y.: Arlington House.

Smith, Christian. 1998. *American Evangelicalism: Embattled and Thriving*. Chicago: University of Chicago Press.

———. 2000. *Christian America?* Berkeley: University of California Press.

Smith, Tom W. 1990. "Classifying Protestant Denominations." *Review of Religious Research* 31(3): 225–45.

Steensland, Brian, Jerry Z. Park, Mark D. Regnerus, Lynn D. Robinson, W. Bradford Wilcox, and Robert D. Woodberry. 1999. "The Measure of American Religion: Toward Improving the State of the Art." *Social Forces* 79(1): 291–318.

Wattenberg, Martin P. 1996. *The Decline of American Political Parties, 1952–1994*. Cambridge, Mass.: Harvard University Press.

Chapter 3

Voting Your Values

WAYNE E. BAKER AND CONNIE J. BOUDENS

THE 2004 National Election Pool (NEP) exit poll, conducted for a consortium of media organizations, propelled moral values to the forefront of the public discussion about the forces that drive political behavior. It asked voters to select from a predetermined list the one issue that mattered most in deciding how they voted for president. Of those voters, 22 percent selected moral values. The other issues included economy-jobs (20 percent), terrorism (19 percent), Iraq (15 percent), health care (8 percent), taxes (5 percent), and education (4 percent). The voters who selected moral values also heavily favored Bush; a large percentage of them were conservative white evangelicals, leading to the widespread perception that attitudes about moral issues among conservative Christians played a major role in Bush's reelection (Langer and Cohen 2005).[1]

By now, the NEP exit poll data have been examined and reanalyzed in multiple ways, causing most analysts to reject the validity of the popular perception that the election turned on moral values (see, for example, Hillygus and Shields 2005; Klinkner 2006; Langer and Cohen 2005). ABC's director of Polling Gary Langer, for example, concluded that the NEP item was a "poorly devised exit poll question" that produced a misleading result (Langer 2004). Christopher Muste, a senior polling analyst at the *Washington Post*, offered another criticism, based on the national exit polls conducted by the *Los Angeles Times* since 1992 ("Hidden in Plain Sight: Polling Data Show Moral Values Aren't a New Factor," December 12, 2004, B4). In the 2004 poll, 40 percent selected moral-ethical values as one of their two most important issues, but this figure is about the same as in the previous two presidential elections: 35 percent in 2000, and 40 percent in 1996. Moreover, fewer moral values voters cast their vote for Bush in 2004 than in 2000. Bob Dole actually garnered more of the values voters in 1996 than Bush did in either 2000 or 2004. Based on these and other results, Muste concluded that values voters are nothing more than a myth.

In contrast, Howard Schuman, an authority on surveys at the University of Michigan Institute of Social Research, argued that the moral values question in the NEP exit poll may have more validity than many critics think and could indicate the rising importance of moral values in future elections (2006). Indeed, the rising influence of values on voting had been noticed and tracked by political scientists and political sociologists well before the 2004 elections (see Layman 1997). For example, the 2000 elections were the source of the first famous red state–blue state map of the nation, a dramatic visual of a country seemingly divided by values and geography. This map was reproduced by the 2004 elections. The media coverage of the 2004 NEP exit poll, and the rhetoric that attaches itself so readily to simple, salient statistics, merely added to the already prevalent perception in America that the nation was deeply divided with respect to moral values and engaged in a culture war about irreconcilable differences in values (see, for example, Baker 2005; Fiorina, Abrams, and Pope 2006; Hunter 1991; Hunter and Wolfe 2006). This deep division was perceived to be related, at least in part, to the strengthening bonds between religion and politics—especially between conservative Christians and the Republican Party. Ralph Reed, a born-again Christian, political activist, and head of the Christian Coalition from 1989 to 1997, was the poster child of the tightening grip of the Religious Right on American politics and a commanding officer in the culture war that would (supposedly) determine the future of America.

Given the ease and élan with which the word *values* is deployed, there is a surprising lack of consistency and clarity about what it means. We therefore attempt to be precise and clear about what we mean by it. We use two scales that define values clearly and measure them in a deeper and more sensitive way than has been done in previous studies of values and political behavior in the United States. These scales—a continuum of traditional versus secular-rational values and another of survival versus self-expression values—are well tested in research on values in America (Baker 2005; Baker and Forbes 2006) and in cross-cultural research (Inglehart and Baker 2000; Inglehart and Norris 2003; Norris and Inglehart 2004). We use them to assess the extent of shared values across groups, especially religious affiliations, using data on the greater Detroit metropolitan area in 2003. We find, for example, that evangelical Protestants in the region tend to have traditional values but that a sizable minority of them have secular-rational values; conversely, we find that seculars (no religious affiliation) tend to have secular-rational values, though some do have traditional values.

We also use the two scales to assess the link between values and political behavior by analyzing data on the United States in 2000 and on the Detroit metropolitan area in 2003 (see appendix). We believe these scales are the "better measures" of values that Geoffrey Layman argued are needed to evaluate the role of values in political beliefs and behaviors (1997, 307). More generally, our analysis contributes to the revival of values as a subject of sociological research (Hitlin and Piliavin 2004), a renewal of interest we believe is part of the cultural turn in sociology—the "increasing attention being given to cultural factors (such as language, symbols, and meanings) in sociological explanations" (Alexander and Thompson 2008, 16). Of course, better measures of values cannot detect an effect that is not there. But, if the effect is there—if people do vote their values—better measures allow us to document the effect more accurately and to assess its strength more fully, compared to other attempts to analyze the values-voting link. Our use of better measures of values yields two surprises. First, the link between conservative Christians and political behavior may be much weaker than previously thought. Second, values that cut across groups may be more important than previously documented. Our findings lead us to suggest that values cannot be reduced to sociodemographic characteristics or social groups. Values may arise from or be socialized through structural positions in society—social class, occupation, education, race, immigrant status, age cohorts, and others (Hitlin and Piliavin 2004, 368–78)—but values may also exist with some autonomy from social structure.

Defining Values Voters and Values

Figuring out the role of values as a predictor of political behaviors and the importance of values voters is plagued by several problems. For example, the terms *values* and *values voters* tend to be associated with particular religious groups, specifically Christian conservatives, and with conservative political, social, and economic values—as if to say that other religious groups, even seculars, do not or could not vote according to their values. But even atheists have values that inform their choices and decisions (Baker 2005, 67). Moral relativists use a system of ethics to make decisions (Fletcher 1966), just as moral absolutists do. Adherents of any religious affiliation, including those without one, can vote their values. We define values voters as voters who use their values—whatever those values may be—to inform political attitudes, to evaluate candidates for political office, and to make decisions about voting. Voters also may take into account their material interests, identity, or other factors to figure out what to think and who to vote for. The relative importance of values may vary from voter to voter and from time to time. One of the key goals is to determine the relative weight values play in decisions about voting. If values voters are playing a major role in elections, as some social scientists and popular journalists argue (for example, Frank 2004), we would expect to see that values are one of the biggest factors in decisions about voting, compared to others, such as class, race, education, and so on.

A deeper problem is that the concept of values is often poorly defined or not defined at all in popular discourse, the media, or even in sociological uses of the concept (Hitlin and Piliavin 2004). For example, the term *moral values* was presented without any elaboration in the NEP exit poll, leaving it up to the respondents and the people charged with analyzing the results to interpret what this meant. One could, for example, think of specific moral issues, such as abortion and gay rights, which were seen by many as the hot-button moral issues behind the 2004 exit poll controversy (Lovett and Jordan 2005). It is easy to assume that these issues were an important basis for vote choice in that election, but voters taking the exit poll could also have interpreted moral values to mean any number of things.

Values are often conflated with attitudes, as well as norms, needs, or traits (Hitlin and Piliavin 2004, 360). For example, feelings about abortion and gay rights are attitudes, not values; attitudes are more specific and concrete than values. Values are often conflated with religious beliefs and moral visions—worldviews about the location of moral authority, the transcendental realm (God or society) or the mundane realm (the individual or local situation) (Baker 2005). The distinctions between values, religious beliefs, moral visions, as well as attitudes, norms, needs and traits, have to be maintained to isolate and evaluate the effects of values on behaviors such as voting (see Baker 2005, for example). For our analysis, we adopt Hitlin and Piliavin's definition of values, based on their comprehensive review of work on the topic: values are ideals; they form an "internal moral compass" used to guide and evaluate behavior; values are trans-situational and more durable than attitudes; values motivate action, even if in an unarticulated, almost subconscious way (2004, 361–65).

This definition, however, elides the most difficult problem facing an analysis of values and voting: What is the content of values? That is, what are values about? There are two systematic attempts to define the content of values that have been tested on an extensive array of samples, one by a social psychologist, Shalom Schwartz, and the other by a political scientist, Ronald Inglehart (Schwartz and Bilsky 1987, 1990; Schwartz 1992, 1994; Inglehart 1997; Inglehart and Baker 2000). Of course, others have developed taxonomies of values, such as Milton Rokeach (1973), but these have not been tested on a large and diverse set of samples.

Schwartz's approach has been applied in surveys in many nations, but almost all of the samples have been of specific categories of people, such as teachers or students. Unfortunately, the approach has not been used in representative national or regional surveys of American voters and hence cannot speak to the question of values voters. Therefore, we adopt Inglehart's, which has been tested in a much larger array of samples—more than eighty nations around the world—and includes representative national and regional samples of the United States. Based on data from the World Values Surveys (WVS), Ronald Inglehart and Wayne Baker identified two fundamental dimensions of values mentioned earlier: a continuum of traditional versus secular-rational values and another of survival versus self-expression values (2000). The first dimension taps a constellation of values about God, country, and family. Traditional values emphasize the importance of religion and God, patriotism and nationalism, absolute standards of morality, and deference to authority. These values include pro-life and pro-family values, manifested, for example, as opposition to abortion, divorce, euthanasia, and suicide, and the belief that it is more important for children to learn obedience and religious faith than determination and independence. George Lakoff's strict father model fits with traditional values (Lakoff 1996; Baker 2005, 68–71; for an extended discussion of Lakoff's work, see chapter 6, this volume). Secular-rational values emphasize the opposite positions on all these topics (see appendix).

There is a good deal of nominal similarity between traditional values and religious traditionalism as described by John Green (2007; volume 1, chapter 4) and again by Geoffrey Layman and Edward Carmines (1997). For example, Layman and Carmines created a religious traditionalism index based on religious salience, born-again experience, church attendance, denomination, and biblical views. Similarly, Green's categories are determined by a combination of religious affiliations and religious beliefs. The traditional versus secular-rational scale is broader in scope, which we believe makes it a better measure for the analysis of values voting. Traditional or secular-rational values are more than just religious values. Thus this scale includes one item about religious beliefs (the importance of God in one's life) plus nonreligious items that capture other traditional or secular-rational values, such as variations of patriotism and family values. Further, religious affiliation is not a component of the scale, making it possible to examine the extent to which traditional values (or secular-rational values) are shared across religious affiliations.

The second dimension—survival versus self-expression values—represents a fundamentally different orientation. One component is Inglehart's materialism-postmaterialism index, which has been included in the quadrennial surveys conducted by the American National Election Studies (ANES). Layman and Carmines used it as an indicator of values-based cultural conflict in the United States: materialist values focus on economic stability, physical security, and domestic order, and postmaterialist values emphasize new social and cultural concerns, such as human rights (1997). Based on data from the ANES surveys from 1980 to 1992, Layman and Carmines found it to have an increasing effect on party identification, political ideology, and presidential vote choice. However, they concluded that, by itself, the index is inadequate as a measure because religion and religious-based cultural differences are more significant sources of cultural conflict. They conceded that the apparent weak effect may be simply because they have better measures of religion and religious differences than of values (1997, 764). Our second dimension is a better measure because it includes Inglehart's index and adds indicators of interpersonal trust, subjective well-being, tolerance of outgroups, and political activism (see appendix). At one end of this dimension, survival values emphasize economic stability, safety and security, domestic order, and distrust of outgroups, immigrants, and foreigners, as well as low levels of political activity, fear of ethnic diversity and cultural change, and low subjective well-being. Self-expression values emphasize the opposite. Self-expression values are expressed in high levels of political activity and concerns about human rights, the quality of life, and the environment. Self-expression values relate to what Robert Fogel called spiritual or immaterial needs (2000, 176–77).

The two dimensions—traditional versus secular-rational values and survival versus self-expression values—are robust. They emerged from analysis of forty-three societies included in the first two waves of the World Values Surveys 1981 and 1990 (Inglehart 1997), from analysis of sixty-five societies once the 1995 third wave was added (Inglehart and Baker 2000), and from analysis of eighty societies when the 2000 fourth wave was included (Inglehart and Norris 2003)—though the broader coverage in each successive wave increased the cultural and economic diversity of the societies analyzed.

Each dimension is correlated in sensible ways with dozens of additional items (Inglehart and Baker 2000, 26–27), lending further support to the validity of these dimensions. For example, those with traditional values tend to believe in heaven, hell, and life after death; they find comfort and strength from religion; they frequently attend religious services and have confidence in the nation's religious institutions; they emphasize work over leisure; and, their political ideology leans to the right. Those with secular-rational values take the opposite position on all these topics. People with survival values tend to be dissatisfied with their financial situations and emphasize a good income and a safe job versus a feeling of accomplishment and working with people one likes, tend to give lower ratings to their overall health, do not support women's rights, and believe the government should take more responsibility for people. Those with self-expression values emphasize the opposite.

These dimensions represent an opportunity to investigate the extent to which values are related to political behaviors and attitudes, and whether or not values are better predictors than such sociostructural factors as income, race, and religious affiliation. We believe that the study of values as a basis for political behaviors and attitudes makes an important contribution to the discussion of the relationship of values, religion, and politics for at least two reasons. First, we can use them to assess the degree to which religious affiliation and values overlap, and to determine if one can truly be used as a proxy for the other, or if religion and values affect political behavior in differential ways. Second, we can include all religious affiliations as well as seculars, based on the values *they* use when making political choices.

Effects of Values on Political Behavior and Attitudes

The two values dimensions influence a wide range of political, social, and economic attitudes and behaviors, according to analyses of the WVS data on the United States (Baker 2005). For example, Americans with traditional values had confidence in more institutions—such as the church, armed forces, press, labor unions, police, civil service, and major companies—than those with secular-rational values, controlling for religious affiliation and many sociodemographic characteristics. Americans with traditional values and survival values attend religious services more frequently than those with secular-rational or self-expression values. They also engage in less political activity.

Church-state separation is a hallowed American principle, enshrined in the U.S. Constitution's First Amendment. But Americans vary in their support of it, based on their values (Baker 2005). Separation of church and state, Baker has observed, is a contentious issue today, pitting the Religious Right against moral progressives and civil libertarians in debate and litigation about prayer in school, public vouchers to support religious schools, religious symbols in public buildings and places, and so forth (2005, 92). Compared to Americans with secular-rational values and self-expression values, those with traditional values and survival values tend to believe that politicians who do not believe in God are unfit for public office, that it would be better for America if more people with strong religious beliefs held public office, and that religious leaders should influence government decisions. In short, Americans with traditional values and survival values favor less separation of church and state; those with secular-rational and self-expression values favor more.

Values also influence voting preferences, as we observed when we analyzed the WVS data on the United States. As shown in table 3.1, Americans with traditional values are significantly more likely to say that they would vote Republican than those with secular-rational values, controlling for religious affiliation, frequency of attendance at religious services, political ideology, and a host of sociodemographic characteristics. Similarly, Americans with survival values are significantly more likely than those with self-expression values to say they would vote Republican, holding constant all the same factors. In the Detroit region, people with traditional values are more likely than those with secular-rational values to report that they voted for Bush in the 2000 elections, controlling for a variety of other factors (see table 3.2). Similarly, they are also more likely to identify as Republican. However, the second dimension of values—survival versus self-expression—does not have a significant effect on the likelihood of voting for Bush or identifying as a Republican for those living in the three-county Detroit region. It does influence the likelihood of having voted at all in the 2000 elections—residents of the Detroit region with self-expression values are more likely than those with survival values to report that they voted in 2000, holding constant other factors (see table 3.2). This finding is consistent with other findings that people with self-expression values exhibit higher levels of political participation than those with survival values (Baker 2005; Inglehart and Baker 2000).

The Effects of Religious Affiliation

Religious affiliation exerts limited effects on political attitudes and behavior when the two values dimensions and a variety of sociodemographic variables are also included in the analysis. Nationwide, for example, religious affiliation does not influence confidence in institutions or levels of political activity, controlling for values and other factors (Baker 2005). Similarly, religious affiliation has no effect on attitudes about church-state separation except one: Protestants are more likely than Catholics to say that it would be better for America if more people with strong religious beliefs held public office (Baker 2005). According to our analysis, Protestants nationwide were more likely than any other religious group to say that they would vote Republican if the national election were tomorrow; Catholics and seculars were neither more nor less likely to vote Republican, holding other factors constant (table 3.1).

The WVS data provide a single category for Protestants, so we cannot separate and compare mainline and evangelical Protestants in this na-

Table 3.1   Intended Voting Behavior

Independent Variables	Would Vote Republican IF Election Tomorrow
Religious affiliation and behavior	
Protestant	.859***
	(.209)
Catholic	−.020
	(.220)
Secular	−.060
	(.259)
Frequency of attendance at religious services	−.101
	(.052)
Race	
Nonwhite	−2.188***
	(.228)
Values	
Traditional or secular-rational values	−.812***
	(.127)
Survival or self-expression values	−.390***
	(.102)
Control variables	
Liberal-conservative scale	.343***
	(.044)
Subjective social class	−.164
	(.101)
Education	.147**
	(.051)
Household income	.046
	(.037)
Age	−.107[a]
	(.054)
Gender (female)	−.427**
	(.158)
Married now	.175
	(.168)
Constant	−6.894***
	(1.154)
−2 Log-likelihood	1058.06
N of observations	861
Nagelkerke Pseudo R^2	.381

Source: Authors' compilation.
Notes: Coding of variables is the same as Baker (2005, 193–95) to ensure comparability. Omitted category for religion is other (not Protestant, Catholic, or secular). Total sample size for the 2000 U.S. World Values Survey = 1200. Respondents who indicated "not applicable" when asked about intended voting preference were excluded from the model. * $p < .05$, ** $p < .01$, *** $p < .001$. Standard errors are in parentheses.

tional sample (see appendix). The Detroit area study was intentionally designed to subdivide Protestants into these categories. The Detroit region, however, is not representative of the United States, and so generalizations must be made cautiously. For example, race is especially prominent in the region. Detroit is the most segregated metropolitan area in the country and it has the nation's most isolated black population. This racial segregation extends to the surrounding counties on a neighborhood-by-neighborhood basis (Farley, Danzinger, and Holzer 2000; Baker and Coleman 2004). Religious affiliation and race interact. It is well known that white and black evangelicals are different when it comes to political ideology and voting, despite doctrinal similarities and agreement on many conservative social issues. In contrast to their white counterparts, black evangelicals are politically liberal and vote for Democrats. Given the prominence of race in the Detroit area, we would expect that this contrast would be especially stark when we consider the effects of religious affiliation on political behavior and attitudes.

Let's continue with simple statistics about religious affiliation and voting. Mainline Protestants in the Detroit region split their vote in 2000: 52 percent said they voted for Gore, 48 percent for Bush. But we see big differences by race. White mainline Protestants favored Bush (53 percent) while almost all black mainline Protestants voted for Gore. Two-thirds of evangelical Protestants voted for Gore—but this simple statistic obscures differences by race: white evangelical Protestants overwhelmingly voted for Bush (70 percent), but only 9 percent of black evangelical Protestants voted the same way. As it does elsewhere in America, race shapes the effects of religious affiliation in the Detroit region.

When we consider the combined effects of religious affiliation, values, race, and other sociodemographic variables in the Detroit region, we find that evangelical Protestants are neither more nor less likely to have voted for Bush than mainline Protestants (table 3.2). Similarly, evangelical Protestants were not more likely than mainline Protestants to identify as Republican or to have voted in the 2000 elections (table 3.2). One reason is the influence of race, as discussed. But it may also be that speculations about the importance of conservative Christians in American politics are overblown. After all, shoals of evidence fail to support the notion of a divided nation—of a culture war based on deep differences in values (see, for example, Williams 1997; Baker 2005; Fiorina, Abrams, and Pope 2006). America is purple, not red versus blue. For example, members of different religious affiliations can share values and, by voting their values, make the same vote choices. Values, as we know from the results above, strongly influence political ideology, party identification, and voting (table 3.2).

There are, of course, significant differences between some of the religious affiliations on the two values dimensions, as shown in figure 3.1

Table 3.2   Voting Behavior and Party Identification

	Voted in 2000	Voted for Bush	Identify as Republican
Religious affiliation and behavior			
Evangelical Protestant	−.800	−.651	.478
	(.512)	(.657)	(.504)
Catholic	.007	.206	−.093
	(.470)	(.506)	(.408)
Other religion	−.674	1.753*	.260
	(.534)	(.659)	(.505)
Secular	.233	1.410*	1.499**
	(.595)	(.714)	(.598)
Frequency of attendance at religious services	.558***	−.053	.084
	(.120)	(.139)	(.114)
Race			
Black	1.235**	−2.168***	−2.980***
	(.419)	(.564)	(.712)
Values			
Traditional or secular-rational values	.148	−.837**	−.703**
	(.223)	(.295)	(.250)
Survival or self-expression values	.808***	−.359	−.571**
	(.217)	(.272)	(.220)
Controls			
Liberal-Conservative scale	.034	1.247***	1.078***
	(.167)	(.253)	(.200)
Republican	.332	2.808***	
	(.402)	(.482)	
Education	.394*	.048	−.064
	(.157)	(.178)	(.144)
Household income	.072	−.101	.185*
	(.082)	(.103)	(.087)
Youth	−1.654**	−.609	.131
	(.602)	(1.070)	(.576)
Middle age	−.451	.589	.534
	(.352)	(.385)	(.339)
Gender (female)	−.898**	.016	−.452
	(.312)	(.402)	(.297)
Married now	.289	−.194	.532
	(.320)	(.380)	(.315)
Constant	2.022*	2.832*	−.279
	(.976)	(1.184)	(.060)
− 2 Log-likelihood	322.26	220.63	320.31
N of observations	387	293	423
Nagelkerke pseudo R^2	.322	.602	.401

Source: Authors' compilation.
Notes: Omitted category for religion is mainline Protestant. Total sample size for 2003 Detroit Area Study = 508. Respondents who were not U.S. citizens or who were younger than eighteen in 2000 are excluded from the models estimating voting. Those did not vote are excluded from models estimating voted for Bush.
* $p < .05$, ** $p < .01$, *** $p < .001$. Standard errors are in parentheses.

Figure 3.1   Religious Affiliation and Values in the Detroit Region

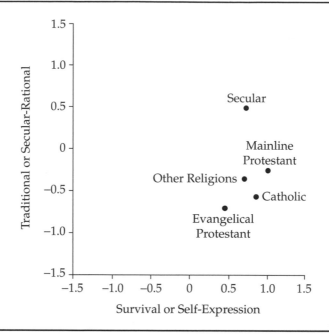

Source: Authors' compilation.

(each point is the average for a group). On average, evangelicals have stronger traditional values than mainline Protestants, other religions, or seculars, but are not significantly different from Catholics. Seculars have stronger secular-rational values than any group. Evangelicals have stronger survival values than mainline Protestants or Catholics, but their survival-oriented values are not significantly different on this dimension from the values of seculars or of members of other religions.

There are differences, but many are not big. Although mainline and evangelical Protestants have different proportions of members with traditional values and secular-rational values, the overlap is considerable. As shown in figure 3.2, a sizable proportion of mainline *and* evangelical Protestants have traditional values. The extent of shared values across political party identification is even higher than it is for religious affiliation. Further, some mainline *and* evangelical Protestants have secular-rational values. The mix of traditionalists and secular-rationalists among Catholics is close to the mix for evangelicals. The extremes are seculars versus evangelicals, but even some seculars have traditional values. Thus, values crosscut religious affiliations, muting the voices of

Figure 3.2   Shared Values in the Detroit Region

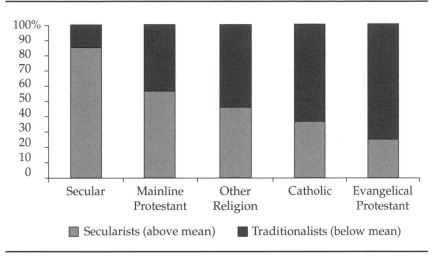

Source: Authors' compilation.
Notes: Secularists are those who are above the mean on the traditional-secular values scale. Traditionalists are those who are below the mean on the same scale. The proportions of respondents in each religious affiliation are secular (11.0 percent), mainline Protestant (16.9 percent), other religion (17.3 percent), Catholic (31.1 percent), and evangelical Protestant (23.6 percent).

specific affiliations. As our analysis demonstrates, values are more important predictors of political behavior and attitudes than religious affiliations (table 3.2).

The Continuing Importance of Race

Our analysis of the WVS data for the United States shows that whites are about nine times more likely than nonwhites to say they would vote Republican if the election were tomorrow, controlling for religious affiliation and behavior, values, political ideology, and a host of sociodemographic characteristics (table 3.1). We expected that the effect of race in the Detroit region would be even stronger, given the role race plays in the area. However, the effect of race is about the same as it is nationwide. Those who are not black are about nine times more likely than blacks to report that they voted for Bush in the 2000 elections. Similarly, blacks are very unlikely to identify as Republican, controlling for many factors (table 3.2).

The lack of support among black voters for Bush does not appear to vary by political ideology. For example, conservative and liberal black voters in the Detroit region exhibit similar low levels of support for

Bush (based on analyses not shown here but available on request). Political ideology does matter for voters who are not black—about 80 percent of conservative nonblacks voted for Bush, versus only 33 percent of liberal nonblacks. In the Detroit region, race trumps religious affiliation and political ideology as bases of vote choice.

What Is the Most Important Predictor of Voting?

Figure 3.3 provides a basis for answering this question. The figure illustrates the difference in presidential vote as the percentage Democratic minus the percentage Republican between categories (for example, black versus nonblack). Think of it as the Democratic premium. The difference in Democratic presidential vote based on income is small—a difference of only 8.1 points between the upper and lower income thirds. In recent elections, the difference in Democratic presidential vote between the upper and lower income thirds has been roughly the same as that between regular churchgoers and those who never attend religious services; in the 2000 elections, however, the difference for religious differences, based on frequency of attendance, was twice as big as the difference for income thirds (Fiorina, Abrams, and Pope 2005, 71). The pattern in the Detroit region for the 2000 election was the same as the national pattern: the difference in Democratic presidential vote between churchgoers and those who never attend was 15.8 points, almost twice as large as the income difference of 8.1 points.

The effect of race is glaring: the difference in Democratic presidential vote between blacks and nonblacks was 35.7 points, much larger than that for religious participation (15.8 points) or economic cleavages (8.1 points). The effect of values is also big. Traditional and secular-rational values are either the strongest predictor of all or second only to race, depending on how it is measured. If we compare the difference in Democratic presidential vote for those above the mean score with those below the mean score on the traditional versus secular-rational scale, we find that the difference is large: 24.4 points. This is considerably larger than the difference for religious participation (15.8 points) or economic cleavages (8.1 points) but less than the difference for race (35.7 points). But values are more important than any factor if we compare the extreme traditionalists and the extreme secular-rationalists (defined, respectively, as one standard deviation below the mean and one standard deviation above the mean). As shown in figure 3.3, the difference is enormous: 48 points.

What did all this mean for the outcome of the 2000 presidential election in the Detroit region? Bush lost the region (and, as a result, the state of Michigan) in 2000, so conservative values voters were not enough to

Figure 3.3   Difference in Democratic Presidential Vote in the Detroit Region

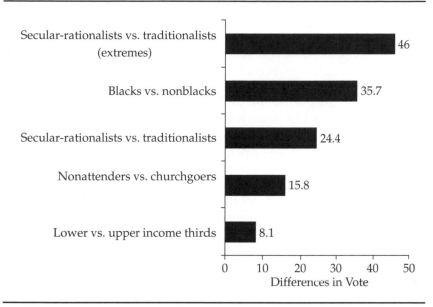

Source: Authors' compilation.
Note: Difference in presidential vote is calculated as the percentage Democratic minus percentage Republican between the respective categories. (See text for definitions of categories.)

swing the region (or state) in his favor. Liberal values voters also mattered and they voted for Gore. Values played a major role in the outcome of the election, but voters of all stripes voted their values—those with traditional values tended to vote for Bush, and those with secular-rational values tended to vote for Gore. Other factors matter. Race, in particular, remains a big predictor of political behavior in the Detroit region. Blacks are more likely to have turned out and voted than nonblacks, and are much less likely than nonblacks to have voted for Bush. Overall, the effect of values voters depends on a variety of factors and their interactions; among these are the proportions of the electorate with shared values, how motivated they are to turnout and vote, and how strongly—and in which direction—their values influence choice of presidential candidate.

Conclusion

For many years, the question of values voters has been moving to the front of debate about American politics. The exit polls from the 2004 elections reporting that conservative values voters swung the election in favor of Bush were only a recent expression of what many consider a long-term transformation of the social bases of political attitudes and behavior. Among political scientists, this transformation is phrased as a shift toward a more cultural or values-based politics (Layman and Carmines 1997, 751). Sociologists of culture may quibble with this cavalier use of the word *culture*, but the point is clear—Americans seem to be increasingly likely to vote their values rather than their pocketbook or group-based interests. This is the theme, for example, of Frank's 2005 *New York Times* bestseller, *What's the Matter with Kansas*? Poor conservative Christians in Kansas (or anywhere in the United States) vote for Republicans who promise to halt abortion, ban gay marriage, outlaw stem cell research, and reinstate prayer in public schools but also make decisions about economic policies that end up hurting the poor. In other words, poor conservative Christians vote their values, not their economic interests, and are willing to do so even when it impoverishes them. We disagree, however, with Frank's assessment that Kansans who vote their values are suckers for doing so; the real point is that values are central in American society (Baker 2005) and voters may vote their values more than their material interests. And, as we have stressed, values voting goes both ways: those with secular values can vote their values just as those with traditional values can vote theirs. Values voting is not a conservative monopoly.

Of course, the issue of what determines vote choice is much more complex than the simple but false dichotomy between values votes and interest votes, as Greeley and Hout have argued (2006, 40). Based on our analysis, we agree with Greeley and Hout that both values and income matter, but emphasize that values are much more important. Better measures of values, as we have used here, reveal the enormous effect of values on voting. Our sensitive measures of values detected an association between values and political behavior that is considerably stronger than the effects of income, religious affiliation, frequency of church attendance, and other factors. The impact of values on political behavior is rivaled only by the effects of race.

The effects of what have been considered important determinants of political behavior, especially conservative Christian religious affiliation and frequency of attendance at religious services, disappear when we have better measure of values in the analysis. This suggests that shared values—not religious affiliation or religiosity—is a key determinant of political behavior. Perhaps religious affiliation and religiosity are only imperfect proxies for underlying shared values. Untangling these relationships would require the use of such methods as structural equation modeling. As John Bartle argued, "the challenge for political science is to shift away from simply describing the relationship between explanatory variables and vote, to examining the causal interrelationships that exist among the explanatory variables themselves" (1998, 503).

What does our study tell us about the future of conservative Christians and American democracy? As Yogi Berra said, "it's tough to make predictions, especially about the future." It is even tougher in our case because our data are snapshots of historical moments in the life of Americans nationwide and Americans in one major metropolitan region. Without longitudinal data, we cannot extrapolate into the future. But our intention was different from the beginning. Our goal was to use better measures of values to produce a deeper, clearer, and more nuanced understanding of the cultural and structural bases of political behavior. Our better measures of values tell us that the link between conservative Christians and political behavior is weaker than previously documented, values that cut across groups are more important than previously documented, and better measures of values should be included in the design of future studies that investigate trends in the changing social bases of political attitudes and behavior.

Appendix: Sources of Data and Coding of Variables

We used data from two representative surveys to analyze the effect of values on political behavior and attitudes: the 2000 World Values Surveys (WVS) and the 2003 Detroit Area Study (DAS). The United States has been surveyed routinely as part of the WVS. The WVS is the only national survey of the American people that includes the survey items necessary to calculate our better measures of values—the dimensions of traditional versus secular-rational values and survival versus self-expression values. A limitation of the WVS is that it includes only basic categories for religious affiliation. For example, Protestant is a single category that contains the various Protestant denominations. We thus cannot separate evangelical from mainline Protestants. We use the latest WVS data available, the 2000 survey, to assess the effect of values in the United States. Voting preferences were ascertained by the question, If there were a national election tomorrow, for which party on this list would you vote? The list included Republican, Democratic, Independent, Libertarian, and Reform. About 80 percent picked the first two (for more information, see http://www .worldvaluessurvey.org; see also Baker 2005, appendix A).

The 2003 Detroit Area Study (DAS) is a representative survey of adults living in Wayne, Oakland, and Macomb counties in the state of Michigan. The 2003 DAS was designed to build on the WVS and to compensate for its limitations. Most important, it includes all the survey items needed to calculate the two values dimensions. It also includes series of questions about religious affiliation that allow us to precisely categorize respondents. Hence, we can compare, for example, the political behavior and attitudes of evangelical Protestants versus mainline Protestants, controlling for the effects of the two values scales and other factors. The DAS asked more questions about voting behavior than the WVS, including whether a person had voted in the 2000 general elections and presidential vote choice. A limitation of these measures of political behavior is the elapsed time between the survey (April through August 2003) and the general elections (November 2000). As a result, respondents may overreport their vote or either intentionally or unintentionally misreport who they voted for; these are common problem in surveys about voting behavior that rely on recall, even those renowned for high-quality data, such as the ANES (Bernstein, Chadha, and Montjoy 2001; see also Belli et al. 1999). Robert Bernstein, Anita Chadha, and Robert Montjoy found that nonvoters who report that they voted are more likely to be educated, partisan, or religious; they also found that the greater the concentration of an ethic or racial group in a district, the more likely members of it overreport voting (2001). This suggests, for example, that African Americans in our DAS sample may be likely to overreport, given that they are a concentrated minority in the Detroit region. These potential limitations should be kept in mind as we report and interpret our findings.

The study population for the DAS is defined to include all adults who were eighteen years and older and lived in households in the Detroit three-county metropolitan area during the survey period, April to August 2003. The geographic area of the survey population includes Wayne, Oakland, and Macomb counties in Michigan. This population includes only eligible adults living in households. Individuals in institutions, living in group quarters or on military bases are excluded from the survey population. The DAS is an area probability sample based on a conventional three-stage sample design: a primary stage sample of area segment units followed by a second-stage sample of housing units within area segments, and a third-stage random selection of one eligible adult respondent in households with one or more eligible persons.

The sample size for the DAS is 508. The American Association for Public Opinion Research (AAPOR) response rate is 56.6 percent, which is about the same as the average response rate for the 1997–2001 DAS studies (Clemens, Couper, and Powers 2002). Sampling weights were constructed to account for variation in probabilities of selection and nonresponse rates, and to adjust sample results to match known census totals for the Detroit three-county area for age, gender, and race. The probabilities of selection varied because a single adult was selected from each household, in effect overrepresenting in the sample persons who live in households with fewer adults. Nonresponse rates were higher in some areas than others, and the inverse of the response rates in sample areas was used as an adjustment factor. Poststratification weights were developed so that the final weighted estimates agreed with census distributions by age, gender, and race for the metropolitan area. A rescaled final weight, which is the product of all three adjustments, was computed which sums to the unweighted sample size of 508. All analyses employ the final rescaled weight.

Dependent and Independent Variables

The dependent variables for the DAS are three dummy variables: *voted in 2000 elections* (1 = yes, 0 = no); *voted for Bush* (1 = yes, 0 = other), and *identify as Republican* (1 = yes, 0 = other). About 90 percent of the 508 respondents were eligible to vote in 2000, based on U.S. citizenship and age (eighteen or older in 2000). Of these, about 77 percent voted in the 2000 general elections. The 55.3 percent majority voted for Gore, 42.3 percent for Bush, and 2.3 percent voted for Ralph Nader or someone else. Among all 508 respondents, about 21 percent identified as Republican, 41 percent as Democrat, 23 percent as Independent, and 15 percent indicated other or no preference.

The independent variables are defined as follows. *Religious affiliation* is a set of dummy variables, where mainline Protestant = 1, 0 = otherwise; evangelical Protestant = 1, 0 = otherwise; Catholic = 1, 0 = otherwise; other religions = 1, 0 = otherwise; and secular (no religious affiliation) = 1, 0 = otherwise. Mainline Protestant is the omitted category in the multivariate analyses. *Frequency of attendance at religious services* is a 5-point scale ranging from 1 = every week or more to 5 = less often than [a few times a year]. This is reversed coded in the analysis. *Race* is a single dichotomous variable, where 1 = nonwhite and 0 = white, using the U.S. Census categories for race. *Socioeconomic class* is indicated by education (1 = less than high school, 2 = some high school, 3 = completed high school or GED, 4 = some college or completed college, 5 = graduate or professional degree) and household income (1 = less than $10,000, 2 = $10,000–$14,999, 3 = $15,000–$19,999, 4 = $20,000–$29,999, 5 = $30,000–$49,999, 6 = $50,000–$74,999, 7 = $75,000–$99,999, 8 = $100,000–$149,999, 9 = $150,000–$199,999, and 10 = $200,000 or more.

Values are represented by two values dimensions: a continuum of traditional values versus secular-rational values, and a continuum of survival values versus self-expression values. These are the first and second components from a factor analysis of the ten items in table 3.3, over all the nations in the World Values Surveys plus the DAS, following the same procedure used by others (for example, Inglehart and Baker 2000, Inglehart and Norris 2003, Norris and Inglehart 2004; Baker 2005).

Political ideology is indicated by choices on a conservative-liberal scale, where 1 = very conservative, 2 = moderately conservative, 3 = middle of the road, 4 = moderately liberal, and 5 = very liberal. This variable is reversed coded in the analysis, so that higher scores indicate a more conservative political ideology. We also use a dichotomous measure of political ideology, where 1 = very or moderately conservative, 0 = middle of the road to very liberal.

Control Variables

The control variables include age, gender, and marital status. Three dummy variables are used for age: *youth* (1 = ages eighteen to twenty-

Table 3.3   Components of Two Values Scales, Results from Factor Analysis

	1	2
Traditional vs. secular-rational values		
Traditional values emphasize the following:		
Abortion is never justifiable.	.670	−.253
It is more important for a child to learn obedience and religious faith than independence and determination [Autonomy index].	.656	−.122
God is very important in respondent's life.	.638	−.057
Respondent favors more respect for authority.	.469	−.093
Respondent has strong sense of national pride.	.452	.241
Secular-rational values emphasize the opposite.		
Survival vs. self-expression values		
Survival values emphasize the following:		
Respondent describes self as not very happy.	.274	.592
You have to be very careful about trusting people.	−.007	.569
Homosexuality is never justifiable.	−.526	.497
Respondent gives priority to economic and physical security over self expression and quality of life [4-item Materialist-Postmaterialist Values Index].	.129	.378
Respondent. has not and would not sign a petition.	−.114	.371
Self-expression values emphasize the opposite.		

Source: Authors' compilation based on World Values Surveys and DAS.
Note: The original polarities vary. The above statements show how each item relates to a given dimension, based on factor analysis with varimax rotation, using individual-level data from all nations in the World Values Surveys plus the DAS (follows the procedure used by, among others, Inglehart and Baker 2000; Inglehart and Norris 2003; Norris and Inglehart 2004; Baker 2005).

five; 0 = ages twenty-six plus), *middle age* (1 = ages twenty-six to fifty-four; 0 = ages eighteen to twenty-five, fifty-five plus), and *older* (1 = fifty-six plus; 0 = other). The older age group is the omitted category. *Gender* is a dichotomous variable, where 1 = female and 0 = male. *Married* is a dichotomous variable, where 1 = married now, 0 = not married now. In the models predicting voting behavior, we also include party identification as a control variable.

Note

1.   Some of the data for this study come from the 2003 Detroit Area Study, funded in part by the University of Michigan and the Russell Sage Foundation. We are grateful for helpful comments and suggestions made by John Green and Brad Wilcox (the official discussants of our paper), the conference organizers and the participants in the conference. We appreciate the helpful, constructive criticism of the anonymous reviewers.

References

Alexander, Jeffrey C., and Kenneth Thompson. 2008. *A Contemporary Introduction to Sociology*. Boulder, Colo.: Paradigm Publishers.

Baker, Wayne. 2005. *America's Crisis of Values: Reality and Perception*. Princeton, N.J.: Princeton University Press.

Baker, Wayne E., and Kenneth M. Coleman. 2004. "Racial Segregation and the Digital Divide in the Detroit Metropolitan Region." In *The Network Society: A Cross-Cultural Perspective*, edited by Manuel Castells. Cheltenham, U.K.: Edward Elgar Publishing.

Baker, Wayne, and Melissa Forbes. 2006. "Moral Values and Market Attitudes." *Society* 43(1)(January/February): 23–26.

Bartle, John. 1998. "Left-Right Position Matters, But Does Social Class? Causal Models of the 1992 British General Election." *British Journal of Political Science* 28(3): 501–29.

Belli, Robert F., Michael W. Traugott, Margaret Young, and Katherine A. McGonagle. 1999. "Reducing Vote Overreporting in Surveys." *Public Opinion Quarterly* 63(1): 90–108.

Bernstein, Robert, Anita Chadha, and Robert Montjoy. 2001. "Overreporting Voting: Why It Happens and Why It Matters." *Public Opinion Quarterly* 65(1): 22–44.

Clemens, Judi, Mick P. Couper, and Kathy Powers. 2002. *The Detroit Area Study: Celebrating 50 Years*. Ann Arbor: University of Michigan Press.

Farley, Reynolds, Sheldon Danzinger, and Harry J. Holzer. 2000. *Detroit Divided*. New York: Russell Sage Foundation.

Fiorina, Morris, Samuel J. Abrams, and Jeremy C. Pope 2005. *Culture War? The Myth of a Polarized America*. New York: Pearson Longman.

———. 2006. *Culture War? The Myth of a Polarized America*, 2nd ed. New York: Pearson Education.

Fletcher, Joseph F. 1966. *Situation Ethics: The New Morality*. Louisville, Ky.: Westminster John Knox Press.

Fogel, Robert William. 2000. *The Fourth Great Awakening and the Future of Egalitarianism*. Chicago: University of Chicago Press.

Frank, Thomas. 2004. *What's the Matter with Kansas?* New York: Henry Holt.

Greeley, Andrew, and Michael Hout. 2006. *The Truth about Christian Conservatives*. Chicago: University of Chicago Press.

Green, John C. 2007. "The Rise of the 'Traditionalist Alliance': Religion and Presidential Voter Coalitions 1960–2004." Paper presented at the Conference on Christian Conservatives and American Democracy, Russell Sage Foundation. New York (April 28, 2007).

Hillygus, D. Sunshine, and Todd G. Shields. 2005. "Moral Issues and Voter Decision Making in the 2004 Presidential Election." *PS: Political Science and Politics* 38(2): 201–10.

Hitlin, Steven, and Jane Allyn Piliavin. 2004. "Values: Revising a Dormant Concept." *Annual Review of Sociology* 30(1): 359–93.

Hunter, James Davison. 1991. *Culture Wars: The Struggle to Define America*. New York: Basic Books.

Hunter, James Davison, and Alan Wolfe. 2006. *Is There A Culture War? A Dialogue* on *Values and American Public Life*. Washington, D.C.: Pew Research Center and Brookings Institution Press.

Inglehart, Ronald. 1997. *Modernization and Postmodernization: Cultural, Economic, and Political Change in 43 Societies*. Princeton, N.J.: Princeton University Press.

Inglehart, Ronald, and Wayne E. Baker. 2000. "Modernization, Cultural Change, and the Persistence of Traditional Values." *American Sociological Review* 65(1)(February): 19–51.

Inglehart, Ronald, and Pippa Norris. 2003. *Rising Tide: Gender Equality and Cultural Change Around the World*. Cambridge: Cambridge University Press.

Klinkner, Phillip A. 2006. "Mr. Bush's War: Foreign Policy in the 2004 Election." *Presidential Studies Quarterly* 36(2): 281–96.

Lakoff, George. 1996. *Moral Politics: How Liberals and Conservatives Think*. Chicago: University of Chicago Press.

Langer, Gary. 2004. "A Question of Values." *The New York Times* (November 6). Available at: http://www.nytimes.com/2004/11/06/opinion/06langer.html.

Langer, Gary, and Jon Cohen. 2005. "Voters and Values in the 2004 Election." *Public Opinion Quarterly* 69(5): 744–59.

Layman, Geoffrey. 1997. "Religion and Political Behavior in the United States: The Impact of Beliefs, Affiliations, and Commitment from 1980 to 1994." *Public Opinion Quarterly* 61(2): 288–316.

Layman, Geoffrey, and Edward G. Carmines. 1997. "Cultural Conflict in American Politics: Religious Traditionalism, Postmaterialism, and U.S. Political Behavior." *Journal of Politics* 59(3): 751–77.

Lovett, Benjamin J., and Alexander H. Jordan. 2005. "Moral Values, Moralism, and the 2004 Presidential Election." *Analysis of Social Issues and Public Policy* 5(1): 165–75.

Norris, Pippa, and Ronald Inglehart. 2004. *Sacred and Secular*. Cambridge: Cambridge University Press.

Rokeach, Milton. 1973. *The Nature of Human Values*. New York: Free Press.

Schuman, Howard. 2006. "The Validity of the 2004 'Moral Values' Question." *The Forum* vol. 4(2): article 5. The Berkeley Electronic Press. http://www .bepress.com/forum/vol4/iss2/art5.

Schwartz, Shalom. H. 1992. "Universals in the Content and Structure of Values: Theoretical Advances and Empirical Tests in 20 Countries." *Advances in Experimental Social Psychology,* 25(1): 1–65.

———.1994. "Are There Universal Aspects in the Structure and Content of Human Values?" *Journal of Social Issues* 50(1): 19–45.

Schwartz, Shalom H., and Wolfgang Bilsky. 1987. "Toward a Universal Psychological Structure of Human Values." *Journal of Personality and Social Psychology* 53(3): 550–62.

———. 1990. "Toward a Theory of the Universal Content and Structure of Values: Extensions and Cross-Cultural Replications." *Journal of Personality and Social Psychology* 58(5): 878–91.

Williams, Rhys H., ed. 1997. *Cultural Wars in American Politics*. New York: Aldine de Gruyter.

Chapter 4

Moral-Values Politics: The Emergence of an Electoral System

STEVEN BRINT AND SETH ABRUTYN

A CENTRAL PARADOX of contemporary political life in the United States is that white evangelical Protestants have expressed a wide variety of views on social and policy issues, including moderate to liberal views on many issues involving inequalities in American society, yet have proven to be a dependable partner in the Republican coalition for more than a quarter century. Studies of the social and political opinions of evangelicals have consistently found that they support spending to improve the nation's health and education and to reduce poverty (Greeley and Hout 2006, 84–90; Wilcox and Larson 2006, 57–58). Most do not think that abortion should be banned in cases of rape or threats to the mother's health (Greeley and Hout 2006, 121–27). They have expressed a variety of views about the proper balance between pluralistic diversity and national unity (Smith 1998, 120–36, 187–203). Moreover, until 1984, most evangelical Protestants were Democrats (Leege et al. 2002, table 10.1), and even today about one-third identify with the Democratic Party. Nevertheless, their yield for Republican presidential candidates has, with a few exceptions, been consistently high since 1972, in recent years 70 percent or higher. In 1992 they replaced mainline Protestants as the most dependable coalition partner of the Republican Party, as measured by net Republican vote (Leege et al. 2002: table 10.1; Leege, Mueller, and Wald 2001; see table 4.1 for results from the 2004 presidential election).[1] In 2008, less religious Catholics and ethnic minority voters swung toward Barack Obama, but white evangelical Protestants and

Table 4.1   Two-Party Presidential Vote in 2004

	Percent Population	Percent Bush	Percent Turnout
A. Bush Groups			
Evangelicals: regular churchgoers[1]	12.6	88	63
Mormons (and "other Christians")	2.7	80	60
Catholics: regular churchgoers	4.4	72	77
Mainline Protestants: regular churchgoers	4.3	68	78
Evangelicals: irregular churchgoers[2]	10.8	64	52
Latino Protestants	2.8	63	49
Mainline Protestants: irregular churchgoers	7.0	58	68
Catholics: irregular churchgoers	8.1	55	58
Total Bush	52.7		
B. Kerry Groups			
African American Protestants	9.6	83	50
Mainline Protestants: infrequent churchgoers[3]	4.7	78	71
Other faiths (e.g. Muslim, Hindu)	2.7	77	62
Jews	1.9	73	87
Seculars & unaffiliated	16.0	72	52
Latino Catholics	4.5	69	43
Catholics: infrequent churchgoers	5.0	69	70
Evangelicals: infrequent churchgoers	2.9	52	65
Total Kerry	47.3		

Source: Authors' compilation based on Fourth National Survey of Religion and Politics 2004, Post-Election Sample (n = 2730).
Notes:
[1] Reported church attendance weekly or more often
[2] Reported church attendance once or twice a month to a few times a year
[3] Reported church attendance seldom or never

other church-attending whites remained virtually unchanged in their levels of support for the Republicans (Green 2009).

In this chapter, we argue that the key to resolving the paradox of Democratic sympathies on domestic policy issues combined with consistently high levels of Republican voting since the mid-1980s can be found in the construction and institutionalization of a system of moral-values politics.[2] Over the last thirty years, moral-values conflict became institutionalized as a regular feature of American political life, embodied in the activities of political parties and social movement organizations throughout the electoral cycle. Building on the cultural sensibilities of evangelical Protestant church communities—sensibilities characteristic of other conservative church communities as well—these changes were largely the result of improved technologies for monitoring and mobilizing public opinion, combined with stronger, albeit imperfect, coordination between the Republican Party, Christian Right social movement organizations, and broader conservative movement organizations. The strength of moral-values politics comes from the resonance of the messages produced by Republican Party tacticians with the values and cognitive style of evangelicals and other religious voters. The strength of moral-values politics also derives—we think just as importantly—from the organizational and network ties binding the Republican Party leadership to social movement elites, social movement elites to local activists, and local activists to ordinary churchgoers.

Previous Interpretations

Previous efforts to understand the defection of white evangelicals from the Democratic Party and the strength of their subsequent support for the Republican Party have adopted either a bottom-up approach, examining evangelicals' perceptions of external threats to their institutions and values, or a top-down approach, examining the symbolic environment constructed by the Republican Party. We argue that, while both of these interpretations contain elements of truth, each is incomplete.

The Politics of Cultural Defense:
A Bottom-Up Approach

The first important explanations for the rise of moral-values politics emphasized the combination of legal actions taken against conservative Protestant institutions and the threatening quality of the egalitarian and countercultural movements of the 1960s. Changing gender roles and greater sexual freedoms were widely condemned in these communities, as were the curricula of secular humanism in the public schools. The threat by the Carter administration to eliminate the tax-exempt status of Christian schools unless they integrated proved an igniting provocation. According to these accounts, evangelicals and other religious conservatives rallied to defend their way of life by mobilizing in the political arena (Conover 1983; Guth 1983; Lorentzen 1980; Moen 1984; Page and Clelland 1978; see also Wald 2003, 205–7). As the political scientist James Guth wrote:

> Cultural defense movements often appear at the conjunction of several economic social and political developments: a degree of social mobility creating a new political constituency, the growth of "indigenous" leadership and communications networks, and, most important, a threat to the traditional values, beliefs, and institutions of that constituency, often from a "secularizing" (or at least secular) political elite. In broad form that is exactly what happened here. Industrialization and urbanization have created a new "evangelical" constituency, traversed by intricate new organization and communication networks. This group (was) then activated by "trigger issues" involving outside threat to its religious values and institutions. And, as often happens . . . the resulting reaction has been used by

both religious and secular conservative entrepreneurs to add to their own power. (1983, 9)

The theme of cultural defense provides a valuable perspective on the origins of the Christian Right and the weakening of evangelicals' ties to the Democratic Party during the 1970s. However, it cannot account as well for what happened after the IRS threat and the Equal Rights Amendment disappeared from the political agenda. The need for cultural defense against movements of the secular Left should seemingly have subsided by the end of the 1970s. Antiwar protest, and with it much of the counterculture, faded with the end of the war in Vietnam. Members of racial and cultural minority groups were not as publicly assertive after the 1970s; instead, they were, for most of the period, on the defensive (see, for example, Jenkins, Jacobs, and Agnone 2003; Piven and Cloward 1982; Wilson 1987). The women's movement, too, grew less visibly militant; so-called postfeminism emphasized the compatibility of traditional norms of femininity with equal treatment in the workplace and vocal opposition to marriage and family declined (see Susan Bolotin, "Voices from the Post-Feminist Generation," *New York Times Magazine*, October 17, 1982; Pollitt 1995; Wolf 1993). Issues did arise to mobilize conservative religious communities—including continuing contestation over abortion and gay rights—but the mobilization of these issues, as we will show, rarely bubbled up from below. The very continuity of moral-values politics over thirty years, in times of social turmoil as well as relative social quiet, suggests the limitation of formulations based on communal responses to historically specific threats.

The Politics of Cultural Differences: A Top-Down Approach

The leading alternative interpretation emphasizes the symbolic underpinnings of partisan mobilization (Leege et al. 2002). Parties are seen as relying on modern campaign technology, including polling, focus groups, test marketing of advertisements, and sophisticated market segmentation, to detect what symbols and associations can be used to create anxiety among susceptible elements of the electorate. The underlying goal of cultural politics is to show that opposing candidates are not "one of us." The doubts created by cultural politics help parties stimulate loyalty among their core constituency groups, depress turnout among the opposing party's constituency groups, and create defections among those who feel anxious about their party's candidate. All three outcomes—loyalty, depressed turnout, and defection—contribute to electoral success.

Because, in this interpretation, partisan politics is primarily about how we should live (or, more abstractly, the bases of moral order), a primary goal of party tacticians is to sharpen the sense of estrangement among voters, that they—the competing party and its candidates—live differently and have different values. In this framework, voters are understood to be "cognitive misers" who work on principles of social categorization and social association; they tend to like people who seem similar to themselves in values or lifestyle and to feel anxiety about people who seem different from themselves. Voters express traditional loyalties to one or another party, but they are also receptive to messages propagated by parties that opposition candidates associate with people unlike themselves or do not share their values. Churches are important organizing sites because they foster repeated interactions. These interactions create conditions for greater common belief and greater shared anxiety about the cultural values of the opposition party and its candidates.

In our view, this interpretation is a plausible explanation for the persistence of moral-values politics over the entire period from 1978 to 2008, including during election years in which we might expect economic issues to show an overwhelming priority in voters' minds. It correctly weights the financial and organizational resources available to party elites in relation to unorganized categories of people like evangelical Protestants. It also correctly observes the importance of church communities as organizing sites.

At the same time, we find the interpretation deficient in several important ways. We question whether us-them social categorization is as central as this interpretation suggests. Survey and interview evidence indicates that politically engaged members of evangelical Protestant communities often act out of principled convictions and emphasize more specific elements of moral order: notably, the need for unchanging moral standards, gender-role traditionalism, and associations between divine purposes and political events. Political messages do, of course, sometimes highlight associations between political candidates and threatening others, but most communications focus on the values and issue positions of the candidates. The vision of voters as basing their decisions on anxieties about threatening "others," therefore, seems to us incomplete.

More important, we question the adequacy of the organizational analysis on which this interpretation is based. It is true that national political parties have the resources to develop cultural appeals that arouse emotional responses in affiliated constituency groups and, more broadly, throughout potentially sympathetic segments of the electorate. But this is not all that parties do. National political parties also control many resources for co-opting and coordinating constituency organizations. They have the financial resources, the data on party identifiers, the recruitment and training networks for candidates and activists, and the policy discussion networks to encourage constituency organizations to embrace the party's electoral and policy objectives. These constituency organizations, in turn, are able to target messages and build on ties to local activists.

Our interpretation therefore includes a broader understanding of the party's role in managing moral-values politics. It also sees actors other than symbol-producing party elites and symbol-consuming voters as playing critical roles in constructing and reproducing moral-values politics. The most important are local activists tied to church communities, the social movement organizations of the Christian Right, and the organizations of the broader conservative movement. These actors have status as well as ideological interests in the system. Parties consequently use both appeals to values and material incentives and organizational rewards to build ties that can help produce electoral victories. Better integration depends, in part, on the success of party leaders in bringing movement organizations and activists into alignment with the potentially winning messages and organizational priorities of the party. In this chapter we therefore examine not only the rhetoric of moral-values politics, but also the mechanisms used by Republican Party tacticians to integrate leaders of movement organizations and local activists.

The Party-Movement-Church Electoral System

Moral-values politics is, then, an organizational as well as a cultural structure. Relationally, it can be described as an interacting system of actors located at levels closer and more distant from the levers of national political power. Actors closer to the center of political power provide rewards and symbolic cues for actors further from the center. At the same time, some important differences in interest naturally exist between religious activists, who often act on principled conviction, and party leaders, who must assemble broad coalitions to gain and keep political power. We therefore use the term *system* advisedly; a social system involves interacting parts, but it does not require a tightly coordinated meshing of these parts.

In the remainder of the chapter, we examine the interests and relationships of actors located at each level in the moral-values system: the white evangelical Protestant social base, local activists who are involved with social movement organizations, the leaders of Christian Right social movement organizations, and the national Republican Party leadership. The chapter draws from a wide range of sources, including analyses of survey data, speeches, websites, and media coverage of moral-values issues.

The White Evangelical Social Base

Social groups are inchoate, but central tendencies do exist that can be activated for political gain. Effective appeals resonate with the concerns, cognitive styles, and social circumstances of the group. Because all large groups contain a diversity of opinion, electoral appeals are more effective with some segments than others. In the case of evangelicals, moral-values politics and Republican voting are more appealing to higher income and more religious segments of the group. But they have considerable appeal as well in the middle of the group's income distribution and among less frequent churchgoers (see Bartels 2008, chapter 3; Frank 2006; Greeley and Hout 2006, 48–52; see also chapter 2, this volume).

Cultural commitments. For religious conservatives, moral values are rooted in traditional (that is, male-headed) family and church-centered patterns of life, and biblical authority. Dozens of studies have documented the characteristic social views of evangelicals: opposed to homosexuality and easy access to abortion; opposed to gender equality at home and, to a lesser degree, in the workplace; less tolerant than other groups of alternative lifestyles, immigrants, and dissenters; sexually restrictive; and highly favorable toward public expressions of religious belief (see, for example, Bolzendahl and Brooks 2005; Greeley and Hout 2006, chapters 8–9; Loftus 2001; Wald 2003, chapter 6; Woodberry and Smith 1998). The support of evangelicals for assertive, sometimes militant nationalism is also notable (Greeley and Hout 2006; 82–84; Layman and Hussey 2007, 191–97); for many evangelicals this, too, has religious roots—in the view of the United States as having a special, divinely inspired mission in the world (Smith 1994; Tuveson 1968).

On these issues, gaps separating evangelicals from more liberal groups in American society can be very wide. Our analysis of 2004 data from three national surveys, the General Social Survey, the American National Election Study (NES), and the Pew Study of the Political Landscape, each of which included at least sixty attitude items, indicated that only a few issues were polarized by party identification or self-described political ideology. But no fewer than 40 percent of the attitude items on each survey were either polarized or borderline polarized by ethnoreligious identities. *Polarized* is defined here as describing issues on which at least two-thirds of one group favor a position and two-thirds of another oppose it and the split is unaffected by the margin of error. *Borderline polarized* is defined as describing issues on which a two-thirds to two-thirds split would be statistically possible within the upper and lower bounds of the 95 percent confidence intervals.[3]

Depending on the survey, between half and two-thirds of all polarized or borderline polarized items involved attitudes on moral-values or national security issues. On these items, the most frequently divided groups were churchgoing white evangelicals, on one side, and religiously unaffiliated or secular people, on the other. On the General Social Survey, for example, gaps of 50 percentage points or more separated these groups on opposition to the sale of pornography, opposition to teenagers' access to birth control, support for traditional gender roles, opposition to abortion, restrictive standards for regulating the end of life, and prayer in school.[4]

The interest of Christian Right organizations and the Republican Party in highlighting cultural differences—and particularly the divergent values of secular elites—undoubtedly helps to fuel moral-values politics, but the values themselves existed long before secular elites came into focus as a symbolic threat (see chapter 5, this volume), On issues such as the permissibility of abortion and teenage sex, the views of churchgoing white evangelicals and the religiously unaffiliated have been sharply divided since at least the early 1970s—before the era of partisan mobilization around the politics of moral values.

Evidence is accumulating that three primary commitments underlie the values of evangelicals and other social conservatives—religiosity, gender-role traditionalism, and moral certainty—and that, of these three, moral certainty, that is, the opposition to changing moral standards and lifestyles in society, has the most consistent and far-reaching effects (see table 4.2). The American National Election Studies survey includes data relevant to the examination of these three major bases of cultural politics. In the analysis, we used pooled NES data from 2000 and 2004. We report here only on attitudes concerning abortion, homosexuality, and national defense. The first model reports standardized regression coefficients and standard errors for ethnoreligious categories only. These models showed sizable effects for evangelical Protestants on all three variables, and sizable effects for all ethnoreligious groups on homosexuality compared to the reference group of secular-unaffiliated respondents. The second models add measures of religiosity, moral certainty, and family ideology, together with a standard battery of sociodemographic controls. In these models, the effects of ethnoreligious category were greatly attenuated or, in the cases of abortion and national defense, disappeared altogether.

By contrast, moral certainty showed sizable effects on abortion, homosexuality and national defense. Both religiosity and gender-role traditionalism also showed significant and sizable net effects on two of the dependent variables: abortion and homosexuality. This analysis suggests that while evangelical Protestantism is strongly associated with conservative views on moral-values and national defense issues, this is largely due to the tendency of evangelicals to be more religious, more traditionalist in their approach to gender and family roles, and, especially, more absolutist in their moral thinking (for further analysis, see Brint and Abrutyn 2009).

Moral certainty as a cognitive style is undoubtedly related to the orthodox theological doctrines to which evangelicals subscribe. An important feature of evangelical Protestant culture has been the vision of ideal social organization that it holds; for many evangelicals, the Christian community is world-transforming on the basis of following God's plan for humanity. Another important feature is the strong feelings of disapproval it directs against individuals and groups perceived to be failing to live up to a righteous way of living. As Andrew Greeley and Michael Hout wrote, "[Evangelicals] tend to emphasize self-reliance and facing the consequences of bad choices over aid of any type. Their churches are strict with them, and they prefer strictness in social policy" (2006, 61). Many evangelicals, of course, have accommodated in everyday life to the less strict social norms of American society, but aspirations for greater purity and concerns about pollution may nevertheless remain psychologically salient in what David Tracy called the analogical imagination of conservative Protestantism (1981).

Social circumstances. For sociologists, feelings of social superiority are the foundation out of which positively privileged status groups develop. White evangelical Protestants indicate feelings of humility in relation to God, yet many feel morally elevated in relation to other groups in American society (Smith 1998, chapter 2). Their claims to status are undoubtedly supported by their membership in the dominant racial and religious groups. But in a more immediate way they are supported by the expectations of their churches that they carry the message of Jesus into the world and attempt to act in harmony with the commands of Christian morality.

These feelings of moral elevation are potently combined, for many, with a sense of exclusion from the mainstream of American culture. Regular churchgoers frequently feel on the periphery of an American culture dominated by secular education and secular entertainment industries, a circumstance not dissimilar to that of an ethnic group whose acceptance by the dominant society is in doubt. They feel that their practices and beliefs are not well understood or respected by secular society. In church communities, those who perceive themselves to be underappreciated by the larger society are more likely to express sympathy with the goals of the Christian Right (Wald, Owen, and Hill 1989). It is no surprise, under the circumstances, that the language of the civil rights movement has come to permeate the language of the Christian Right, including demands for equality, respect, and acceptance of cultural diversity (see Smith 1998, chapter 5).

A long line of research shows divisions between people anchored, either by experience or loyalty, in the moral traditions of religious, middle- and lower-middle-class, small town, Heartland white America and those whose lives are not anchored in these experiences and loyalties (see, for example, Brint 1994, chapter 5; Brooks 2002; Brooks and Manza

Table 4.2 Attitudes about Abortion, Homosexuality, and National Defense, U.S. Adults, 2000 to 2004

	Abortion[1]		Homosexuality[2]		National Defense[3]	
	Model 1 B (S.E.)	Model 2 B (S.E.)	Model 1 B (S.E.)	Model 2 B (S.E.)	Model 1 B (S.E.)	Model 2 B (S.E.)
Ethnoreligious groups						
Evangelical Protestant	.24*** (.12)	.05 (.07)	.63*** (.16)	.26*** (.15)	.25** (.15)	.03 (.16)
Mainline Protestant	-.05 (.12)	-.05 (.07)	.28*** (.16)	.11 (.14)	.06 (.15)	-.02 (.15)
Black Protestant	.06 (.13)	-.06 (.08)	.36*** (.17)	.13 (.15)	.01 (.16)	-.13 (.16)
Catholic	.09 (.11)	.07 (.06)	.55*** (.15)	.20* (.14)	.18 (.14)	.03 (.15)
Secular-unaffiliated	Ref	Ref	Ref	Ref	Ref	Ref
Religiosity[4]	—	.28*** (.02)	—	.22*** (.04)	—	.05 (.04)
Moral certainty[5]	—	.18*** (.02)	—	.26*** (.04)	—	.20*** (.04)
Family ideology						
Gender roles[6]	—	.14*** (.01)	—	.16*** (.02)	—	-.07 (.02)
Obedient children[7]	—	.06* (.04)	—	-.04 (.06)	—	.09* (.06)
Controls						
Year	—	.05 (.01)	—	NA	—	NA
Age (+= older)	—	-.05 (.00)	—	.05 (.00)	—	.15*** (.00)
Sex (+= male)	—	.09** (.04)	—	.07 (.06)	—	.18*** (.06)

Income (+ = high)	—	-.07*	—	-.03	—	.06
		(.01)		(.02)		(.02)
Manager	—	-.02	—	-.00	—	.05
		(.05)		(.09)		(.08)
Education (+ = high)	—	-.11***	—	-.22***	—	-.25***
		(.01)		(.02)		(.02)
South	—	-.02	—	-.02	—	.01
		(.03)		(.06)		(.06)
Rural	—	.04	—	.21***	—	-.01
		(.04)		(.07)		(.07)
Small town	—	.01	—	.05	—	-.00
						(.07)
N	1109	1109	506	506	487	487
R-square	.06	.27	.13	.42	.04	.20
Adj. R-square	.05	.26	.12	.40	.03	.17

Source: Authors' compilation based on National Election Studies, 2000 to 2004.

Notes:

[1] Abortion (attitude toward abortion), is based on an item indicating the conditions under which respondents would permit abortion (never, in cases of rape and incest, only when need established, or always).

[2] Homosexuality (attitudes toward homosexuality), is a factor-weighted scale based on four items: support or opposition to gay marriage, for laws protecting homosexuals; support or opposition to banning homosexuals from the military, and support or opposition for allowing homosexuals to adopt children. Alpha = 79/Omega = .91.

[3] National defense (attitudes toward national defense issues) is a factor-weighted scale based on three items: support/opposition to government increases in defense spending; support/opposition to using military force as "the best way" to ensure peace; and support/opposition for increasing spending to fight terrorism. Alpha = .74/Omega = .75.

[4] Religiosity is a factor-weighted scale based on by six items: belief in the Bible as the literal word of God, views of the importance of religion in life, use of religion to guide action in everyday life, frequency of prayer, frequency of church attendance, and participation in church activities outside of services. Alpha = .66/Omega = .75.

[5] Moral certainty is a factor-weighted scale based on three items: support or opposition to the view that moral views should adjust to a changing world, support or opposition to the view that people should be more tolerant of different moral standards, and support or opposition to the view that newer lifestyles are causing societal breakdown. Alpha= .64/Omega = .69.

[6] Gender role traditionalism is based on a seven-point scale item asking whether men and women should have equal roles in society where 1 is "men and women should have an equal role" and 7 is "a woman's place is in the home."

[7] Children's obedience is based on an item asking respondents to identify the relative importance of obedience as a quality in children.

*** p < .001 ** p < .01 * p < .05

2004; Hunter 1992; Layman 2001). Class and locale are no longer as determining as they once were, however; many evangelicals have experienced social and geographical mobility. Evangelicals now have an income and education profile more similar to that of mainline Protestants, and are not as concentrated as they once were in the Bible Belt (Greeley and Hout 2006, 91–100; Smith 1998, 75–82). But another tradition-preserving social process has come into play. Americans who are unhappy with the values environment of the denominations of their youth frequently change churches to find those that more closely express their outlooks. Thus, conservative mainline Protestants join evangelical churches, and conservative Catholics find parishes that value religious belief and practice over social reform, leading to a sorting out along lines of sociocultural affinity, rather than of inherited circumstances (Bishop 2008).

The Activist Stratum

Activists are the most important stratum within church communities from the point of state and national conservative political leaders. A decade ago, the activist periphery was estimated at 4 million people, or about one in seven religious voters (Green 2000). Members of the activist periphery provide material support for Christian Right movement organizations through donations and purchases, and by providing an audience for revenue-producing Christian television and radio programs. They provide the organizing energy for political activities, ranging from letter writing to get-out-the-vote campaigns to pro-administration demonstrations.

A more deeply involved activist core follows politics closely, donates to Christian Right organizations at higher levels, and is more active in movement political actions. One recent study defined the activist core as those members of the voting-age public who said they felt favorably toward all major Christian Right organizations (Green, Conger, and Guth 2006). In this study, core activists were notably more religious than other activists: they were much more likely to say the Bible is the literal word of God and to attend church more than once a week. Nearly half were women. They included a high proportion of southerners and Southern Baptists. More than two-thirds were college educated and, although they were also more affluent than evangelicals generally, they differed more in educational levels than in income levels (Green, Conger, and Guth 2006). The activist core was estimated at 200,000 people a decade ago (Green 2000), and, although no authoritative estimates of its current size exist, it seems likely that the number of core activists expanded during the run-up to the 2004 presidential election (Wilcox, Merolla, and Beer 2006; Campbell and Monson 2007) and has declined in numbers since that time.

Until the 2000s, evangelicals' awareness of opportunities for political action, other than through the distribution of voter guides, may have been lower on average than in other religious communities (Chaves 2004, 112–20; compare Welch et al. 1993). However, in 2004 grassroots efforts to reelect George Bush and to pass initiatives banning gay marriage led to markedly higher participation in political action in evangelical church communities. These efforts included large-scale GOP-organized task forces devoted to personal contact with evangelical (Monson and Oliphant 2007, 100) and Catholic (Hudson 2008, 193–96) activists who could lead door-to-door get-out-the-vote drives. The determined mobilizing work of Christian Right organizations and the Bush campaign created a new peak in the number of local activists. In 2000, 14 percent of the electorate self-identified as Religious Right. In 2004, according to one study, more than 20 percent did so (Rozell and Das Gupta 2006).

Traditions of weeknight meetings for a pot-luck dinner and Bible study, self-help discussions, and church committee work provide the small group settings in which political conversations naturally arise and in which volunteers can be recruited for letter-writing campaigns or get-out-the-vote canvassing (Wald, Owen, and Hill 1988). Many activists are interested primarily in changing the direction of American society to better represent their personal convictions. At the same time, activists can gain status in the church community as opinion leaders who are willing to stand up and motivate others on the basis of the information they have gained about issues of the day.

Activists are the sinews of the party-movement-church system. Their efforts to inform and mobilize others are essential to the success of causes supported by movement organizations and the Republican Party. In our model, activists' energies are stimulated not only by powerful images and rhetoric designed by party and movement tacticians, but also by personal interactions focusing around the communication of knowledge and conviction. Activists' influence can be amplified by the effects of church cultures that promote political action in support of traditional moral values.

Christian Right Social Movement Organizations

Beginning in the late 1970s, social movement organizations mobilized and indeed constructed the politicized evangelical community. However, by the late 1980s, these organizations became increasingly incorporated into the organizational structure of the national Republican Party leadership. For this reason, the analysis of social movement organizations as actors in the emergence and institutionalization of the moral-values system must be divided into two periods: one encompassing the era of Jerry Falwell's Moral Majority (1979–1988) and the other the era of the Robertson-Reed Christian Coalition and the George W. Bush administration (1989–2008).

Constructing and mobilizing a constituency.   Christian Right social movement organizations, such as the National Christian Action Coalition (founded in 1977), the Christian Voice (1978), the Moral Majority (1979), Concerned Women for America (1979), the Religious Roundtable (1979), the American Coalition for Traditional Values (1980), and the Family Research Council (1983), all grew in the wake of disappointments with the Carter administration. As Rogers Smith shows in volume 1 (chapter 11), the formation of the Christian Right was closely related to court decisions threatening the tax exempt status of Christian broadcasters and Christian private schools.

As they focused on issues with appeal in evangelical communities, Christian Right organizations created a public identity and narrative for evangelicals to impel political action. Like other forms of identity politics, those of the Right emphasized the valuable qualities and central importance of a group unfairly marginalized by the dominant powers in society. But in these narratives the dominant powers were secular, liberal, and attached to culture-producing industries, not the conservative white males who figured so prominently in the identity politics of the Left. In a complex society, every individual holds multiple identities— occupational, class, gender, and others. Social movement leaders heightened the salience of religious identities by focusing on the centrality of church communities and the threats to religious values posed by secular elites. Statements by Jerry Falwell before the 1980 election captured this emphasis: "We're not trying to jam our moral philosophy down the throats of others. We are simply trying to keep others from jamming their amoral philosophy down our throats" (quoted in William Greider, "Would Jesus Join the Moral Majority?" *Washington Post*, October 13, 1980, D1). In a separate statement, Falwell called for a vigorous response: "The day of the silent church is passed. . . . Preachers, you need as never before to preach on the issues, no matter what they say or what they write about you" (quoted in Doug Willis, "Pastor Says God Opposes ERA," *Associated Press*, October 30, 1980).

Social movement leaders also developed a narrative about the perils facing American society and the role evangelicals could play in opposing these perils. This narrative drew on the long-standing theme in evangelical discourse about the need to assert godly values to overcome a world in moral decline. This theme was given new energy by evangelicals' sense of a world turned upside down by sexual experimentation, gender equity, and an aggressive secularism that gave no quarter to religious sensibilities. The branch of the movement focusing on opposition to secular elites grew out of the work of the Religious Roundtable and the Moral Majority, and the pro-family branch out of Eagle Forum's opposition of the Equal Rights Amendment (Hudson 2008, 3–12, 62–65).

Early movement leaders such as Falwell began to speak not only of the need for spiritual renewal and the approaching end of times, but also of what believers could do to return morality to a society in need of it. As Nancy Ammerman writes in volume 1, "Evangelicals have never stopped believing that spiritual salvation is the key to long-lasting change, but they became convinced that they might lose the ability to preach that gospel and preserve their way of life if they did not also act politically" (chapter 2). The sense of fighting an immoral power with only the force of divine favor and moral justice on one's side has, of course, deep roots in Christianity, and has frequently given rise to powerful movements for social change.

Leaders of the Christian Right learned to tailor the same basic narrative structure to the interests of those they hoped to influence. During the Robertson-Reed era, the Christian Coalition made a conscious effort to reach out beyond older religious conservatives to younger, suburban, and more affluent people with children. These people were strongly motivated by concerns about the cultural environment to which their children were exposed in the media and the schools (Wilcox and Larson 2006, 47–49). The fight to protect children and families consequently became a central motif of the narrative when the target audience consisted primarily of young suburban families.

Much of the organizational technology of the contemporary system of moral-values politics was pioneered by leaders of social movement organizations. These included congressional scorecards (borrowed from the American Conservative Union), targeted mailers, and building grassroots local chapters (a rarity in recent American political life). Between 1992 and 2000, the voter guide was the chief asset of the Christian Right as a grassroots electoral enterprise. Estimates of the distribution of these voter guides vary, but it is safe to say that they were distributed to tens of millions of voters in 1992, each one showing where candidates stood on issues such as abortion, gay rights, prayer in schools, and other issues appealing to religious conservatives (Wilcox and Larson 2006, 99, 133). The 40 million voter guides prepared in the watershed year of 1994 were designed to be distributed to 100,000 churches, though many were undelivered or left unopened in bulk. During this period, Republican politicians credited the voting guides with changing electoral margins by as much as 5 to 7 percentage points. In the early and mid-1990s, church directories were often used for get-out-the-vote telephone drives and door-to-door canvassing. The Christian Coalition claims to have made calls to three million evangelical voters during the 1994 election season (Wald 2003, 213). Christian Right organizations also pioneered techniques for reaching voters on the issues they cared most about through sophisticated surveying and targeted mailing. They held regional and national conferences to build commitment and social ties among sympathetic ministers and church leaders. These methods were later adopted by Republican Party tacticians.

Sharing and ceding control.   The image of an independent social movement exercising influence on a resistant Republican Party establishment is not accurate for the Reagan era, and it is less accurate for the period following the formation of the Christian Coalition in 1989. Movement organizations encouraged evangelical Christians to align with the Republican Party, because Republican Party leaders, beginning with Ronald Reagan, took positions on moral-values issues consistent with movement positions. Reagan declared his endorsement of the agenda of the Christian Right in a meeting of the Religious Roundtable in 1980. However, divisions within his administration led to an incomplete embrace of that agenda and strenuous objections to it among some (Hudson 2008, 234–38).

The Christian Coalition, under the leadership of the televangelist and 1988 Republican presidential candidate Pat Robertson and his chief lieutenant Ralph Reed, spearheaded the second wave of organization. Unlike the Moral Majority, the Christian Coalition received funds from the Republican National Committee, and Reed worked closely with party leaders throughout the period of his involvement with the organization (Easton 2000). Beginning in earnest at this time, the Republican Party and its allied organizations nurtured and trained movement leaders and contributed directly to their success.

In the early 1990s, para-party organizations, such as Empower America and the Heritage Foundation, played a distinct role in forging a bond between Christian Right leaders and Republican Party politicians. These groups specialized in marketing, data dissemination, and (in the case of Empower America) candidate training. Empower America provided data about what it called moral decline through its influential *Index of Leading Cultural Indicators* (Bennett 1993), and trained politicians to run campaigns that could be perceived as moderate enough to appeal to independents, but conservative enough to gain the enthusiastic support of evangelicals. According to a one-time staffer, Empower America helped focus Republicans on culture, realizing that issues such as religious discrimination, abortion, and so-called Hollywood values appealed strongly to religious conservatives. In 1993 and 1994, Empower America trained more than 600 candidates on how to run for office. More than 300 won in the Republican tide of 1994. Empower America told candidates to use code to keep religious discussion general, not specific, and to use "softer, more nuanced language such as phrases from parables" to signal religious voters without alienating Republican moderates and independents (Kuo 2006, 62–63).

In the mature party-movement-church system of the 1990s and 2000s, social movement organizations continued to mobilize conservative Christians through fundraising appeals and newsletters that cast secular liberalism as intent on the destruction of religious and family values. However, the position of national social movement organizations shifted subtly, and they became a more coordinated and cooperative partner of the Republican Party electoral organization (for further analysis, see chapters 9 and 11, this volume). Facing upward toward party elites, social movement organizations acted as pressure groups advocating appointments and more vigorous efforts to change social policies in the direction favored by religious and pro-family voters. Facing downward toward local church communities, they acted as conduits for party messages to activists.

In principle, social movement organizations should be able to address a wider range of issues than party leaders because they are not required to worry as much about alienating moderates. Nevertheless, national social movement organizations have focused in recent years on issues that are most advantageous to the Republican Party. Our analysis of Christian conservative websites in early 2007 indicate that the issues of abortion and homosexuality received the most attention in the 2007 data (see table 4.3, January 2007), as one would expect in a coordinated system, because these issues have the greatest traction in the electorate. Second-tier issues of public expression of religious symbols, support for traditional families, and opposition to judicial activism were addressed, but less frequently. Politically unpopular moral values issues, such as restriction on stem cell research, teen sexual abstinence, pornography, and divorce laws were, by contrast, rarely mentioned.

Data from mid-2008 (see table 4.3, August 2008) show less activity on the websites and splits emerging in the movement as the presidential election neared. The National Association of Evangelicals removed all overt political content and added links to newspaper articles about evangelicals, many indicating a more liberal view on issues such as the environment. By contrast, other websites, such as the Traditional Values Coalition, focused much more attention on militant Islam and implicitly linked the Democratic candidate, Barack Obama, to Islam. Others, such as Concerned Women for America, continued to focus on the familiar staples of moral-values politics. Party influence continued to be evident in these websites; as in 2007, none of the websites focused on moral-values issues with limited appeal in the broader electorate.

One further indicator of the growing role of the party can be found in the massive shift in responsibility for informing voters about the issues from Christian Right social movement organizations to the Republican

Table 4.3   Topics on Christian Conservative Websites, 2007 and 2008

Values Coalition	Traditional Women of America	Concerned Legal Action	Christian Coalition Family Action	AFA/ Focus on the News Links	Nat. Assoc. Evang.
January 2007					
Homosexuality/ gay rights	11	3	0	>20	6
Abortion	4	>20	0	1	0
Judicial activism	1	2	1	5	2
Public religion	4	2	2	1	1
Traditional families	0	3	1	4	1
Terrorism	7	0	0	0	0
Stem cell research	2	0	0	1	0
Pornography	0	2	0	0	0
Sexual abstinence	1	0	0	0	0
Divorce laws	0	0	0	0	0
Poverty	0	0	0	0	0
August 2008					
Homosexuality/ gay rights	8	4	1	5	0
Abortion	1	12	0	2	0
Islam	6	0	1	1	0
Obama	4	4	1	1	1
Energy	4	0	1	1	0
Judicial activism	3	0	2	1	0
Public religion	1	2	4	1	1
Traditional families	1	1	0	1	1
Terrorism	1	1	0	0	0
Stem cell research	0	0	1	1	0
Pornography	0	1	0	1	0
Sexual abstinence	0	1	0	1	0
Divorce laws	0	0	0	0	0
Poverty	0	0	0	0	0

Source: Authors' compilation.

National Committee. A 2004 campaign communications survey showed that the Republican National Committee was responsible for the over-whelming majority of mailers sent to voters by conservative organizations; 75 percent of the pieces of mail received by respondents in the survey were sent by the RNC (Monson and Oliphant 2007, 107). Four major Christian Right social movement organizations—the National Right to

Life Committee, Focus on the Family, the Christian Coalition, and the Traditional Values Coalition—together sent fewer than 17 percent of the mailers. In the mailers sent by both the RNC and other conservative organizations, just four issues dominated, each a proven winner with religious conservatives: abortion, same-sex marriage, nomination of judges, and family values. These four were among sixteen issues mentioned in the mailers, but comprised 85 percent of all issue mentions (Monson and Oliphant 2007, 109).

The National Republican Party

National parties cannot win elections by appealing to the sentiments of a single group, and particularly not to one as controversial as the Christian Right. Appeals to the public good, rather than to narrower interests, are necessary for success in political life. For this reason, most politicians avoid the appearance of a close association with voters who are motivated primarily by intense religious convictions. Nevertheless, in the mature party-movement-church system, the national Republican Party proved an able manager of conservative Christian support. The electoral technology of the party is expressed in its issue management, message design, outreach efforts, and patronage.

Issue management. In our model of the moral-values electoral system, the Republican Party filters and edits policy ideas with public opinion in mind. Before endorsing policy ideas, analysts consider the distribution of public opinion, the degree to which issues create strong emotions for activists on either side of the issue, and the likelihood of divisions among members of the opposing party. The party emphasizes only a handful among all possible moral-values issues, and then works to keep the focus on those issues. It redirects moral-values policies that have a more limited appeal to those who have a special interest in them and attempts to minimize their salience at the national level.

For Republicans, the most important feature of polarized issues is the extent to which positions supported by white evangelicals are also supported in the broader population. Our analysis of General Social Survey data between 1972 and 2006 shows that the majority of Americans tilted toward evangelicals on issues related to homosexuality. They also became somewhat less willing to support abortion under any circumstances. By contrast, Americans tilted toward seculars on issues of premarital sex, divorce, pornography, and end of life. Polarized issues favoring the evangelical position have been featured in partisan political conflicts advanced by Republican Party politicians, and those that tilt toward the Democratic Party have typically been minimized.

Examined from the point of view of the Republican Party, these winning, contentious issues have had the following characteristics: public opinion is trending in the direction of the party; divisions exist in the opposing party's coalition; and a constituency subgroup feels very strongly about the issue. In the 1990s and early 2000s, the issues of gay marriage and abortion fit the profile, as did tough-minded foreign policies, including the PATRIOT Act and (until early 2005) the war in Iraq. A major discovery by Republican tacticians has been that wedge issues can be winning issues even if the public is closely divided. Wedge issues not only turn out fervent supporters but also opponents, who thereby become visible and can be demonized for the benefit of attracting moderate, but conservative-leaning swing voters. This process of symbolic interaction requires visible, threatening others to activate fears. Wedge issues reliably create these visible others.

The issue of gay marriage is a contentious issue that has played favorably for the moral-values electoral system. At least two-thirds of Americans say they are opposed to gay marriage. White evangelicals are almost unanimously opposed and half of these people tell polling organizations that they feel very strongly about the issue. Division exists among Democrats on this issue. At the same time, supporters of gay marriage will naturally exercise their First Amendment rights to support efforts to legalize gay marriage, thereby visually activating the opposition of values voters to gay influence. Thus, the widely disseminated images of parades of gay activists in San Francisco, some dressed as transvestites, following the legalization of gay marriage served as a stimulus to antigay backlash among conservative Christians in 2004.

A legal strategy sometimes used to help mobilize the vote is to put measures on the ballot that will increase voter turnout among constituencies that feel strongly about the issue. The gay marriage initiatives that appeared on the ballot in eleven states in 2004 are an example of the effective use of this strategy. A similar strategy was pursued by the Republican Party in 2006. It included initiatives on gay marriage in eight states, including two southern states with tightly contested senatorial elections, as well as initiatives to restrict abortion in three states and to ban illegal immigration in two southwestern states, where such a ban has wider support among Republicans and conservative-leaning independents. Six similar initiatives were on state ballots in 2008.

The Republican Party has also benefited from a second type of moral-values issue: exploitable, consensus issues, such as support for faith and family. In the highly rationalized system of American political campaigning, it may seem surprising that these issues can provide advantages to a particular political party. However, advocacy of consensus positions can be effective if the opposition party does not counter, either because mobilized minorities within the party coalition are opposed to adopting the consensus position, or because statements would violate matters of party principle. Republican emphasis on the importance of having two parents raising children is a good example of an exploitable consensus issue. Four out of five Americans agree with this position, including a sizable majority of Democrats. Key constituencies within the Democratic coalition represent single parents and poor people and would like to keep the focus of social policy on poverty rather than family structure. Similarly, many Democrats have been reluctant to talk about faith for fear of alienating secular supporters, or because of principled positions about the separation of church and state. Because Democrats have been reluctant, until recently, to express majority views about faith and family, Republicans have found it easy to paint them as members of an irreligious, antifamily party.

With the cooperation of social movement organizations, party leaders can keep issues on the agenda by mentioning them in press releases and speeches, or reduce their visibility if they are unpopular issues. The rhetorical emphases and themes of party leaders, as transmitted by the press corps, are signals to allies in social movement organizations about issues that are politically viable. Our content analysis of speeches given by eight Republican politicians to Christian Right organizations shows that three topics were most frequently mentioned: homosexuality, multiple references in half of the speeches; abortion, multiple references in half of the speeches; and traditional families, at least one reference in five of the speeches. Other moral-values issues, such as divorce laws, pornography, and abstinence, were rarely mentioned. The references in these speeches to Christian Right organizations also differed from those speeches to broader conservative movement audiences. In the latter cases, references to national security, terrorism, and government spending were far more common, and moral-values issues were rarely mentioned. Terrorism, judicial activism, and public religious expression were the only issues that crossed audience lines.[5]

In table 4.4, we present the results of a Lexis-Nexis search for the period March 1 through Election Day 2004 on a set of moral-values issues. The table shows that coverage of moral-values issues in the months leading up to the election was both extensive and skewed to the issues that split Democrats and aroused strong emotions among Christian conservatives. One as-yet unanswered question is why the press corps was so interested in these issues at election time. The most likely reason is the dependence of journalism on the narrative power of drama and conflict; stylized controversies help to sell papers because they evoke strong feelings in readers.

Message design.   Candidates and political parties spend enormous sums to ensure that their messages are communicated effectively. As David

Table 4.4   Newspaper and Magazine Coverage of Moral-Values Issues, 2004

Issue	Lexis-Nexis Counts
Abortion	6000+
"Christian values"	6000+
Family values	6000+
Gay marriage	6000+
Gay adoption	330
Divorce law	322
Prayer in school	198
Pornography laws	166
Abstinence pledges for teens	82
Decency laws	21

Source: Authors' compilation based on Lexis-Nexis U.S. Newspaper and Magazine Database, March 2004 to Election Day 2004.

Leege and his colleagues (2002) emphasized, these efforts sometimes involve associating the opposing party with images and personalities considered by most voters to lie outside the cultural mainstream. National Republican party tacticians have worked hard to associate Democratic candidates with Hollywood celebrities and "party girls" (as in the Britney Spears and Paris Hilton ads aired against Barack Obama), with "out-of-touch" intellectuals (as in the characterizations of Al Gore as the ozone man), with "angry liberals" who "hate" America (as in the association of Obama with his former pastor Jeremiah Wright), with foreign enemies of the United States (as in the well-publicized support of a Hamas leader for Obama), and even with violent criminals (as in the Willie Horton ad used against Michael Dukakis). The association of President Bill Clinton with the countercultural lifestyle of the 1960s became a potent symbol for conservative movement activists during the 1990s.

Although such messages are emotionally arousing, they can also come in for criticism as unfair or below-the-belt blows. Perhaps as a result, most messages focus on voters' values and issue preferences, not on their social aversions. A study of political mailers in the 2004 election showed that, of the top ten mailers, only one drew out negative associations between the rival candidate and public figures outside the cultural mainstream, in this case liberals such as the film personalities Michael Moore and Jane Fonda. The rest focused on differences in the values or issue positions of the candidates. A very common theme of these microtargeted mailers was that the candidate shared the values of the mailer's recipient (Monson and Oliphant 2007, 113–16). Studies of broadcast advertising show similar results: at least two-thirds are issue based (Franz et al. 2007, 69; Geer 2006, 61).

As they provide information about the candidates' positions on issues, political parties attempt to place their issues and candidates on the normative end of three important quality dimensions in American political culture: strength-weakness, integrity-corruption, and belonging-separation (compare Alexander and Smith 2003, chapter 5). Of these three, the strength-weakness dimension may be particularly meaningful to evangelicals, who are sensitized to the discipline required to improve the world and overcome moral weaknesses. But the appearance and reference to strength clearly also resonates far beyond the evangelical Protestant community, particularly during periods of international challenge and war.

Because religious people do not constitute a majority of voters, the Republican Party has faced the difficult task of appealing simultaneously to swing voters, who have relatively moderate views on moral-values issues, at the same time that it appeals to the sensibilities of religious voters. Republican Party candidates have been willing to declare their commitment to the culture of life and to the idea that marriage is between a man and a woman. But even the born-again George W. Bush played down his religious faith in public. Christian Right leaders, beginning with the Christian Coalition's Ralph Reed, counseled their candidates throughout the 1990s to follow the same course.

Rhetoric used in national campaigns must have wide appeal. Compassionate conservatism, a George W. Bush campaign slogan in 2000, is the most important recent example of rhetoric that builds beyond the evangelical base to other religiously inclined groups. According to those close to the Bush campaign, politically motivated evangelicals were not the primary target for compassionate conservatism. Instead, this rhetoric was aimed at Catholics, suburban women, and minorities—all groups with a propensity to support people in need (Kuo 2006, 60–61; Morris and Slater 2006, 96–98).

Given the variety of groups that make up the American electorate, narrowcasting to subcultural constituencies is as important as broadly targeted messaging. Through surveys, focus groups, and the knowledge of culturally sensitive local informants, the Republican Party has developed techniques for tailoring messages to subcultural constituencies. Thus, Catholic audiences for Republican politicians heard the word *scripture* instead of *Bible* and the phrase *social renewal* rather than *moral decline*, and their evangelical Protestant counterparts typically heard the opposite. The phrase *culture of life* crosses religious cultures, but it has special meaning for Catholics because it repeats a key term in Pope John Paul II's 1995 encyclical, *Evangelium vitae*. In general, Republicans attempt to guard against self-righteous and haughty-sounding rhetoric when communicating with Catholics, because this language and tonality is reminiscent of the Southern Baptist culture that many Catholics grew up distrusting (Morris and Slater 2006, 99–100).

Similarly, images that would be considered inflammatory in a national campaign can be used effectively when targeted to a narrower population. One 2004 poster familiar to members of conservative evangelical churches, for example, showed a picture of a gay couple with the caption "allowed" and next to it a picture of the Bible with the caption "banned." By defining and directing rhetoric at several levels within the polity, based on breadth of appeal, the party can aggregate supporters within a pluralistic society while restricting exposure to messages with limited appeal to the core constituencies who are most sympathetic to them (see also Hillygus and Shields 2008; Monson and Oliphant 2007).

Outreach and network expansion.   Political coalitions require personal as well as symbolic interchanges to prosper. The narrative of struggle between virtue and the agents of immorality has proven exceptionally durable, but social relations of trust are necessary to keep the primary advocates of the narrative committed and energized. These relations are embedded in social networks. From the perspective of national party leaders, networks provide channels for listening and responding to concerns, testing ideas, communicating priorities, and building a sense of common interest.

Religious leaders are an important constituency in the United States and special briefings have been organized for them at least since the beginning of the modern era. The extent of outreach to religious communities expanded significantly in the George W. Bush White House. A steady stream of national Christian leaders were given briefings and presented with presidential mugs and pins. The briefings were often led by Timothy Goeglein, special assistant to President Bush and deputy director of the Office of Public Liaison and Intergovernmental Affairs. One such briefing, for thirty leaders of the national Apostolic (Pentecostal and Charismatic) church associations, was described by an official of the Assemblies of the Lord Jesus Christ: "The consistent theme presented throughout the day was that the United States is at a critical point in history. Strong, value-oriented leadership must be continued. America is at an important crossroads and the right path must be taken" (Robert Martin, "Apostolic Leaders Given Exclusive White House Briefing," Ninety andnine.com, 2004). During the meeting, church leaders were briefed by a national security advisor on the war on terror by a State Department official on Israel and the Middle East, by a political affairs official on President Bush's "strong leadership" and the "imperative" that people of faith remain engaged in politics, and by a domestic policy advisor on the social consequences of same-sex marriage in Sweden. Goeglein ended the session by discussing the need to end filibusters on pro-life judges and by emphasizing that the main issue in the United States was the "issue of values, values that must be preserved." During the years of Republican ascendancy, annual events such as the National Prayer Breakfast, begun in 1953, have grown into larger enterprises, with 3,000 church and international dignitaries now attending (Jeffrey Sharlet, "Jesus Plus Nothing," *Harpers Magazine*, March 2003).[6]

The Republican Party and the White House also sent out emissaries to church communities. As part of its efforts to inform religious and nonprofit leaders about what it called its compassion agenda, the White House held dozens of conferences in politically important states. According to a former White House aide, an average of 1,500 people per conference received information, materials, and resources. All were leaders of larger organizations—and "most went back to their organizations impressed by how much the President and his staff cared about their concerns" (Kuo 2006, 171–72).

As part of the outreach effort, White House deputies held weekly—sometimes more frequent—conference calls with leaders of the Christian Right to provide updates on administration projects and priorities, and to solicit feedback. Regulars on the call included the director of public policy for Focus on the Family, the head of the National Association of Evangelicals, the publisher of the conservative Catholic magazine *Crisis*, the director of Pat Robertson's American Center for Law and Justice, the head of the Family Research Council, the president of the Southern Baptist Convention's Ethics and Religious Liberty Commission, and two Christian radio talk show hosts (Kuo 2006, 170–71).

In addition to White House–directed conversations and events, conservative evangelicals convened weekly meetings with congressional leaders and Republican officials to discuss public policy and specific strategies. Invitation-only meetings of groups like the Values Action Team and the Arlington Group are attended by both Senators and representatives of the White House and cover topics in social policy and message design (Karen Tumulty and Matthew Cooper. "What Does Bush Owe the Religious Right?" *Time*, January 30, 2005; Alan Cooperman. "Gay Marriage as 'The New Abortion.'" *The Washington Post*, July 26, 2004). Other Christian elite policy discussion networks provide forums for consensus-building and elite cohesion across institutional sectors. The most important of these organizations is the Council for National Policy, founded by the Reverend Timothy LeHaye in 1981. The council meets three times a year and publishes a weekly newsletter and semiannual journal. In the recent past, council membership has included CEOs of major American corporations, top Republican officials and congressmen, and leaders of Religious Right social movement organizations, such as Sam Moore, Sun Myung Moon, Pat Robertson, Rousas John

Rushdoony, Phyllis Schafley, Jay Sekulow, Louis Sheldon, and Donald Wildmon (David Kirkpatrick, "Club of the Most Powerful Gathers in Strictest Privacy," New York Times, August 28, 2004, A10). Prominent evangelicals have also been drawn into the party's orbit through invitations to events like the Americans for Tax Relief Wednesday meetings (John Cassidy. "Wednesdays with Grover." The New Yorker, July 25, 2005), Heritage Foundation and American Enterprise Institute seminars, and the Conservative Political Action Conference. Policy forums like these help to build elite cohesion through their focus on a common set of topics, the sense of belonging they encourage, and the informal social ties they can produce (Domhoff 2002).

Policy discussions and strategy sessions are probably not the principal source of cohesion in the upper echelons of the party-movement-church system, however. As Michael Lindsay argues in this volume, in these upper reaches cohesion is more often based on personal friendships outside the political sphere (see chapter 10). Serving on the boards of evangelical nonprofit organizations together and having personal ties with leaders and their families cement bonds of loyalty and mutual commitment. Some key leaders, such as Edwin Meese, the attorney general under Ronald Reagan, Charles Colson, an advisor to Richard Nixon, and Senator Dan Coates of Indiana, have cultivated very extensive informal networks among evangelicals. Participation in these networks has, in turn, often led to important jobs in the executive branch. Michael Gerson, the chief speechwriter during the first George W. Bush term, was, for example, a protégée of Colson, and Timothy Goegelin, Bush's liaison to the Christian Right, was a protégée of Coates.

In addition, Christian fellowships exist in many organizations of government, including the Air Force Academy (U.S. Air Force Headquarters Review Group 2005) and the Pentagon (Jeffrey Sharlet, "Inside Christian Embassy," Theraveler.org, 2006). Daily Bible study was held also at the U.S. Department of Justice during the first George W. Bush administration (Dan Eggen. "Ashcroft's Faith Plays Visible Role at Justice." The Washington Post, May 14, 2001). A cross-institutional Christian fellowship of Republican leaders gathers at the Cedars mansion in suburban Virginia (Kuo 2006, 91–92; Lindsay 2007, 35–36). Many of these Christian fellowships, notably the Cedars, are apolitical and invite members of both political parties. Some, however, such as Christian Embassy, a significant presence in the military, are explicitly political in support of both social movement and Republican Party objectives. Whether political or not, personal ties forged through Christian fellowships have fostered many mentoring relationships and contributed "to a shared sense of identity among leaders who, without that common faith, probably would have not worked together at all. That cohesion has contributed greatly to the rise of American evangelicalism" (Lindsay 2007, 62).

Patronage and policies.   Political parties can provide assurance that they are responding both to the personal convictions and material interests of their supporters in how they distribute their patronage. Parties in power have two key forms of patronage to bestow: appointments to office and funding of policies supported by constituency groups. The George W. Bush administration used each of these tools to further institutionalize the moral-values system.

Some 2,600 political appointees were at work in the Bush administration before the 2004 election (Stephen Barr, "Appointees Everywhere, But Try to Count Them," *Washington Post*, October 17, 2004, C2). These appointees do not include members of blue-ribbon commissions or delegations. It is impossible to know how many appointees, commission members, or members of delegations were closely associated with the Christian Right, because most appointees do not advertise their connections to controversial organizations. Some high-profile appointees had close ties, including the first attorney general, John Ashcroft; the director of the Office of Personnel Management, Kay James Cole (former vice president of the Family Research Council and Dean of Pat Robertson's Regent University); and Michael Gerson, the presidential speechwriter. Christian conservatives have been particularly interested in judicial appointees and in policy arenas close to the moral-values agenda, and have gained some important appointees in these areas. Early appointees of the Bush administration included Michael McConnell, an opponent of the separation of church and state, to the federal bench; the Religious Right activist Eric Treene as special counsel in the Justice Department for religious discrimination; and several Religious Right leaders as members of a delegation to change UN policy on abortion. The two Supreme Court justice appointments were conservative Catholics and members of the Federalist Society, an association of religious and political conservatives (for other key evangelical appointees, see Lindsay 2007, 26).

Encouraged by a general trend toward public-nonprofit partnerships, some evangelical nonprofits have been funded by the U.S. government since the 1970s. But this funding grew significantly during the administration of George W. Bush. In 1981, for example, the evangelical humanitarian relief and development organization, World Vision, provided $60 million in overseas aid, of which 6 percent came from federal government sources. By 2003, World Vision's expenditures had risen to $513 million, 37 percent of which came from the government (World Vision 2007).

The Bush administration initially indicated ambitious plans to provide federal funding for faith-based organizations involved in domestic social services. Allocated funds, however, failed to live up to expectations. The Bush administration originally promised a Compassion Capital Fund for faith-based organizations at a level of $200 million per year, but this fund was cut down to $30 million in later appropriations (Kuo 2006, 212). The fund functioned as a venture capital source for charities and represented all of the new funding received by faith-based organizations. The funds, although theoretically open to representatives of all faiths through peer review, went almost exclusively to evangelical Christian organizations (215–16). A second policy initiative, the Healthy Marriage Initiative, received a higher level of funding ($150 million annually) with bipartisan support to promote education about the benefits of marriage and skills for creating strong marriages (U.S. Department of Health and Human Services 2007). Studies of the distribution of these funds have not yet been conducted. Congress earmarked $150 million for religious groups during the session that included the 2004 election (Diana Henriques and Andrew Lehren, "Religious Groups Reaping Share of Federal Aid for Pet Projects," New York Times, May 13, 2007, A1). Not surprisingly, religious groups began to hire lobbyists to pursue congressional earmarks during this period.

Conclusion

By effectively deploying its symbolic and material resources, the Republican Party has demonstrated a capacity for activating and suppressing social conflicts along politically profitable lines. At the same time, new issues and a newly competitive opposition have created challenges to the party's aspirations for a stable, long-term electoral advantage among voters who are regular churchgoers. Are projections of a collapse of the party-movement-church system likely to come true?

The environment has the potential to become a divisive issue within the movement. In recent years, influential evangelical ministers have begun to argue that the environment is a values issue. This position is known within the Christian conservative community as creation care. A National Association of Evangelicals vice president, Richard Cizik, observed that creation care is "not a Red State issue or a Blue State issue or a green issue. It's a spiritual issue" (Karen Breslau and Martha Brant, "Eco-Evangelism: God's Green Soldiers," Newsweek, February 5, 2006). To a lesser degree, other issues that do not fit the traditional agenda of the Christian Right have also emerged in the evangelical Protestant community. The most important of these is poverty. Rick Warren, the best-selling author and pastor of a southern California megachurch, has called for a new war on global poverty, and his views have been widely circulated in the Christian conservative community (Holly Rossi, "Evangelicals Embrace New Global Priorities," Beliefnet.com, 2005).[7] Other prominent evangelical ministers, including Pat Robertson, have begun to raise money to alleviate poverty in the developing world. Although it is possible that issues like the environment and poverty could create rifts between younger evangelicals and the Old Guard, a more likely outcome may be the expansion of the issue base of the movement. Many evangelical leaders, including Warren, have argued for an expanded conception of moral values, rather than a choice between old issues and new. However, the eventual resolution of this tension is not yet clear.

The willingness of Democrats to talk about faith and family issues could also pose a challenge to the moral-values system. Before the 2006 congressional elections, Democratic Party leaders recruited candidates who could speak authentically about faith and family issues. Several candidates, including Senator Bob Casey in Pennsylvania, Representative Heath Shuler in North Carolina, Representative Brad Ellsworth in Indiana, and Governor Ted Strickland in Ohio, campaigned on pro-life, pro-marriage platforms. Leading Democratic candidates for president also began to appear on stages of mega-churches and to discuss the role of religion and traditional family values in their lives (Mark Totten, "A New Agenda for U.S. Evangelicals," *Christian Science Monitor*, December 18, 2006).[8] Through these efforts, Democrats have shown the capacity to reconnect with religiously oriented ethnic minority voters, and to compete again for moderate white Catholic voters. President-elect Obama showed that he intended to continue to compete for the votes of religious conservatives when he chose the evangelical leader Rick Warren to deliver the opening prayer at his inauguration.

A party-led system requires motivation and energy to manage effectively. The George W. Bush administration provided a blueprint for mobilizing and managing the religious constituency, but future Republican Party candidates may not place the same priority on religious voters, or may not be capable of generating the will and resources to mobilize them effectively. If they fail to do so, the bonds joining religious voters to the Republican Party will loosen. It is very likely that Republican presidential candidate John McCain would have fared much worse with evangelicals in 2008 had he not picked a running mate the movement supported.

Nevertheless, a number of factors weigh against the collapse of the party-movement-church system of moral-values politics. Most evangelicals have shown no signs of changing their minds about abortion or traditional families, and Republican outreach to conservative churches remains impressive. For a generation, the carefully designed symbolic environment of moral-values politics and the social networks that energize religious voters around these symbols have persisted even in the face of economic downturns, sensational sex scandals, and policy disappointments. The reputation of Republicans as supporters of moral-values issues and the reputation of liberal Democrats as opponents of these issues is by now so well engrained that religious voters need few reminders that the Republican Party supports their causes or that the Democratic Party is run by people who oppose them.[9] The support of evangelicals for McCain is, in this respect, telling. McCain, who publicly criticized leaders of the Christian Right in 2000 and was never known for his religious convictions, outpolled Barack Obama by three to one among evangelicals, in spite of Obama's efforts to reach out to religious conservatives and to highlight the centrality of Christianity in his own life.

White evangelical Protestants gain symbolic support for their vision of self and society through successful political activity. At the same time, we have argued, moral-values politics cannot be understood primarily either as the expression of status group interests or as a form of cultural defense. Instead, the project of moral-values politics has over the last two decades come under the management of the national Republican Party leadership, working through its sophisticated cultural technologies and its dense and expanding political networks. Nor do hard times necessarily harm church-based organizing. Indeed, attendance at evangelical churches climbed during the fall and winter of 2008, as people sought answers for economic hardships in spiritually comforting places (Paul Vitello, "Bad Times Draw Bigger Crowds to Churches," New York Times, December 13, 2008). On the basis of the evidence, political sociologists would do well to acknowledge the strength of the bonds joining white evangelical Protestants, and other like-minded religious voters, to conservative movement organizations and the Republican Party. It would be unwise to expect an imminent demise of the moral-values system.

Notes

1. We thank Nancy Ammerman, John Green, Michael Hout, Martin Johnson, Michael Lindsay, Michele Renee Salzman, Kenneth Wald, Bradford Wilcox, Clyde Wilcox, Rhys Williams, Robert Wuthnow, and three anonymous reviewers for comments and bibliographical references that helped to improve the quality of this chapter.
2. The capacity of Christian Right and Republican Party activists to associate the term *moral values* with evangelical Protestant meanings is itself a significant achievement. After all, every religious tradition has distinctive teachings about right and wrong, and every tradition also has a complex history of exegetical and hermeneutic texts related to these teachings. Traditions of secular ethics also exist, of course, and have offered bases for grounding morality, not in religion, but rather in universalistic principles of Enlightenment (Kant 1784/1985), social obligations (Durkheim 1893/1997), dialogical ethics (Buber 1923/1958), a utilitarian calculus (Smith 1759/1986; Bentham

1789/1973), or neural hard-wiring acquired during human evolution (Hauser 2006).

3. In this analysis, ethnoreligious categories were based on a modified version of the Pew framework, which divides the three major white Christian groups (evangelical Protestants, mainline Protestants, and Catholics) by frequency of church attendance (regular, irregular, and infrequent). Ethnoreligious categories include also black Protestants, Latino Protestants, Latino Catholics, Jews, members of other faiths, and unaffiliated and secular people. Among the seventy-three Pew Research Center items we examined, thirty (41 percent) were polarized (four items) or borderline polarized (twenty-six items) by ethnoreligious category. Regular church attending white evangelical Protestants divided on one side and unaffiliated and secular people on the other on seventeen of these issues (23 percent of the total). These latter issues involved homosexuality, abortion, free speech, the importance of religion, national security, and the Iraq War. Among the sixty-four General Social Survey items we examined, twenty-six (40 percent of the total) were polarized (two items) or borderline polarized (twenty-four) by ethnoreligious identification. Again, the most common of these divisions were between regular churchgoing white evangelical Protestants and unaffiliated and secular people. These two groups were divided on seventeen items (20 percent of the total) involving gender roles, abortion, birth control, premarital sex, pornography, prayer in school, confidence in television, and confidence in the military. The American National Election Study data were anomalous in showing more frequent patterns of polarization. Of the sixty NES items we examined, more than half were polarized (three) or borderline polarized (thirty-one) by ethnoreligious categories. Fully one-third of the items divided regular churchgoing white evangelical Protestants from unaffiliated and secular people on items involving traditional families, gender roles, desired qualities in children, abortion, homosexuality, immigration, the importance of religion, the role of religion in forming morality, the use of military force, and strength of patriotic feelings. The 2004 NES sample included a relatively high proportion of lower-income and less educated white evangelical Protestants. The differences between NES and the other two surveys could consequently be due, at least in part, to sampling variation.

4. Previous research has established that levels of ethnoreligious polarization decline when demographic characteristics, such as the age and education of respondents, are controlled (see, for example, several of the essays in Nivola and Brady 2006). Insofar as evangelicals are older and less educated than seculars, this has an impact on polarization. We report the bivariate comparisons because, at least on the side of evangelicals' polarization, organization occurs in church communities. The polarization of seculars also occurs within organizational contexts associated with specific demographic characteristics, such as college campuses and professional associations. This suggests to us that, from an organizational perspective, bivariate comparisons are meaningful.

5. This analysis is based on content analysis of eight speeches given to Religious Right organizations such as the Traditional Values Summit and the Christian Coalition by eight Republican speakers—President George W. Bush, Governor Mitt Romney, Governor Mike Huckabee, Senator George

Allen, Senator Sam Brownback, Representative Mike Pence, and Press Secretary Tony Snow. It also includes speeches given to the Conservative Political Action Council (CPAC) by seven Republican speakers—Vice President Dick Cheney, Governor Rick Perry, Senator George Allen, Representative Tom DeLay, Representative Sam Johnson, Representative Mike Pence, and Representative Paul Ryan. The analysis of speeches to broader conservative audiences also includes speeches given by Senator Rick Santorum to the Heritage Foundation, Representative Newt Gingrich to the Wednesday morning club, and Representative Tom DeLay to Vision America. We are grateful to Carol Kay for making recordings and transcripts of several of these speeches available for analysis.

6. http://www.harpersmagazine.org/jesusplusnothing.html.
7. http://www.beliefnet.com/story/168/story_16822_1.html.
8. http://www.csmonitor.com/2006/12211218/p09s02-coop.html.
9. True institutionalization is based on automatic cognition (DiMaggio 1997). For many religious voters, the Republican Party is automatically associated with "right living" in the world—and has been for a long time. Neuroscience studies show automatic associations with political images differ markedly among self-described conservatives and liberals (Kaplan, Freedman, and Iacaboni 2007). But the circuits of automatic cognition are incomplete. Among evangelicals, the proportion voting for Republican candidates over the last two decades has varied between the high 70 percent range and the mid to high 60 percent range; this difference is enough to swing the balance of an election in a closely divided polity like the United States.

References

Alexander, Jeffrey C., and Philip Smith. 2003. "The Discourse of American Civil Society." In *The Meanings of Social Life: A Cultural Sociology*, edited by Jeffrey C. Alexander. New York: Oxford University Press.

Bartels, Larry M. 2008. *Unequal Democracy: The Political Economy of the New Gilded Age*. New York: Russell Sage Foundation.

Bennett, William J. 1993. *The Index of Leading Cultural Indicators*, vol. 1. Washington, D.C.: Heritage Foundation and Empower America.

Bentham, Jeremy. 1789/1973. *The Utilitarians. Introduction to the Principles of Morality and Legislation by Jeremy Bentham and On Liberty by John Stuart Mill*. Garden City, N.Y.: Doubleday.

Bishop, Bill. 2008. *The Big Sort: Why the Clustering of Like-Minded Americans Is Tearing Us Apart*. New York: Houghton-Mifflin.

Bolzendahl, Catherine and Clem Brooks. 2005. "Polarization, Secularization, or Differences as Usual? The Denominational Cleavage in U.S. Social Attitudes since the 1970s." *Sociological Quarterly* 46(1): 47–78.

Brint, Steven. 1994. *In an Age of Experts: The Changing Role of Professionals in Politics and Public Life*. Princeton, N.J.: Princeton University Press.

Brint, Steven, and Seth Abrutyn. 2009. "Who's Right about the Right? Comparing Competing Explanations for the Links between Conservative Religion and

Politics in the United States." Unpublished paper. Department of Sociology, University of California, Riverside.

Brooks, Clem. 2002. "Religion, Politics, and Concern with the Decline of the Family." *American Sociological Review* 67(2): 191–211.

Brooks, Clem, and Jeff Manza. 2004. "A Great Divide? Religion and Political Change in U.S. National Elections 1972–2000." *Sociological Quarterly* 45(3): 421–50.

Buber, Martin. 1923/1958. *I and Thou*, translated by Ronald Gregor Smith. New York: Charles Scribner's Sons.

Campbell, David E., and J. Quin Monson. 2007. "The Case of Bush's Reelection: Did Gay Marriage Do It?" In *A Matter of Faith: Religion in the 2004 Presidential Election*, edited by David E. Campbell. Washington, D.C.: Brookings Institution Press.

Chaves, Mark. 2004. *Congregations in America*. Cambridge, Mass.: Harvard University Press.

Conover, Pamela Johnson. 1983. "The Mobilization of the New Right: A Test of Various Explanations." *Western Political Quarterly* 36(4): 632–49.

DiMaggio, Paul. 1997. "Culture and Cognition." *Annual Review of Sociology* 23(1997): 263–87.

Domhoff, G. William. 2002. *Who Rules America? Power and Politics*, 4th ed. New York: McGraw-Hill.

Durkheim, Emile. 1893/1997. *The Division of Labor in Society*. New York: Free Press.

Easton, Nina J. 2000. *Gang of Five: Leaders at the Center of the Conservative Crusade*. New York: Simon & Schuster.

Frank, Thomas. 2006. "Class Dismissed." Available at http://www.psci.unt.edu/enterline/franksdismissd.pdf (accessed in January 2007).

Franz, Michael, Paul B. Freedman, Kenneth M. Goldstein, and Travis N. Ridout. 2007. *Campaign Advertising and American Democracy*. Philadelphia, Pa.: Temple University Press.

Geer, John G. 2006. *In Defense of Negativity: Attack Ads in Presidential Campaigns*. Chicago: University of Chicago Press.

Greeley, Andrew, and Michael Hout. 2006. *The Truth about Conservative Christians: What They Think and What They Believe*. Chicago: University of Chicago Press.

Green, John C. 2000. "The Christian Right at the Millennium." New York: American Jewish Committee.

———. 2009. Personal communication based on analysis of the Fifth National Survey of Religion and Politics, Post-Election Sample.

Green, John C., Kimberly H. Conger, and James L. Guth. 2006. "Agents of Value: Christian Right Activists in 2004." In *The Values Campaign? The Christian Right and the 2004 Elections*, edited by John C. Green, Mark J. Rozell, and Clyde Wilcox. Washington, D.C.: Georgetown University Press.

Guth, James L. 1983. "The Politics of the Christian Right." In *Religion and the Culture Wars: Dispatches from the Front*, edited by John C. Green, James L. Guth, Corwin E. Smidt, and Lyman A. Kellstedt. Boulder, Colo.: Rowman & Littlefield.

Hauser, Marc D. 2006. *Moral Minds: How Nature Designed Our Universal Sense of Right and Wrong.* New York: HarperCollins.

Hillygus, D. Sunshine, and Todd G. Shields. 2008. *The Persuadable Voter: Wedge Issues in Presidential Campaigns.* Princeton, N.J.: Princeton University Press.

Hudson, Deal W. 2008. *Onward, Christian Soldiers: The Growing Political Power of Catholics and Evangelicals in the United States.* New York: Simon & Schuster.

Hunter, James Davison. 1992. *Culture Wars: The Struggle to Define America.* New York: Basic Books.

Jenkins, J. Craig, David Jacobs, and Jon Agnone. 2003. "Political Opportunities and African American Protest 1948–1997." *American Journal of Sociology* 109(2): 277–303.

Kant, Immanuel. 1784/1985. "Answering the Question: What Is Enlightenment?" In *Foundations of the Metaphysics of Morals and What is Enlightenment?* New York: Macmillan.

Kaplan, Jonas T., Joshua Freedman, and Marco Iacoboni. 2007. "Us Versus Them: Political Attitudes and Party Affiliation Influence Neural Response to Faces of Presidential Candidates." *Neuropsychologia* 45(1): 55–64.

Kuo, David. 2006. *Tempting Faith: An Inside Story of Political Seduction.* New York: Free Press.

Layman, Geoffrey. 2001. *The Great Divide: Religious and Cultural Conflict in American Party Politics.* New York: Columbia University Press.

Layman, Geoffrey, and Laura S. Hussey. 2007. "George W. Bush and the Evangelicals: Religious Commitment and Partisan Change among Evangelical Protestants, 1960–2004." In *A Matter of Faith: Religion in the 2004 Presidential Election,* edited by David E. Campbell. Washington, D.C.: Brookings Institution Press.

Leege, David C., Paul D. Mueller, and Kenneth D. Wald. 2001. "The Politics of Cultural Differences in the 2000 Presidential Election." Unpublished paper. Presented at the annual meeting of the American Political Science Association. San Francisco (September 2001).

Leege, David C., Kenneth D. Wald, Brian S. Krueger, and Paul D. Mueller. 2002. *The Politics of Cultural Differences: Social Change and Voter Mobilization Strategies in the Post-New Deal Period.* Princeton, N.J.: Princeton University Press.

Lindsay, D. Michael. 2007. *Faith in the Halls of Power: How Evangelicals Joined the American Elite.* New York: Oxford University Press.

Loftus, Jeri. 2001. "America's Liberalization in Attitudes toward Homosexuality, 1973 to 1998." *American Sociological Review* 66(5): 762–82.

Lorentzen, Louise J. 1980. "Evangelical Life-Style Concerns Expressed in Political Action." *Sociological Analysis* 41(1): 144–54.

Moen, Matthew C. 1984. "School Prayer and the Politics of Life-Style Concern." *Social Science Quarterly* 65(4): 1065–71.

Monson, J. Quin, and J. Baxter Oliphant. 2007. "Microtargeting and the Instrumental Mobilization of Religious Conservatives." In *A Matter of Faith: Religion in the 2004 Presidential Election,* edited by David E. Campbell. Washington, D.C.: Brookings Institution Press.

Morris, James, and Wayne Slater. 2006. *The Architect: Karl Rove and the Master Plan for Absolute Power.* New York: Crown.

Nivola, Pietro, and David W. Brady, eds. 2006. *Red and Blue Nation? vol. 1, Characteristics and Causes of America's Polarized Politics.* Washington, D.C.: Brookings Institution Press and the Hoover Institution.

Page, Ann, and Donald Clelland. 1978. "The Kanawha County Textbook Controversy: A Study in Alienation and Lifestyle Concern." *Social Forces* 57(1): 265–81.

Pew Research Center. 2005. *Mapping the Political Landscape 2005.* Washington, D.C.: Pew Research Center. Available at: http://www.pewresearch.org/assets/files/politicallandscape2005.pdf.

Piven, Frances Fox, and Richard A. Cloward. 1982. *The New Class War: Reagan's Attack on the Welfare State and Its Consequences.* New York: Pantheon Books.

Pollitt, Katha. 1995. *Reasonable Creatures: Essays on Women and Feminism.* New York: Vintage.

Rozell, Mark J., and Debasree Das Gupta. 2006. "'The Values Vote': Moral Issues and the 2004 Elections." In *The Values Campaign? The Christian Right and the 2004 Elections,* edited by John C. Green, Mark J. Rozell, and Clyde Wilcox. Washington, D.C.: Georgetown University Press.

Smith, Adam. 1759/1976. *The Theory of the Moral Sentiments.* Indianapolis: Liberty Classics.

Smith, Christian S. 1998. *American Evangelicalism: Embattled and Thriving.* Chicago: University of Chicago Press.

Smith, Tony. 1994. *America's Mission: The United States and the Worldwide Struggle for Democracy in the 20th Century.* Princeton, N.J.: Princeton University Press.

Tracy, David. 1981. *The Analogical Imagination.* New York: Crossroads.

Tuveson, Ernest Lee. 1968. *Redeemer Nation: The Idea of America's Millennial Role.* Chicago: University of Chicago Press.

U.S. Air Force Headquarters Review Group. 2005. *The Report of the Headquarters Review Group Concerning the Religious Climate at the U.S. Air Force Academy.* Washington, D.C.: U.S. Department of the Air Force. Available at: http://www.af.mil/pdf/HQ_Review_Group_Report.pdf

U.S. Department of Health and Human Services. 2007. *The Healthy Marriage Initiative.* Washington, D.C.: Administration for Children and Families. Available at: http://www.acf.hhs.gov/healthymarriage.

Wald, Kenneth D. 2003. *Religion and Politics in the United States.* Lanham, Md.: Rowman and Littlefield Publishers.

Wald, Kenneth, Dennis E. Owen, and Samuel S. Hill. 1988. "Churches as Political Communities." *American Political Science Review* 82(3): 531–48.

———. 1989. "Evangelical Politics and Status Issues." *Journal for the Scientific Study of Religion* 28(1): 1–16.

Welch, Michael R., David C. Leege, Kenneth D. Wald, and Lyman A. Kellestedt. 1993. "Are the Sheep Hearing the Shepherds? Cue Perceptions, Congregational Responses and Political Communication Processes." In *Rediscovering the Religious Factor in American Politics,* edited by Lyman A. Kellestedt and David C. Leege. Armonk, N.Y.: M. E. Sharpe.

Wilcox, Clyde, and Carin Larson. 2006. *Onward Christian Soldiers: The Religious Right in American Politics,* 3rd ed. Boulder, Colo.: Westview Press.

Wilcox, Clyde, Linda M. Merrola, and David Beer. 2006. "Saving Marriage by Banning Marriage? The Christian Right Finds a New Issue in 2004." In *The*

Values Campaign? The Christian Right in the 2004 Elections, edited by John C. Green, Mark J. Rozell, and Clyde Wilcox. Washington, D.C.: Georgetown University Press.

Wilson, William Julius. 1987. *The Truly Disadvantaged: The Inner City, the Underclass, and Public Policy.* Chicago: University of Chicago Press.

Wolf, Naomi. 1993. *Fire with Fire: The New Female Power and How It Will Change the 21st Century.* New York: Random House.

Woodberry, Robert D., and Christian S. Smith. 1998. "Fundamentalism et al.: Conservative Protestants in America." *Annual Review of Sociology* 24(1998): 25–56.

World Vision International. 2007. *World Vision International 2007 Review.* Federal Way, Wash.: World Vision International.

PART II

DISCOURSES OF MOBILIZATION AND PUBLIC REASON

Chapter 5

Politicized Evangelicalism and Secular Elites: Creating a Moral Other

RHYS H. WILLIAMS

I~N THE~ discourse of much contemporary conservative Protestant evangelicalism, particularly that concerned with the place of religion in politics and the public sphere, one group stands out—portrayed as perhaps a singular threat to evangelical religion specifically, religion in general, and America's social and moral well-being. Under a variety of names, much of politicized evangelicalism has constructed "secular elites" as its primary political opponent, and even more expansively, as the primary threat to our societal health. This chapter examines the construction of secular elites as a moral "other," and the ways in which that construction works as a resource for political mobilization and resonates within evangelical culture. In particular, I argue that a construction labeled secular elites has become the primary foil and moral other for organized political evangelicalism. To do so, I discuss general features of social movement rhetoric as it is used to mobilize adherents and to wage political battles, review briefly the construction of various moral others in American religious and political history, and examine the features of evangelical religious culture that make the "othering" of secular elites so resonant as an oppositional group and symbol.

Political Culture and the Rhetoric of Mobilization

A truism in sociology is that people's definition of a situation plays a large role in shaping social reality. A definition may begin as a subjective perception, but if it is acted upon, or is picked up and shared by others and regarded as an accurate understanding of the world, the consequences are decidedly real—the definition of the situation moves from subjective understanding to objectively understood social reality. Shared definitions can in essence create their own reality.

The sociology of social movements has gained great understanding of collective action by studying how advocacy groups collectively define their situations, their opponents, and themselves. Social movements develop and promote *frames*—bundles of rhetorical claims and symbols that together represent a movement's attempt to communicate to its members and to others. Scholars have spent considerable energy examining the social movement frames that define issues, as well as studying framing processes through which collective actors develop these definitions (for useful overviews, see Benford and Snow 2000; Snow 2004; Williams and Benford 2000). Effective movement frames are definitions of social situations and social identities that accomplish two tasks: they mobilize those who agree with the frames to take action—that is, they mobilize "internally" the movement's supporters; and they become generally and publicly accepted as the proper understandings of the issue among broader publics, such as news media or neutral bystanders—that is, they have "external" resonance in public discourse (Williams 1995, 125–27; 2004, 93). Any given movement's frames are almost always countered by opponents who sponsor alternative frames. Thus, a significant aspect of public politics is the struggle over whose definition of the situation will dominate.

Effective social movement rhetoric, and the frames that comprise it, have several key components.[1] First, movement frames must present a persuasive diagnosis of the social conditions the movement seeks to rectify—"here is the problem and here is why it is a problem." This diagnosis must identify the problem as an injustice, adding a moral valence to the situation, and assign responsibility for it—that is, who is to blame for the problem. Thus, movement frames are inherently moral claims—there is an injustice and a villain identified (Williams 1994, 2002, 2003a). Second, effective frames must offer a prescription for solving the diagnosed problem. The seeds of the solution are often implied in the elements that go into the definition of the problem, but the diagnosis does not always determine the prescription. For example, Joseph Gusfield noted that solving the problem of alcohol-related traffic accidents could have resulted in a push for more mass transit; however, when the diagnostic frame became "drunk drivers," with an attendant moral condemnation, the prescription more easily became a legal crackdown and moral suasion aimed at individuals (1981).[2]

In addition to prescribing the solution, a movement's framing must be clear that a solution is possible—that is, provide activists a sense of agency by arguing that the problem is not so big as to be inevitable. This stands in a bit of tension with the diagnostic needs for emphasizing the seriousness and urgency of a problem. If a problem becomes constructed as too big, too entrenched, or inevitable, that framing undercuts the sense of agency that empowers people to feel that collective action can make a difference.

Finally, a good framing must motivate people to take action with regard to the cause. Partly this comes from a sense of agency—the conviction that things can change. But importantly, it makes those who are listening responsible for action and solving the problem. Just as responsibility for causing the problem is assigned, so must the responsibility for participating in the solution be accepted and borne willingly. One dimension of this motivation is constructing the basis for a collective identity, a sense of we that is connected to the issue at hand, and is clearly differentiated from those responsible for the problem. A collective identity is a distinction, and for movements it separates *them* as villains of the problem from *us* as the solution. A movement's collective identity can be an existing social category, but more often emerges during mobilization[3] and is a cornerstone for the solidarity and commitment necessary for collective action (Polletta and Jasper 2001; Hunt and Benford 2004).

Such definitional work is most effective when the boundaries between us and them are drawn clearly, but neither the we nor the they is defined too clearly. Specifying too clearly who constitutes the us may discourage some sympathetic constituents from joining, thinking they are not welcome, or else preclude forming alliances with other groups in the future. For example, one-time Christian Coalition director Ralph Reed (1996) consistently referred to the coalition's constituency as "people of faith." By not making explicit sectarian references, Reed implicitly expanded the forces of good to those with faith—without specifying which faith—while making those without faith the primary enemy. Similarly, one wants some flexibility in defining one's opponents in order to be able to adapt to circumstances.

Thus, social movement framings produce boundary-drawing distinctions between us and them. They are responsible for the problems identified, and those problems pose a threat and an injustice. But the problem can be solved and we are the ones with the moral responsibility for solving it. They are the problem, we are the solution, and there is a moral boundary dividing us. This distinction is seldom pregiven and unchanging; rather the differences emerge as a collective product of attempts at defining the situation (for an example, see Paul Lichterman and his colleagues, chapter 6, volume 1). One way of accomplishing this identity distinction is to create *demons*—identify another social group as the moral other against which one's own group stands as a bulwark (see Rogin 1987). Thus political demonizing is a common outcome of the symbolic discourse of politics.

Creating the Moral Other

The dynamic of creating an other is a broader phenomenon, however, and need not be confined to explicit attempts at a movement mobilization (see, for example, Edgell, Gerteis, and Hartmann 2006). One way to understand the discourse that shapes, and is shaped by, the evangelical worldview, as with any worldview, is to view it as a collection of symbolic boundaries that serve to distinguish those within the group or subculture from those outside it. Social groups create and maintain their collective identity at least in part by comparing and contrasting themselves to other groups. In that sense, collective identity is largely relational—its particular content may be centered in specific ideas, rituals, or ascribed characteristics, but those features are socially meaningful only because they serve comparatively to make one group distinct from others. As social creatures, we know who we are—in particular, who fits within the category of we—because we can determine who we are not based on certain socially significant features. Making these distinctions through comparison and contrast are key features of any group's ability to define itself. Thus it is not surprising that in political and social conflict, competing groups often mobilize themselves around a definition of their enemy (Michael Lindsay in chapter 10 of this volume cites Eric Hoffer's observation that politics may not require a God, but surely require a devil)—and rivals demonize each other with remarkably similar terms. Collective identity, particularly among people who do not share obvious social background characteristics, emerges and is defined in relation to others.

There is an important corollary to this relational logic when it concerns the world of politics. As Pierre Bourdieu persuasively argued, distinctions do not just order the social world horizontally—that is, by helping group members distinguish one group (us) from others (them) in the social landscape (1984, 1991). Distinctions also have a vertical dimension in that this sorting has clear implications for social and institutional hierarchies (see also Rogin 1987). Bourdieu understood the cultural realm, the definition and enforcement of distinctions, as a key way in which inequalities are reinforced. Those with the ability to define standards apply them to others, leaving the others wanting, and in turn, reaffirming the worthiness of those in control. They create the "normal." Social movement culture similarly creates moral metrics that allocate worthiness and condemnation, and movements use these in the quest for change.

It seems as though it should be possible to make identity distinctions without implying normative differences between better and worse, privileged and despised. With some distinctions, that may be the case. However, when the markers of distinction—the things about which groups are judged differently—are loaded with normative meaning (such as who is moral, or who represents the one true religion, or who is responsible for a social threat), identity distinctions help create, reinforce, and challenge hierarchy and inequality. In the case I examine here, for reasons that I argue are integral to the American evangelical worldview, the distinctions being created—implicitly or explicitly—are marked as religious differences. These differences are theologized, and divide the social world not just into separate groups, but as well into the religious and the secular, the moral and the immoral—or in stark terms, good and evil. A binary classification scheme, which is commonly found in fundamentalist religious thought, though not only there, totalizes the world and infuses it with religious significance (see Marty and Appleby 1991, 814–42). The boundaries creating these distinctions pull together in powerful and easily comprehended terms the injustice frames needed for movement rhetoric, assign moral responsibility for public politics and social problems, and align moral identity with hierarchy and legitimacy

If boundaries become identified as sacred, their importance and need for protection is that much greater. Impermissible boundary crossing becomes a violation, and can be seen as pollution (Douglas 1966). For exclusivist religions—those that claim all divine truth for themselves—rival faiths can form just that sort of polluting menace. If one has the whole truth, other systems of belief can only be unwelcome and threatening. This often translates into a suspicion of religious pluralism in society, because most religious faiths have clear ideas about organizing human relationships and social institutions. Similarly, the secular world and its pleasures can also hold a polluting danger. And yet, in contemporary societies, religious people must live in that world and are often surrounded by other faiths, as well as those who are not religious. This condition helps explain the proliferation of what might be called "defensive fundamentalisms"—groups that are primarily interested in keeping the secular world out (Williams 1994, 805). For these groups, there is an easily identified and comprehended threat because secular modernity seems so ubiquitous. But whether the threats are rival religions or the secular world, totalizing groups must constantly be guarding their social boundaries and their worldviews.

However, many religions have as one of their missions changing this world to be in more accord with Divine Will, and they may have to interact with religious others or the secular to achieve that. This presents a paradox—the threat of pollution means that boundaries must be sharp and distinct, but many boundaries need to be potentially permeable to allow the faithful to reach out, organize, and convert the world. In practice, this dilemma can heighten, rather than lower, the need for clear marks of distinction.

This makes it clear why, for evangelical Protestants, the boundaries separating themselves from others are both important and potentially problematic. If one pursues an evangelical and universalistic faith, one is committed to the idea that others can be, potentially, converts. Christianity has an inherent universalism in its message, with the idea that the non-Christian can and should be brought into the fold. The conversion event is a key part of the evangelical identity. Further, there is a deep religious duty to help create a godly society, even if that goal is ultimately not achievable through human striving. But the risk of pollution is always present. Thus the boundaries between the godly and the secular are always tenuous and often fluid. The godly have certain responsibilities for reaching across boundaries to the other, but must be careful not to fall themselves (see Williams 2002).[4] Given this ambiguity, and the accompanying need for clear boundaries to mark the path of righteousness, it is small wonder that issues of subversion or infiltration are seen as such a threat (compare Rogin 1987). Those who might be a threat, but are disguised or hidden, make boundary issues all the more of a concern.

In sum, who gets constructed as other, especially religiously other in a deeply religious country whose moral tradition is constructed around differences between them and us (Morone 2003, 13–14), has implications for national identity, claims to public legitimacy, and political authority (Edgell, Gerteis, and Hartmann 2006; Morone 2003).

Not all mobilizing rhetoric is negative—warning of threats, defining enemies, and predicting disasters. Leaders use and people respond to positive visions that embody aspirations and hope as well. Movement frames must say that a solution is possible and hold out a path for recreating the world as it should be. This is particularly true for religiously based movements, which often promise some type of better life, and perhaps eventually Paradise, as a part of their mobilizing appeal. But it is also true that in politics people often mobilize to stop a perceived collective threat, and do so by clearly articulating an opponent. It may be that negative frames are more effective immediately, but that long-term mobilization requires a more inspiring positive vision. Nonetheless, it is hard not to notice in the discourse of contemporary politicized evangelicalism the consistent reference to the urgent and serious dangers posed by secular elites.

A Brief Definitional Consideration

It is important to be clear about my references to "evangelicalism" and, more specifically, public or politicized evangelicalism. Much media discourse and everyday references often lump together conservative religious people as being basically alike—and often label them all as "fundamentalists." But Protestant evangelicalism is not a single denomination or a unified group; there are both religious and political differences among people labeled evangelical. And there are significant differences between those who are publicly politically active—even leaders of advocacy groups—and others who are less involved. Given this volume's thematic purpose of examining evangelical Protestantism and American democracy, I focus here primarily on public discourse and opinion leaders and activists. However, no movement succeeds only with leaders: mobilizing appeals need to motivate a rank-and-file as well. Thus, some consideration about who evangelicals are and what they commonly believe is in order.

Evangelicalism is a religious orientation found among a significant part of the American people, depending upon how one measures, a quarter to a third. As an orientation, evangelicalism stresses Scripture as the dominant—even sole—source of religious authority. Thus, emphasis on inerrant or literal interpretation of the Bible is constitutive of the evangelical identity; and it follows that evangelicals also hold traditional Christian beliefs, such as in the virgin birth and physical resurrection. Further, evangelicalism emphasizes experiential approaches to faith, often expressed emotionally, and makes a conversion or born-again experience one of the qualifying marks of faithfulness. Finally, evangelicals usually have a commitment to sharing their faith, that is, to evangelize others with the good news of the Christian message (Greeley and Hout 2006; Smith 1998). Although denominations such as Baptists and Churches of Christ are often categorized as evangelical or as conservative Protestants (see Roof and McKinney 1987), people who share evangelical religious orientations can be found in most Protestant denominations (Steensland et al. 2000). As Robert Wuthnow and others have argued, American religion has been "restructured" in recent decades so that theological and political differences within denominations are often more important than affiliational differences across denominations (Wuthnow 1988). Thus, denominational affiliation as such is not as important to note when classifying individuals as evangelicals as their approach to Scripture, beliefs, and religious experience.

Many scholars, and in fact many evangelicals, distinguish evangelicals from fundamentalists, despite the popular conflation of the two terms. They define contemporary evangelicalism as a mid-twentieth century reaction to fundamentalism (see Carpenter 1997, 189–96; Smith 1998, 2–3, 9–15). The fundamentalist response to modernism and liberal Christianity in the early twentieth century was an affirmation of traditional belief and practices in the face of an urbanizing, liberalizing society and the modernist hermeneutics of the biblical criticism then gaining ground in American Protestant seminaries (see Marsden 1980). Fundamentalism produced, particularly after the 1925 Scopes trial in Tennessee, a type of separatist worldview in which the purity of the faith was maintained by refusal to fellowship with nonbelievers or even other conservative Christians considered not sufficiently fundamentalist. The pollution taboo became paramount and there was a disengagement from "the world" that was reinforced for many by the regional marginalization of the South and other rural areas and the establishment of separate, parallel, fundamentalist organizations (on fundamentalist schools, see Peshkin 1988).

By the early postwar period, many Protestants wanted to maintain their conservative faith without such separatism. Evangelicalism emerged as a label and a set of religious associations, such as the National Association of Evangelicals, founded in 1942, in distinction to the separatism of the fundamentalists, on one hand, and the modernism of liberals, on the other. Evangelicalism became a religious response marked by its critical involvement with the world—what Christian Smith called an "engaged orthodoxy"—that is "in the world but not of it" (1998, 126, 151). This has of necessity mitigated some of the inflexible conservatism that marks fundamentalism. Evangelicals are religiously more conservative than mainline Protestants because their theology is more traditional and orthodox, their reading of Scripture draws less from academic approaches to literary analysis than from personal faith and experience, and they tend to be relatively certain of the truth of their beliefs and their religion. On the other hand, those who call themselves evangelicals are less politically and socially conservative than those who consider themselves fundamentalist (see Hunter 1987; Woodberry and Smith 1998).

Another important distinction is that between the political elites and activists who are regularly involved in public politics, and those ordinary citizens who are the bulk of people captured in surveys. Russell Neuman estimated that only about 5 percent of the American public are consistently active in and engaged with politics (1986). Another 20 percent are resolutely nonpolitical. The remaining 75 percent do things such as vote, and often have opinions on public and political issues, but are only occasionally mobilized beyond that. Thus, studies of the intensely politically active are studies of a small proportion of the American people. Christian Smith's surveys and interviews with ordinary evangelicals reveal a certain political moderation; for example, most do not want a "Christian America" in any kind of theocratic or governmental sense (2000). Like most Americans, evangelicals regard politics and religion as distinct, if related fields of activity. Public figures such as Jerry Falwell were not always popular among ordinary evangelicals because of their divisiveness and what seemed to be an inappropriate mixture of faith and politics. Thus, phrases such as *the Christian Right* or *politicized evangelicals* capture but a small slice of the conservative Christian population, which may not be representative of grassroots evangelical public opinion.

However, if 20 percent of the American population is thoroughly apolitical, the activist-involved core of any social group assumes much greater importance in public life than its small numbers indicate. Activist minorities often make up in influence what they lack in numbers—at least in part because they largely dictate the discourse with which the public and the media discuss political life, events, and issues. But these activists face a consistent challenge in translating their concerns to coreligionists in ways that will mobilize political involvement. Thus, movement rhetoric needs to stress danger, urgency, and a clear villain using cultural symbols and language that resonate with ordinary people.

Clearly, politicized evangelical leaders have been successful in finding sympathetic ears and mobilizing voters. When activists and political leaders write and publish books about the threats posed by secular elites to Christian America they must have some audience. And that audience is often passionate. The extent to which conservative and religious talk radio now dominates the airways (particularly AM frequencies) is one sign of that. Moreover, local churches issue voter guides that use information from groups such as the Christian Coalition or the Traditional Values Coalition to rate candidates, assuming some alignment between the ideas promoted by the social movement organization and the beliefs and values of their laity. But it is important to recognize that Christian Right groups generate commercials, slogans, and talking points largely with the purpose of creating shared understandings that will mobilize rank-and-file voters and others who have some political interests but are not highly active.

In sum, it is dangerous to generalize too directly from the political discourse generated by activists and political professionals to the ideas and beliefs of ordinary citizens, even if the latter are sympathetic with movement groups.[5] But it is also the case that if discourse has no resonance with the public, it would fade in prominence. That politicized evangelicalism has become a key constituency in the Republican Party, and that publishers believe there is a consistent market for books extolling the threats that secular elites, liberals, and others pose, clearly indicate that something and someone is connecting with these messages. Evangelicalism as a segment of American religious life is marked by some shared concerns, attitudes, and values. Many people who identify as evangelicals have gotten politically involved. Thus I use the terms *evangelicals* or *evangelicalism* in this chapter to refer to a group of people, and their worldview, engaged with public life, attendant to politics, and sharing a broad set of religio-political understandings.[6]

A Short History of Religious Others in America

I argue here that a construction labeled secular elites has become the primary foil and moral other for organized political evangelicalism. On the one hand, I claim that the process of creating a moral other is a typical dynamic common to many movement mobilizations. On the other, I argue that the development of the secular elite, as the primary moral other for politicized evangelicalism, is a fairly recent phenomenon specific to social and political developments since the 1970s. To illustrate both points, I offer a short review of the construction of "others" by public evangelicalism in American history.

The creation of moral others has been closely linked to the perfectionist idealism of theologically conservative Protestantism in the United States. The European colonies in North America that went on to become the United States were founded by Christians, overwhelmingly Protestants. Many of those founders viewed the American settlement as "an errand into the wilderness," a wilderness in which they would build a "city on a hill" that would be to God's glory (Miller 1956). The New England Calvinists found the established Church of England, though Protestant, too established, liturgical, and corrupt for their religious standards. And they left the Netherlands for the New World at least in part because of their fear that Holland's religious tolerance would threaten the boundaries and rigor of their faith. They saw themselves as New Hebrews, experiencing their own exodus, and coming to an unformed world in which they could engage anew in the project of creating the kingdom of God on earth (Hughes and Allen 1988; Hughes 2003). Their goal was a promised land of Zion, and they had little doubt that religious homogeneity in a community of saints was the way to accomplish that.

The dominant colonial religious cultures of the Anglican South and the Presbyterian mid-Atlantic regions were Protestant, but different from Puritan New England. The Presbyterians were Calvinist, but not generally as strict, often coexisting with Quakers. The Anglican colonies of the South had established colonial churches, but they did not have the thorough penetration of religion into society that marked Massachusetts or Connecticut, and they kept ties to the liturgical Church of England. They expressed a churchly integration, not a separatism. Given the key role played by New Englanders in leading the war of independence, and the discredited position of the Anglican Church because of its connections to the Crown, it is easy to point to the tremendous influence of New England Puritan culture on what became the United States, and to see it as the source of what seems like generic American civil religious thinking and belief (Hughes 2003; Kelly 1984; Reichley 1985).[7]

New England Calvinism and its revivalist progeny were marked by a cultural tendency to divide the social and moral world into Manichean dualisms (see Williams 1999, 2002) and to see the American nation as bound in a "covenanted" relationship to God (Hughes 2003; Morone 2003; Williams 1999, 4–5). The latter concept understands the United States as God's chosen nation, charged with bringing God's kingdom to realization here on Earth, and blessed with a certain prosperity as long as it is faithful in that charge (Handy 1984; Williams 1999). There is a clear corporatist dimension to this belief—the nation as a body politic is responsible for this mission, and suffers as a whole for transgressions or wandering from the way, just as Jews were covenanted after the Exodus. Although the religious individualism that developed in pietist Protestant traditions has diluted this notion of corporate sin, there are clear covenantal dimensions in politicized evangelicalism's understanding of its mission. It is common for evangelical Protestants to argue that our nation's collective forsaking of the Christian path is the cause of many of our national social problems.

These two features—binary boundaries and covenanted relationships—together led to a thorough identification of Protestant religious affiliation and American national identity. So, not only was America of the early national period overwhelmingly composed of Protestants, it is not a stretch to say that a rigorous and generically sectarian Protestant worldview was indelibly stamped on the national identity.

The first half of the nineteenth century saw two significant changes in the American religious landscape. Through immigration and revival, an enthusiastic, experiential, pietist Protestantism emerged that challenged many aspects of the Calvinist established churches (Hatch 1989; Fischer 1991). One key difference was Pietism's populism, often led by laity or clergy with little formal theological training, and it harbored an attendant distrust of established institutional elites. Further, Pietism made the emotional dimensions of religion paramount—particularly the conversion event. Formal education took a distinct backseat to immediate, emotional, experiential faith. Groups such as the Disciples of Christ, Baptists, and Methodists, the forebears of today's evangelicals, grew quickly and spread throughout the nation, especially in the West and in rural areas.

Second, beginning in the 1840s, significant religious diversity began to arise as large numbers of Irish and German Catholics began emigrating to the United States, increasing the Catholic percentage of the population tenfold in just two decades (Dolan 1983). The development of nativist and religious backlash against this immigration has occupied many scholars, most noting that the conflict developed along religious lines as Protestants resisted Catholic newcomers (Higham 1955/1963; Bennett 1988; Shea 2004). There was anti-Catholic personal and property violence, the rise of a nativist political party (the American Party, a.k.a. the Know-Nothings), and numerous anti-immigrant and anti-Catholic civil associations.

The nativist critique of immigrants—the basis for the moral other—was clearly their Catholic faith, and involved a number of issues. Several features received attention as the markers on which distinction with the other was defined. Catholics were suspected of not being capable of assimilation into American national identity. Their differences—seen as deficiencies—were often articulated as involving a lack of commitment to democracy. They were charged with having a first allegiance to a foreign potentate, the Pope, rather than to the United States. Two areas in which this played out were in public schools and in the status and interpretation of the Bible, and they were often intertwined.

Catholics, Protestants charged, were not allowed to read the Bible, and thus based their faith on a worldly authority—the Church—rather than the word of God. Catholics worked hard to dispute this claim, noting the extent to which clerical training was scriptural, and explaining that they read the Bible, "not as autonomous individuals but under authority" (Noll 1998, 205). They argued that they were faithful Catholics and still freedom-loving Americans, who considered the Bible as the inspired word of God. Nonetheless, the importance of Church teachings and the existence of a Catholic Bible different from the King James Version that was becoming standard among Protestants, continued to be fuel for anti-Catholicism. Evangelical Protestants were people who had "sola Scriptura" (by Scripture alone) as their basis for religious legitimation and believed, at least in theory, in the populist democratic reading and interpretation of the Bible. Evangelical Protestants saw their approach to Scripture as consistent with American democratic ideals, and Catholic authority as too similar to an Old World monarchy. These debates, Jay Dolan noted, were also happening among Catholics themselves and the many Catholics who were wary of "Americanism" as a dilution of their true faith gave anti-Catholic nativists ammunition for their charges (1998).

The public schools were also a focal point of Protestant-Catholic conflict, in many cases because Catholic parents objected to the mandatory readings and lessons from the so-called Protestant Bible. Virginia Lieson Brereton (1998) and Mark Noll (1998) showed the extent to which battles and challenges over the Bible in schools were the symbolic center of fights over control of the schools and assimilation into American culture. Public schools were becoming more important to the educational system, and to the economic prospects of many who would be looking for jobs in an industrializing and modernizing economy, and were themselves becoming a representation of American culture and national identity. Further, of course, schools involved children, a fact certain to make political issues passionate.

Thus schools and Scripture came together in ways that made them an identity issue at the intersection of religion and national culture. Combined with many of the lurid tales told about Catholics—particularly those involving sexuality, children, and Catholic convents and seminaries—a distinct moral other was created and labeled *Romanist* (Franchot 1994). Jenny Franchot showed how the creation of a coherent Romanism as the ideological, political, and moral foil to American evangelicalism helped solidify both those cultural identities (1994). The Romanist other elided the racial, ethnic, national, and class differences among actual Catholics—making French Jesuits, Irish peasants, Native American converts, and the Spanish landed gentry equivalent in their foreignness and in their threat to the nation. Concomitantly, this process of creating moral others rhetorically unified an increasingly fractious Protestant culture, as Calvinists, Pietists, the beginnings of modernism, and the divisions between North and South divided Protestant orientations. With Romanism as the other, differences among Protestants could be submerged, and unifying factors—such as Protestants' assumptions about their status as true Americans—could be highlighted.

The creation of this moral other, using religious markers for distinction, helped reinforce the assumed connection between religion and national identity. Laurence Moore noted that a series of religious "outsiders"—such as Mormons, Christian Scientists, and Adventists, along with Catholics and Jews—were thought to be both "aberrational or not-yet-American" by Protestants who considered themselves the mainstream (1986, 208).[8] Given their opposition to Catholicism, and the important role played by many evangelicals in the abolition and other moral reform movements (Young 2006), evangelicals, for a significant period of American history, assumed themselves to be the moral guardians of the nation (Marsden 1980; Penning and Smidt 2002, 19; Smith 1998, 4). Further, they assumed that the alignment of their religious commitments with national identity was the clear cornerstone of American democracy. Indeed, into the second half of the twentieth century, many Protestants continued to voice concerns about Catholic threats to the American political system (see Blanshard 1950).

In the late nineteenth century, as immigration began to resume after the Civil War ended, so did nativist anti-Catholicism, though now joined by an emerging anti-Semitism as significant numbers of eastern European Jews arrived. Much of this anti-Semitism retained the charges common to it in European societies, and were based in Jews' "failure" to recognize Christ, or more pointedly, to be responsible for his death. Some anti-Jewish stories moved into the familiar niches occupied by anti-Catholicism. For example, whereas Catholic convents were posited as sites of abduction and abuse of Protestant young women, by the early twentieth century, rumors began to allege that Jews were the organizing minds and financiers of the "white slavery" trade (Morone 2003, 2–3, 260–65). These stories also attached themselves to Mormon polygamy. Although levels of anti-Jewish prejudice have attenuated, it is generally true that there have been markedly higher levels of anti-Semitism among conservative Protestants than among many other groups of Americans (Glock and Stark 1966; Jaher 1994).[9]

In the nineteenth and early twentieth centuries, much of the evangelical othering of Judaism, like nativist suspicions about Catholicism, concerned the fact that it is part of, and seen as essentially, an international religion. Its headquarters is foreign, and the integration into American culture of its adherents is questionable. Again, the natural alignment that seems to exist for many Americans between Protestant faith and national identity is missing for Jews. This international character made Jews part of the Old World—the fallen world that Americans, especially, according to national mythology, those who came here seeking religious freedom (Hughes 2003), had left to begin their New Eden in North America. Moreover, Jews had no one particular national identity, making the idea of a truly international network that much more plausible. Thus, Jews' foreignness was potentially polluting, and a threat to America's Christian identity as well as its national security. Anti-Semitic conspiracy theories emphasizing how Jews could undermine the United States abounded.

As American anti-Semitism grew, communism was also beginning to become a key political fear. The first Red Scare is often dated as early as 1917, with the rise of the Soviet Union. By the late 1940s to early 1950s, communism had become the nation's primary political enemy. Its threat to free market capitalism was obvious, and much was made of its hostility to civil liberties and liberal democracy. But significantly, the term *godless communism* was used so often it became a cliché. One of the key threats Communism posed, and one of its defining deficiencies, was its commitment to atheism. Many credit the addition of the words *under God* to the Pledge of Allegiance in 1954 to the importance of displaying that very distinction. Evangelicals were not alone in their concern: Americans of many political and religious stripes were concerned about communism. But evangelicals clearly articulated how religious differences distinguished the two political systems and national identities:

> Conservative theologians such as [Billy] Graham and [Billy James] Hargis stressed the moral evils of Communism. Every conflict was a battle between good and evil, between the Godly and the damned. "Either Communism must die, or Christianity must die," wrote Reverend Graham in 1954, "because it is actually a battle between Christ and anti-Christ." When Fred Schwartz [leader of the Christian Anti-Communist Crusade] declared that "Stalin is the fulfillment of Communism," or Billy Graham

described Communism as "Satan's religion," each created a broad caricature—a metaphor that everyone could understand. Leaders such as
Schwartz, Graham, and Hargis took relative American pietism and made
it absolute. (Aiello 2005)

Communism and Jews were linked in many strands of American conservative political and religious thought. The structural parallel between
theories about international conspiracies by Jews, such as in banking
and finance, and theories of international communism as a threat to infiltrate and gain political control, are easy to see (Oldfield 1996, 92–95).
Aaron Beim and Gary Alan Fine noted that the association between Jews
and communists was not completely fictional; many Jewish immigrants
to this country had socialist backgrounds, and many members of the
American Communist Party were secularized Jews (2007). Further, the
eastern European Judaism that immigrated to the United States from the
1880s to the 1920s had a communalist religious culture rather than
Protestant individualism, which added fuel to those fears. And, in the
postwar era, many efforts to secularize public institutions in the United
States were also initiated by Jews (Hollinger 1996), giving conspiracy
thinkers more concern that a clear thread ran through European-
Judaism-communism-secularism and was clearly antagonistic to native-
born American Protestantism.

These ideas have been submerged since the height of the Red Scare,
but they have not gone away. For example, in 1991, Reverend Pat
Robertson published a book, *The New World Order*, that recapitulated
many of the theories regarding Jews and international banking conspiracies common among European anti-Semites for decades and thought to
have receded from American public politics after World War II (Robertson 1991; see also Lind 1995, 1997).[10] Another example includes the 1980
declaration of the Reverend Bailey Smith, at the time president of the
Southern Baptist Convention, that "Almighty God does not hear the
prayer of the Jew." Also, at the National Governors' Conference in 1992,
Mississippi Governor Kirk Fordice was reported to have referred to the
United States as a "Christian nation." A colleague suggested gently that
he surely meant a Judeo-Christian nation. "If I meant that," Fordice re-
portedly replied, "I would have said that."[11]

The point here is not to assess the levels of anti-Catholic or anti-
Semitic prejudice among contemporary evangelicals. Rather, it is to note
several historical examples of evangelical Protestants creating religious
others, and some of the features of the religious distinctions used in that
process, to illustrate several aspects of the claims that are now turned on
a new moral other—secular elites. For evangelical Protestants, most of
whom are the religious descendants of Calvinists or Anabaptist Pietists,
in-group and out-group distinctions are crucial because they are easily

theologized as the differences between the elect and the nonelect, the saved and the unregenerate. Social distinctions become overlaid with religious distinctions, making the normative evaluation of in-group and out-group that much clearer. These distinctions figure prominently, through differentiation, in making the evangelical subculture what it is. A constituent part of what separates evangelicals from "the world" involves these distinctions, and they are important tools in maintaining subcultural vitality.

In form, evangelical identity distinctions are binary, moralized, in-group and out-group differences, with closely monitored boundary lines; in content, evangelical identity is centered in its alignment with American national identity, and a populist celebration of experience and the emotional over formal education and a cosmopolitan worldview.

The Emergence of a New Other:
The Secular Elite

Anyone reading the books, advocacy literature, activist interviews, letters to the editor, or weblogs from contemporary evangelicals in the last decade or so cannot help but notice how seldom the descriptions of their current opponents, or the descriptions of those who threaten America's moral health, are named as Catholics, Jews, or communists. Certainly suspicion of religious others has not disappeared, but it is not difficult to claim that the demonizing of other religions within the Judeo-Christian tradition[12] has diminished, particularly as a dimension of public political culture. Justin Watson summarized this transition in the primary other:

> [The Christian Coalition wants] a return to the de facto or quasi-establishment of evangelical Protestantism of the nineteenth century. The anti-Catholic nativism and anti-Semitism of that era would be dismissed by [Pat] Robertson and [Ralph] Reed because they define their enemies in terms of *hostility to religion* rather than by different religious beliefs. Catholics and Jews with a conservative or traditionalist orientation are seen as cobelligerents against secularism. (1997, 120–21 [emphasis added])

Rather than demonize rival faiths,[13] much of the current rhetoric of outrage generated by politicized evangelicalism, the mobilizing frames calling American Christians to active political engagement, is directed at liberals, Hollywood, the media, the American Civil Liberties Union, and often, academics. These enemies are not associated with a competing religious faith or its people; instead, they are identified with secular professions or political ideologies that advocate secularizing public and political life. The opponents are said to be elites, and are regularly accused of being antireligious; sometimes they are called secularists. Thus, even though the term secular elites is only occasionally used as invective, I use it here because it encapsulates the fears of evangelical activists, and pulls together the two basic critiques of their opponents—that they are hostile to religion and they are antipopulist. Both qualities show them to be fundamentally un-American.

A quick skimming of the writings of several high profile conservatives who are either part of or aligned with the Christian Right reveals how their opponents are categorized.[14] For example, Dick Armey, the former Republican leader, divided the country into virtuous "doers" and sinister "talkers." He considered the latter the members of the "new class" and divides it into subspecies, "politicians, educators, journalists, lawyers, and entertainers" (1995, 3–18). The Reverend David Limbaugh, conservative radio personality Rush Limbaugh's brother, castigated "liberals" and the "social engineers" who "inculcate hostility toward Christianity" (2003, 3). The journalist David Kupelian put his opponents in the subtitle of his book *The Marketing of Evil*, warning of "radicals, elitists, and pseudo-experts" (2005). Alan Sears and Craig Osten did much the same with *The ACLU vs. America*, "exposing the agenda to redefine moral values" (2005). Gary Demar, the editor of *Bible Worldview* magazine, claimed in his book *America's Christian Heritage* that this heritage is ignored or denied by "media and academic elites" whom he also referred to on occasion as secularists. James Dobson and Gary L. Bauer discussed protecting America's children from the corrupting influence of the media and "value-free education" (1994). Rush Limbaugh offered a number of criticisms of "the American Civil Liberties Union and its radically secular allies" because of their opposition to abstinence and moral values curricula in public schools (1993, 276). Tim LaHaye worried that "atheistic, amoral, one-world humanists [may] succeed in enslaving our country" (1980, 23), and noted that a "humanist, whether he is a politician, government official, or educator . . . does not think like a pro-moral American, but like a humanist" (31). And Frank Pastore, a radio show host in Los Angeles who won the 2006 National Religious Broadcasters Talk Show of the Year award, noted that America is threatened by "the Left" in the "strongholds of the Academy, Hollywood, and Old Media" but remains united as "one nation under a God they reject" ("The Envy of the World," *Los Angeles Times*, November 4, 2004).

This collection of quotes could be supplemented by many more.[15] But they are enough to demonstrate the central characteristics of those who form the secular elite in the politicized conservative evangelical worldview. Hollywood, the coastal news media, the academy, and those with connections to international organizations or social networks are most often labeled as part of the elite. It is worth noting, however, the imprecision with which these activist leaders use the term secular elites.

Indeed, attempts at definition are usually minimal. For example, pundit and TV host Bill O'Reilly, in the wake of the controversy surrounding Mel Gibson's *Passion of the Christ*, used his regular feature called *Talking Points Memo* to "define the elite media" (March 8, 2004, http://www.foxnews.com/story/0,2933,113614,00.html). Although O'Reilly clearly labeled the *New York Times*, National Public Radio, and PBS as elite media, there were more examples of elite perfidy than there was sustained attempt at defining who counted as elite. The closest O'Reilly got was the assertion that one can discern the elite media because of the conviction that "It [*sic*] knows—you don't" and the media's belief that the "majority in this country—white Christian Americans—are prone to oppressing the minority." Similarly, Rush Limbaugh eschewed careful definitions or categories when he offered a laundry list of the causes of America's social problems, locating them in the cultural ideals of liberalism: "Liberalism propagates a very different vision of America [from 'real' Americans' vision]. Among the ideas it celebrates are multiculturalism, humanism, secularism, feminism, racial quotas in hiring, political correctness in the university, special rights based on sexual behavior, sensitivity, fairness, and equality not of opportunity but of outcomes" (1993, 276).

Tim LaHaye, whose 1980 book *The Battle for the Mind* is often credited with bringing the term *secular humanism* into the discourse of conservative Protestantism (Oldfield 1996; Shuck 2005), is equally expansive. At some point in the book, humanism entails atheism, communism, liberalism, socialism, Freudianism, higher criticism, feminism, sexual liberation, art, self-determination, rock music, tolerance, evolution, rationalism, empiricism, situational ethics, and Unitarianism.

It is tempting to dismiss these loose and shotgun definitions, except that such ambiguity is neither trivial nor inconsequential. To the contrary, lack of precision is a strength of social movement rhetoric. There is an "artful ambiguity" that must be maintained for a mobilizing discourse to make the most of its potential audience (Williams 2003b, 179). Too much specificity can open rhetorical claims up to debunking or ridicule. For example, Tim LaHaye once made the claim that just 275,000 dedicated humanists hold the media, the schools, and nearly the entire country under their control—a claim that could not possibly be substantiated and even supporters found exaggerated (1980, 181). Too much precision and specificity thus increases the potential for disconfirmation.

Those interested in mobilizing groups tend to avoid specificity and nuance in movement claims for two other reasons. First, well-defined frames may lead some sympathizers to conclude that they do not fully agree with activists' calls to action. Leaving the framing symbols open enough for some individualized interpretation maximizes the number of potential supporters. Second, one power of symbols is to help produce unity; a symbol's emotive power can reach across cognitive differences in meanings and blur those differences until agreement seems to exist. In that way, an effective symbol can help create its own unity as it keeps people centered in a moral and affective core, rather than focusing on the cognitive differentiation that specificity entails. It is not in these activists' interest to generate tomes on exactly who forms their elite opposition—they want to generate activism and it is enough to know that they are secular and elites and we are Christians, believers, and Americans. It provides the necessary social and religious distinctions for collective identity and effective movement frames. And academic analysts who find it maddeningly vague simply demonstrate that their elite culture is out of touch with our emotive, populist sensibilities.

There are several explanations for why secular elites have replaced rival religions as the primary moral other. One factor is that some of the fervor has gone out of anti-Catholicism and anti-Semitism over time as Catholics and Jews have become integrated into American culture, raised families, fought in the country's wars, and generally become "good Americans." American national identity has widened over time beyond the exclusive provenance of Protestants. Concomitantly, many public institutions lost some of their Protestant character in the last half of the twentieth century, as Bible reading and school prayer were declared a violation of the First Amendment's establishment clause, nativity scenes often disappeared from public grounds, and religious commitment was increasingly thought irrelevant to one's public identity. Religion certainly has not disappeared from American society, but the public sphere is less conspicuously Protestant than it once was, allowing a more expansive construction of who counts as American.

Academics and liberals in other culture industries have spearheaded or applauded many of the changes that de-Protestantized and secularized the public sphere. Groups such as the American Civil Liberties Union (ACLU), often representing secular plaintiffs, have challenged many dimensions of public religiosity since the 1960s. Evangelical Protestant values and attitudes have not disappeared, but there is more room for secular lifestyles and expressions in public and political culture. Further, as Robert Wuthnow and others have noted, the main political cleavages dividing American religion have shifted from denominational affiliations to ideological and cultural coalitions that cut across religious affiliation groups (Wuthnow 1988; see also volume 1, chapter 4). The expansion of higher education and the cultural conflicts of the 1960s divided liberal and conservatives within many religious groups.

Thus, politicized evangelicalism is not wholly inaccurate in identifying secular elites as their political rivals. Highly educated, upper-middle-class people with looser ties to religious communities, and with deep suspicions of conservative Protestantism, have worked to make the American public square more secular and more diverse. Whereas those who value public religious expressions now see the public square as "naked" (Neuhaus 1984), more secular people find it more diverse, more accommodating, and less oppressive. There are different visions of the proper role of religion in American public life, and the visions of politicized evangelicals and politically progressive secular people conflict. The opponents are real, even if the rhetorical constructions of them as all-powerful and ubiquitous are exaggerated and fuzzily defined.

It is worth recognizing that there is what might be called an almost self-perpetuating cycle of complementary demonizing between activists in the Christian Right and the cultural Left, wherein each defines the other as its primary enemy. Fundraising and promotional literature by groups such as the ACLU often feature Christian Right proposals as the primary threat to American civil liberties. The group Political Research Associates, a progressive think-tank, focuses particularly on the Christian Right as its primary political opponent and clear other in fundraising. Although the argument that claims that America is wracked by culture wars is overblown and often a piece of mobilizing rhetoric (Williams 1997), it is true that activists on opposing sides of many sociocultural political issues have made common cause across class, gender, ethnic, or religious lines to form coalitions with ideologically compatible groups. Thus, for many evangelical activists, conservative Catholics or Jews are more sympathetic allies on public cultural issues than are those progressives whose secular worldview cast doubt on the reasonableness and value of religion itself.

Evangelicals as an Embattled and Persecuted Minority

A noticeable feature of the public evangelical discourse about secular elites is a set of complaints that America was and in some ways still is a Christian nation, but that through the actions of a secular elite critically placed in key institutions, evangelicals—the most "American" of all religious groups—are an embattled minority facing a certain peril (Demar 2003; Kennedy and Newcombe 2003). This theme has been apparent since the late 1970s, and is prominent in the many recent books recounting attacks on American morality, Christian values, and even Christians themselves, by elites that usually include the American Civil Liberties Union, Hollywood, and higher education with its political correctness, multiculturalism, and secularism (Folger 2005). This persecution claim went high profile during the winter holiday season of 2005 when a number of conservative leaders and media stars, such as Fox News' Bill O'Reilly and John Gibson, decried what they called a "war on Christmas" led by "American Civil Liberties Union lawyers, professional atheists, and Christian haters" (Gibson 2005, jacket cover).

The evangelical claim to being a persecuted minority is not new. For example, Jerry Falwell asks this in his *Listen, America!* manifesto: "If the vast majority of Americans . . . still believe the Ten Commandments are valid today, why are we permitting a few leading amoral humanists and naturalists to take over the most influential positions in this nation?" (1980, 258–59).

Phyllis Schafley made a similar claim in a 1987 speech: "You can call this [secular public education and its values neutral' curricula] secular humanism, you can call it situation ethics, you can call it group therapy, you can call it psychological manipulations, you can call it counseling. . . . But whatever it is, it is completely prevalent and widespread in the public schools, and it is a direct attack on the First Amendment rights of those who believe that God created us, and that He created a moral law that we should obey" (2007, 100). Later in her speech she explained this succinctly: "What we want is the same rights for people who believe in God and His commandments as the atheist has already established. Whatever you call it, this no-name ideology, it all boils down to an attack on religion" (2007, 103).

The schooling activist Norma Gabler asked the question this way: "Why shouldn't we fight? It's our children, our tax money, and our government. And it's our rights that are being violated" (quoted in Kater 1982, 66).

There is a clear logic, both strategic and cultural, in the rhetorical framing of embattled persecution. It helps establish the urgency of the situation and justifies the importance of involvement and activism. It has important resonance with aspects of evangelical religious culture and works well as a rhetorical mobilizing tool. The persecution claim, what Nathaniel Klemp and Stephen Macedo in this volume call a "narrative of victimization," identifies both who suffers and who is to blame (see chapter 7).

In addition, the claim resonates with recent trends in American political language, as well as in American law. Since the 1960s, the violation of rights has become a major motif in American political claims-making. Whereas claiming entitlements in the public square has an ambiguous status in American political individualism, protesting when one's rights are abridged is recognized and highly legitimate. Further, legal remedies are more available to protect individuals and their liberties than they are to enforce a particular cultural vision in the public sphere. Evangelicals can say their rights are violated, and invoke the First Amendment, as well as evoke populist sympathies as the political underdog facing an arrogant elite, rather than fight accusations that they want to impose their values on others.

Beyond those strategic advantages, persecution rhetoric resonates with Christian and evangelical theology and culture. Elizabeth Castelli analyzed how the purported war on Christians and the idea of the persecuted church align with the martyr narratives deeply built into Christianity; it can be buttressed by scriptural references that predict persecution and reward those who endure it, and historical examples of heroes who have forfeited worldly success or approbation for faithfulness to an unpopular righteousness are numerous (2005, 2007). If the world is fallen, persecuted Christians demonstrate that they are not "of" it even as they try to save it. Christian Smith concluded that the sense of being embattled helps shore up evangelical identity by brightening the boundary lines between evangelicals and the secular world, so that evangelicals can be engaged, yet safe from pollution (1998). At the same time, identifying their cause with the interests and values of the nation's Christian majority, or its heritage, puts evangelicals in a position of leadership and opens the door for numerous potential allies—in sum, they can be part of the majority and an embattled minority at the same time.

Klemp and Macedo recognize that claims to persecution allow politicized evangelicals to portray their own agenda as merely a defense of rights (see chapter 7). As self-styled political outsiders, evangelical activists are thus not tainted by power, nor can they be accused of compromising their moral agenda by playing politics and making insider deals (see also Williams 1994, 2003a). Claims to persecution and victimization work to mobilize a constituency at the same time they can be persuasive to bystander publics. It is a resonant stance.[16]

Why Othering Secular Elites Works

Constructing a secular elite as their primary political and cultural opponent has a number of advantages for politicized evangelicalism. As part of a social movement mobilizing frame, secular elites as other works just as sociologists argue such frames should. Christian Right advocacy groups find the nation beset by a number of social problems, many of them connected to changes in sex, gender, family relations, and raising children. They identify the retreat of evangelical Protestantism from the public square and a general secularization of society (in that major institutions such as schools do not reinforce what they consider a correct moral code) as the cause. That claim aligns convincingly with elements of evangelical culture, particularly the notion of a covenanted relationship between God and nation—if the nation neglects God's will, the Almighty removes his protection and the nation's favored status.[17]

These diagnostic frames identify the social problems as well as those responsible for the situation. Demonizing secular elites—and naming the secular dimension as the salient qualifying adjective—clearly identifies that group, however vaguely defined, as responsible for these significant changes in American society, and thus the creators of the social problems that evangelical advocacy groups care about. Along with positing an identifiable agent responsible for causing the problem, the causal story about the secular elite establishes, through oppositional relation, evangelical Christians as responsible for the solution. Evangelicals become the hero of the frame in two ways—both as solving critical social problems caused by others, and, with their religious identity reaffirmed, proving their status as the quintessential American Christians.

Although naming secular elites as the moral other has the strategic and solidarity-building advantages identified by social movement framing theory, it may or may not have been developed deliberately with that in mind. Such calculating and strategic thinking is not unheard of,[18] but it is also not necessary to document intention to understand why this construction has had resonance among evangelical Protestants. As I illustrated in examining historical incidents of religious othering, and in examining the defining characteristics of American evangelicalism, the secular elite construction and the attitudes and values it condenses, fit neatly into the reigning cultural forms of evangelicalism.

For example, the charge of elitism resonates deeply with evangelicalism's populism. Evangelicalism's original religious impulse was rooted in the rejection of the ecclesiastical authority of religious prelates. If this has not always translated into general democratic impulses, it has yielded a consistent suspicion of institutional authorities, and instead places trust in the commonsense knowledge of righteous people. At various times, the elites in question were members of religious hierarchies or, in the days of nineteenth-century American populism, economic "plutocrats" (see Williams and Alexander 1994). More recently, the focus has been on cultural elites, particularly those who run institutions or industries that reach into people's lives and affect how they raise their children.[19] Elites are accused of arrogance and of telling people how to live with an air of condescension based on their formal educational credentials. American democratic impulses always react against those thought to be putting on airs, particularly in cultural realms, but more specifically evangelicalism has a distrust of worldly power and status. As with all religions, it incorporates a basic unwillingness to accept the world as it is as an ultimate value and offers a transcendent standard with which to criticize extant social arrangements (Williams 2002).

Thus, the elitism charge, and the idea that the elites are conspiring against us in the hidden recesses of institutional power, resonates. Elite and conspiracy theories appeal because they assign blame to a definable group, cannot be falsified, and are parsimonious in that they explain many things with very few causal factors. But for evangelical Protestants, tales of conspiracies by elites align with many millennial religious accounts of evil being directed by a hidden, shadowy force, and the belief in an active evil in the world—as Satan disguises himself, often using ordinary people to infiltrate society and undermine God's kingdom.

Important to the resonance is the areas in which these elites are thought to operate. Three institutions in particular—Hollywood, the media, and higher education—are major sites of knowledge and symbol production in our society. These institutions value education, cosmopolitan attitudes, and international perspectives, and the people in them are part of a new class that seems less connected to traditional communities (Horowitz 2003). Further, they seem, to many evangelicals, to exude arrogance combined with a hedonistic disregard for the cultural proscriptions of Victorian bourgeois culture. This helps explain why the 1960s and their excesses remain so vivid to many on the Christian Right (see Brint and Proctor, forthcoming).

Moreover, Hollywood, the mainstream news media, and elite higher education are located on the coasts, the sources of liberalism and home to urbanism and immigrants, and are often portrayed as antithetical to the "real America" that exists in the Heartland (the historically Protestant-heavy Midwest and South). Finally, these institutions also have significant numbers of people who are secular, many of whom are secularized Jews, who have tried to dislodge evangelicalism from its formerly privileged position (Hollinger 1996). There is no doubt that many in the academic and entertainment industries are equally suspicious of evangelical Protestants (Oldfield 1996). As noted above, there is mutual demonizing that is useful to both sides in their efforts to mobilize constituencies.

Evangelism and the Significance of 'The Word'

Evangelicals are "people of the word" religiously. They take words seriously and believe in the power of messages. Institutions whose business it is to produce images, ideas, knowledge, symbols, and messages strike directly at what evangelicals believe to be important. It is not just arrogance or lifestyle—or even their secularism—that makes these elites a threat. It is because they work in institutions that evangelicals cannot avoid, and produce ideas, which evangelicals take very seriously, that so-called new class cultural elites pose a threat.

One of the great issues of the Reformation, and something that continues to inform Protestant-Catholic differences, was the status of the Bible in informing and justifying the faith of ordinary Christians. The Catholic tradition, although it takes Scripture as the word of God, also places great stock in Church doctrine and traditions, which are the result of the systematic application of human reason and faith. For many Protestants, by contrast, sola scriptura, by Scripture alone, is the only legitimate religious authority from which truth may be derived. This focus on the Word accompanied a de-emphasis on liturgy and ritual, and the spread of literacy and printing presses that put copies of the Bible in more of the faithful's hands. In addition, Reformation faiths put a great emphasis on sermons—in distinction to the often brief homilies that define the Catholic mass; Protestant religiosity was also marked by songs, not just by sacred instrumental music (Pettegree 2005). All these religious forms emphasized the Word and its transformative power, in contrast to high church approaches to tradition, liturgy, and ritual.

This emphasis on Scripture is still apparent among evangelical Protestants, and found consistently in survey and interview data with ordinary American laity who identify with evangelicalism. For example, as Andrew Greeley and Michael Hout noted, evangelicals are in many ways "heirs to the Reformation" in their constellation of beliefs and practices (2006, 11–38). Greeley and Hout found evangelicals to be much more likely than mainline Protestants or Catholics to subscribe to a literal interpretation of Scripture, to believe in the natural depravity of humans and the harshness of God toward evil, and to report that they have no doubts about the truth of their faith (2006, 22, 28–29). Similarly, Smith found that evangelicals (distinct from fundamentalists) are significantly more likely than mainline Protestants, liberal Protestants, or Catholics to view the Bible as "literally true" (1998, 23). Similarly, they are also more likely to view human nature as "sinful" and to hold that there are absolute standards of morality and that it is the Bible, rather than "church teachings" or "human reason" that informs them "how God wants them to live" (23–25).

In sum, evangelicals treat Scripture with great seriousness, and regard it as one of the great markers between them and others—others who are of other faiths or no faith. Again, considering the relational aspect of collective identity, the importance of biblical inerrancy becomes clear: "Conservatives are . . . constrained to denounce [mainline Protestants] for their questioning of the authority of the inspired word of God in the Bible. If they give that up, they believe they will be no different from other 'compromisers' with Darwin and modernity. One either accepts Genesis as written word-for-word, or the game is lost" (Greeley and Hout 2006, 12).

Evangelicals take the Word seriously—those who seek to convert unbelievers must themselves believe in the potentially transformative power of messages. If cultural messages do not reflect Christian ideas and values, they can have seriously negative effects on those hearing them. Thus, if a culture has too many secular messages—and those who control cultural industries are not people of faith—the damage can be substantial.

This is a clear rationale behind the evangelical antagonism to popular culture and media. To defend, as many liberals do, popular culture as a marketplace of ideas, is to assume that truth can be discovered collectively over the long run as people use reason and argument to sort through various types of information. Truth is emergent and communal, and may involve missteps along the way. But if truth is revealed, and revealed to individuals through their personal relationship with Jesus, and if a misstep can lead to error that gives in to temptation or involves sin, then the marketplace is an unacceptable risk. Further, thinking of ideas for sale in a market could imply that whatever is most popular is ipso facto most likely true; the number of times secular elites and liberalism are accused of moral relativism speaks to how seriously this threatens an evangelical worldview.

In this light, evangelicals' objections to school curricula, popular books, and other elements of contemporary culture make more sense. There is a clear recognition of the difference between their religious meaning systems and the cultural meanings of the world, and a clear recognition that evil is tempting and cunning. Raising children so that they also become full members of their Christian community is a considerable task, and the costs of wandering or backsliding are significant. Thus, the sense that secular people control major cultural industries— Hollywood, the media, and the academy— makes the elite in those institutions dangerous beyond their numbers.

Conclusion: Evangelical Protestants and Secular Culture

I have explored the relationship between evangelical Protestants and nonreligious others such as secularists, agnostics, and atheists. Evangelicals and secularists are the two groups often thought to be on the opposing poles of the culture wars dichotomy, and they have an assortment of symbolic boundaries and identities arrayed between them. These boundaries have in many ways become theologized and politicized, and this has a number of implications for evangelicalism's approach to public political and cultural life.

A number of indicators suggest that many evangelical Protestants find those with no religion particularly threatening. Secularism or secular humanism is often portrayed as a specific ideological threat that is oppressive to evangelicals and a threat to their children. Secular media and those that control cultural industries are often portrayed as enemies of American culture and a nefarious force in the nation's politics. It may be that evangelicals feel constrained to not level public attacks against members of rival religious groups: anti-Catholic and anti-Jewish prejudice is not as acceptable or normative in public discourse as it once was, and most evangelical political leaders avoid it. But such a taboo does not seem to apply to seculars, and for at least some sector of the evangelical population the appetite for books that criticize secularists as America's most dangerous enemy is seemingly insatiable. This suggests that evangelical culture finds its particular bête noir in the ranks of seculars, agnostics, and atheists. They have been constructed as political demons in ways that make that imagery a powerful mobilizing rhetoric and an idea that aligns closely with some long-standing elements of evangelical religious culture.

This rhetoric has potentially deleterious consequences for political life in a religiously pluralistic society, but the dynamics of the construction of this moral other has been a significant political resource for political mobilization, capturing attention in the public sphere and reaffirming evangelical identity. It is hard to believe that we will see it disappear any time soon.

Notes

1.   This summary integrates the insights generated by William Gamson (1992) and David Snow and Robert Benford (1988).
2.   Deborah Stone, using a slightly different language about "causal stories," made a similar point with an interesting angle (1988, 148–54). She noted that attributing cause has two aspects—whether an action is purposeful versus unguided, and whether the consequences of the action were intended or unintended. Arguing that a social problem arises from an intentional cause alleges both purposeful action and intended consequences. This both diagnoses a problem and assigns responsibility for its cause, and is a strong claim in public politics. However, even if one removes the idea of an intentional cause—and admits that consequences may be unintentional or inadvertent—the responsibility and causal connection of the story are still clear. Thus, evangelicals need not argue that secular elites intended to cause social and moral breakdown when they secularized society to keep their focus on these elites as the agents responsible for causing our current situation as the result of their purposeful actions.
3.   Paul Lichterman, Prudence Carter, and Michele Lamont explore exactly this process—the emergent construction of a collective identity through making distinctions and drawing boundaries between "people like us" and "people not like us" (volume 1, chapter 6).
4.   Michael Lindsay describes many evangelical political persons as having an "elastic orthodoxy" that helps navigate this terrain—they have a core set of deeply held beliefs with which to anchor themselves, but they can be elastic enough to stretch many beliefs and values in order to deal with others and importantly, make potential allies (chapter 10, this volume). But this is a cognitive practice that takes some dexterity to accomplish successfully,

and Lindsay also notes that what he calls "cosmopolitan evangelicals"—well educated, middle class, and often in high-level institutional positions—often handle it better than "populist evangelicals."

5. I have argued elsewhere that the conservative religious movement known as the Promise Keepers was a movement of tremendous internal diversity, abetted by a loose organizational style, a reliance on local congregations, and a focus on religious revivalism rather than policy or political outcomes (Williams 2001). Thus, relying on the statements of organizational leaders for understanding rank-and-file attitudes can be misleading. Even in a more tightly organized activist group, individualized interpretation of movement ideology is still abundant (Williams and Blackburn 1996).

6. One can make similar definitional distinctions among those that are considered secular in American life. That label could potentially include a number of people who agree only on a few issues. Atheists are decidedly secular in that they do not believe there is a God. Agnostics, on the other hand, do not necessarily deny the existence of some type of supreme being or divine power, but do not believe that any existing human religion understands it or captures it in formal religious doctrine. There are also some who, whatever their beliefs, are committed primarily to keeping religion a private matter of beliefs and actions and out of the public sphere. Others are not opposed to all public religion, but want government not to appear to sponsor, endorse, or favor religion over nonreligion; thus, civil society's expressions of religious commitment are not a concern. All of these people are in some way seculars. It is characteristic of the mobilizing rhetoric of politicized evangelicalism to elide these distinctions to amplify the sense of threat posed by seculars and to unify its oppositional other.

7. Laurence Moore noted that some of this influence may have as much to do with the historiography of American religion as with the history of American religion (1986). The New England Puritans themselves were prolific writers, lending itself to a great deal of historical scholarship about them. That the Puritans wrote so much could be taken as evidence of their commitment to reading, writing about, and focusing on the Word (as opposed to a commitment to ritual, for example), a point to which I return.

8. Probably no religious group in the United States has been as vilified as the Church of Jesus Christ of Latter-Day Saints (Mormons). In the latter half of the nineteenth century, Congress passed a series of laws designed to wipe out the practice of polygamy, then a distinguishing tenet of the Mormon faith. These acts—the 1862 Morrill Anti-Bigamy Act, the 1882 Edmunds Act, and the 1887 Edmunds-Tucker Act—not only prohibited the practice of polygamy, but also revoked polygamists' right to vote, to serve on juries, and to take political office. Women, who had been enfranchised by the territorial legislature, also were disenfranchised. The laws also allowed for the seizure of church property and took partial control of the public schools and the local judiciary. However, the Mormon concentration in the mountain west, away from population centers, meant that relatively few Americans had to live directly with that form of religious diversity.

9. By the twentieth century, conservative Protestants' particularistic self-regard—their conviction that their own faith was the only true religion—led

them to consistent levels of distrust of Jews for not being Christian, as well as widespread evangelical support for efforts to evangelize them (Smith 1999).

10. Michael Lind notes, however, that in many places in Robertson's book he substitutes the term *German* or *European* where his sources used *Jewish* (1997, 101). Although Aaron Beim and Gary Fine argued that these attitudes have receded in American culture generally, they are still easy to find on many Christian-themed websites (2007; see, for example, http://www.biblebelievers.org.au, or "Weekly Updates for Christians on the New World Order" at http://www.cuttingedge.org/news/headlines.html or http://www.worldslastchance.com). And many Christian Identity movement groups continue to be fairly open with their anti-Semitism (Barkun 1996). Robertson and Ralph Reed, then the director of Robertson's Christian Coalition, defended Robertson from claims of anti-Semitism—but the charges themselves came from mainstream media and liberal groups, not the evangelical community. Robertson has become less influential, but this is due more, in my view, to his general unpredictability and numerous public gaffes than to anti-Semitism per se.

11. A more recent incident shows the fluid dynamics in religious and political alliances among evangelicals, Catholics, and Jews. Mel Gibson's 2004 movie *The Passion of the Christ*, and the tactics Gibson and others used to drum up a media buzz about the movie before its release, raised questions about anti-Semitism. Whether the film, or Gibson, or the pre-release publicity, was anti-Semitic is open to debate. It is a fact, however, that Gibson, a traditionalist Catholic, marketed the film adroitly among evangelical congregations and para-church organizations. And several evangelical Protestant leaders emerged as Gibson's main defenders in the media (see Landres and Berenbaum 2004). Two aspects of this are significant for my argument here. First, evangelical Protestants seemed completely comfortable publicly defending a conservative Catholic, while evangelicals flocked to a movie with a decidedly Catholic sensibility about the passion. Politics trumped older Protestant-Catholic tensions. Second, in defending himself from charges of anti-Semitism, Gibson often referred to "certain forces" in Hollywood that opposed him, called the *New York Times* "anti-Christian," and claimed that Jewish interest groups pressured him to delete a scene (Frank Rich, "The Greatest Story Ever Sold," *New York Times*, September 21, 2003; "The Pope's Thumbs Up for Gibson's Passion," *New York Times*, January 18, 2004). These could easily be taken as allusions to classic beliefs about the power of a Jewish elite who control the entertainment and media industries. The claims resonate clearly with widespread evangelical concern about control of culture industries.

12. How Islam fares post-9/11 is another issue. There have been some notable expressions of intolerance toward Islam by a variety of evangelical leaders, including Franklin Graham, son of and heir to Billy Graham. On the other hand, many such statements have been criticized for their intolerance. Blogs and letters to the editor are often careful to oppose "militant Islam" or to adopt a version of President George W. Bush's Islamo-fascists. Most of the political establishment, and many evangelical opinion leaders, have

tried consistently to separate terrorism from Islam as a religion. Nonetheless, things are said publicly about Muslims—by evangelicals and nonevangelicals alike—that are not said about Catholics and Jews.

13. One recent study, however, found that among evangelicals bias against Mormons is comparable to their bias against atheists (Carrie Moore, "As Romney Prepares Speech, Poll Shows Bias Against Mormons," *Deseret Morning News*, December 5, 2007). This was enough of an issue for Mormon Mitt Romney in the 2008 Republican presidential primaries that he addressed those concerns in a major speech.

14. Most of the people I quote are publicly identified as evangelical Protestants, and are recognized as speaking from that community (if not necessarily for it). Others have posted on religiously themed websites. However, I also include some other voices of conservatives that find much support in the Christian Right, even if not publicly established as evangelical themselves. I include some of these figures, such as Bill O'Reilly, because their claims-making identifies secular elites as a major source of our societal problems, and often defends evangelical Christians as persecuted. For example, David Kupelian is publicly identified as a journalist, but his book is published by WND Books, the publishing arm of WorldNetDaily.com, a conservative news website that prominently features Christian Right authors and religiously themed merchandise in its online gift shop. The WND imprint was launched in 2002 through a partnership with Thomas Nelson Publishers, now based in Nashville, Tennessee, a prominent Christian publishing house. It is also the case that othering secular elites is not confined to evangelicals. Conservative commentator Laura Ingraham is a converted Roman Catholic, but her recent book *Shut Up & Sing: How Elites from Hollywood, Politics and the UN are Subverting America* (2006) shows many of the themes delineated here—particularly focusing on both the antireligiousness of the elite and their social location in media, entertainment, and international organizations.

15. The rhetoric that emanated from conservative radio, political blogs, Fox News, and other outlets during the 2008 vice presidential candidacy of Alaska Governor Sarah Palin would be another good source of evidence for my argument. In particular, the extent to which Palin supporters castigated the media and Washington elites for being out of touch with real Americans (who were disproportionately in the Midwest and South) was telling.

16. Klemp and Macedo's reference to *narrative* (as opposed to my use of frames) is more that just semantics, and is worth examining. Narratives are, by definition, stories; they have plots, characters, and moral lessons embedded in them. Frames, as bundles of claims or symbols, are too easily thought of as static packages assembled purely strategically by movement leaders—and that agreement with frames is primarily cognitive (see Williams 2002). Frame theory makes the important point that the claims-making is successful when a movement's framing simultaneously accomplishes a number of tasks (diagnosing problems, proposing solutions, and motivating members). But humans are storytelling creatures, and people understand their situations and develop the motivations for collective ac-

tion through narratives. The persecution theme is important in the claims of contemporary politicized evangelicals, but Klemp and Macedo are correct to note that it is expressed in a narrative of victimization.

17. Many, of course, recognize that evangelical Protestantism does not have the place in American life it once did. The story of American history can be told as public, established religion retreating in the face of an advancing modern, pluralist, and secular society. For many evangelicals this is a declension narrative, as a righteous community goes astray as it loses a societal commitment to the true faith. For many liberals and secularists, it is a progress narrative that understands religion as differentiating into the private sphere of personal and family commitments, as modernity ushers in a secular age of science, reason, and social diversity and a pluralistic public sphere becomes religiously neutral (see Shea 2004).

18. Michael Lind (1997, 154) noted that Republican organizer, former Congressman, and confirmed cultural warrior Newt Gingrich gave activists advice to use the term *homosexual* rather than *gay* because of the differing emotions the two terms evoked.

19. Duane Oldfield quoted Gary Bauer's claims that the centrality of children, and evangelicals' abilities to raise their children in their faith, is the centering principle in all of the social issues raised by Christian Right advocacy groups (1996, 62–65).

References

Aiello, Thomas. 2005. "Constructing 'Godless Communism': Religion, Politics, and Popular Culture, 1954–1960." *Americana: The Journal of American Popular Culture (1900–present)* 4(1)(Spring). Available at: http://www.americanpopu larculture.com/journal/articles/spring_2005/aiello.htm (accessed on July 20, 2007).

Armey, Dick. 1995. *The Freedom Revolution*. Washington, D.C.: Regnery Publishing.

Barkun, Michael. 1996. *Religion and the Racist Right*. Chapel Hill: University of North Carolina Press.

Beim, Aaron, and Gary Alan Fine. 2007. "The Cultural Frameworks of Prejudice: Reputational Images and the Postwar Disjuncture of Jews and Communism." *The Sociological Quarterly* 48(3): 373–97.

Benford, Robert D., and David A. Snow. 2000. "Framing Process and Social Movements: An Overview and Assessment." *Annual Review of Sociology* 26(2000): 611–39.

Bennett, David 1988. *The Party of Fear*. Chapel Hill: University of North Carolina Press.

Blanshard, Paul. 1950. *American Freedom and Catholic Power*. Boston, Mass.: Beacon Press.

Bourdieu, Pierre. 1984. *Distinction: A Social Critique of the Judgement of Taste*. Cambridge, Mass.: Harvard University Press.

———. 1991. *Language and Symbolic Power*. Cambridge, Mass.: Harvard University Press.

Brereton, Virginia Lieson. 1998. "Education and Minority Religions." In *Minority Faiths and the American Protestant Mainstream*, edited by Jonathan D. Sarna. Chicago: University of Illinois Press.

Brint, Steven, and Kristopher Proctor. Forthcoming. "Middle-Class Respectability 'After Thrift': Work and Lifestyle in the Professional-Managerial Stratum." In *After Thrift*, edited by Joshua J. Yates and James Davison Hunter. New York: Columbia University Press.

Carpenter, Joel A. 1997. *Revive Us Again: The Reawakening of American Fundamentalism*. New York: Oxford University Press.

Castelli, Elizabeth. 2005. "Praying for the Persecuted Church: U.S. Christian Activism in the Global Arena." *Journal of Human Rights* 4(3): 321–51.

———. 2007. "Persecution Complexes: Identity Politics and the War on Christians." *differences: A Journal of Feminist Cultural Studies* 18(3): 152–80.

Demar, Gary. 2003. *America's Christian Heritage*. Nashville, Tenn.: B&H Publishing.

Dobson, James, and Gary L. Bauer. 1994. *Children at Risk*, 6th ed. Nashville, Tenn.: Thomas Nelson.

Dolan, Jay P. 1983. *The Immigrant Church: New York's Irish and German Catholics, 1815–1865*. Notre Dame, Ind.: University of Notre Dame Press.

———. 1998. "Catholicism and American Culture: Strategies for Survival." In *Minority Faiths and the American Protestant Mainstream*, edited by Jonathan D. Sarna. Chicago: University of Illinois Press.

Douglas, Mary. 1966. *Purity and Danger: An Analysis of Concepts of Pollution and Taboo*. London: Routledge and Kegan Paul.

Edgell, Penny, Joseph Gerteis, and Douglas Hartmann. 2006. "Atheists as 'Other': Moral Boundaries and Cultural Membership in American Society." *American Sociological Review* 71(2): 211–34. Available at: http://www.soc.umn.edu/pdf/atheistAsOther.pdf.

Falwell, Jerry. 1980. *Listen, America!* New York: Bantam Books.

Fischer, David Hackett. 1991. *Albion's Seed: Four British Folkways in America*. New York: Oxford University Press.

Folger, Janet L. 2005. *The Criminalization of Christianity: Read This Book Before It Becomes Illegal!* Sisters, Ore.: Multnomah Publishers.

Franchot, Jenny. 1994. *Roads to Rome: The Antebellum Protestant Encounter with Catholicism*. Berkeley: University of California Press.

Gamson, William A. 1992. *Talking Politics*. New York: Cambridge University Press.

Gibson, John. 2005. *The War on Christmas: How the Liberal Plot to Ban the Sacred Christian Holiday Is Worse Than You Thought*. New York: Sentinel/Penguin.

Glock, Charles Y., and Rodney Stark, 1966. *Christian Beliefs and Anti-Semitism*. New York: Harper and Row.

Greeley, Andrew, and Michael Hout. 2006. *The Truth about Conservative Christians: What they Think and What they Believe*. Chicago: University of Chicago Press.

Gusfield, Joseph. 1981. *The Culture of Public Problems*. Chicago: University of Chicago Press.

Handy, Robert. 1984. *A Christian America: Protestant Hopes and Historical Realities*. New York: Oxford University Press.

Hatch, Nathan O. 1989. *The Democratization of American Christianity*. New Haven, Conn.: Yale University Press.

Higham, John. 1955/1963. *Strangers in the Land: Patterns of American Nativism, 1860–1925*. New Brunswick, N.J.: Rutgers University Press.

Hollinger, David A. 1996. *Science, Jews, and Secular Culture: Studies in Mid-Twentieth-Century American Intellectual History*. Princeton, N.J.: Princeton University Press.

Horowitz, David A. 2003. *America's Political Class Under Fire: The Twentieth Century's Great Culture War*. New York: Routledge.

Hunt, Scott A., and Robert D. Benford. 2004. "Collective Identity, Solidarity, and Commitment." In *The Blackwell Companion to Social Movements*, edited by David A. Snow, Sarah A. Soule, and Hanspeter Kriesi. Malden, Mass.: Blackwell Publishing.

Hughes, Richard T. 2003. *Myths America Lives By*. Chicago: University of Illinois Press.

Hughes, Richard T., and Leonard Allen. 1988. *Illusions of Innocence: Protestant Primitivism in America, 1630–1875*. Chicago: University of Chicago Press.

Hunter, James Davison. 1987. *Evangelicalism: The Coming Generation*. Chicago: University of Chicago Press.

Ingraham, Laura. 2006. *Shut Up & Sing: How Elites from Hollywood, Politics and the UN are Subverting America*. Washington, D.C.: Regnery Publishing.

Jaher, Frederic Cople. 1994. *A Scapegoat in the New Wilderness: The Origins and Rise of Anti-Semitism in America*. Cambridge, Mass: Harvard University Press.

Kater, John L., Jr. 1982. *Christians on the Right: The Moral Majority in Perspective*. Boston, Mass.: Seabury Press.

Kelly, George Armstrong. 1984. *Politics and Religious Consciousness in America*. New Brunswick, N.J.: Transaction Books.

Kennedy, D. James, with J. Newcombe. 2003. *What if America Were a Christian Nation Again?* Nashville, Tenn.: Thomas Nelson Books.

Kupelian, David. 2005. *The Marketing of Evil: How Radicals, Elitists, and Pseudo-Experts Sell Us Corruption Disguised as Freedom*. Medford, Ore.: WND Books.

LaHaye, Tim. 1980. *The Battle for the Mind*. Grand Rapids, Mich.: Baker Book House.

Landres, J. Shawn, and Michael Berenbaum, eds. 2004. *After the Passion is Gone: American Religious Consequences*. Walnut Creek, Calif.: Altamira.

Limbaugh, David. 2003. *Persecution: How Liberals Are Waging War Against Christianity*. New York: HarperCollins.

Limbaugh, Rush III. 1993. *See, I Told You So*. New York: Pocket Books.

Lind, Michael. 1995. "Rev. Robertson's Grand International Conspiracy Theory." *The New York Review of Books* 42(2): 21–25.

———. 1997. *Up From Conservatism*. New York: The Free Press.

Marsden, George M. 1980. *Fundamentalism and American Culture: The Shaping of Twentieth-Century Evangelicalism, 1870–1925*. New York: Oxford University Press.

Marty, Martin E., and R. Scott Appleby, eds. 1991. *Fundamentalisms Observed*. Chicago: University of Chicago Press.

Miller, Perry. 1956. *Errand into the Wilderness*. Cambridge, Mass.: Belknap Press.

Moore, R. Laurence. 1986. *Religious Outsider and the Making of Americans*. New York: Oxford University Press.

Morone, James A. 2003. *Hellfire Nation: The Politics of Sin in American History*. New Haven, Conn.: Yale University Press.

Neuhaus, Richard John. 1984. *The Naked Public Square: Religion and Democracy in America*. Grand Rapids, Mich.: William B. Eerdmans.

Neuman, W. Russell. 1986. *The Paradox of Mass Politics: Knowledge and Opinion in the American Electorate*. Cambridge, Mass.: Harvard University Press.

Noll, Mark A. 1998. "The Bible, Minority Faiths, and the American Protestant Mainstream, 1860–1925." In *Minority Faiths and the American Protestant Mainstream*, edited by Jonathan D. Sarna. Chicago: University of Illinois Press.

Oldfield, Duane Murray. 1996. *The Right and the Righteous: The Christian Right Confronts the Republican Party*. Lanham, Md.: Rowman & Littlefield.

Penning, James M., and Corwin E. Smidt. 2002. *Evangelicalism: The Next Generation*. Grand Rapids, Mich.: Baker Academic.

Peshkin, Alan. 1988. *God's Choice: The Total World of a Fundamentalist School*. Chicago: University of Chicago Press.

Pettegree, Andrew. 2005. *Reformation and the Culture of Persuasion*. New York: Cambridge University Press.

Polletta, Francesca, and James M. Jasper. 2001. "Collective Identity and Social Movements." *Annual Review of Sociology* 27(2001): 283–305.

Reed, Ralph. 1996. *Politically Incorrect: The Emerging Faith Factor in American Politics*. Nashville, Tenn.: W Publishing Group.

Reichley, A. James 1985. *Religion in American Public Life*. Washington, D.C.: Brookings Institution Press.

Robertson, Pat. 1991. *The New World Order*. Dallas, Tex.: Word Publishing.

Rogin, Michael Paul. 1987. *Ronald Reagan, the Movie, and Other Episodes in Political Demonology*. Berkeley: University of California Press.

Roof, Wade Clark, and William McKinney. 1987. *American Mainline Religion: Its Changing Shape and Future*. New Brunswick, N.J.: Rutgers University Press.

Schafley, Phyllis. 2007. "Child Abuse in the Classroom." In *Landmark Speeches of the American Conservative Movement*, edited by Peter Schweizer and Wynton C. Hall. College Station: Texas A&M Press.

Sears, Alan, and Craig Osten. 2005. *The ACLU vs. America: Exposing the Agenda to Redefine Moral Values*. Nashville, Tenn.: B&H Publishing.

Shea, William M. 2004. *The Lion and the Lamb: Evangelicals and Catholics in America*. New York: Oxford University Press.

Shuck, Glenn W. 2005. *Marks of the Beast: The Left Behind Novels and the Struggle for Evangelical Identity*. New York: New York University Press.

Smith, Christian. 1998. *American Evangelicalism: Embattled and Thriving*. Chicago: University of Chicago Press.

———. 2000. *Christian America? What Evangelicals Really Want*. Berkeley: University of California Press.

Smith, Tom W. 1999. "The Religious Right and Anti-Semitism." *Review of Religious Research* 40(3): 244–58.

Snow, David A. 2004. "Framing Processes, Ideology, and Discursive Fields." In

The Blackwell Companion to Social Movements, edited by David A. Snow, Sarah A. Soule, and Hanspeter Kriesi. Malden, Mass.: Blackwell Publishing.

Snow, David A. and Robert D. Benford. 1988. "Ideology, Frame Resonance, and Participant Mobilization." *International Social Movement Research* 1: 197–218.

Steensland, Brian, Jerry Z. Park, Mark D. Regnerus, Lynn D. Robinson, W. Bradford Wilcox, Robert D. Woodberry. 2000. "The Measure of American Religion: Toward Improving the State of the Art." *Social Forces* 79(1): 291–318.

Stone, Deborah A. 1988. *Policy Paradox and Political Reason*. New York: Harper-Collins.

Watson, Justin. 1997. *The Christian Coalition: Dream of Restoration, Demands for Recognition*. New York: St. Martin's Press.

Williams, Rhys H. 1994. "Movement Dynamics and Social Change: Transforming Fundamentalist Ideology and Organizations." In *Accounting for Fundamentalisms: The Dynamic Character of Movements*, edited by Martin E. Marty and R. Scott Appleby. Chicago: University of Chicago Press.

———— 1995. "Constructing the Public Good: Cultural Resources and Social Movements." *Social Problems* 42(1): 124–44.

————, ed. 1997. *Cultural Wars in American Politics: Critical Reviews of a Popular Myth*. Hawthorne, N.Y.: Aldine de Gruyter.

————. 1999. "Visions of the Good Society and the Religious Roots of American Political Culture." *Sociology of Religion* 60(1): 1–34.

————, ed. 2001. *Promise Keepers and the New Masculinity: Private Lives and Public Morality*. Lanham, Md.: Lexington Books.

————. 2002. "From the 'Beloved Community' to 'Family Values': Religious Language, Symbolic Repertoires, and Democratic Culture." In *Social Movements: Identity, Culture, and the State*, edited by David S. Meyer, Nancy Whittier, and Belinda Robnett. New York: Oxford University Press.

————. 2003a. "Religious Social Movements in the Public Sphere: Organization, Ideology, and Activism." In *Handbook of the Sociology of Religion*, edited by Michele Dillon. New York: Cambridge University Press.

————. 2003b. "The Language of God in the City of Man: Religious Discourse and Public Politics in America." In *Religion as Social Capital: Producing the Common Good*, edited by Corwin Smidt. Waco, Tex.: Baylor University Press.

————. 2004. "The Cultural Contexts of Collective Action: Constraints, Opportunities, and the Symbolic Life of Social Movements." In *The Blackwell Companion to Social Movements*, edited by David A. Snow, Sarah A. Soule, and Hanspeter Kriesi. Malden, Mass.: Blackwell Publishing.

Williams, Rhys H., and Susan M. Alexander. 1994. "Religious Rhetoric in American Populism: Civil Religion as Movement Ideology." *Journal for the Scientific Study of Religion* 33(1)(March): 1–15.

Williams, Rhys H., and Robert D. Benford. 2000. "Two Faces of Collective Action Frames: A Theoretical Consideration." *Current Perspectives in Social Theory* 20(1): 127–51.

Williams, Rhys H., and Jeffrey Neal Blackburn. 1996. "Many Are Called but Few Obey: Ideological Commitment and Activism in Operation Rescue." In *Disruptive Religion: The Force of Faith in Social Movement Activism*, edited by Christian Smith. New York: Routledge.

Woodberry, Robert D., and Christian S. Smith. 1998. "Fundamentalism et al.: Conservative Protestants in America." *Annual Review of Sociology* 24(1998): 25–56.

Wuthnow, Robert. 1988. *The Restructuring of American Religion: Society and Faith Since World War II.* Princeton, N.J.: Princeton University Press.

Young, Michael P. 2006. *Bearing Witness Against Sin: The Evangelical Birth of the American Social Movement.* Chicago: University of Chicago Press.

Chapter 6

Mobilizing Evangelicals: Christian Reconstructionism and the Roots of the Religious Right

JULIE INGERSOLL

S TUDIES THAT date the origins of the Christian Right to the late 1970s and early 1980s have generally failed to explore the groundwork that prepared the way for the movement throughout the 1960s and into the 1970s. In this chapter, I argue that a small group within fundamentalism known as Christian Reconstructionists played an important but underexplored part in the rise of the Christian Right and that, though unacknowledged, the influence of this group continues today. The published works of the Reconstructionists influenced the leaders of the Christian Right. These works made their way into evangelical and fundamentalists churches in the forms of study guides and into Christian school (and homeschool) curricula (Ingersoll 2006). The ideas of Reconstructionists helped to frame the worldview of the Christian Right, and helped weave together the issues that have dominated the Christian Right's political agenda while grounding those issues in a specific understanding of the family.

Briefly, Christian Reconstruction is a label for a small group of conservative Christians who want to reconstruct society to conform to biblical law: they wish, that is, to build a theocracy. Many consider Rousas John Rushdoony the father of this movement. More than other Christians, Reconstructionists emphasize the Old Testament; they have their roots in the Calvinist wing of the Reformation, and see themselves as the intellectual heirs of the Puritans and of the early-twentieth-century theologians from Old Princeton.[1]

I begin by discussing the movement's history, noting several of its most important thinkers, and exploring the central theological themes and political strategies. Drawing on George Lakoff's *Moral Politics* (1996) and *Whose Freedom* (2006), I argue that the influence of Reconstructionism stems, in large measure, from its success at implanting a particular image of the ideal patriarchal family at the heart of Christian Right thinking. I tease out the Strict Father metaphor that underlies the discourse of the Christian Right because it is framed in the efforts of Rushdoony to develop a biblical worldview. This image of the family not only provides guidance for Christian Right family practices, but is also a metaphor that shapes much of the worldview and political agenda of the movement.

Although many scholars have noted the importance of Reconstructionism, albeit without developing any lengthy analysis, some contend that it is only a fringe movement (Wilcox 1996, 124–25; see also Shupe 1977; Juergensmeyer 2000; Diamond 1995, 1998; Balmer 2006; Goldberg 2006).[2] This is certainly true in terms of the numbers, in that few conservative Christians openly embrace the label Reconstructionism, and the recognizable leaders of the Christian Right, more often than not, deny ties to the Reconstructionists. However, I am suggesting a more subtle form of influence. In previous work, I have held that Christian Right leaders deny ties to Reconstructionists, because Reconstructionist writings are often so extreme that identification with them could be delegitimating.

I suggest here that Lakoff's model offers a lens for understanding the important influence of Reconstructionism on the Christian Right, in spite of these denials of ties. The popular translation of the core ideas of Christian Reconstructionism into Christian Right thinking is so consistent (including even the very language the Reconstructionists use), and the evidence of ties between the Reconstructionists and the early leaders of the Christian Right common enough, that the influence is, I argue, undeniable (see also Ingersoll 2006). Howard Phillips of the Conservative Caucus, one of the Washington-based organizations that has been at the core of the Christian Right since its inception,[3] has called Rushdoony the most influential man of the twenty-first century and asserted that Rushdoony catalyzed "historic changes in the thinking of countless leaders."[4] We need not agree with Phillips to see the impact Rushdoony and those he trained had on Phillips and his colleagues. Finally, even those who consider the movement fringe recognize the important role Reconstructionists have played in framing the debate over the characteristics of civil society in terms of biblical law. The political scientist Clyde Wilcox wrote that "the Christian Reconstructionists are but a tiny fringe of the

Christian Right. [However,] their arguments are being . . . incorporated in mainstream writing, including in recent books by Pat Robertson. . . . This does not mean that many Christian Right activists advocate stoning incorrigible youth, but it does indicate that serious discussions are taking place among Christian Right activists of how to go about restructuring society to conform with biblical law" (1996, 125).[5] That emphasis on bringing society into conformity with biblical law is rooted in the work of Rushdoony and other Reconstructionists.

It is important to be clear about the limitations of my claim.[6] First, I do not argue that the influence of the Christian Reconstructionists takes the form of clearly identifiable leaders who embrace an organization known as Christian Reconstruction. The influence I point to is much more subtle, implicit, and hidden. Second, I do not argue that Rushdoony's early formulation of Christian Reconstruction remains unchanged. In fact, several important areas of disagreement have developed, especially over the centrality of the family. Third, I do not argue that this influence is consistent across the movement we know as the Christian Right. On the contrary, conservative American Protestantism is a diverse, complex movement that has developed from a variety of sources (Ingersoll 2003; see also Marsden 1991; Woodberry and Smith 1998).

Reconstructionist Worldview and Early Influence

As early as the 1960s, Rushdoony and other Reconstructionists framed what they see as a biblical worldview in terms of the family. They wrote about it extensively and made their writings widely available, actively promoting what they called epistemological self-consciousness and a blueprint for transforming society along those lines. Although many scholars have dated the origins of the Christian Right to the disappointment of evangelicals with the presidency of Jimmy Carter, Reconstructionists were publishing and disseminating books in churches and Christian schools through much of the 1960s and all of the 1970s, building what would become a reservoir of support for the Christian Right. Certain names and dates are important in establishing that their work appeared well before the conventionally dated beginnings of the Christian Right.

Rushdoony's Chalcedon Foundation, founded in 1960, is the central institutional expression of Christian Reconstruction. It employed many Reconstructionist writers early in their careers, most importantly in writing for its publication *The Journal of Christian Reconstruction* (JCR). At least twenty of Rushdoony's books predate 1980. The most important of these is the two-volume *The Institutes of Biblical Law* (1973). I examine this study, which places the family at the center of a biblical worldview, at length in the next section. Gary North, married to Rushdoony's daughter, was already writing for JCR in 1974 and had completed two important Reconstructionist works, including his 1973 *Introduction to Christian Economics*, by 1980.

Perhaps more than any other figure, North dedicated himself to promoting the application of Reconstruction to politics, family, and church. He typically wrote for nontheologians, and his publishing house, Dominion Press, focused on accessibility. This is best exemplified by the Biblical Blueprint series he edited and published in the mid-1980s. Targeted to a broad Christian audience, the series is an excellent example of the intentional development and strategic dissemination of a worldview based in Rushdoony's work—a worldview grounded in notions of the biblical family. Topics for these volumes include money and banking, economics, political action, the role of government, the ownership of the family, education, poverty, and political activism.[7] By the 1970s, the Reconstructionist network was fully developed and their biblical worldview was being widely disseminated in churches.

Core Ideas of Christian Reconstruction

The Reconstructionist system is anchored in a few core ideas, which are expressed theologically as postmillennialism and presuppositionalism, and politically as dominionism and theonomy. Christian Reconstructionist writers like North present these ideas in accessible popular terms as a critique of secular humanism and as an effort to restore America as what they call a Christian nation.[8]

The overwhelming majority of contemporary conservative Christians are premillennialist. In fact, they subscribe to a very particular version of premillennialism that dates to the mid-nineteenth century. Popularized in the revivals of the nineteenth and early twentieth centuries, premillennial dispensationalism teaches that God dispenses grace in different ways during different periods of history. According to dispensationalism, we are now living in the end of the second to last age—the church age. In this period, the world will tumble in decline until things are so bad that Jesus must return to establish the kingdom of God (thus his return is premillennial). Evangelicals debate the details of this decline, but they include the Great Tribulation, the Battle of Armageddon, and the Rapture (during which, it is thought, Christians will be rescued from the chaos of the Tribulation). Many scholars consider this End Times theology to be the unifying characteristic of the various groups that make up the core of theologically conservative Protestantism in America.

Unlike most contemporary evangelicals, Reconstructionists are postmillennialists—that is, they believe that the kingdom of God is an earthly reality and that the second coming of Jesus will mark the culmination of that period. For postmillennialists, Jesus defeated death (and Satan) at the cross, thereby establishing the kingdom of God. Postmillennialists teach that it is the work of Christians to restore the damage done by the fall, to bring the blessing of the gospel to the whole earth. Because they did so, the kingdom of God will be increasingly made manifest. The work of building the kingdom of God, the literal transforming of the world, becomes the fundamental purpose of the Christian life. This view was prevalent throughout much of the American history. The Puritans understood their "errand into the wilderness" as an effort to expand the kingdom of God. This was a common view among nineteenth-century evangelicals, and in fact, evangelical efforts to build the kingdom of God led to many of the social reform movements of that period, including abolition and temperance.[9]

One of the paradoxes noted by those who study the rise of the Christian Right is that premillennialists who believe that the end of the world, and the return of their savior, are imminent (and who enthusiastically looked forward to those developments) were mobilized to build a Christian nation that conforms to postmillennialist views. One of the more interesting dimensions of the story of the rise of the Christian Right is the way in which Reconstructionists framed postmillennialism as dominion theology so that that many evangelicals could be convinced to help rebuild a Christian America even as they continued to embrace a premillennial eschatology.

For Reconstructionists, dominion theology is closely tied to postmillennialism. In simple terms, God created Adam and Eve to have fellowship with him and have dominion over the garden of Eden. With the fall, both their fellowship with God and their place in the garden were broken. In postmillennialism, all of creation is restored with the resurrection, and because the garden is now the whole earth, Christians are to exercise dominion over it in the name of Christ. The notion of dominion in Reconstructionist writing is developed from the notion of stewardship[10] found in the larger context of Reformed thinking, giving its meaning a slightly different cast than it might have outside this context. It really does not explicitly mean *to dominate*, though certainly it does not mean only *to care for* either (see for example, North 1983a, 1983b, 1986a, 1986b, 1987d). It is, rather, a paternalistic caring for that includes both ideas. Gary North wrote that "the will to dominion is . . . not the quest for power apart from ethical law, but the quest for authority by means of ethical action" (1986b, 126). In fact, North saw power and dominion as opposing characteristics representing, respectively, humanistic and godly religion (1985).

In some ways, North's postmillennialism is typical of other Reconstructionists and nineteenth-century postmillennialists. In *Conspiracy: A Biblical View*, for example, he argued that only the "covenantal faithfulness" of the people can save society:

> It's not our job to "throw the rascals out" in one glorious national election. Our job is to replace them steadily by our own competence. God did not promise Moses that the Hebrews would conquer the Canaanites over night. . . . God promised them victory and he promises us victory too. . . . A counter-offensive is called for. Not a defensive holding action [premillennial dispensationalism]. Not a retreat into the historical shadows. A counter-offensive. It must be a *bottom-up* decentralized offensive campaign. The top-down centralized strategy is the strategy of our opponents [communists]. What we need is a long-term grass roots campaign at very level of politics, economics, and institutional influence, in every region of the country—indeed every region of the world. (North 1986b, 141, 143, italics in original)

In concrete terms, Reconstructionists believe that since the resurrection, we have been living in the kingdom of God. This is a reality that is increasingly real as Christians exercise dominion and a reality that has, as one of its most immediately observable examples, the Christianization of America. With the help of Reconstructionists like Gary North, the lines between the postmillennialism of the Reconstructionists and the premillennialism of the larger conservative Protestant subculture in America have blurred. The two groups have made common cause in returning America to its Christian roots while smoothing over the theological division between pre- and postmillennialism. Whether it is a gradual replacing evil with good, or the faithful remnant picking up the pieces after an apocalyptic cataclysm, Reconstructionist postmillennialism, framed as dominionism and translated at a popular level as the reestablishment of America as a Christian nation, is now a rallying cry for the Christian Right.

The second key idea of Reconstructionism is presuppositional epistemology. According to Rushdoony, there can be no knowledge without presuppositions based in religion. There can therefore be no religious neutrality. There can be no religiously neutral legal systems or economic systems, because all law is someone's view of what is right imposed on others. The originator of law can be God or man, but it can never be impersonal. Nor can there be religiously neutral educational systems or curricula. Believers and nonbelievers have no common ground on which to engage. All presuppositions not derived from God (that is, from the Bible) are derived from human beings' desire to be gods unto themselves, determining good and evil for themselves—in other words, humanism. Sometimes explicitly acknowledged, but often not, the intellectual-theological foundation for the Christian Right's critique of secular humanism is presuppositionalism, as translated through Reconstructionist writings.

Strategies for Change

Reconstructionists developed a two-pronged strategy to bring the nation, in their words, under the lordship of Christ. In the short run, they put efforts into electoral politics and then attempted to bring pressure on elected officials. Their more long-term strategy was to "raise up a generation of leaders" with the skills and the worldview to "usher in the kingdom of God." This is nicely illustrated in the book Ray Sutton wrote for North's Biblical Blueprint Series. Sutton laid out a perfect illustration of the strict family. The family is hierarchical. The father is the undisputed head who exercises biblically based authority. The training of children in right and wrong and the controlling the inheritance of property are important considerations. Sutton saw the state as intrusive and often usurping the legitimate function of the family. The book concluded with a chapter on what families should do in terms of exercising dominion to rebuild a biblical society. These strategies fall into three categories: go to church, separate your children from the humanistic influence of public school, and be involved in politics. After finding a Bible-believing church,

> the second most important thing you and your family can do is to get involved in the *Christian School Movement*. Creationism and a moral environment are the two great forces of Christian education. These have been unleashed on humanist society, and are also challenging a stagnant, compromising brand of Christianity that is all the last generation knew.
> Let's face it, we're just beginning a new program of cultural renewal with our generation. Most of us, and most of the people who read this book, will be first generation Christians who were educated in public schools. Our children will be the ones to begin to see the true resurgence of Christianity and its cultural effects. . . . If we're going to return the family to what God has given it, we will have to put our children in Christian schools and join the fight. . . . *Parents, not the state, have the responsibility of choosing what method of education they'll use.* . . . If we pay the price . . . we can win back ownership of the family. (1986, 138, italics in original)

Rus Walton is another disseminator of Christian Reconstructionist thinking. Each of his works—*In the Spirit of 76* (1975a), *Fundamentals for American Christians* (1979), and *One Nation Under God* (1975b)—lays out a critique of secular humanism, puts forth a biblical political philosophy, and cites Rushdoony and North throughout. Walton's works were widely used in churches in Christian schools. In the foreword to *In the Spirit of 76*, Walton explained his purpose this way: "This is a . . . 'how to' book about winning elections. . . . It is written for those Americans—especially Christians—who want America to be truly a government of and by and for the people; based on God's laws and Christ's teachings that were the foundation of this republic. . . . It is a handbook for political action designed primarily for use in home and group study courses" (1975, xi–xii).

In the Spirit of 76 begins by explaining how small, home-based study groups can develop political sophistication among Christians, and how those study groups can be expanded to become precinct organizations. It details how to contact local party officials, how party structures work, and how to find candidates and "interview" them for appropriateness. Subsequent chapters deal with the various roles within a campaign, conducting polls, organizing a precinct, running a campaign office, producing campaign literature, and using reverse phone directories: all the details of running a political campaign in 192 pages.

Walton also relied on works that were important in disseminating these ideas in churches and Christian schools: Rosalie Salter and Verna Hall's three book series (affectionately called the big red books), Slater's 1965 *Teaching and Learning America's Christian History*, and Hall's1966 *The Christian History of the Constitution of the United States*. Although Slater and Hall were not Reconstructionists, they were figures in patriotic anti-communist movement of the 1950s and 1960s, when Reconstructionists encountered their work and incorporated it into their own efforts to promote the vision of America as a Christian nation. In *The Separation Illusion*, another writer who aligns himself with Christian Reconstructionists, John Whitehead, "documents" the shift from America as a "nation founded on God's law," to one founded on secular humanism.[11] In the prologue, he wrote that:

> in recent years Christians and non-Christians alike have been questioning whether American ever was a Christian nation. Without a doubt it was, but secular historians have eradicated as much Christian influence as possible from history. While they profess to write history objectively, it is a fact that no man is objective about religion. Since all men are made in the image of God, all men are thereby religious, whether it is the Christian religion or the religion of secular humanism they profess. (1977, 17)

The book contains a foreword written by Rushdoony, references his work throughout, and, in the acknowledgments, thanks Rushdoony for the use of his library. Although Tim LaHaye's most recent books are rooted in premillennial dispensationalism (the Left Behind series), his early books—*The Battle for the Mind*, *The Battle for the Family*, and *The Battle for the Public School*—develop the critique of secular humanism (1980, 1982, 1983). The early titles also cite Rushdoony, as well as Whitehead, specifically Whitehead's work drawing on Rushdoony, and illustrate the incorporation of Reconstructionist work and its translation to fundamentalist popular culture. LaHaye took presuppositionalism and theonomy to argue that there are only two sources of knowledge—God and human. All that is not God based (in their understanding of God and the Bible) is humanism. This is all based on Rushdoony, and LaHaye's sources bear that out. The framing of the LaHaye series itself borrows from the Rushdoony's typology, in which biblical authority resides in three distinct—and limited—spheres, namely, family, church, and civil society. This is even more true in LaHaye's later book, *Faith of Our Founding Fathers* (1987), which argues for a Christian nation—published, incidentally, by a small if short-lived press with Reconstructionist ties: Wolgemuth and Hyatt.

Christian Reconstructionists produced much of the early materials to help churches start Christian schools and to help parents home school their children. Some consider Rushdoony to be the father of the contemporary homeschool movements. Rushdoony's 1981 work, *The Philosophy of the Christian Curriculum*, begins with a foreword that puts his efforts in context:

> The chapters of this book were delivered as one or more lectures to a variety of groups. These include the Christian Schools of Ohio conferences; Pensacola Christian College summer session; Via Vera School in North Hollywood, California; the Alabama Christian Schools conventions; the Southern Association of Christian schools; Christian Educations Association of the Southeast conventions; Fairfax Christian School; Trinity Christian School of Mesa, Arizona; the Michigan Association of Christian Schools; and the Church and School of Christian Liberty, Brookfield, Wisconsin. The contents were written over a period of fifteen years, and sometimes expanded as Christian school teachers and administrators by the hundreds discussed these matters with me in question and answer sessions. (1)

The significance of this is that, as early as 1981, Rushdoony's influence in the Christian school and homeschool movements spanned the country, from Virginia (Fairfax) to California (Hollywood) and Florida (Pensacola) to Michigan.

Materials developed by Reconstructionists included why-to and how-to start a school, as well as ready-made curricula. Fairfax Christian School and Pensacola Christian College (PCC) produced much of the early curriculum. PCC remains an important source for curriculum and now has one of the largest programs for training teachers for Christian schools. *The Light and the Glory*, by Peter Marshall and David Manuel, details American history from this perspective, and was widely used as a textbook in home schools and Christian schools (1977). The book sets the stage for exploring "God's hand in American history" with a revisionist version of the voyage of Columbus, and serves as a useful illustration of the curricular materials and their approach. Although history records Columbus having found the Americas while looking for a trade route, Marshall and Manuel claimed that his journals reveal a different motivation. Describing how they came to write the book, they tell a story of a lecture in which Marshall quoted from Columbus:

> "It was the Lord who put into my mind (I could feel his hand upon me) the fact that it would be possible to sail from here to the Indies. All who heard of my project rejected it with laughter, ridiculing me. There is no question that the inspiration came from the Holy Spirit, because he comforted me with rays of marvelous inspiration from the Holy Scriptures. . . . For the execution of the journey to the Indies, I did not make use of *intelligence*, mathematics or maps. It is simply the fulfillment of what Isaiah had prophesied." (17)

They then describe the response of the audience:

> Stunned amazement swept the chapel audience. Did Columbus really think that way? All we had ever read or been taught indicated that Columbus had discovered the New World by accident, while seeking a trade route to the Indies. No mention had ever been made of his faith, let alone that he felt he had been given his life's mission directly by God. Not had we suspected that he felt called to bear the Light of Christ to undiscovered lands and fulfillment of biblical prophecy, or that he had been guided by the Holy Spirit every league of the way—and knew it. Moreover, this was not wishful thinking of some overly enthusiastic fundamentalist; *these were Columbus' own words*. (17).

One needs to turn to the back of the book to learn that the source for this quotation is the "original journal of Christopher Columbus," which "has now been lost," but had been "retold" by a sixteenth-century bishop (Marshall and Manuel 1977, 360).

Reconstructionists quickly learned that to run their schools free from humanistic influence they had to develop legal resources. One of the very first of the organizations founded to promote the Christian Right's agenda through the courts was the Rutherford Society. Founded by the Reconstructionist John Whitehead, the Rutherford Society sought to defend Christian homeschoolers and church-run Christian schools that failed to comply with state truancy and certification laws. Rushdoony's involvement with the Christian Schools of Ohio included serving as an expert legal witness on their behalf in the courts. In 1977, Alan Grover published *Ohio's Trojan Horse: A Warning to Christian Schools Everywhere*. Grover was the executive director of Christian Schools of Ohio, and the book came at the end of a lengthy court battle over the rights of Christian schools. Rushdoony's books, taped lectures, and an unpublished work were cited throughout. Intriguingly, Bob Jones University Press published this book a couple of years before Bob Jones himself famously called Jerry Falwell "the most dangerous man in America" for his involvement in politics, an involvement which Jones thought violated Baptist principles of separation.

Metaphors that Shape Political Thought

People are not often directly aware of the sources for their ideas, and in this case have an interest in hiding links between their views and Christian Reconstructionism. The work of the cognitive scientist George Lakoff offers a useful way of understanding the underlying sources of political discourse. Lakoff used the notion of folk theories to articulate the distinction between what we think is going on in our everyday reality from what studies in cognitive linguistics suggests is really going on. Folk theories about how language works are based in the assumption that words have single, clearly delineated meanings that are related to conditions "out there" (2006, 22). According to Lakoff, abstract notions, those most central to moral and political discourse, consist of simple uncontested "cores" surrounded by unspecified details. "Simple freedom," is relatively uncontested but the "unspecified details" of freedom, such as what counts as illegitimate coercion, are disputed. When someone asserts that "freedom is freedom is freedom," he or she is in part right, as long as we're talking about "simple freedom" (2006, 21–27). Yet when we talk about freedom as it bears on moral and political discourse, that is, when we are filling in the unspecified details, the meaning is much less clear.

Much of our thinking, Lakoff wrote, is not conscious. "We think using conceptual systems not readily accessible to our consciousness and . . . conceptual metaphor is part of our normal thought process" (1996, 32). Moral thinking is imaginative and depends fundamentally on metaphorical understanding (41). For example, one might argue that justice is necessary for freedom. In Lakoff's model, the logical rational connection between these two ideas depends on metaphors that precede them and give them content: justice for some has to do with equal rights but for others is centrally punishment for criminal behavior; freedom might be the opportunity to flourish as a creative human being or an absence of outside constraints. The meanings we bring to these words determine the possible logical connection between them. Summarizing with regard to freedom, he wrote that "freedom is a frame based concept, defined within a mental structure and not just free floating. And even in its simple uncontested form, it is thoroughly metaphorical, which means that, though it is abstract it is grounded viscerally in bodily experience" (38).

Lakoff argued that family model metaphors provide the basis for contemporary political worldviews, and he specified two versions: the strict father and the nurturant parent. Lakoff discussed these two models at length. In his view, the strict father metaphor underlies the conservative understanding of basic values and political discourse. The strict father ideal justifies not only particular arrangements in the family, but also, more broadly, commitments to rewarding compliance with social rules, a pessimistic view of human nature, distrust of the welfare state as enabling dependencies, and support for "bright line" morality in social life, including tough attitudes toward crime. By contrast, the nurturant parent metaphor underlies the liberal and progressive understanding of basic values and political discourse. For Lakoff, the nurturant parent ideal leads to commitments to the common good, an optimistic view of human perfectibility, support for the welfare state as a guarantor of decent standards of living for all citizens, and acceptance of cultural differences.

Although Lakoff's articulation of the dimensions of the nurturant parent metaphor and the progressive worldview is clear and convincing, his explication of the strict father metaphor and the conservative worldview, while correct in some respects, is also deeply flawed.[12] In particular, Lakoff did not trace the origins of this metaphor to the biblical worldview, as interpreted by Reconstructionists. I argue that this connection is essential for understanding the power of the metaphor among evangelicals and other conservative Christians, and, further, for assessing the true influence of Christian Reconstructionists.

Christian Reconstruction and the Christian Right's Family Metaphor

Lakoff argued that conservatives are clearer than liberals are about their views on family and the implications of those views for their political worldview. On this point, Lakoff is correct: the Christian Right's worldview is grounded in a particular understanding of family. Furthermore, it is no accident that their political agenda is clearly connected to the family metaphor. As early as the 1960s, and well into the 1980s, Christian Reconstructionists developed their version, consciously woven into a biblical worldview, and advocated that Christians should go about transforming the world, by bringing it "under the lordship of Christ." This transformation was to have a decidedly political cast: Christians should run for office and elect other Christians, and Christians should remove their children from the influence of the world so as to raise them up to be a generation of leaders to complete the task.

In the forty years that Christian Reconstructionists have been writing and promoting their views, there have been significant changes, developments, variations, and even divisions within the movement. In looking at the early formulation of the Reconstructionist system, I draw primarily on the work of Rushdoony. His earliest works laid the epistemological foundation, and argued that theonomy (that is, God's Law as revealed in the Old and New Testaments) is the necessary foundation for all knowledge (1958, 1961, 1963, 1967). After having developed his critique of all systems of thought not rooted in biblical revelation, in other words, having explained what is wrong with the world, Rushdoony moved to explicate the biblical worldview in his *Institutes of Biblical Law* (1973), that is, lay out a vision for a world based on biblical principles.

Rushdoony began his project with a development of the presuppositionalist epistemology of Cornelius Van Til, a professor of apologetics at Westminster Seminary.[13] For Rushdoony, the fundamental question concerned authority: what is its source and how do we live appropriately in terms of it? His answer was that there are only two possible sources for authority, and therefore law: God (leading to life) and man (leading to death). With Lakoff's model in mind, we see readily that this emphasis on authority lends itself to a strict father metaphor. The family, with the father as authority, mirrors the cosmos with God as authority. Rushdoony makes this explicit in his exploration of the recognition that all legitimate authority for the family, and by extension, for all of society, comes from God.

Rushdoony's *The Institutes of Biblical Law* (*IBL*), something of a culmination of his previous work, is a lengthy commentary on the Ten Commandments and the relevant "case law" from other parts of the Bible.[14] The particular family model developed in *IBL* grounds Rushdoony's worldview and shapes Reconstructionism generally. The larger biblical worldview promoted among fundamentalists and, later, by Christian Right activists flows from this model.

In the introduction, Rushdoony explains that the contemporary Christian notion that the New Testament replaced "the Law" with "Grace" is heresy:

> It is modern heresy that holds that the law of God holds no meaning nor any binding force for man today. It is an aspect of the influence of humanistic and evolutionary thought on the church, and it posits and evolving, developing god. This "dispensational" god expressed himself in an earlier age, then expressed himself by grace alone, and is now perhaps to express himself in some other way. But this is not the God of scripture who grace and law remain the same in every age. (1973, 2)

The purpose of Rushdoony's *IBL* was to institute the "consideration of that law which must govern society, and which shall govern society under God" (1973, 2). He explained that the Ten Commandments lay out general principles of law, which he said even the most antinomian of Christians accept, but that a true understanding of biblical law requires the detailed examination of the application of the principles in specific cases found throughout the Bible. "The law, then, *first* asserts principles, *second*, it cites cases to develop the implications of those principles, and, *third*, the law has as its purpose the direction and *the restitution of God's order*" (1973, 12, italics in original).

We must conclude that authority is not only a religious concept but also a total one. It involves the recognition at every point of our lives of God's absolute law-order. The starting point of this recognition is the family: honor they father and thy mother. Out of this commandment, with its requirement that children submit to and obey their parents under God, comes the basic and fundamental training in religious authority. If the authority of the home is denied, man is in revolution against the fabric and structure of life, and against life itself. Obedience thus carries the promise of life (Rushdoony 1973, 218).[15]

According to Rushdoony, biblical authority is God's authority, delegated to humans who exercise dominion under God's law. He argued that God has ordained that legitimate authority will function in three distinctly separate spheres—civil, ecclesiastical, and familial—but that familial authority is the most fundamental and, in many ways, the model for the others.[16] He went on to write that "*the meaning of the family is thus not to be sought in procreation but in a God-centered authority and responsibility in terms of man's calling to subdue the earth and exercise dominion over it*" (Rushdoony 1973, 164, italics in original).

Although he argued against making too much of the traditional division of the Ten Commandments into the two tablets, one governing the relationship of humans to God and the other relations among humans, he did point out that there are as many commandments dealing with the family as there are in the first tablet:

In the Ten Commandments, four laws deal with the family, three of them directly: "Honor they father and mother," "Thou shalt not commit adultery," "Thou shalt not steal," and "Thou shalt not covet thy neighbors house, thou shalt not covet thy neighbors wife, nor his man-servant, nor his maid-servant, nor his ox, nor his ass, nor anything that is thy neighbor's (Ex 20: 12, 14, 15, 17). The fact that property (and hence theft) were family oriented appears not only in all the law, but in the tenth commandment: to covet, whether property, wife or servants of another was a sin against the neighbor's family. The family is clearly central to the Biblical way of life, and it is the family *under God* which has this centrality. (1973, 159, italics in original)

For Rushdoony, the centrality of the family's authority is evident in the creation account. Before there were gatherings of God's faithful or civil societies, there was the family with its primary function: to exercise dominion over the earth and subdue it. The whole life purpose of humans is seen in the very the calling given Adam, and by implication Eve, in Genesis, and that calling rests on the God given authority to the family.

> Although originally only Adam was created (Gen 2:7), the creation mandate is spoken to Adam in the married estate, and with the creation of woman in mind. Thus, essential to the function of the family under God, and to the role of the man as the head of the household, is *the call to subdue the earth and exercise dominion over it.* . . . Man must bring to all creation God's law-order, exercising power over creation in the name of God. The earth was created "very good" but it was as yet undeveloped in terms of subjugation and possession by man, God's appointed governor. This *government* is particularly the calling of the man as husband and father, and of the family as an institution. (Rushdoony 1973, 163, italics in original)

It might seem obvious that from these views of the family flow certain notions about the relationships between men and women and the relationships between parents and their children. Submission and obedience figure prominently in both relationships. Rushdoony was explicit about this and found in the Fifth Commandment—"honor thy father and mother that thy days may be long upon the land"—much more than one might expect. When men fail to exercise their godly authority, in both the family and in civil society, social chaos ensues. Rushdoony pointed to Isaiah 3:16–26 as an illustration of what happens when men fail to exercise their God-given prerogative of dominion in the family: "Women rule over men; children then gain undue freedom and power and become oppressors of their parents; the emasculated rulers in such a social order lead the people astray and destroy the fabric of society" (1973, 200). His analysis comes from an essentialist view of male and female—a view in which males, by nature, fight for territory and status, and the females' instincts are personal and anarchistic: "The woman becomes absorbed with problems of law and order in a personal way, i.e. when her family and her family's safety are endangered by its decay. The man will be concerned with the problems of society apart from the condition of crisis" (201). In a passage that could be lifted from a Promise Keepers tract more than thirty years later, he wrote this: "Today men have abdicated extensively their masculinity, are less concerned with order and more with gratification. As a result, women, because their security and that of their children is at stake, become involved with the problem of social decay and law and order. Social and political action thus becomes a pressing feminine concern. Their concern underscores the decay of society and the failure of men" (201).

Because this commandment is directed to children, Rushdoony's main focus in this chapter of *IBL* was on discussing the implications of children's place in the family and the mutual relationship and responsibilities between them and their parents. At the center of children's responsibilities is to be obedient. Chief among the parents' responsibilities is to provide an education "in the broadest sense of the word," which means chastisement and schooling (1973, 182). Lakoff's strict father model could have no clearer expression. In a hearty endorsement of corporal punishment, Rushdoony wrote that "parents then [in biblical times] were as inclined to be tenderhearted as now, but the necessity for chastening cannot be set aside by a foolish pity. Chastisement can be a lifesaver to the child" (182).

The Family and the School

In the discussion of schooling, Rushdoony laid out what has become for many in the Christian Right the basic framework for understanding education:

> It needs more than ever to be stressed that the best and truest educators are parents under God. The greatest school is the family. In learning, no act of teaching in any school or university compares to the routine task of mothers in teaching a babe who speaks no language the mother tongue in so short a time. No other task in education is equal to this. The moral training of the child, the discipline of good habits, is an inheritance from the parents to the child which surpasses all other. The family is the first and most basic school of man. (1973, 185)

Rushdoony argued that not only is the family the most influential school, but it is also to the family, and not the church or the state, that God has given the authority to train children. Public schools, according to Rushdoony, usurp the authority of the family, and in the process destroy the family. Furthermore, he argued, public schools contribute to the destruction of society: "The statist school, moreover, basically trains women to be men; it is not surprising that so many are unhappy to be women. Nor are men any happier, in that dominion in modern education is transferred to the state, and man is progressively emasculated" (1973, 191). In words that could have come from the conservative commentator and author Christina Hoff Sommers, he asserted that "the major casualty in modern education is the male student, since any education which diminishes man's calling to exercise dominion also diminishes man to the same degree" (1973, 184). Reconstructionists largely agree on this point. Somewhat more contentious, however, is Rushdoony's view that church-run schools usurp the authority of the family.

Just what does this family-centered education look like? Remember that Rushdoony's presuppositionalism asserts that all truth is rooted in biblical Christianity. Education is to be Bible-centered. Efforts at critical thinking and concerns over freedom of inquiry are humanistic—rooted in a false religion. Students are to learn in obedience; teaching the value of questioning, let alone the value of challenging authority, is not part of the curriculum. Even student government would seem to violate the biblically mandated structure: "The child has no right to govern his parents, the student their school, nor the employees their employer" (1973, 192).

The Family and "Economic Freedom"

Not only does this assertion illustrate the epistemological basis for education and the relationship between the family and education, it also shows the use of this family metaphor for filling out the contested areas of what Lakoff called economic freedom. Lakoff developed a general notion of economic freedom and laid out his understanding of the conservative framing of economic freedom (2006, 149). He saw clearly that conservative views of economic freedom are individualistic, private, fundamental to other freedoms, and that they are based in nature. What he missed, although it provides evidence for his larger theory, is that very specific ideas about the family lie behind these views. The commission given to Adam and Eve in the garden is, in essence, an economic mission: be fruitful and multiply; fill up the earth and subdue it. Rushdoony found this in the Fifth Commandment, about which he said, the "first general principle inherent in this law . . . is the law of inheritance" (1973, 165–66).

> What we inherit from our parents is life itself, and also the wisdom of their faith and experience that they transmit to us. . . . we do not enter an empty world. The houses, orchards, fields and flocks are all the handiwork of the past, and we are richer for this past and must honor it. . . . The basic and central inheritance of culture and all that it includes, faith, training, wisdom, wealth, love, common ties and traditions are severed and denied where parents and elders are not honored. (166)

Rushdoony explored the relationship between family, property, and liberty. Here, family members have property rights in each other. "It can be said that a man holds his wife as his property and his children also. But because his wife and children have certain, individual, particular, special, and continuing claims on him, they have a property right in him" (175). Western metaphors of progress, and even postmillennialism, are the second general principle derived from the family metaphor rooted in the Fifth Commandment (166).

> In Biblical faith, the family inherits from the past in order to grow firmly into the future. . . . Scripture declares, "Therefore shall a man leave his father and mother and cleave unto his wife; and they shall be one flesh" (Gen. 2:24). Marriage calls for a move forward by the man and his wife; they break with the old families to create a new one. They remain tied to the old families in that both represent a cultural inheritance from two specific families. They remain tied further by their religious duty to honor their parents. The growth is real, and the dependence is real: the new clearly and plainly grows out of and realizes the potentiality of the old. (Rushdoony 1973, 167)

Opposition to abortion is rooted in the family as understood by Rushdoony, and he tied his views to biblical law. In a discussion often cited by his opponents, Rushdoony examined the law in Deuteronomy 23:17 pertaining to incorrigible youth. The rebellious youth are to be chastened and, if they will not reform, they are to be brought before the elders of the city who are to put them to death. Rushdoony carefully explained this in detail—although the explanation is not likely to make the solution seem more reasonable to modern ears. Following the explanation closely, however, is necessary to illustrate the relationship to abortion. In fact, he said, the passage actually limits parental authority to chastisement and only the representatives of the community as a whole had the right to execute the death penalty. In a legal-cultural context, it is in Roman law, not Christian law, that fathers had an absolute right over the life and death of their children (1973, 186). Rushdoony argued against the legalization of abortion (remember, this is before Roe v. Wade) as a return to Roman pagan law in which fathers were the life givers, and had, therefore, the right to take life.

Rushdoony grounded his conservative notions of limited government in this aspect of the law:

> Life is created by God, governed by His law, and to be lived only in terms of His law-word. All transgression faces ultimate judgment; capital offenses require the death penalty here and now, by civil authorities. *Neither the parents nor the state are the creators of life, and therefore cannot fix the terms of life.* In this fact is man's greatest safeguard for freedom; the godly state does indeed deal severely with offenders, but it strictly limits the power of the state . . . the power of the parents is similarly limited. (1973, 190, italics in original)

In a section that clearly fits Lakoff's model, Rushdoony argued that freedom itself is found most fully in obedience, as understood in the familial relationship described in the Fifth Commandment: "It is commonly held, by the humanistic mind, that the unquestioning and faithful obedience required by law of children is destructive of the mind. . . . But the best functioning mind is the obedient and disciplined mind. The child who is disciplined into obedience is not the servile youth but the free man" (1973, 104–5).

Contemporary Influence

As we move into the twenty-first century, the influence of Christian Reconstruction on the Christian Right is evident. I note three dimensions of that influence here: groups that seek to promote a biblical worldview through workshops, seminars, and publications; efforts focused on young people to train them to be a generation of dominion takers; and the impact of Reconstructionists on parts of the right-to-life movement. Each of these efforts is rooted in the Christian Right's understanding of traditional family values. Although these influences are important, I argue that the most important source of influence of Christian Reconstructionism is through the family ideal it developed and promulgated.

Promoting the Biblical Worldview

Organizations like American Vision, Summit Ministries, and Christian Worldview Network train parents, teachers, pastors, and activists in developing family-oriented biblical worldviews at conferences around the country, some of which are called Worldview Weekend. Each of these organizations illustrates the contemporary expression of the influence of Reconstructionists.

The Reconstructionist leader, author of more than twenty books, and radio host Gary DeMar founded American Vision in 1978. On its website, the organization describes its vision as the effort to build "an America that recognizes the sovereignty of God over all of life and where Christians apply a Biblical worldview to every facet of society. This future America will be a 'city on a hill' drawing all nations to the Lord Jesus Christ and teaching them to subdue the earth for the advancement of His Kingdom."[17]

Much of the website is devoted to promoting postmillennialism, which they do through books, a monthly magazine, *The Biblical Worldview,* various DVDs, and seminars. The banner headline for the website announces to reprinting of David Chilton's postmillennial commentary on the book of Revelation, *Days of Vengeance* (1987). DeMar's website boasts of his connections to the larger world of conservative Protestantism. DeMar has been interviewed by *Time* magazine, *CNN*, *MSNBC*, *FOX*, the *BBC*, and *Sean Hannity*. He has held numerous radio and television interviews, including the *Bible Answer Man*, hosted by Hank Hanegraaff. Newspaper interviews have also appeared in the *Washington Times*, *Toledo* (Ohio) *Blade*, the *Sacramento Bee*, the *Atlanta Journal/Constitution*, and the *Chicago Tribune*.

In terms of the relationship of Reconstructionists to the larger world of the Christian Right, another point of interest is that Brandon Vallorani recently joined American Vision after leaving the organization Answers in Genesis, which is widely known for its new, 45,000 square foot Creation Museum in Cincinnati, Ohio. According to Vallorani, the Answers in Genesis website receives more than 5 million hits each year and produces a creationist radio show heard on more than 650 Christian radio stations.

In another example, the gateway to the Worldview Weekend conferences is an online worldview test developed by Brannon Howse, president and founder of Worldview Weekend.[18] The test is on a website sponsored by Worldview Weekend, Summit Ministries, and the American Family Association (Donald Wildmon's organization known for its boycotts of television shows and movies deemed to be antifamily). The purpose of the test seems to be to rate test-takers' worldviews in relationship to what the organizations see as a biblical worldview, and then to encourage test-takers to attend conferences and buy books that will help them develop more biblical worldviews. The test consists of eighty-five questions that cover issues relating to civil government, economics, education, family, law, religion, and science. The questions are phrased as statements with which test-takers are asked to agree or disagree. Sometimes the answer they consider to be correct is strongly agree, and sometimes it is strongly disagree. I took the test, answering as if I were a Reconstructionist, and scored a ninety-eight.[19] Many of the questions, indeed, presume answers that would be common among most evangelical and fundamentalist Christians: abortion, homosexuality, science and creation, the nature of Jesus and the Holy Spirit, and the reliability of the Bible. Other questions move closer to promoting the political views of Reconstructionists on issues less likely to be recognized by evangelicals and fundamentalists in general: concern over the United Nations and opposition to control of education at the federal level. Still other questions, especially when taken together, represent rather distinct perspectives that tie directly to Reconstructionist views (this is a sampling rather than an exhaustive list):

- "The Bible, rightly divided, should be the foundation for all our beliefs, actions, and conduct." Reconstructionists would strongly agree. Not only is this an example of presuppositionalism and theonomy, it also uses a phrase commonly found in Reconstructionist discourse: the Bible "rightly divided."

- "Since God is not the author of law, the author of law is man. In other words, the law is the law simply because the highest human authority, which is the state, has said it's the law and is able to back it up by force."

- "Both secular Humanism and Marxism are religious worldviews." Reconstructionists would strongly agree. Although many Christians see secular humanism as a religion, I contend that it was Rushdoony who made it a popular view. My claim is bolstered by the extent to which he and Gary North wrote about Marxism as religion.

- "Legislating morality is a violation of the separation of church and state." Rushdoony argues that all law is someone's view of morality.

- "The Bible is a consistent revelation from beginning to end." Reconstructionists would strongly agree. This is a challenge to dominant fundamentalist dispensationalism, which teaches that God reveals himself differently at different ages.

- "A Christian can develop a biblical worldview for every major area of life by studying the Bible from beginning to end in context." Reconstructionists would strongly agree. They call this "making every thought captive to Christ."

- "Ultimately every individual will bow their knee and confess with their mouth that Jesus Christ is Lord." Reconstructionists would strongly agree; this is a favorite text to support postmillennialism.

- "Biblically minded Christians should look at the issues of the world as falling into two categories, the secular and the sacred." This is the presuppositionalism that Reconstructionists popularized as the myth of neutrality.

- "The more a government resembles a pure democracy the more disorder and confusion occur." Although Reconstructionists debate this point among themselves, Rushdoony has been quite public about his critique of democracy as an ungodly political system.

- "Family, church and state are institutions ordained by God." These are Rushdoony's three spheres of biblical authority ordained by God. This is perhaps the clearest example.

The point is not that only a Reconstructionist could hold these views, but that these views are central tenets of Reconstruction—rooted in Rushdoony's notions of the family—and are promoted here in exactly the same phrasing as they have been promoted by Reconstructionists for forty years.[20]

Developing a New Generation of Leaders

At the same time, the strategy of transforming the world by developing a generation of leaders not "polluted" by the humanism in secular education is also bearing fruit. Families are considered the central bulwark against secular education, and many of the Christian Right's organizations and institutions exist solely to assist in this task. One well-known example is Patrick Henry College (PHC) in Purcellville, Virginia. Home School Legal Defense Association founder and president Mike Farris founded this college to reach out to students who had been educated in home schools and Christian schools. Institutions like PHC seek to provide an alternative to the liberalism and humanism of secular higher education. The college has received considerable media coverage, given its proximity to Washington, D.C., and is said to have placed more interns on Capitol Hill than any other institution of higher education in the country. Articles about PHC have appeared in the *Chronicle of Higher Education*, the *New York Times*, *USA Today*, the *Economist*, and the *New Yorker*.[21] The school has also been the subject of a documentary film titled *God's Next Army*.

Rushdoony's biblical law seems to have contemporary expression in a recent controversy at the college. As reported in the *Chronicle*, the controversy arose after a student complained about the weight given to nonbiblical sources in the liberal arts curriculum. Presuppositionalist in its epistemology, the college faced controversy over academic freedom. One faculty member was fired over the incident, and others resigned in support. "They have also raised questions that cut to the heart of Christian higher education, such as can a Christian find truth in the writings of non-Christians?" *Chronicle* writer Tom Bartlett observed. "What role should the Bible play in the classroom? . . . The controversy has pitted the college's president and founder . . . against many of its professors. He has challenged their fidelity to a biblical worldview" (2006).

Steeped in dominionism, the school trains students, to borrow the words of Gary North, to "replace evil with good," and to "replace [the radicals] steadily with our own competence" (1986b, 141). The *New Yorker's* Hannah Rosin explained it this way:

> Of the school's sixty-one graduates through the class of 2004, two have jobs in the White House; six are on the staffs of conservative members of Congress; eight are in federal agencies; and one helps Senator Rick Santorum of Pennsylvania and his wife Karen home-school their six children. Two are at the F.B.I., and another worked for the Coalition Provisional Authority in Iraq. Last year, the col-

lege began offering a major in strategic intelligence; the students learn the history of covert operations and take internships that allow them to graduate with a security clearance ("Annals of Education God and Country: A College Trains Young Christians to be Politicians," June 27, 2005).[22]

The Right-to-Life Movement

Finally, in what conservative Christians understand as the cornerstone of family values, the abortion issue remains a key component of the political agenda, the organizing strategy, and the very identity of many. No doubt, many sources have shaped the Christian Right's approach to this issue. Some parts of the right-to-life movement that identify directly with Reconstructionists: Randall Terry, founder of Operation Rescue, the group that used nonviolent civil disobedience to block access to abortion clinics in the 1980s and 1990s, but also more radical activists who advocate or defend the use of violence to stop abortion. For example, Mike Bray, who served time in Virginia for firebombing clinics and who has defended the Army of God in print and in the news, and Paul Hill, who was executed in Florida for killing an abortion provider, have identified themselves with Christian Reconstruction. Terry has since converted to Roman Catholicism and presumably has left his Reconstructionist leanings behind.[23] His conversion was cheered by Gary North, who said, "Our gain is their loss," citing Terry's infidelity and apparent political ambitions.[24] Mike Bray's views are documented in Mark Juergensmeyer's *Terror in the Mind of God* (2000) and Paul Hill's ties to the Reconstructionist movement in Carol Mason's *Killing for Life* (2002). It is interesting, however, that Gary North carried on a written correspondence with Paul Hill, while Hill was in prison, arguing that Christian Reconstruction did not justify Hill's violence and then repudiated Hill in the same essay in which he wrote about Terry: "On September 4, 2003, I sent the following information to this mailing list: Two men virtually eliminated anti-abortion activism in the United States after 1994: Paul Hill and Randall Terry. They became the visible symbols of anti-abortion activism, both for the pro-abortionists and for anti-abortionists. The two of them cut the heart out of the activists" (Juergensmeyer 2000, 29).

Four years after Hill's crime, in 1998, Terry, the founder of Operation Rescue, abandoned his wife of nineteen years, along with their four children, three of whom were adopted, and then declared bankruptcy, so that the National Organization of Women would stop legal suits against him.[25]

Conclusion

The influence of the Christian Reconstructionists in the Christian Right persists today, though it is far more explicitly present in some places than in others. Although some contemporary groups do embrace the label Reconstructionist, others do not. Personal identifications are, however, not the most important source of Christian Reconstructionist influence on the Christian Right. As Lakoff argued, we think in metaphors, and Christian Reconstructionists shaped the underlying metaphor of the Christian Right in the 1960s and 1970s, long before the movement had a public presence.

Through the 1960s and 1970s, Christian Reconstructionists developed a critique of contemporary culture, a critique rooted in Rushdoony's defense of biblical law and his interpretation of it in terms of the role of the family in God's plan for humans. From the family flows the dominion mandate and postmillennialism. Other Reconstructionist work either fills out the meaning of this basic commitment or develops a strategy for addressing the social-political problems they see through political engagement and education. Through the end of the twentieth century, conservative Christians returned to the political process, and both home-schooling and Christian schooling exploded. Underneath both of those developments was the Reconstructionists' framing of the problems and the solutions.

Glossary

- *Dominion*: From Genesis. God told Adam and Eve to have dominion over the earth. Reconstructionists understand this as the basic reality of human existence: created for dominion, inhibited by the Fall, but restored to that purpose by the resurrection. It is tied to traditional notions in reformed theology about stewardship and work in general.

- *Millennialism*: Refers to the Christian belief in the thousand-year reign in the Kingdom of God. Some believe that it will be in heaven and others believe it will happen on earth. Some believe it will be a thousand years, and others "very long time."

- *Postmillennialism*: Refers to a particular belief about the millennium. Postmillennialists believe that the Kingdom of God was established, when Jesus rose from the dead, but that Christians must work to make the Kingdom real, and that Jesus will return when the work is completed. Thus his return is postmillennial. Many of the Puritans who came to build a model of the Kingdom, as well as the nineteenth-century social reformers in America who thought they were building God's Kingdom had this view. This also is the view of the subjects of this paper.

- *Premillennialism*: Refers to a particular belief about the millennium.

This is the dominant view in contemporary American Protestantism. Premillennialists believe that life on Earth will get worse until there is a great cataclysm after which Jesus will return and establish the Kingdom. Thus his return is premillennial.

- *Presuppositionalism:* A philosophical view that is the basis of reconstruction. Presuppositionalists believe that knowledge always starts with assumptions, which are not prove-able. In this case, the relevant assumptions are from either the God of Revelation or human reason. This is how Reconstructionists conclude that there is not middle ground and that all systems of thought not based in their understanding of the Bible are really one system: humanism.

- *Theonomy:* Literally, God's Law. Also called biblical law by Reconstructionists. Reconstructionists believe that all law should be from the Bible, which is the appropriate basis for all of society. This would be the legal system governing a theocracy.

Notes

1. Old School Presbyterians, such as Archibald Alexander and Charles Hodge at Princeton, maintained that strict Calvinist orthodoxy was essential to the Christian faith. They opposed New School Presbyterians. Hall in his chapter writes about Lyman Beecher, a preeminent New School Presbyterian. The Old Presbyterians also opposed voluntary associations, such as those developed by Beecher and other New School Presbyterians. Old School Presbyterians believed that such activities belonged within the church where they could be guided by a confessional stance that emphasized the sovereignty of God and man's debased natural state.

2. My research has been strongly encouraged Juergensmeyer (see also Barron 1992; English 2003).

3. Phillips has been also been president of the U.S. Taxpayers' Party, recently renamed the Constitution Party, and twice its candidate for the U.S. presidency.

4. Howard Phillips made this comment at a birthday celebration for Rushdoony's eightieth. The text of Phillips's speech is available at: http://www.ustaxpayers.org/hp-rushdoony-bday.htm (accessed February 3, 1998).

5. Wilcox is referring to Rushdoony's commentary on a passage from Leviticus in which the death penalty prescribed when a young man refuses to reform.

6. My emphasis on Reconstructionists is not an attempt to undermine the importance of Francis Schaeffer as a figure. Some call Schaeffer the most important evangelical theologian of the twentieth century and his influence in terms of encouraging evangelicals to engage the world is undeniable. Schaeffer's work, however, remained largely philosophical and theological— promoted though books and the retreat centers. There developed no move-

ment that included anything comparable to the Reconstructionist's efforts at strategies for application (for more on his work and life, see Schaeffer 2007).

7. Also on staff at Chalcedon Foundation was Greg Bahnsen, whose *Theonomy and Christian Ethics* was in press by 1974. Two years later, Bahnsen was teaching at Reformed Theological Seminary in Jackson Mississippi, and the future Reconstructionist pastor and theologian James Jordan was one of his students. Jordan also wrote for JCR. By 1978, one of the earliest dates set for the beginnings of the Christian right, David Chilton, who would later write the definitive works on Reconstructionist postmillennialism (1985, 1987) had joined the staff at Chalcedon and was writing for JCR. Also by 1978, Rus Walton had already founded his Plymouth Rock Foundation to disseminate Reconstructionist ideas in churches and Christian schools and by 1975 had written *One Nation Under God*, which advocated Christian involvement in politics for the purpose of returning American to its biblical roots.

8. Among evangelicals, Schaeffer popularized the critique of secular humanism. In fact, Schaeffer and Rushdoony were aware of each other (1968, 1976). When I visited Schaeffer's L'Abri fellowship in Switzerland in the late 1980s, the staff and other guests readily discussed the Reconstructionist movement.

9. Reconstructionalist postmillennialism is based on an early work by J. Marcellus Kik (1955). Kik was a faculty member at Westminster Seminary where many of the Reconstructionists studied. His later book was a full blown defense of postmillennialism and had an introduction by Rushdoony (1971). The biographical note on the back cover states that Kik had been an associate editor of *Christianity Today*. Rushdoony's own postmillennial exposition was also published in1971. Then in 1984, David Chilton wrote a much more detailed and accessible postmillennial work.

10. The classic reformed theology view of stewardship and dominion focused on constructing a Christian world, a prerequisite for the Second Coming. Among the evangelical left, stewardship has a somewhat different meaning. Drawing on Genesis 1:26, they argue that man is holding the world in trust for God and will be judged on the basis of their stewardship. When man allows environmental degradation to occur, he is being a poor steward and will be found wanting. The liberal view of stewardship, however, has made inroads among more conservative groups, most notably the National Association of Evangelicals, which has taken a strong environmental stance.

11. John Whitehead gained fame as the attorney for Paula Jones in her legal dealings with President Bill Clinton.

12. Lakoff is a progressive and sees his work as a blueprint for reinvigoration of the Left. In fact, some of his critics have charged that his solution is too simple, that we cannot just overhaul American political culture by simply changing the frame of the debate. I have no such agenda and the limitations of his political strategy are not my concern. I am interested in a theoretical model that helps explain how our political culture works, and I

think his model offers that. What I think needs to be developed, however, is the portrait of conservatives made possible by this model. Despite his efforts, Lakoff often details conservatism through his own progressive worldview, and therefore, still ends up with a caricature.

13. Apologetics is the field of study devoted to the systematic defense of Christianity from attacks. In the 1920s, van Til developed what came to be known as presuppositionalist apologetics. Unlike evidentiary apologetics, this form of apologetics did not marshal evidence in any effort to convince non-believers of the rightness of their beliefs. Instead, it relied on faith, and adherents argued that Christians could find no common ground with nonbelievers (for more on van Til, the Orthodox Presbyterian Church, Westminster Seminar, and Old Princeton, see Marsden 1987).

14. The first two volumes run 890 pages. It is a quaint bit of lore in Reconstructionist circles that Rushdoony, through the end of his life, wrote in longhand. In the preface, he thanks his wife for typing the manuscript.

15. This is, of course, a reference to the second part of the Fifth Commandment: "honor thy father and mother that thou days shall be long upon the land."

16. It is on exactly this point that the most significant division exists within Reconstruction. Later thinkers, North and Jordan especially, have argued that the Church, with its ecclesiastical authority, is preeminent. This disagreement has implications for education, such as whether church related Christian schools are permissible (see, for example, Jordan 1986).

17. http://www.americanvision.org/about/ministry (accessed March 19, 2009).

18. http://worldviewweekend.com/test (accessed March 19, 2009).

19. The one question I "missed," had to do with whether the notion "God helps those who help themselves" is in the Bible. Apparently, it is not, but I had in mind such texts as I Corinthians 15:58 "Labor is not in vain in the Lord," Proverbs 13:11 "He that gathereth by labor shall increase," and 2 Thessalonians 3:10 "For even when we were with you, this we commanded you, that if any would not work, neither should he eat."

   The correct answer seems challengeable from inside the worldview they are espousing; in other words, I out-proof-texted them; I think I got 100 percent.

20. I know of no Conservative Christian group promoting postmillennialism that does not have ties to Reconstructionists.

21. My thanks go to Bethany Daniel, at the time a student in my Religion as Culture class at the University of North Florida, for these citations.

22. http://www.newyorker.com/archive/2005/06/27/050627fa_fact?currnet Page=all (accessed June 13, 2008).

23. "Randall Terry Converts to Catholicism," June 9, 2006, http://unscripted remars.blogspot.com/2006/06/randall-terry-converts-to-catholicism-html (accessed June 20, 2007).

24. Gary North, http://www.operationsaveamerica.org/articles/articles/world-mag-exposes-randall-terry.htm (accessed June 20, 2007).

25. Ibid.

References

Balmer, Randall. 2006. *Thy Kingdom Come*. New York: Basic Books.

Bartlett, Thomas. 2006. "Give Me Liberty or I Quit." *The Chronicle of Higher Education* 52(37)(May 17): A.10.

Barron, Bruce. 1992. *Heaven on Earth?* Grand Rapids, Mich.: Zondervan.

Chilton, David. 1985. *Paradise Restored*. Tyler, Tex.: Reconstruction Press.

———. 1987. *Days of Vengeance*. Ft. Worth, Tex.: Dominion Press.

Diamond, Sara. 1995. *Roads to Dominion*. New York: Guilford Press.

———. 1998. *Not by Politics Alone*. New York: Guilford Press.

English, Adam C. 2003. "Christian Reconstruction after Y2K: Gary North, the New Millennium, and Religious Liberty in America." In *New Religious Movements and Religious Liberty*, edited by Derek Davis and Barry Hankins. Waco, Tex.: Baylor University Press.

Goldberg, Michele. 2006. *Kingdom Coming*. New York: W. W. Norton.

Grover, Alan N. 1977. *Ohio's Trojan Horse*. Greenville, S.C.: Bob Jones University Press.

Hall, Verna M. 1966. *The Christian History of the Constitution of the United States*. San Francisco: Foundation for Christian Education.

Ingersoll, Julie. 2003. *Evangelical Christian Women: War Stories in the Gender Battles*. New York: New York University Press.

———. 2006. "Religion and Politics: The Impact of the Religious Right." In *Faith in America*, edited by Charles Lippy. New York: Praeger Press.

Jordan, James B. 1986. *The Sociology of the Church: Essays in Reconstruction*. Tyler, Tex.: Geneva Ministries.

Juergensmeyer, Mark. 2000. *Terror in the Mind of God*. Berkeley: University of California Press.

Kik, J. Marcelus. 1955. *Revelation Twenty: An Exposition*. Philadelphia, Pa.: Presbyterian and Reformed Publishing.

———. 1971. *An Eschatology of Victory*. Philadelphia, Pa.: Presbyterian and Reformed Publishing.

LaHaye, Tim. 1980. *The Battle for the Mind*. Old Tappan, N.J.: Fleming H. Revell.

———. 1982. *The Battle for the Family*. Old Tappan, N.J.: Fleming H. Revell.

———. 1983. *The Battle for the Public School*. Old Tappan, N.J.: Fleming H. Revell.

———. 1987. *Faith of our Founding Fathers*. Old Tappan, N.J.: Fleming H. Revell.

Lakoff, George. 1996. *Moral Politics: How Liberals and Conservatives Think*. Chicago: University of Chicago Press.

———. 2006. *Whose Freedom?: The Battle over America's Most Important Idea*. New York: Farrar, Straus and Giroux.

Marsden, George. 1987. *Reforming Fundamentalism*. Grand Rapids, Mich.: William B. Eerdmans.

———. 1991. "Preachers of Paradox," in *Understanding Fundamentalism and Evangelicalism*. Grand Rapids, Mich.: William B. Eerdmans.

Marshall, Peter and David Manuel. 1977. *The Light and the Glory*. Mantoursville, Pa.: Lamp Post Publishing.

Mason, Carol. 2002. *Killing for Life*. Ithaca, N.Y.: Cornell University Press.

North, Gary. 1973. *Introduction to Christian Economics*. Vallecito, Calif.: Craig Press.

———. 1976. *None Dare Call It Witchcraft*. New Rochelle, N.Y.: Arlington House.

———. 1983a. *The Last Train Out: The Essential Survival Manual for the 80s and Beyond*. Ft. Worth, Tex.: American Bureau of Economic Research.

———. 1983b. *Government by Emergency*. Ft. Worth, Tex.: American Bureau of Economic Research.

———. 1985. *Moses and Pharaoh: Power Religion Versus Dominion Religion*. Tyler, Tex.: Institute for Christian Economics.

———. 1986a. *Fighting Chance: Ten Feet to Survival*. Cave Junction, Oregon: Oregon Institute of Science and Medicine.

———. 1986b. *Conspiracy: A Biblical View*. Ft. Worth, Tex.: Dominion Press.

———. 1986c. *Honest Money*. Biblical Blueprint Series. Forth Worth, Tex.: Dominion Press.

———. 1986d. *Marx's Religion of Revolution: Regeneration Through Chaos*. Tyler, Tex.: Institute for Christian Economics.

———. 1987a. *Healer of the Nations*. Biblical Blueprint Series. Forth Worth, Tex.: Dominion Press.

———. 1987b. *Inherit the Earth*. Biblical Blueprint Series. Forth Worth, Tex.: Dominion Press.

———. 1987c. *Liberating Planet Earth*. Biblical Blueprint Series. Forth Worth, Tex.: Dominion Press.

———. 1987d. *The Pirate Economy*. Ft. Worth, Tex.: American Bureau of Economic Research.

Rushdoony, Rousas John. 1958. *By What Standard?* Philadelphia, Pa.: Presbyterian and Reformed Publishing.

———. 1961. *Intellectual Schizophrenia*. Philadelphia, Pa.: Presbyterian and Reformed Publishing.

———. 1963. *The Messianic Character of American Education*. Nutley, N.J.: Craig Press.

———. 1967. *The Mythology of Science*. Nutley, N.J.: Craig Press.

———. 1973. *The Institutes of Biblical Law*. Philadelphia, Pa.: Presbyterian and Reformed Publishing.

———. 1981. *The Philosophy of the Christian Curriculum*. Vallecito, Calif.: Ross House Books.

Schaeffer, Francis. 1976. *How Should We then Live*. Old Tappan, N.J.: Fleming H. Revell.

———. 1968. *The God Who is There*. Downers Grove, Ill.: Intervarsity Press.

———. 2007. *Crazy for God*. Cambridge, Mass.: Carroll and Graf.

Shupe, Anson. 1977. "Christian Reconstruction and the Angry Rhetoric of Neo-Postmillennialism." In *Millennium, Messiah's and Mayhem*, edited by Thomas Robbins and Susan J. Palmer. New York: Routlege.

Slater, Rosalie. 1965. *Teaching and Learning America's Christian History*. San Francisco: Foundation for Christian Education.

Sommers, Christian Hoff. 1994. *Who Stole Feminism?* New York: Simon & Schuster.

Sutton, Ray. 1986. *Who Owns the Family? God or the State*. Tyler, Tex.: Biblical Blueprint Series.

Walton, Rus. 1975a. *The Spirit of 76*. Washington, D.C.: Third Century Publishers.

———. 1975b. *One Nation Under God*. Nashville, Tenn.: Thomas Nelson.

———. 1979. *Fundamentals for American Christians.* Nyack, N.Y.: Parson Publishing.

Wilcox, Clyde. 1996. *Onward Christian Soldiers? The Religious Right in American Politics.* Boulder, Colo.: Westview Press.

Woodberry, Robert, and Christian Smith. 1998. "Fundamentalism and Conservative Protestants in America." *Annual Review of Sociology* 24(1998): 25–56.

Chapter 7

The Christian Right, Public Reason, and American Democracy

NATHANIEL KLEMP AND STEPHEN MACEDO

O VER THE last thirty years, the Christian Right has become an increasingly powerful voice in American democracy. From Jerry Falwell's Moral Majority to Pat Robertson's Christian Coalition to James Dobson's Focus on the Family, Christian Right organizations have mobilized conservative Christians into political action, largely though not exclusively on behalf of a conservative moral agenda. Throughout this period of heightened engagement, the rhetoric of Christian Right activists on issues like same-sex marriage and abortion has been couched in what we call a *narrative of victimization*. Religious citizens, it is claimed, have been unfairly silenced and marginalized by liberal elites on the courts, in the academy, and in Hollywood.

Christian Right activists portray people of faith as an embattled minority—victims of a subtle form of religious persecution. This narrative has been echoed by academic critics of liberalism and deliberative democracy, who suggest that the primary threats to democracy come not from overzealous religious groups seeking to impose their sectarian agenda, but from the exclusionary ideals of democracy and public discourse espoused by liberal elites (Eberle 2002; Stout 2004; Young 1990). On this account—popular both in activist circles and the academy, and which is also explored by Rhys Williams's essay in this volume—norms of advocacy promoted by liberal elites have made the public realm hostile to religious persons and religious discourse (chapter 5). This narrative helps activists mobilize supporters while eliciting the sympathies of fellow citizens concerned about the alleged exclusion of Christians from the public square.

We argue that such narratives of victimization obscure the complex interactions among Christian Right political organizations and democratic politics. Drawing on Nathaniel Klemp's interviews with Christian Right activists and critics, we describe the actual rhetorical strategies of the Christian Right, and find that some leaders of the Christian Right support and practice the ideals of public reason and democratic deliberation that are supposed to be the instruments of their marginalization.[1] Our account is thus part critique and part defense of the rhetorical practices of Christian Right activists. The Christian Right's victim narrative should be greeted with skepticism. We cautiously applaud those leading Christian Right figures who defend liberal democratic ideals of public reason and public justification while speaking in the language of shared faith to fellow believers. Some argumentative strategies deployed by the Christian Right do, however, furnish some cause for concern.

To defend this mixed assessment, we first examine what we call the Christian Right's *two-tiered rhetoric*. When speaking to internal audiences, Christian Right activists often frame their political grievances and ambitions around scripture and explicit appeals to faith. In James Dobson's newsletter to members of Focus on the Family, for instance, he argues that same-sex marriage is wrong because "God designed marriage between a man and a woman as the first system of interdependent relationships" (2003). This internal tier of rhetoric enables leaders to reinforce a sense of moral separation between conservative Christians and the broader public.

When speaking to more pluralistic outside audiences, however, leaders of the Christian Right invoke a second tier of rhetoric. They recast their agenda in more widely accessible terms—in language that appeals to commonly shared public values and empirical evidence (Hardisty 1999; Herman 1997; Hertzke 1998; Klemp 2007; Moen 1992; Shields 2007). Rather than invoking the word of God or scripture, leaders like Dobson will publicly oppose same-sex marriage on the grounds that it opens the door to polygamy and harms children. This second tier of public rhetoric enables activists to reach out to nonbelievers on common terms that all citizens, not just Christians, can accept.

Several subsidiary aspects of the Christian Right's two-tiered rhetorical strategy are also worthy of attention. First, the Christian Right's public arguments are often couched in the language of social science. Second, the Christian Right selectively chooses issues that have the greatest likelihood of success. Finally, despite their reliance on public arguments and social scientific evidence when advocating policies in the public realm, Christian Right activists believe that their positions are also supported by religious "truths" or postulates of faith. For many, these grounds—which are not readily or straightforwardly subject to empirical verification or scientific refutation—seem to be the ultimate religious reasons for the positions they advocate.

The Christian Right's two-tiered strategy and its various supporting elements might be interpreted as an inauthentic and manipulative attempt to conceal the Christian Right's true political ambitions. According to critics like Jean Hardisty, for instance, the deployment of two tiers of rhetoric represents a "stealth" effort, in which Christian Right activists in the public realm manipulate fellow citizens by "camouflaging" their "Christian agenda" (1999, 114). Some also suspect that reliance on social scientific evidence is insincere: that evidence plays no independent role for those on the Christian Right, but is only cited opportunistically—as a sort of cherry-picking—to bolster established dogmatic claims. Moreover, it might be charged that the Christian Right has hidden its real agenda and its real reasons by seeking to advance only those policies that have broad appeal, and then defending them in terms of public arguments even when religious reasons are held in the background. Democratic debate and deliberation are undermined when a group's real agenda is camouflaged, and when citizens and groups offer reasons with the intent to manipulate and distract others from the real reasons that are thought to establish the merits of the case. If figures on the Christian Right retain ultimate religious grounds for the laws they advocate, and exercise selectivity in devising a public agenda, does this render Christian Right advocacy duplicitous or otherwise problematic from a democratic standpoint?[2]

Attempts to discern real reasons or motivations, or hidden agendas, can be hazardous. Nevertheless, we argue in contrast to many critics of the Christian Right that the two-tiered rhetoric often seems to represent a sincere effort to engage fellow citizens on the basis of common reasons and shared standards for evidence. When particular groups with particular agendas enter the political arena, it is inevitable that they must consider which of their favored issues might permit the formation of a wider coalition and so have some promise of success. All interest groups face prudential political calculations when seeking to devise a platform that has a chance of succeeding, and securing the respect of others, in America's pluralist democracy. Similarly, when members of a particular group go outside the group to speak to a wider public in the language shared by that wider public, a two-tiered discourse will often be inevitable. On the face of it, there is nothing novel or insidious about this, as we explain. We argue that there is a danger of applying standards of assessment to Christian Right groups that are higher than those applied to other interest groups in democratic politics. We believe, in other words, that there is some evidence that prominent Christian Right leaders and organizations have embraced public rhetoric in public forums for their own prudential and principled reasons—to succeed in persuading others and winning political contests, but also to respect citizens of other faiths.

The two-tiered rhetorical strategy thus offers grounds for applause as well as concern. Advocates for deliberative democracy and civic virtue can applaud the Christian Right for mobilizing citizens and injecting publicly accessible ethical values into a politics too often dominated by self-interested appeals. This facilitates rather than undermines public deliberation on the merits of proposed legislation. Yet there is also a risk that more extreme activists will use the rhetorical strategies we describe to propagate deeply flawed pseudoscientific claims while concealing their religious agenda from fellow citizens.

We conclude that the Christian Right's narrative of victimization rings hollow, as does the companion complaint of some that the religious voice in our politics has been unfairly marginalized or silenced by liberal elites in the courts and elsewhere. The Christian Right's rhetorical strategy is better understood as an adaptation to the pluralist character of American democracy, in which all groups who wish to succeed must speak a language that appeals broadly to those outside the group.

Democracy and Public Reason

Before turning to our critical explication of the Christian Right's rhetorical practices, we briefly describe the liberal—or closely related deliberative democratic—ideals of public reason and public justification. We do this because the normative principles implicit in such ideals help make sense of controversies surrounding the appropriateness of religious discourse in public life. Ideals of public reason have been defended not only by political philosophers but also by the courts and public figures. These ideals are held by some to unfairly silence or marginalize the religious voice in public life.

Philosophical accounts of public reason have been articulated by liberal political philosophers (such as John Rawls), theorists of deliberative democracy (such as Amy Gutmann and Dennis Thompson), and civic republicans.[3] These accounts elaborate the judgment, familiar in democratic practice, that when seeking to pass a law that will be binding on all, public officials and citizens should offer one another supporting reasons and evidence whose force can be appreciated by all reasonable fellow citizens, and not only by co-religionists. Rawls puts it this way, "Our exercise of political power is proper only when we sincerely believe that the reasons we would offer for our political actions—were we to state them as government officials—are sufficient, and we also reasonably think that other citizens might reasonably accept those reasons" (1999b, 137). By offering reasons for the laws we advocate, not only our preferences (or threats, or force, or manipulation), we display an appropriate form of respect for our fellow citizens as free and equal citizens. Rawls says that offering reasons of the right sort manifests an important form of civility among citizens, though reason giving is not of course a legal duty of any sort.

The ideal of public reason also reflects the deep conviction characteristic of modern liberal democracies that political association is an association for some purposes and ends, and not others. The social contract that John Locke said underlies our political association aims at securing our civil interests, such aims as civil peace, the rule of law, and secure rights to life, liberty, and property (1689/1983, 1690/1988). Nowadays, we would include the promotion of health, welfare, and prosperity, as well as social justice. The preamble to the U.S. Constitution declares America's political aims in similar terms.[4] Our political partnership aims at securing these and other common or public interests and not, for example, salvation or holiness. Because citizens have different and incompatible convictions about religious truth, we agree to disagree and leave questions of religious truth to one side in politics. The First Amendment reinforces this by disallowing government establishment of religion.

Practices of reason-giving and reason-demanding are familiar, and indeed pervasive, features of ordinary politics. We expect the merits of issues to be thoroughly discussed and debated before decisions are taken. Institutions such as the separation of powers and judicial review allow officeholders and ordinary citizens to demand reasons for the way power is exercised (Holmes 1995; Macedo 1990).

Liberal constitutionalists emphasize the importance of public reasons—demanding and supplying reasons—in the context of constitutional controversies concerning fundamental rights. Deliberative democrats argue for public reasoning in the context of morally important policy controversies, such as decisions about health care or welfare policies. Both camps would tend to agree with John Rawls that laws and institutions should be justified in terms "that others can reasonably be expected to endorse" (1993, 226), and with Gutmann and Thompson that citizens should "try to find mutually acceptable ways of resolving moral disagreements" (1996, 2).

Seeking to persuade others based on common reasons is not only a moral idea, but in many circumstances, a matter of prudential common sense. When I appeal to my self-interest or to reasons that have force only in my faith community or narrow ideological circle, my arguments are unlikely to be broadly persuasive. When the president of General Motors comes into the public realm to advocate legislation, he says, "What's good for General Motors is good for America." E. E. Schattschneider noted decades ago that appeals to the naked self-interest of

General Motors may work well enough within the organization, but not when speaking to outsiders (1975). Effective public advocacy requires the invocation of considerations that are good for all. And so Kwame Anthony Appiah is right to say that ideas of public reason may appear to resemble debating tips: "rhetorical advice about how best, within a plural polity, to win adherents and influence policies . . . the spirit behind these liberal strictures is less Madalyn Murray O'Hair than Dale Carnegie" (2005, 81).

Yet, the idea of public reason is controversial, not as practical advice, but as a moral expectation: as the idea that we owe others reasons of an appropriate sort for the way we would have the law formulated and applied. We expect legislators to deliberate in terms of the public good. We expect political parties to lay out the case for the legislative agendas based on public reasons and evidence. These expectations furnish the basis for critical appraisal even though we know that legislators and parties are also influenced by narrower and self-serving factors.

The conviction that public reasons ought to be offered for laws and policies shapes expectations and behavior. Consider the example of conservative opposition to same-sex marriage nationally. Opposition to same-sex marriage has been highly moralistic, but the importance of finding broad common ground has been apparent. In April 2003, Senator Richard Santorum (R-PA) caused an uproar when commenting on the impending Supreme Court decision in Lawrence v. Texas, 539 U.S. 558 (2003), representing a challenge to Texas's antisodomy criminal statute: "If the Supreme Court says that you have the right to consensual [sodomitical] sex within your home, then you have the right to bigamy, you have the right to polygamy, you have the right to incest, you have the right to adultery. You have the right to anything." Many commentators accused Santorum of equating homosexual conduct with bigamy, polygamy, incest, and adultery, and the senator, a devout Catholic, quickly became a symbol of intolerance.[5] Santorum's arguments failed to resonate with the public. When Lawrence was decided—overruling Bowers v. Hardwick, 478 U.S. 186 (1986), and striking down laws across the country that criminalized sodomy—it failed to generate a broad public outcry. This seemed to reflect greater public acceptance or at least tolerance of homosexuality (see Macedo 1997).[6]

When Republican senators took up the Federal Marriage Amendment (FMA), in the summer of 2004, they sought to justify the FMA by pressing two claims reflecting broad public values: first, that traditional heterosexual marriage fosters the well-being of children, and, second, that same-sex matrimony would weaken marriage and harm children. Senators cited apparent evidence that those countries in Europe that recognized same-sex partnerships also experienced higher rates of cohabitation, out-of-wedlock births, and divorce. These arguments seemed designed to make a broadly appealing public case based on evidence and reason, though they also ignored the far more direct role of no-fault divorce legislation and generous welfare benefits for single mothers in explaining increased rates of out-of-wedlock births and single parenting.[7]

The idea of public reason is familiar and, we believe, widely acknowledged. Does the fact that particular citizens or public officials retain their own nonpublic ultimate religious basis for certain public moral convictions and arguments—concerning the wrongness of homosexual conduct, for example, or the proper nature of marriage—compromise the commitment to public reason? Not necessarily.

It is inevitable that persons of faith will often have religious as well as public reasons for favoring a given law or policy, whether concerning flood relief for hurricane victims or restrictions on abortion. It is an inevitable but familiar complexity of democratic politics that, in addition to common reasons and common language, participants will have private reasons of their own. If my brother-in-law runs for president, I may hope he wins both because he is my brother-in-law and because I believe that he is the best qualified. The president of General Motors' belief that what is good for GM is good for America may be quite sincere (and right). Or the GM president and I may be delusional or hypocrites. People often fool themselves into thinking that the greater good coincides with their own good. There are tendencies toward corruption in the overlap of personal and public interests and convictions. All we can do is to try to identify and guard against it as best we can.

In his mature statement of the philosophical ideal of public reason, Rawls argued that in addition to offering public reasons and evidence sufficient to justify laws or policy choices, it is fine to also offer religious reasons (1999b). We fail in our duty of civility or good citizenship only when we argue for laws based solely on sectarian grounds, that is, based solely on grounds peculiar to a religious or philosophical worldview that other citizens reasonably reject (for a more elaborate exposition and defense of the idea of public reason, see Macedo 1998; George and Wolfe 2000). If an argument for restricting marriage to heterosexuals or for prohibiting stem cell research can only be made sense of based on sectarian religious beliefs, or sectarian philosophical systems that are widely rejected on reasonable grounds by other citizens, then one is not acting as a good citizen when one seeks to secure passage of a law based only on such narrow and peculiar grounds.

A few scholars, such as Christopher Eberle (2002) and Jeffrey Stout (2004), argue that, at the end of the day, a citizen whose only reasons for supporting a law are sectarian, even a law touching on basic rights, does no wrong as long as he or she has made a sincere effort to find public reasons. Eberle's example is a citizen who supports legislation based solely on the belief that homosexuality is an abomination to God. Having tried conscientiously but failed to discern public reasons—in terms of harm to society or a straightforward account of moral wrongness— citizens do no wrong, Eberle and Stout assert, if they act solely on sectarian religious grounds.

We deem it a failure of civic virtue when citizens seek to legislate for the entire community based only on sectarian grounds that make sense only within a religious or moral framework that is peculiar to a part of the community. We also think this is rare, and that when it does happen, ordinary citizens often object to law being used to impose some people's religious beliefs on the rest. Even Eberle and Stout believe that citizens ought to try to discern public reasons, which indicates all agree that something is amiss when public reasons are unavailable. It is also common ground that citizens have a right to advocate legislation on sectarian or indeed self-interested grounds. No one should stop them. At stake is a claim about civic virtue.

Eberle and Stout make one valuable point. Ideals of public reason give rise to practice-oriented expectations that are hard to apply in particular cases and can lead to hasty ascriptions of bad faith. Liberals may sometimes be too quick to charge their conservative opponents with being moved only by religious convictions, ignorance, and prejudice. Conservatives take umbrage insofar as they believe that evidence and morality are on their side. Some believe they face a Catch-22: having been admonished to supply public reasons and evidence, they are then told that their reasons and evidence are not of the right sort (George and Wolfe 2000). The idea of public reason can pose the danger that opposing sides will question each other's motives and good faith, rather than debate the merits of issues. We agree that it is generally important to focus on the merits of opposing arguments and evidence, and to avoid hasty ascriptions of bad faith. Nevertheless, many (though not all) will allow that when religious convictions (or naked self-interest) are all that justify a law then the law is illegitimate. Partisans—liberal and conservative—often believe what they want to believe, and zeal leads people to accept lousy arguments and flawed evidence. Hypocrisy often takes a back seat to self-deception.

It is rare in practice in the United States for candidates for major political figures to argue for the confinement of marriage to heterosexuals or for prohibitions on abortion based strictly on religious grounds. This would require arguing, after all, that abortion and same-sex relations are an abomination to God, but not seriously harmful to society.[8] No significant national political figure or movement leader in America argues that way.[9] In national political debates, opponents of same-sex marriage and abortion try to make publicly reasoned arguments. Local communities are more homogeneous, and so strictly sectarian appeals may more often occur there. Even so, the charge that liberal elites unfairly constrain religious voices in public debate is a convenient rhetorical ploy.

As we will see, the actual political practices of Christian Right activists illustrate that a norm of public reason may be all but inevitable in any moderately well working diverse democracy. Of course, groups with strongly shared faith-based convictions may well experience tensions when formulating positions and rhetorical strategies for a wider public. We consider how some on the Christian Right seem to negotiate such tensions. We also examine whether religious convictions are, in this respect, much different from other deep partisan, ideological, or moral commitments. We argue that the Christian Right should not be held to a higher standard than other participants in democratic politics, including those who are apt to be moved by deep moral or ideological convictions.

Populist and Religious Narratives of Victimization

Before examining how Christian Right activists negotiate the tensions that arise in presenting publicly accessible reasons before wider audiences, we outline the Christian Right's narrative of victimization. Although this narrative is not unique to the Christian Right, it plays a vital role in the movement's mobilizing efforts as well as in its appeals to the sympathies of the broader public. It also plays an important role in the philosophical objections to the ideal of public reason leveled by academic critics of Rawls. Christian Right activists and these critics of liberal democracy portray the values of liberal elites as having marginalized people of faith by pushing them out of the public political forum.[10] Yet we argue that in both academic debates and in broader democratic politics, this narrative has an obscuring effect. This narrative vastly overstates the power of liberal elites and obscures the ways Christian Right organizations adapt to the pluralist nature of American democracy. Lost in the simple narrative of religious exclusion is a more nuanced understanding of the Christian Right's efforts to engage fellow citizens by appealing to publicly accessible reasons.

The 1950s, 1960s, and early 1970s were an era of rapid social change. The principal elements of the profound transformation of American life included significant strides with respect to race and gender equality, significant measures to address poverty and promote equality of opportunity, greater freedom and openness (eventually) for gays and lesbians, and also a children's rights movement (Macedo 1997; Macedo and Young 2003). Increased federal spending in the 1960s and early 1970s issued in a host of new programs and agencies, many targeted at poverty reduction and the cities. This era is also associated with profound changes in family life: women working outside the home, the spread of birth control, increased divorce, a rise in single parenting, extramarital sex, and a more assertive youth culture. Challenges to parental and governmental authority by young people were spurred by the domestic unrest brought about by the civil rights movement and the Vietnam War.

The federal courts, and especially the Supreme Court, of this era often helped lead social and political reforms: civil rights, greater rights for those accused of crimes, and efforts to reform and equalize political representation. The Court also sought to police the constitutional boundaries between church and state more vigorously, including by prohibiting government-sponsored prayers in public schools.

The greatest philosophical expressions of the principles that animated this era's liberal reformism were published in the 1970s, by liberal political philosophers such as John Rawls (1999a) and Ronald Dworkin (2005). Long before his extensive writings on public reason, Rawls argued for a theory of justice that prioritizes the basic rights and liberties of individuals, and fundamental commitments to equality. Using the *original position* as a thought experiment, he argued that inequalities in wealth could only be justified if they arise from institutions that also work to enhance the position of the worst off in society. Rawls and Dworkin also accorded the courts a special role as the expositors of the fundamental principles of political morality in a constitutional democracy. Both insisted that the special authority of the Supreme Court rests on its insulation from partisan politics and its need to justify its decisions in publicly reasoned opinions, open to the criticism of the wider polity.

The political and social changes and the ideas associated with this era incited a populist backlash. Barry Goldwater invoked the old idea of states rights against federal activism. Richard Nixon invoked the silent majority whose interests had been unfairly ignored: members of the middle class fed up with urban social unrest, high crime, and taxes. White urban ethnics played an important part, driven in part by opposition to forced integration of schools and neighborhoods (Reider 1997). Especially important to Nixon's success and the subsequent rise of the Republican Party was what was known as a southern strategy, designed to appeal to disaffections associated with race and civil rights. Also helpful to Republicans were the rising numbers of suburbanites who fled the cities and opposed federal efforts—and taxation—to address urban poverty. As Thomas Byrne Edsall and Mary Edsall make clear, the increasingly geography-based organization of class and race in America—"white flight" and the increasing isolation of poor blacks in inner cities—allowed the old anti–civil rights language of "states rights" to give way to a gentler and less obviously race-based language of "home rule," keeping government "close to the people," and shrinking the size of the federal government, the main engine of distributive justice and integration (1991). These themes were central to Ronald Reagan's success and had obvious appeal to suburbanites who had left behind the problems of inner cities.

The backlash against the 1960s helped shape and reinvigorate an old populist political narrative pitting a virtuous but marginalized middle class against a powerful liberal elite (see Brint and Proctor, forthcoming). The Christian Right embraced these themes to portray itself as an excluded group besieged by remote and powerful liberal cultural and political elites. These narratives stress the substantive failures and procedural illegitimacy of elite-driven federal interventions in local politics.

This victim narrative focuses both on the substance and process of liberalism. The substantive element emphasizes the corrosive effects of modern liberal philosophy on the traditional values associated with families and local communities, including churches. Critics charge that the liberal philosophy elevates personal choice and social permissiveness over the stricter community-based virtues on which a healthy society depends. In the words of Christopher Lasch, "Liberals have always taken the position that democracy can dispense with civic virtue" (1995, 85). Similarly, Robert Bork argues that modern liberalism's radical egalitarianism and hedonistic individualism—"unhindered in the pursuit of pleasure"—is at war with traditional religious and moral convictions about personal and sexual morality (1996, 5).[11] No matter that these claims are caricatures, bearing little resemblance to the liberal tradition or the substance of much reformism (Berkowitz 2000; Macedo 1990).

Conservative populists criticize not only the substance of liberal reform, but also the process by which these changes were brought about. They argue that these changes arose as the result of political and cultural elites working through nondemocratic channels and contrary to the wishes of the majority. The prime culprit is reliance on an unelected federal judiciary. Liberal activist judges, they argue, have used their positions to impose their values on the political community without running the normal, demanding process of persuasion and legislation. Bork argues that by disregarding moral decency in the name of protecting pornography and hate speech, abortion and gay rights, the court has illegitimately imposed its permissive sexual morality on states and local communities: "the Supreme Court has usurped the powers of the people and their elected representatives. We are no longer free to make our own fundamental moral and cultural decisions" (1996, 109).[12] Not only the Court, but also the media, the movie industry, and the academy, are all seen as playing a part in the antidemocratic effort to impose liberal elite values on the majority of Americans.[13]

This victim narrative issued on behalf of the cultural or Christian Right also bears some resemblance to arguments advanced by multiculturalists and theorists of difference on the left, or nearer the political center (Benhabib 1992; Fraser 1992; Young 1990, 2000). Iris Marion Young, for instance, argued that liberal theories of social justice are too abstract and acontextual—that they ignore group differences (1990, 3). Like Bork and others on the right, Young sometimes argued that ideals of liberal theorists are based upon culturally specific values that privilege elites: "most theorists of deliberative democracy assume a culturally biased conception of discussion that tends to silence or devalue some people or groups" (1996, 120). Supposedly universal norms of deliberation and reason fail to recognize the perspectives of groups at the periphery.

A strand of the victim narrative that has enduring potency is the charge—heard from the political Right, but also the Center and Left—that courts and other elites have marginalized religious people and silenced religious voices in the public square. Whereas theorists of difference worry that liberal values and practices exclude the perspectives of racial minorities, women, and other disadvantaged social groups, others argue that the groups whose claims are unfairly devalued are religious minorities, including the Amish, supporters of creation science or intelligent design, or fundamentalist Christians whose distinctive biblical hermeneutic is alien to liberal reason. These themes are central to widely read books by centrists such as Yale law professor Stephen Carter (1993), cultural conservatives including Bork (1990, 1996), Richard John Neuhaus (1984), James Davison Hunter (1992), and several Left academics, including Jeffrey Stout (2004).

Yet this sentiment of religious victimization reaches far beyond the realms of academia and policymaking. Since its emergence in the late 1970s, the modern Christian Right movement has appealed to this narrative to mobilize conservative Christians at the grassroots and to elicit the sympathies of fellow Americans. Like other expressions of this narrative, Christian Right activists depict religious citizens as a persecuted minority that has come under attack by everyone from gays and lesbians to feminists to judicial activists (Diamond 1998; Hedges 2007; Wilcox and Larson 2006; Moen 1992). According to this narrative, such liberal groups seek to relegate Judeo-Christian values to the sidelines of American democracy.

Early Christian Right leaders, such as Jerry Falwell, used this theme to warn fellow Christians about the dangers of secular humanism and liberal elite values. In Susan Friend Harding's account of a 1986 sermon, for instance, she observed Falwell warning members of the corrosive effects of secular values:

> Why is this secularizing [of America] taking place? It is a part of the global conquest against our little children, to teach them there is nothing absolutely right or absolutely wrong, there are no absolutes in society, that there is no infallible Bible, there is no biblical standard of righteousness,

that situational ethics is the better code for successful living. If it feels good, do it. And you know, and I know, that once you adopt that philosophy and join that secular society, you also become victimized by every other problem today that is destroying our young people. (2000, 160)

Falwell's depiction of religious persecution radicalizes many of the sentiments expressed in intellectual circles.

One component of the Christian Right's recent rhetoric of victimization is that it frequently appeals to language of warfare. In Jon Shields's content analysis of direct mail from the Christian Coalition and Concerned Women for America, he found that half of these documents compare "contemporary moral conflicts to a war" (2007, 95). In sermons, direct mail, and radio programs, Christian Right leaders describe their political struggles as a culture war, they call their opposition militant homosexuals, and they portray the values of Christians as having come under siege by the Left. In a 1990 campaign advertisement in the *Christian American*, for example, the Christian Coalition warned: "Danger! Christian Americans are under siege. Schoolchildren are being threatened and adults jailed for the peaceful practice of God-given rights. It's time to say, enough. Time to regain a voice in government and raise a righteous standard. . . . Now Christians can be united behind a grassroots movement that will change the status quo" (Diamond 1998, 77).

In these documents and others, Christian Right leaders portray liberal groups as having waged a war against Christianity—a war that can be won only through intense political activism.

This rhetoric of victimization has reached its apotheosis in current discussions of gay and lesbian issues. Focus on the Family and other groups describe the efforts of gay and lesbian political activists in almost conspiratorial terms. As Dobson wrote in a 2004 newsletter to Focus members:

For more than 40 years, the homosexual activist movement has sought to implement a master plan that has had as its centerpiece the utter destruction of the family. . . . These goals include universal acceptance of the gay lifestyle, discrediting of Scriptures that condemn homosexuality, muzzling of the clergy and Christian media, granting of special privileges and rights in the law, overturning laws prohibiting pedophilia, indoctrinating children and future generations through public education, and securing all the legal benefits of marriage for any two or more people who claim to have homosexual tendencies.

As we have seen, criticisms of the Supreme Court and judicial activism are staples of conservative and populist politics. Following Bork and others, the Christian Right portrays activist judges as eager participants in this war against traditional values and religion. Conservatives portray themselves as champions of the little guy, even while opposing groups long subject to prejudice and discrimination. Following the Supreme Court's decision to not intervene in the case of Terri Shiavo, James Dobson accused the high court of "the cold-blooded, cold-hearted extermination of an innocent human life," and declared that Supreme Court justices are "unelected and unaccountable and arrogant and imperious and determined to redesign the culture according to their own biases" (Eric Gorski, "Schiavo Case Tests Faiths," *Denver Post*, April 1, 2005, A-01).

Some politically centrist and even progressive scholars echo the Christian Right's complaints. Jeffrey Stout argues, for example, that some secular liberals "have strongly urged people to restrain themselves from bringing their religious commitments with them into the political sphere." As a result, "many religious people have grown frustrated at the unwillingness of the liberal elite to hear them out on their own terms, and have recently had much to say against the hypocrisies and biases of secularism" (2004, 63). On Stout's view, we may have only begun to see the blowback from the philosophical effort to diminish religion's role in American democracy:

> We are about to reap the social consequences of a traditionalist backlash against contractarian liberalism. . . . Because most of the Rawlsians do not read theology or pay scholarly attention to the religious life of the people, they have no idea what contractarian liberalism has come to mean outside the fields of legal and political theory. . . . One message being preached nowadays in many of the institutions where future preachers are being trained is that liberal democracy is essentially hypocritical when it purports to value free religious expression. . . . Over the next several decades this message will be preached in countless sermons throughout the heartland of America. (2004, 76)

The victim narrative offers Christian Right activists several important strategic benefits. Within the movement, such narratives cultivate a sense of outrage, fear, and resentment, all of which help mobilize political action and unify activists sympathetic to the cause (Simmel 1903). As Sara Diamond points out, "the perception among evangelicals that they are underdogs, ignored if not abused by the establishment, is part of the mindset that keeps activists from becoming complacent" (1998, 5). Fostering a sense of perpetual crisis can be an effective mobilizer. When we asked Glenn Stanton, Focus on the Family's primary spokesman on same-sex marriage, how his organization counters the efforts of activist judges, for instance, he remarked, "Our main primary vehicles have been a kind of pamphleteering. It's education and a bit of outrage. We inform the democratic crisis—that where we're losing our democracy because courts are becoming an oligarchy" (Interview, July 19, 2005).

This combination of education and outrage couched within the rhetorical frame of persecution appears to be an effective mobilizing strategy.

The victim narrative also enables Christian Right activists to influence the terms of debate when engaging the general public. First, the victim narrative enables the Christian Right to frame itself as a group on the periphery of the political establishment, untainted by power (Diamond 1998). In short, it dissolves the tension between the Christian Right's increasingly powerful role within the Republican Party—exerting influence as political insiders—and its efforts to portray itself as a grassroots, outside-the-Beltway movement. By continually reasserting its victim status, leaders can obscure the Christian Right's close connection to political leaders at all levels of government and its influence over the Republican Party Platform. The victim narrative conceals these facts beneath the carefully manicured façade of Christians as perpetual outsiders, all but ignored by the powerful liberal elites who control culture and politics.

Second, the victim narrative enables the Christian Right to counter the view that the 1960s and 1970s were a period of unqualified social progress toward equal rights. As we have seen, this was an era in which women, blacks, and other ethnic minorities won greater civil liberties and a more equal standing as citizens in U.S. politics. The narrative of victimization, however, suggests that that such progressive advances came at a high price to the equal rights and standing of people of faith. It suggests that, as the result of increased federalization and the rise of more liberal and secular values, conservative Christians and others who embrace more traditional and faith-centered worldviews became a marginalized class. Abortion rather than civil rights takes center stage, and people of faith are the new oppressed class.

Third, it frames the substantive political agenda of the Christian Right as purely defensive. When viewed as responses to religious persecution, efforts to prohibit same-sex marriage and abortion take on the appearance of a protectionist strategy to defend the family, rather than an offensive effort to strip away the rights of fellow citizens. Clyde Wilcox and Carin Larson point out that this framing contest—over whether the Christian Right is an offensive or defensive movement—has profound significance (2006, 10–19). When viewed offensively, the Christian Right's agenda appears to diminish democracy by seeking, as Wilcox and Larson put it, "to deprive gays and lesbians of their civil rights, to limit dramatically the public and private role of women in society, and to impose a prescientific worldview on public education" (2006, 14). When viewed defensively, the movement might appear to be engaged in a legitimate effort to uphold the core democratic value—entrenched in the First Amendment—of the free exercise of religion.[14]

Finally, the narrative of victimization enables the Christian Right to obscure the racial undertones of the Right's political agenda. Obscured, in this way, is the association of the conservative moral agenda of the Christian Right with other forces that have aided the Republican resurgence: the southern resistance to civil rights, opposition to race-conscious remedies for the effects of past discrimination, and opposition to federal taxes and further growth in federal redistributive programs.

In this regard, we note one important claim advanced by Rogers Smith in volume 1, chapter 11, and elsewhere by Randall Balmer. Smith cites the testimony of Paul Weyrich to the effect that it was not Roe v. Wade, 410 U.S. 113 (1973), or other front-burner values issues that mobilized the Christian Right. Weyrich asserts that the Christian Right really took off when the IRS tried to deny tax-exempt status to Christian schools that practiced racial discrimination. These included those Christian academies founded in the wake of Brown v. Board of Education, 347 U.S. 483 (1954), and Bob Jones University, which banned interracial dating. Leaders of the Christian Right saw the IRS's proposal to end tax-exempt status for schools practicing racial discrimination as the thin edge of a liberal wedge, which put at risk other practices, including favoring fellow believers in hiring, unequal opportunities for women in many churches, and so on.[15] "It seemed clear to many conservative evangelicals," Smith writes, "that their organizations were indeed at risk of losing beneficial forms of government treatment" (volume 1, chapter 11). So, if we follow the money, an important mobilizer for the Christian Right was the risk of the loss of tax exemptions for schools and other institutions that discriminate on grounds of race.

By casting themselves as victims of liberal elites, Christian Right activists obscure the role played by race and class in efforts to oppose such federal interventions. In short, this narrative helps them win the allegiance and sympathies of citizens who might otherwise oppose their substantive political ambitions.

The victim narrative furnishes a convenient rhetorical tool, and as such, should not be accepted at face value. That people feel treated unfairly by liberal elites tells us little about whether they really are treated unfairly. And yet the Christian Right has not gotten much that it has sought in politics. Roe v. Wade and abortion rights are largely intact as a matter of constitutional law. Republicans have not made the Federal Marriage Amendment, defining marriage as a relation between a man and a woman, a high priority. Leaders of the Republican Party are concerned about alienating moderates, and thereby losing elections.

To assess the contribution of the Christian Right to American democracy we need to look beneath its narrative of victimization. Rather than accepting what Christian Right activists say about their role in democratic politics, we examine their concrete rhetorical practices. This involves a deeper exploration into the positive rhetorical strategies the

Christian Right adopts. By examining rhetorical practices, we can better assess how the Christian Right has comported itself with respect to the idea of public reason, and whether that idea imposes unfair constraints on believers. We turn, therefore, to the central features of the two-tiered rhetorical strategy. We will return to the question of assessment after we have more fully described the Christian Right's style of participation in American politics. The Christian Right's own rhetorical practices cast doubt, as we shall see, on the proposition that liberal elites have relegated religious citizens to the sidelines of public debate.

Two-Tiered Political Rhetoric

During the last thirty years, the Christian Right's public rhetoric has undergone an important shift. Whereas earlier activists openly expressed religious motivations and scriptural arguments, their counterparts today often steer clear of expressions of religious conviction when speaking in public settings, and instead, rely on public reasons and empirical evidence. We now examine this strategy.

When speaking to fellow Christians, activists appeal to arguments based on scripture and religious conviction. Consider, for example, the arguments Dobson uses to express his opposition to same-sex marriage in a newsletter to Focus members: "Throughout Scripture, God's intention for human sexual relationships is clearly limited to the heterosexual union between a man and a woman in marriage (see Genesis 1:27–28, and 2:18, 23–24). By stark contrast, sex outside of that relationship, whether it be of a heterosexual or homosexual nature, is clearly identified as a sin" (2003). In addressing fellow Christians, these kinds of religious arguments provide movement leaders with a powerful tool for mobilizing conservative Christians to take up political action.

Although references to scripture and religious reasons mobilize the faithful, leaders of the contemporary Christian Right understand the need to appeal to a second tier of reasons when engaging the general public. Rather than appealing to religious conviction, such public arguments rest upon reasons that, as Rawls might say, "others can reasonably be expected to endorse" (1993, 226). Dobson explains in the same 2003 newsletter: "As Christians, we believe that the Bible's admonitions against homosexual behavior, along with the design for marriage put forth in Genesis and affirmed by Paul, are reasons enough to oppose gay marriage. However, it is often said that God speaks to us through two books: the Bible and the 'book of nature.' Even for those who do not know Christ, the book of nature provides numerous reasons why homosexual behavior is harmful to individuals and to society as a whole."

To encourage fellow Christians to use such "natural" reasons when talking to outsiders, Dobson's group trains members to use public arguments. As Focus's leading expert on same-sex marriage, Glenn Stanton explained, "It is our desire to bring people up to a different level and argue more intelligently and more persuasively. You've got to do re-education. You've got to retrain people in that way. It's not so much what you do say but what you don't say" (Interview, June 6, 2006).[16] As we will see, this two-tiered rhetorical strategy shows that religious citizens have not been unfairly excluded from political debate. When engaging in political debate, they willingly adhere to norms of civility and public reason.

The two-tiered rhetorical strategy that we describe is in some ways similar to what Rogers Smith describes (chapter 11, volume 1) as a second-best litigation strategy designed with an eye toward political efficacy. Although many Christian Right leaders would have preferred to express their political claims using religious language, their concerns over the effectiveness of religious language led them to adopt this second-best strategy of two-tiered rhetoric. In a 1989 interview conducted by Michael Moen, for instance, Gary Bauer, then director of the Family Research Council, explained, "today the [Christian Right] movement realizes that it must employ the language that the American people feel comfortable with." Yet Bauer also expressed regret that such considerations prevent conservative Christians from using religious language. "It is unfortunate," Bauer remarked, "that leaders cannot use the words and phrases that were once part of the national dialogue" (quoted in Moen 1992, 132).

The Christian Right's shift toward a second tier of discourse based upon publicly accessible reasons was most evident in the mid-1980s. During this period, the Christian Right's early emphasis on Christianizing America began to give way to more publicly accessible forms of political rhetoric. As Michael Schwartz of the Free Congress Foundation remarked in a 1989 interview, "today, Christian Right activists speak of the need for citizens to work for the public good, rather than speak of the need for Christians to clean up a morally decadent country" (quoted in Moen 1992, 132).

During the mid-1980s, the traditionally liberal language of civil rights and equality supplanted talk of biblical mandates and language deemed excessively moralistic. For instance, the Moral Majority recast its primary arguments in support of school prayer. Rather than emphasizing the religious or moral benefits of school prayer, it was presented as an issue of choice. The Moral Majority's legislative director explained it this way: "We pushed school prayer three years in a row, but we framed the issue in terms of how prayer in schools is good. But some people feel that prayer in school is bad. So we learned to frame the issue in terms of 'student's rights,' so it became a constitutional issue. We are pro-choice for students having the right to pray in schools" (quoted in Moen 1992, 129).

The Moral Majority's arguments against abortion also shifted. Instead of appealing to religious arguments to oppose abortion, the Moral Majority of the late 1980s emphasized basic rights. To have an abortion, it claimed, was to deprive the unborn of their basic right to life. As Jerry Falwell declared in a 1985 interview, "We are reframing the debate [on abortion]. This is no longer a religious issue, but a civil rights issue" (quoted in Moen 1992, 129). This framing of abortion as a rights issue has resulted in an important divergence between the language of pro-life and pro-choice advocates. As Shields points out, "One of the great unrecognized ironies of the abortion debate is that pro-choice leaders want to frame abortion as a religious issue, while their pro-life opponents want to highlight philosophical and scientific objections to abortion" (Shields 2007, 103). Pro-life activists understand that if the moral status of embryos is regarded as a purely religious matter, then their opposition to abortion will fail to persuade judges, policymakers, and the public. Pro-choice activists, by contrast, often seek to exploit this vulnerability by insisting that the Christian Right's arguments concerning the moral status of embryos are guided solely by religious considerations (Shields 2007, 103).

The Christian Right's appropriation of liberal discourse also transformed its arguments in gay rights debates. During the 1992 debate over Amendment 2, an amendment to the Colorado state constitution that sought to strike down all state and local antidiscrimination ordinances based on sexual orientation, the Christian Right appealed to the liberal language of equal rights. The campaign literature of Colorado for Family Values (CFV), the group that crafted the amendment, never mentions scripture or religious reasons. Instead, CFV argued against gay right's protections using the slogan No Special Rights.[17] The centerpiece of its claim was that antidiscrimination ordinances based on sexual orienta tion extended special rights to gays and lesbians, treating homosexuals as a privileged class. As Jean Dubofsky, head legal council in Romer v. Evans, 517 U.S. 620 (1996), in which Amendment 2 was declared unconstitutional, remarked, "the 'no special rights' spin had a tremendous impact because at that point there was a lot of unhappiness about affirmative action for blacks and for women" (Interview, June 23, 2006; for another important analysis, see Diamond 1998).

CFV also used this message to reach out to racial minorities, claiming that extending civil rights protections for gays and lesbians would devalue existing racial classifications. It argued that gays were a privileged group, who earn almost two times as much as average Americans and take four times as many overseas vacations (see Colorado for Family Values 1992; Herman 1997). Given the significant economic privileges homosexuals enjoy and the fact that being gay is a lifestyle choice, argued CFV, they had no legitimate claim to special rights. In a fundraising letter, former Senator Bill Armstrong put it this way: "to equate the self-created personal miseries of pleasure-addicted gays—who sport average incomes of nearly $55,500 a year—with the innocent sufferings and crippling poverty of legitimate minority groups is an insult to those who've struggled to achieve true civil rights in America" (quoted in Lesage 1998, 347).

Leading contemporary Christian Right organizations, such as Focus on the Family and the Family Research Council, continue to deploy empirical evidence in public debates. Their concerns are targeted less at the intrinsic immorality of homosexual relations than at the potentially destructive social consequences of the gay agenda, particularly as concerns the welfare of children. In the 2004 document "Debate-Tested Sound Bites on Defending Marriage," for example, Focus on the Family outlined a number of public reasons to oppose the practice (Stanton 2004, 1):

1. Same-sex families always deny children either their mother or father.

2. Same-sex family is a vast, untested social experiment with children.

3. Where does it stop? How do we say "no" to group marriage?

4. Schools will be forced to teach that the homosexual family is normal.

Evident here is the worry that same-sex marriage will erode the traditional family, harm children, and foster socially harmful sexual permissiveness.

The rhetoric used by today's Christian Right to address outside audiences on issues like same-sex marriage not only avoids explicit religious references, but also what others might perceive to be excessive moralism, as we saw in the discussion of same sex marriage. By the late 1980s and 1990s, groups such as the Moral Majority and the Christian Coalition were already speaking the language of civil rights, and basic their claims on public argument and evidence.

The two-tiered rhetoric of the Christian Right is open to two possible interpretations. The first—the manipulative interpretation—views its use of public reasons as an inauthentic and purely strategic ploy. On this view, the Christian Right's concealment of religious reasons in public debates is a clandestine strategy to push America toward theocratic rule. Jean Hardisty, for instance, calls the Christian Right's public rhetoric an effort to "camouflage" its Christian agenda (1999, 114).

The journalist Chris Hedges goes even further. He likens this rhetoric to the stealth tactics used by the Nazis and other totalitarian movements, whereby the movement seeks gradually to appropriate the language of ordinary citizens. In his description, "this slow, gradual and often imperceptible strangulation of thought—the corruption of democratic concepts and ideas—infects society until the new, totalitarian vision is articulated in the old vocabulary. This cannibalization of language occurs subtly and stealthily" (2007, 16). A central tenet of the manipulative interpretation is notion that these public reasons arise out of a hidden religious agenda. According to Hedges, this is precisely what is occurring. This manipulative rhetorical strategy is based on a hidden ethos of militant biblicism—on the notion that America is "an agent of God, and all political and intellectual opponents of America's Christian leaders are viewed, quite simply, as agents of Satan" (12).

Critics can point to instances in which movement leaders have indeed advocated stealth tactics. For instance, when speaking at a 1992 meeting of the Montana Christian Coalition, Ralph Reed, former head of the Christian Coalition, advised members that "the most important strategy for evangelicals is secrecy. We're involved in a war. It's not a war fought with bullets, it's a war fought with ballots. You must paint your face and travel at night. You must move underground and don't stick your head out of the foxhole until the sun is beyond the horizon" (Joan Lowy, "Stealth Christian Coalition is Making Inroads in Politics," *Houston Chronicle*, January 3, 1993).

Although some associated with the Christian Right have used public reasons to manipulate and perhaps deceive, we argue that the public rhetoric of leading figures is mostly consistent with a second, less insidious and more democratic, interpretation. On this view, the public dimension of the Christian Right's discourse represents an authentic effort to engage fellow citizens using reasons that, as Rawls would say, "others can reasonably be expected to endorse" (1993). When we asked Glenn Stanton, Focus on the Family's lead analyst on same-sex marriage, how he approaches public political debate, he explained it this way: "When I debate, I try to think how can I speak to my own people (the religious crowd), but also speak to my thoughtful opponent at the other end of the spectrum. I do that by seeking to make universal human arguments" (Interview, June 24, 2004). When asked whether his public rhetoric has a manipulative side, he insisted that "It's not tricky. It is just thinking, 'alright what do we all have in common.' If you go into a room and they are all Elvis fans, use a rationale like his favorite book was such and such. In the culture war, why can't we have more of that? Let's find our common starting place rather than starting with our divisions" (Interview, June 6, 2006).

Stanton insists that Focus's public arguments arise from a genuine desire to engage fellow citizens with different religious or philosophical convictions. Of course, prudence also argues for such a discursive strategy.

Interestingly, some Christian Right activists go so far as to invoke scriptural grounds for their use of public reasons in politics. Daniel Weiss, Focus's leading expert on pornography policy, told us this:

> In the book of Acts, the apostle Paul is credited largely with the amazing spread of Christianity through the Roman Empire because he traveled everywhere and was such an eloquent and prolific writer. Paul goes to one town in Greece spends some time there and then goes to the market place where all of the folks talk and he starts talking to them about their own traditions. He's speaking to them in their own language—Greek was the common language—he's referencing their Gods and he's making a reasoned case for believing in Jesus Christ as the true God based on their own faith, their own philosophers. So he's speaking the way they can understand. Now I think right now—for good or ill—not a lot of people understand the way Christians talk, so we speak their language. (Interview, July 6, 2006)

On Weiss's account, the two-tiered rhetoric of the Christian Right is not motivated by the desire to transform America's democracy into theocracy covertly but by a theology that calls for engaging non-Christians on their own terms.

These kinds of sentiments are not unique to activists at Focus on the Family.[18] In Shields's interviews with activists in the Christian Coalition and Concerned Women for America, he reaches a similar conclusion that Christian leaders "argue that appeals to theology should be scrupulously avoided in public forums" (2007, 104). His findings also support our more democratic interpretation of the Christian Right's two-tiered rhetorical strategy. He observes that Christian Right leaders not only aspire to train members in the use publicly accessible reasons but also to cultivate an ethos of civility toward opponents (100). He also notes that organizations like Stand to Reason, which trains 40,000 Christian activists each year to engage in the public square, encourage trainees to become what they call Christian ambassadors and that Tom Minnery, Focus's vice president of public policy, has encouraged group members to "bless those who persecute you" (100). Such efforts to cultivate civility call into question the manipulative interpretation of the Christian Right's use of public reasons. They show that many conservative Christians use publicly accessible claims to engage respectfully fellow citizens who do not share their religious convictions.

In a pluralist democracy like America, it is hardly surprising (but nonetheless encouraging) that religiously devout citizens view themselves as having religious as well as public moral reasons for addressing their fellow citizens in commonly accessible terms. But what of the fact that figures on the Christian Right deploy two tiers of rhetoric: does the deployment of religious argument alongside public argument run against the liberal injunction against voicing religious reasons in politics? Are liberal constitutionalism and deliberative democracy really consistent only with a single tier of discourse concerning the law—an exclusively public discourse? To characterize the liberal position this way, critics like Jeffrey Stout have had to ignore Rawls's mature and explicit statements and substitute an exclusionary and cramped view of the logic of public reason (Stout 2004; Rawls 1999b). The crucial thing for liberals and deliberative democrats generally—including Rawls—is that citizens advocating a coercive law that will be binding on all should seek out reasons that will be good for all who are similarly motivated, that believers also hold and express ultimate religious reasons as well is hardly surprising.[19]

The two-tiered pattern of discourse and advocacy we have observed among some prominent Christian Right leaders seems consistent with the expectations of liberal constitutionalists and deliberative democrats. Contrary to those critics who suggest that liberal public reason has unfairly silenced religious voices and marginalized religious citizens, important figures in the Christian Right seem to embrace public reasons for several reasons, including sensible political calculations about how to win over people of other faiths, principled reasons based on mutual respect among citizens, and religious reasons. At least so far as those whom Klemp has spoken with are concerned, the liberal democratic settlement championed by Rawls and others seems to be working in a way that is neither exclusionary nor unfair. We do not find evidence of duplicity. Christian Right leaders are responding to the discursive incentives built into a pluralistic Madisonian polity and their own growing sense of the appropriateness of public appeals when making binding law for a diverse polity.

The Fraught Marriage of Faith and Empirical Research

As we have seen, the rhetoric of Christian Right activists has shifted from arguments based on scripture and moralism to those about social consequences. One result of this rhetorical shift is that the movement has become increasingly reliant on social scientific evidence. When discussing issues like same-sex marriage, activists now rely heavily on sociological and demographic studies. This fusion of external arguments with internal arguments based on religious conviction prompts important questions: Should Christian Right activists be applauded for their willingness to appeal to scientific evidence? Or does this intermingling of allegedly scientific empirical research and religion threaten to undermine the objectivity of the scientific process and the epistemic quality of public debate? Are claims being tested by all the relevant evidence or is evidence being cited selectively—cherry-picked—to support conclusions that faith has already established?

The Christian Right's appeals to empirical evidence are most evident in its opposition to gay rights. In the 1990s, during battles over antidiscrimination ordinances such as Amendment 2, as we noted, Christian Right groups based much of their opposition on the claim that gays are a privileged group with no need for special rights. More recently, same-sex marriage has been opposed based on evidence pertaining to children's well-being.

Christian Right activists in the 1990s also appealed to research that reinforced the stereotype of gays as deviants and sexual predators. To shock and disgust potential voters, for instance, CFV's 1992 election tabloid detailed lurid statistics concerning the sexual habits of gay men (Colorado for Family Values 1992).[20] During this era, the primary source of many of the Christian Right's so-called scientific claims about gays and lesbians was Paul Cameron—a Christian Right psychologist prominently touted during the 1990s as an authority on homosexuality. Among other things, Cameron's studies, which were based on deeply flawed research methodologies, have purported to show that homosexuals are ten to twenty times more likely to be child molesters, twenty times more likely to commit bestiality, and fifteen times more likely to commit murder (Bull and Gallagher 1996, 27).

Among mainstream activists in today's Christian Right, these claims are no longer disseminated and their appeals to empirical evidence are less antagonistic. Although Paul Cameron, now head of the Family Research Institute, continues to produce such questionable "research" on the habits of gay men, we could not find a single instance of Focus citing his studies in its recent publications. Instead, activists like Glenn Stanton, Focus's lead analyst on marriage and sexuality, cite social scientific literature on childhood development to bolster claims against same-sex parenting and marriage. Stanton has argued that these studies show that depriving children of a mother or a father can be deeply destructive: "These children suffer from much higher levels of physical and mental illness, educational failure, poverty, substance abuse, criminal behavior, loneliness, as well as physical and sexual abuse. Children living apart from both biological parents are eight times more likely to die of maltreatment than children living with their mother and father" (2004).

Based on evidence such as this, Stanton argues that same-sex marriage ought to be prohibited. But note that such evidence is hardly on point: it speaks only to the question of whether children who are adopted, or raised in single-parent homes, tend for that reason to be at a disadvantage compared with children raised by two biological parents. Children raised by two biological parents, or even one, are not likely to be adopted by same-sex couples, so the comparison is misleading, and tells us nothing about whether the relevant pool of children are made worse off by same-sex adoption. It would be more pertinent to know how children raised by same-sex adoptive parents fare as compared with children being reared in orphanages.[21]

An important tension seems to lurk beneath the Christian Right's appeals to supposed scientific empirical evidence. The ethos of science includes a determination to follow the evidence where it leads, and an openness to having one's views refuted (Popper 2002). Yet many Christian Right leaders and rank-and-file conservative Christians believe in the primacy of revealed religion and of truths known before and independently of scientific investigation (or, indeed, public deliberation). This is far from the spirit of science.

This tension between science and religion is illuminated by survey data on the beliefs of theologically conservative Christians. Although these surveys do not isolate the beliefs of Christian Right activists, they do show that within the broader set of theologically conservative Christians, belief in biblical literalism and distrust of science are widespread, though far from universal. Andrew Greeley and Michael Hout find that though the belief in biblical literalism has declined somewhat throughout the last thirty years, 54 percent of theologically conservative Protestants endorse the statement, "The Bible is the actual word of God and is to be taken literally, word for word" (2006, 15). Christian Smith finds that 52 percent of evangelicals and 61 percent of fundamentalists believe that the Bible is "literally true" (1998, 23).

These surveys also show that theologically conservative Christians express a greater than average distrust for the results of scientific research. Greeley and Hout observe that 45 percent of theologically conservative Protestants believe that science changes our lives too fast and are more likely than average Americans to endorse the statement, "We trust too much in Science, not enough in Faith" (2006, 35). For our purposes, it is worth noting that these findings simply suggest that within the broader community of theologically conservative Christians, many believe in biblical literalism and distrust science. These findings do not give us a direct window into the beliefs of Christian Right activists who are theologically and politically conservative and deeply engaged in politics.

So just how do Christian Right activists who believe in revealed truth attempt to reconcile this belief in biblical literalism and inerrancy with the scientific method? We asked both Stanton and Cameron to describe their understanding of the relationship between faith and science. In both cases, they argued that they see these two worlds as tightly connected—that empirical research and religious convictions go hand in hand. Stanton explained it this way: "We just don't have a belief in fideism—of pure faith. It's faith tied to something. The value of Christianity is that at the center of it is the incarnation—is the fact that the God of Christianity became the creation. Christianity brings these worlds together. We cannot be disinterested in what God created or designed, what he is redeeming, what he became, and what he is one day going to renew. So this is a Christianity that is very well connected with fleshly everyday earthly existence" (Interview, June 6, 2006).

Stanton's reflections need not suggest that Focus manipulates or "massages" the data to bring it into conformity with God's will. These remarks point to a view of science and faith as interconnected without clarifying whether independent evaluation of evidence in the spirit of science leads to revisions on matters where faith had been thought to provide the answer.

Stanton's holistic understanding of the connection between faith and science might prompt us to ask scientific questions, which might in turn lead to scientific findings that place religious convictions in a new light. But how far is the back and forth process allowed to go with respect to religious convictions? Does scientific inquiry ever lead to reinterpretations of scripture or revisions of dogma? To return to a question we posed at the outset, does social scientific evidence play an independent role for those on the Christian Right?

Dogmatic religious conviction may furnish a ground for discounting the reliability of evidence that does not fit revealed truths. Paul Cameron sees faith and scientific empirical research as so tightly intertwined that the findings of sound empirical research should cohere with religious precepts. "In the ultimate sense," he explained, "assuming that we have correctly gotten material from the real world, as a Christian I believe that it cannot be incompatible with God's intent and what the universe is about." Cameron is explicit about the primacy of faith in his empirical research. As he told us, "religious convictions are foundational in that they suggest where I should spend my energy. Obviously, you could ask questions about trees and use the same methodology. I'm interested in homosexuality because the Christian tradition and scripture have pointed to it as a terrible evil. And I want to see to what degree that's the case" (Telephone interview, June 6, 2006).

Note the ambiguity of that last remark. If it were enough to know that Christian tradition and scripture have been understood to point to homosexuality as a terrible evil, then empirical evidence would be superfluous. A resort to empirical (or normative) inquiry to see "to what degree that's the case" as a matter of social consequences (or as a matter of moral reasoning) suggests a certain open-mindedness about what will be discovered. The worry, however, is that the dogmatic conviction will drive the empirical inquiry, including perhaps the selection of a methodology and the interpretation of evidence, perhaps even to the point of suppressing or manipulating evidence. Although there is nothing wrong insofar as religious motivations lead researchers to important and interesting questions, nearly any kind of scientific or scholarly inquiry would be put at risk if the inquirer claimed to know the "right" conclusion in advance. Given ex ante dogmatic convictions about the conclusion, it is equally unclear why one would enter into genuine public deliberation, that is, a discussion about the merits of the case at hand in which one is open to persuasion.

Nevertheless, as noted, the conviction that revealed truth must be compatible with the evidence need not imply a manipulative attitude toward the evidence. This tension can be negotiated several ways. One might be open to revision in one direction only, such that if the evidence points toward the "wrong" conclusion, it will be assumed that the evidence must be wrong (and we will keep running the experiment until it comes out right). One might also be open to revision in both directions. Or, consider another alternative: faith might encourage varying degrees of rigidity, obduracy, or "stickiness" with respect to particular religiously grounded convictions, perhaps depending on their centrality or importance in one's faith, or the clarity with which scripture or religious authorities have spoken on the matter. A degree of rigidity or obduracy raises the bar with respect to the weight of scientific evidence needed to trigger the revision of religious beliefs, but it need not altogether preclude revision.[22]

We might think of faith as introducing the sort of stickiness of beliefs associated with Thomas Kuhn's idea of a scientific paradigm, or a reigning orthodoxy in science (1996). On Kuhn's account, the ideal world of self-critical scientists seeking to refute their own convictions is not the real world of science: actual scientists are themselves often committed to a certain view of the world based on certain widely shared fundamental convictions, assumptions that resist incremental shifts in the evidence, and which may even resist for a time an accumulation of counterevidence. A massive accumulation of counterevidence is necessary, on Kuhn's account, to unseat one reigning scientific paradigm in place of another.

Assuming that some Christian Right activists take up this nonmanipulative approach to research, what affect does such stickiness of religious convictions have on the scientific and democratic enterprise? The approach may often establish a bias in favor of certain conclusions— understood to conform to religious dogma—that at least partially undermines the scientific ethos of objectivity but need not undermine the conditions of democratic debate. From the perspective of science, the reflections of Stanton, and particularly those of Cameron, ought to cause concern. Although both might be open to revising religious convictions in the face of massive accumulations of empirical evidence against their position, both also appear to hold firmly to particular convictions that flow from their religious beliefs. In this sense, their threshold for revising existing religious beliefs appear to bias research, even if the conscious aim is not to manipulate the evidence. Rather than embodying the scientific ideal of disinterested and objective inquiry that follows the evidence wherever it may lead, such activists and researchers approach empirical research with a clear preference for evidence that coheres with their religious convictions.

It should be noted, however, that members of the Christian Right are not the only participants in partisan politics who fall short of scientific ideals of self-criticism and objectivity. In research and scholarship, even in areas seemingly remote from the partisan fray, ideology and deep moral convictions may lead people to overlook flaws in research whose conclusions they find agreeable, or unfairly to discount research supporting conclusions deemed objectionable. Left-leaning academics are frequently accused (and sometimes with cause) of allowing political correctness to influence their scholarship or their judgments. None of this should be excused, but we would need to engage in careful study before concluding that Christian Right advocates in politics are more likely than others to manipulate evidence (on the tendency of empirical evidence to be distorted by political convictions in the context of school choice, see Henig 2008).

From the perspective of partisan politics, the tendency to adhere to time-worn principles and policies is common. Party platforms and materials generated by interest and advocacy groups should not be confused with nonpartisan studies that seek only the truth. Partisan and interest-group competition can be acceptable and legitimate part of democracy as long as it is clear that that is what they are, and as long as the conditions of competition are fair. Candidates for office and the parties that support them are understood to have the role of making their strongest case, while emphasizing their opponent's weaknesses. The justification for such partisan political roles, insofar as they can be justified, is that in fair competition, all claims are vigorously contested, similar to the adversarial system in trials (Applbaum 1999). Likewise, advocacy groups such as Focus on the Family play a role in defending a point of view alongside other groups that contest their claims.

Even within the sphere of partisan politics and interest and advocacy group competition, there is an important difference between seeking out all the evidence that bolsters one's view and assembling it in a persuasive manner for the sake of engaging in vigorous public debate, and citing research known to be deeply flawed. The first practice is an inevitable part of party politics, and is understood on all sides to be acceptable. The second practice, by contrast, is widely understood to be improper and it undermines the quality of democratic deliberation by injecting untruths into the public marketplace of ideas. Politicians, advocates, and debaters are not supposed to lie and manipulate to advance their interests, and they suffer loss of credibility when they are caught lying.

The corrective process of fair debate—according to which peddlers of falsehoods are scorned, and credible sources are listened to—may not work as well as it should under conditions of intense polarization, when activists have a tendency to drift to extreme views (Sunstein 2000, 2006). We do, however, find it encouraging that groups like Focus on the Family, which once relied heavily on the research of extremists such as Cameron, no longer appeal to such clearly flawed research. It is, of course, unclear whether this shift arose from strategic motives or from genuine concerns about the quality of scientific research. Nevertheless, the turn toward more legitimate social science research lends some support to the notion that vigorous contestation and debate may discourage political groups from using such deeply flawed research.

Issue Selectivity and Hidden Agendas

Christian Right political organizations like Focus tend to be selective in choosing which issues to emphasize in political deliberations. Although the Christian tradition warns against myriad vices, groups such as Focus place far more emphasis on the claimed "evils" of homosexuality than those of other issues like divorce. In our interview with James White, former minister at the First Congregational Church in Colorado Springs and long-time friend of Dobson, he described the strategic considerations that shape the issue selection of the Christian Right:

> There is a certain sense in which you push that which will sell. If you were really concerned about the family, you would come out against divorce. But divorce is so popular now that you can't come out against that. So you've got to come out against something that your constituency isn't engaged in. Forty or fifty years ago, the religious Right was poisoned on alcohol, lipstick, music, movies, and Sunday closings. Now all their people drink, divorce, go to Wal-Mart on Sundays, watch movies—they can't come out against that. So you find issues that their constituency isn't really involved in like gay marriage. But yet everybody has their own hang-ups about sexuality. So let's blame these other people. (July 7, 2006)

White makes a persuasive case that one major reason for the prominence of discussions of same-sex marriage is the fact that in contrast to divorce, the gay and lesbian lifestyle is alien to many Americans. As a result, the Christian Right's opposition to what they consider the evils of homosexuality is a far more effective tool of political mobilization than other issues.

Critics might worry that a danger inherent in issue selectivity is that the real or full agenda of the Christian Right may not be made apparent. Here again, the issue of deception or manipulation rears its head. Ideology-driven political groups are often charged with harboring deeper and darker agendas; the Christian Right levels such charges against liberal groups. Julie Ingersoll's essay in this volume reveals some evidence that some Christian right leaders have been influenced behind the scenes by radical Christian Reconstructionist theology (see chapter 6). Such critics should indeed describe how, insofar as it is true, Christian Right principles point beyond immediate agendas toward wider and deeper transformations of society. Insofar as there are worries about the true aims of the Christian Right, we see no alternative but to trust in the normal workings of democratic politics, aided by vigilant scholars, journalists, and other investigators.

A quite different danger concerns not the public realm but the non-public realm of faith. The moral integrity of faith-based communities may be corrupted when politics dictates which purported moral evils are spoken of in public. Religious leaders since Roger Williams in the seventeenth century have counseled remaining aloof from political partisanship on account of the dangers of corrupting faith. But our focus has been on the political side of the ledger, and we leave the question of the consequences for the integrity of faith to others.

Conclusion: The Christian Right and American Democracy

How should we assess the foregoing account of Christian Right activism from the standpoint of American democracy? Like other groups with less than majority status, the Christian Right seems—for its own combination of strategic, theological, and moral reasons—to have embraced a two-tiered rhetorical strategy, which involves appealing in public settings to arguments and reasons that have wide appeal. We found little ground for crediting the Christian Right's victim narrative, or the parallel charges leveled by critics of liberalism. The Christian Right is neither silenced nor marginalized and powerless in American politics.

We have argued that the idea of two-tiered rhetoric is not necessarily problematic from the standpoints of liberal constitutionalism or deliberative democracy. For members of a group to speak one way when speaking to fellow members of the group, and another way when speaking to outsiders, is in many ways altogether natural in a diverse democracy. As we noted, the whole notion of liberal public reason assumes that, along with a shared public discourse, groups with divergent ultimate religious and philosophical conceptions will have reasons of their own for favoring one policy or another. Although it is important that there be some consistency and that the outward directed reasons are not deceptive, in the materials we have examined and the interviews Klemp has conducted, contemporary Christian Right activists did not seem to be using publicly accessible arguments to manipulate.

We found some reason to be concerned about the use of empirical evidence by Christian Right groups, though it is hard to tell whether the source of the problem is faith, ideology, wishful thinking, sloppiness, or some combination of these. It is also not easy to say whether Christian Right groups or the Christian Right as a whole is more prone to misuse evidence than comparable groups at other points on the ideological spectrum. Political leaders and activists often cite deeply flawed statistics. Countries have been known to go to war based on what has turned out to be deeply flawed evidence marshaled uncritically.

Finally, we have also argued that the Christian Right's victim narrative too often goes unchallenged, including by academic critics of liberal public reason who seem to embrace unreflectively the canard that liberal elites make the rules of public speech—how exactly?—and thereby silence and marginalize American Christians. The Christian Right's willingness to engage in political discussion using public reasons and evidence calls into question its own appeals to the narrative of victimization. The Christian Right is anything but silent in our politics, and professions of religious faith are not only permitted, but also mandatory among aspirants to high public office. In these ways, religious believers and beliefs appear to be treated with reverence by nearly everyone in public life.[23] The victimization charge serves certain rhetorical purposes for the Christian Right, and that it is repeated by centrist and even left of center academics, if anything, attests to a certain hegemonic power on the part of the Christian Right.

The vehemence and popularity of the charge of victimization may, nevertheless, be a cause for concern about political polarization. It is generally argued that the polarization that infects elite politics in the United States does not extend to the general population, perhaps with some limited exceptions, such as the abortion issue (Fiorina, Abrams, and Pope 2006). But those who are active constituents of organizations such as Focus on the Family—the views of which are shaped by its extensive Christian media infrastructure—and who tend as a consequence to participate in repeated conversations with groups of like-minded others may well be prone to group polarization.[24]

The Christian Right's establishment of a robust infrastructure of Christian media outlets, advocacy groups, schools, and universities reinforces this worry. Over the last thirty-five years, the number of Christian radio stations has increased from 399 in 1972 (Diamond 1998, 21) to nearly 2,000 in 2005 (Blake 2005). Focus on the Family alone broadcasts James Dobson's daily radio on 2,000 stations throughout America, and estimates that this broadcast reaches upwards of 200 million people worldwide through its international broadcasts in ninety-eight countries. Focus also produces books and DVDs, and distributes twelve magazines with a nationwide paid circulation of 3.5 million people (Buss 2002). The Christian Right has also established television networks, such as Pat Robertson's Christian Broadcasting Network (CBN), and institutions of higher education such as Regent College, Liberty University, and Patrick Henry College. Uniting these subcultural institutions is a common aspiration to cultivate traditional values and to counter the secular humanism that they see as pervasive in Hollywood, academia, and the news media.

This extensive infrastructure may reinforce existing conditions of intellectual insularity and intolerance toward other groups. Although there are few comprehensive studies of Christian Right activists, one of the largest conducted found evidence of widespread intolerance. When asked about members of liberal groups, such as the National Organization for Women, American Civil Liberties Union, and People for the American Way, Wilcox and Lanson notes that "only 61 percent of Christian Right activists would allow them to speak in their communities, 57 percent would allow them to demonstrate, and a disconcerting 14 percent would allow them to teach in public schools" (2006, 138). And though liberal groups often attack the Christian Right with equal animosity, this study found that Left-leaning activists are more likely to grant their opponents these basic political rights (Wilcox and Larson 2006, 138). Of course, such studies do not show that the Christian Right's emerging media infrastructure has heightened attitudes of polarization and intolerance. They do, however, illustrate the pervasiveness of such attitudes and point to the importance of encouraging engagement with other citizens and groups rather than cultural isolation.

These conditions of polarization—cultivated and encouraged by the Christian Right's vast cultural infrastructure—may help explain the staying power of the narrative of victimization, and the feeling that liberal elites have conspired to push them out of the public square. Yet, as we have argued, that this narrative of victimization continues to thrive within the conservative Christian subculture does not prove its validity. To the contrary, the Christian Right's own political successes and positive rhetorical practices call into question its status as a victim of powerful liberal elites.

Notes

1.   These interviews were conducted primarily in Colorado between 2004 and 2006. We interviewed six Christian Right leaders, three Colorado Springs lawmakers, and sixteen liberal opponents of the Christian Right. We sought to diminish the numerical imbalance in favor of liberal activists by

soliciting interviews with a wide range of activists and policy analysts at Focus on the Family, the Family Research Council, and other Christian Right organizations. We found, however, that though liberal opponents of the Christian Right were eager to grant interviews, Christian Right activists were much more hesitant. More often than not, they turned down interview requests or simply never responded. Despite this imbalance, we have structured this essay's analysis to ensure that the reflections of Christian Right leaders are considered equally alongside the reflections of liberal opponents. In many cases, our analysis concerns the political rhetoric of activists in the late 1980s and early 1990s. To evaluate the self-reflections of Christian Right activists during this period, we rely on historical accounts of the Christian Right political movement (see Diamond 1998; Freeman 1993; Hardisty 1995, 1999; Herman 1997; Hertzke 1988; Wilcox and Lesage 1998; Moen 1992; Penning 1994).

2. Deliberative democrats often place special emphasis on the importance of sincere efforts to engage with one another on the merits of public issues. Amy Gutmann and Dennis Thompson argued that candidates, advocacy groups, and citizens should offer one another reasons and arguments that are *"accessible* to all the citizens to whom they are addressed" (2004). Jurgen Habermas argued that the primary virtue of deliberations guided by what he calls 'communicative action' is their orientation toward understanding (1984). Discourse should be aimed toward finding "reasons that are persuasive to all" (Cohen 2002).

3. For Rawls's early articulation of public reason, see *Political Liberalism* (1993). For his later articulation of public reason, see "The Idea of Public Reason Revisited" (1999b). For an excellent overview of public reason that spans both the early and later Rawls, see Charles Larmore (2003) as well as Amy Gutmann and Dennis Thompson (1996). For critical discussions, see Stephen Macedo (1999). For a "republican" account, see Philip Pettit (2000).

4. "We the People of the United States, in Order to form a more perfect Union, establish Justice, insure domestic Tranquility, provide for the common defense, promote the general Welfare, and secure the Blessings of Liberty to ourselves and our Posterity, do ordain and establish this Constitution for the United States of America."

5. This paragraph and the next draw on Stephen Macedo and Frederick Liu (2005). This article in turn draws heavily on Liu's excellent senior thesis at Princeton University (2005).

6. There are complex questions concerning whether natural law arguments are "public" in the right ways, or philosophically sectarian (for a discussion, see Macedo 1998; George and Wolfe 2000).

7. For a critical discussion of the empirical evidence, and the analogies with European countries, see William Eskridge, Darren R. Spedale, and Hans Ytterbergin "Nordic Bliss," in which they point out that the rise of single parenting followed, not same sex partnership legislation (which often excluded adoption rights in any case) but rather, the much earlier introduction of no-fault divorce and the extension of welfare benefits and public child support to single heterosexual parents (2004).

8. Christopher Eberle claims that some argued this way in the controversy

over Colorado's Amendment 2, which sought to eliminate all state and local protective ordinances or policies protections homosexuals against discrimination (see Eberle 2002, 3–5). Supporters of Amendment 2 certainly offered public reasons and arguments—albeit not very good ones—at various stages in the controversy over Amendment 2, especially when the Amendment was challenged in state and federal courts.

9. Andrew Sabl suggests, in an otherwise interesting essay, that public reason is a recipe for hypocrisy, requiring people to "recast" religious arguments in non-religious terms. It happens because religious activists seek "the overrated legitimacy of secular legal and intellectual elites." We think this is a misdiagnosis of practice, at least in general, perhaps not in some isolated cases (see Sabl 2007, 41).

10. Somewhat ironically, in volume 1, chapter 7, John Evans argues that Christian conservatives have to a large extent captured the public debate over moral values, resulting in to a large extent the exclusion of mainstream Protestants from the moral values discussion.

11. Emblematic, say the critics, is the privacy rights jurisprudence deployed by the Supreme Court to strike down state laws prohibiting contraceptive use by married couples, then unmarried couples, and later to provide access to abortion. Griswold v. Connecticut, 381 U.S. 479 (1965); Roe v. Wade, 410 U.S. 113 (1973).

12. See also Cohen v. California, 403 U.S. 15 (1971), and Texas v. Johnson, 491 U.S. 397 (1989). To combat these alleged encroachments, conservative populists call for a "return" to an "originalist" or "strict constructionist" theory of constitutional interpretation, which would narrowly construe the rights of minorities and various freedoms (Bork 1990).

13. See Gabriel Rossman's analysis in chapter 10 of volume 1 on the Christian Right's attempts to reshape the cultural realm to reflect their values. As Robert Bork declared, "Modern liberalism is powerful because it has enlisted our cultural elites, those who man the institutions that manufacture, manipulate, and disseminate ideas, attitudes, and symbols" (1996, 7). Christopher Lasch, Gertrude Himmelfarb, and others have expressed similar sentiments. As Lasch put it, "those who control the international flow of money and information, preside over philanthropic foundations and institutions of higher learning, manage instruments of cultural production and thus set the terms of the public debate—that have lost faith in the values, or what remains of them, of the West. . . . the new elites, the professional classes in particular, regard the masses with mingled scorn and apprehension" (Lasch 1995, 28).

14. Of course, it may be difficult to portray efforts to deny marriage rights to gays, or demands for the federal government to intervene in the Terry Schaivo case, as defenses of the free exercise of religion. Perhaps this works better for local efforts to post the Ten Commandments in schools or courthouses, or for calls to fund religious schools through vouchers.

15. See Green v. Connolly, 330 F. Supp. 1150 (1971), and briefs filed for Bob Jones by National Association of Evangelicals, American Baptist Churches, and Trent Lott, which Rogers Smith discusses in chapter 11 of volume 1.

16. Note here Evans's evidence on the resonance for religious believers of arguments from nature.

17. Though the National Legal Federation, a prominent conservative legal group, advised CFV to avoid this phrasing in the text of the amendment, they confirmed that the "no special rights" slogan served as the perfect centerpiece for public messaging (see Hardisty 1995).

18. When we interviewed Alan Wisdom, vice president of the conservative Christian Institute on Religion and Democracy, he also emphasized the necessity of publicly accessible arguments. As he told us, "For democratic decisions to be legitimate, there must be a perception of principles higher than self-interest. This means that Christians will have to use arguments in the public square that go beyond what we alone recognize. You have to appeal to things that people who don't accept your view of scriptural authority accept" (interview, June 28, 2005).

19. They also portray this it as a major revision of the view presented in the original edition of *Political Liberalism*. Rawls there addressed examples such as Abraham Lincoln's Second Inaugural Address, with its invocation of Old Testament themes, and Martin Luther King Jr.'s political speeches, laced with Biblical allusions. He seemed (to some) to emphasize that the resort to religious reasons and arguments needed a special justification, which was provided by times of constitutional crisis, and in response to grave injustice. For Rawls's final statement, see "The Idea of Public Reason Revisited." Stout chooses to criticize what he takes to be the original rather than the revised or clarified version of Rawls's argument, see *Democracy and Tradition*.

20. CFV's empirical claims include the following: "Overall, surveys show that 90% of gay men engage in anal intercourse—the most high-risk sexual behavior in society today. (No wonder 83% of Colorado AIDS cases have occurred in gay males—it's a tragedy, but it's true.). . . . 80% of gay men surveyed have engaged in oral sex upon the anus of partners. . . . Well over a third of gays in 1977 admitted to 'fisting.'" (Colorado for Family Values 1992).

21. Questions concerning adoption are typically based on the best interests of the child. That a couple seeking to adopt is married may well be a relevant consideration, but it is hardly dispositive (see Woodhouse. 2003).

22. For a discussion of the "stickiness" of religious beliefs about gender roles and how the concept of male headship is being revised to accommodate greater diversity in gender roles, see chapter 5 of volume 1.

23. Of course, there are a few other important exceptions in the academy, recently, Richard Dawkins and Daniel Dennett. Is the lack of more direct debate part of the problem? No doubt, for many academic philosophers, the subject is simply not very interesting.

24. Cass Sunstein usefully summarizes the empirical evidence for the tendency of conversations and deliberation among like-minded people to lead to lead to polarization, such that people's views subsequent to deliberation are more extreme than those they brought with them to the discussion (2002).

References

Applbaum, Arthur Isak. 1999. *Ethics for Adversaries*. Princeton, N.J.: Princeton University Press.

Benhabib, Seyla. 1992. *Situating the Self*. New York: Routledge.

Berkowitz, Peter. 2000. *Virtue and the Making of Modern Liberalism*. Princeton, N.J.: Princeton University Press.

Blake, Mariah. 2005. "Stations of the Cross." *Columbian Journalism Review* 3(May/June): 32–39.

Bork, Robert H. 1990. *The Tempting of America*. New York: The Free Press.

———. 1996. *Slouching Towards Gomorrah*. New York: Regan Books.

Brint, Steven, and Kristopher Proctor. Forthcoming. "Middle-Class Respectability 'After Thrift': Work and Lifestyle in the Professional-Managerial Stratum." In *After Thrift*, edited by Joshua J. Yates and James Davison Hunter. New York: Columbia University Press.

Bull, Christopher, and John Gallagher. 1996. *Perfect Enemies*. New York: Madison Books.

Buss, Dale. 2002. "The Counter Counterculture." *PRIMEDIA Company* (January). Available at: http://findarticles.com/p/articles/mi_m3065/is_1_31/ai_8213 7279 (accessed April 20, 2009).

Carter, Stephen. 1993. *Culture of Disbelief*. New York: Basic Books.

Colorado for Family Values (CFV). 1992. "STOP Special Class Status for Homosexuality: Vote YES! On Amendment 2." *Colorado for Family Values Election Tabloid*. Colorado Springs: Colorado for Family Values. Available at: http://www.coloradoforfamilyvalues.org.

Cohen, Joshua. 2002. "Deliberation and Democratic Legitimacy." In *Democracy*, edited by David Estlund. New York: Blackwell Publishers.

Diamond, Sara. 1998. *Not By Politics Alone*. New York: Guilford Press.

Dobson, James. 2003. "Marriage on the Ropes." *Dr. Dobson's Newsletter* (September 2003). Focus on the Family. Available at: http://www.focusonthe family.com/docstudy/newsletters/A000000771.cfm (accessed in January 2005).

———. 2004. "In Defending Marriage: Take the Offensive!" *Dr. Dobson's Newsletter* (April 2004). Focus on the Family. Available at: http://www.focusonthe family.com/docstudy/newsletters/A000000334.cfm.

Dworkin, Ronald. 2005. *Taking Rights Seriously*. Cambridge, Mass.: Harvard University Press.

Eberle, Christopher. 2002. *Religious Conviction in Liberal Politics*. New York: Cambridge University Press.

Edsall, Thomas Byrne, and Mary D. Edsall. 1991. *Chain Reaction: The Impact of Race, Rights, and Taxes on American Politics*. New York: W. W. Norton.

Eskridge, William N., Darren R. Spedale, and Hans Ytterberg. 2004. "Nordic Bliss? Scandinavian Registered Partnerships and the Same-Sex Marriage Debate." *Issues in Legal Scholarship*. Berkeley, Calif.: Berkeley Electronic Press.

Fiorina, Morris P., Samuel J. Abrams, and Jeremy C. Pope. 2006. *Culture War? The Myth of a Polarized America*. New York: Pearson Longman.

Fraser, Nancy. 1992. "Rethinking the Public Sphere: A Contribution to the Critique of Actually Existing Democracy." In *Habermas and the Public Sphere*, edited by Craig Calhoun. Cambridge, Mass.: MIT Press.

Freeman, Matthew. 1993. *The San Diego Model: A Community Battles the Religious Right*. Washington, D.C.: People for the American Way.

George, Robert, and Christopher Wolfe. 2000. *Natural Law and Public Reason*. Washington, D.C.: Georgetown University Press.

Greeley, Andrew, and Michael Hout. 2006. *The Truth about Conservative Christians*. Chicago: University of Chicago Press.

Gutmann, Amy, and Dennis Thompson. 1996. *Democracy and Disagreement*. Cambridge, Mass.: Belknap Press.

Habermas, Jurgen. 1984. *The Theory of Communicative Action*, translated by T. McCarthy. Boston, Mass.: Beacon Press.

Harding, Susan Friend. 2000. *The Book of Jerry Falwell*. Princeton, N.J.: Princeton University Press.

Hardisty, Jean. 1995. "Constructing Homophobia: Colorado's Right-Wing Attack on Homosexuals." In *Eyes Right!*, edited by Chip Berlet. Boston, Mass.: South End Press.

———. 1999. *Mobilizing Resentment*. Boston, Mass.: Beacon Press.

Hedges, Chris. 2007. *American Fascists: The Christian Right and the War on America*. New York: Free Press.

Henig, Jeffrey. 2008. *Spin Cycle: How Research Is Used in Policy Debates, The Case of Charter Schools*. New York: Russell Sage Foundation.

Herman, Didi. 1997. *The Antigay Agenda: Orthodox Vision and the Christian Right*. Chicago: University of Chicago Press.

Hertzke, Allen D. 1988. *Representing God in Washington*. Knoxville: University of Tennessee Press.

Holmes, Stephen. 1995. "Gag Rules and the Politics of Omission." In *Passions and Constraints*. Chicago: University of Chicago Press.

Hunter, James Davison. 1992. *Culture Wars*. New York: Basic Books.

Klemp, Nathaniel J. 2007. "Beyond God-Talk: Understanding the Christian Right from the Ground Up." *Polity* 39(4)(October): 522–44.

Kuhn, Thomas. 1996. *The Structure of Scientific Revolutions*. Chicago: University of Chicago Press.

Lasch, Christopher. 1995. *The Revolt of the Elites & The Betrayal of American Democracy*. New York: W. W. Norton.

Lesage, Julia. 1998. "Christian Coalition Leadership Training." In *Media Culture and the Christian Right*, edited by Linda Kintz and Julia Lesage. Minneapolis: University of Minnesota Press.

Locke, John. 1689/1983. *Letter Concerning Toleration*. Indianapolis, Ind.: Hackett Publishing.

———. 1690/1988. *Two Treatises of Government*, edited by Peter Laslett. New York: Cambridge University Press.

Macedo, Stephen. 1990. *Liberal Virtues: Citizenship, Virtue, and Community in Liberal Constitutionalism* New York: Oxford University Press.

———. 1997. *Reassessing the Sixties*. New York: W. W. Norton.

———. 1998. "In Defense of Liberal Public Reason: Are Abortion and Slavery Hard Cases?" *American Journal of Jurisprudence* 42(1997): 1–29.

Macedo, Stephen, and Iris Marion Young. 2003. *Child, Family, and the State: Nomos XLIV*. New York: New York University Press.

Moen, Michael. 1992. *The Transformation of the Christian Right*. Tuscaloosa: University of Alabama Press.

Neuhaus, Richard John. 1984. *The Naked Public Square*. Grand Rapids, Mich.: William B. Eerdmans.

Penning, James. 1994. "Pat Robertson and the GOP: 1988 and Beyond." *Sociology of Religion* 55(3): 327–45.

Pettit, Philip. 2000. "Democracy, Electoral and Contestatory." In *Designing Democratic Institutions*, edited by Iris Marion Young and Stephen Macedo. New York: New York University Press.

Popper, Karl. 2002. *The Logic of Scientific Discovery*. New York: Routledge.

Rawls, John. 1993. *Political Liberalism*. New York: Columbia University Press.

———. 1999a. *A Theory of Justice*. Cambridge, Mass.: Harvard University Press.

———. 1999b. "The Idea of Public Reason Revisited." In *The Law of Peoples with "The Idea of Public Reason Revisited."* Cambridge, Mass.: Harvard University Press.

Reider, Jonathan. 1997. *Canarise: The Jews and Italians of Brooklyn vs. Liberalism*. Cambridge, Mass.: Harvard University Press.

Sabl, Andrew. 2007. "Blastocyst Rights: What Science?" *Society* 44(4)(May/June): 38–42.

Schattschneider, E. E. 1975. *Semisovereign People*. New York: Harcourt Brace.

Shields, Jon A. 2007. "Between Passion and Deliberation: The Christian Right and Democratic Ideals." *Political Science Quarterly* 122(1): 89–113.

Simmel, Georg. 1903. "The Sociology of Conflict: II." *American Journal of Sociology* 9(1903): 672–89.

Smith, Christian. 1998. *American Evangelicalism*. Chicago: University of Chicago Press.

Stanton, Glenn. 2004. "Debate-Tested Sound Bites on Defending Marriage." *Focus on Social Issues* (May). Available at: http://www.citizenlink.org/FOSI/marriage/ssuap/A000000984.cfm (accessed in January 2005).

Stout, Jeffrey. 2004. *Democracy and Tradition*. Princeton, N.J.: Princeton University Press.

Sunstein, Cass. 2000. "Deliberative Trouble? Why Groups Go to Extremes." *The Yale Law Journal* 110(1): 71–119.

———. 2002. *Designing Democracy: What Constitutions Do*. New York: Oxford University Press.

———. 2006. *Infotopia*. New York: Oxford University Press.

Wilcox, Clyde, and Carin Larson. 2006. *Onward Christian Soldiers?* Boulder, Colo.: Westview Press.

Woodhouse, Barbara. 2003. "Children's Rights in Gay and Lesbian Families: A Child-Centered Perspective." In *Child, Family, and the State: Nomos XLIV*, edited by Stephen Macedo and Iris Marion Young. New York: New York University Press.

Young, Iris Marion. 1990. *Justice and the Politics of Difference*. Princeton, N.J.: Princeton University Press.

———. 1996. "Communication and the Other: Beyond Deliberative Democracy." In *Democracy and Difference*, edited by Seyla Benhabib. Princeton, N.J.: Princeton University Press.

———. 2000. *Inclusion and Democracy*. New York: Oxford University Press.

PART III

CYCLES AND THE EVOLUTION OF A MOVEMENT

Chapter 8

The Decline, Transformation, and Revival of the Christian Right in the United States

PETER DOBKIN HALL

I have remarked, that the American clergy in general even excepting those who do not admit religious liberty, are all in favor of civil freedom; but they do not support any particular political system. They keep aloof from parties and from public affairs. In the United States religion exercises but little influence upon the laws and upon the details of public opinion; but it directs the customs of the community, and, by regulating domestic life, it regulates the state.

Alexis de Tocqueville, *Democracy in America*, I: 314–15

*D*EMOCRACY IN *America* offers an idealized portrayal of the role of religion in politics, in which churches supported religious toleration, kept aloof from politics, and had little influence on public opinion. We would never guess from de Tocqueville's account that the country was in the midst of a second Great Awakening of religion—one that, in little more than two decades, transformed it from one in which barely one in ten of its citizens were "churched" to being one of the most religious nations on earth (Finke and Stark 1992). Nor would we guess that the nation was at the beginning of an epoch of reform in which social and political movements like temperance and abolitionism, most of them faith-based in their origins, would revolutionize both the methods and motives of political action.

Any account of the role of the Christian Right in public life has to begin in the during the half century preceding the Civil War, which marked the emergence of the fundamental dynamics shaping the relationship of religion and politics. Disestablishment—legal and constitutional prohibitions on government support for religion—forced churches to compete for adherents in a religious marketplace. Subject to the preferences of believers, churches faced a strategic dilemma: on the one hand, success in attracting believers required a degree of flexibility in doctrine and practice; on the other, such flexibility threatened the integrity of their religious mission. Posed in the context of churches' public role, this dilemma offered the choice between a rigid sectarian purity that limited their capacity to form inclusive alliances with other religious bodies on issues of common concern and the pragmatism and flexibility essential to alliances and coalitions that undercut their doctrinal and moral authority. Understanding the history of religion in American politics requires that we recognize the persistent tension between the maintenance of doctrinal integrity and the willingness to accept the compromises essential to public influence in market democracies.

What links earlier instances of religious activism, like the evangelical united front of the antebellum period and post–Civil War revivalism, to today's Christian Right? Certainly, their greatest commonality has been their commitment to saving the nation and its citizens, rather than humanity in general, from immanent peril through redemptive activism. Even when they have worked through secular instrumentalities, their primary goal has always been to build faith communities rather than to strengthen civil institutions—and moving those faith communities to reshape public life. This focus on national redemption through mobilizing the faithful, along with adherence to the core tenets of evangelical Protestantism, is a continuity that links a succession of religious activist movements from the early national period to the present.[1]

Although today's Protestant activists are labeled conservative, I do not suggest that the combination of national redemptionism and evangelical theology invariably aligned its adherents with forces of political conservatism. As the evidence I offer suggests, evangelical Protestants were as likely to engage their activist energies in progressive causes, like antislavery or the social gospel, as in conservative ones like anti-Catholicism. My analysis of these strains of Protestant activism is not concerned with the programmatic substance of the political movements with which adherents affiliated, but with the inherent tensions between religious convictions and political engagement in the context of American democracy. I am less interested in constructing a narrative account of the political activities of a particular group of Protestant sects than in showing how a relatively unchanging set of religious beliefs and practices have produced very different kinds of public activism, depending on social, economic, and political contingencies.

I will focus on three episodes of civic activism among evangelicals: Lyman Beecher's voluntary system, which proved a powerful force from the mid-1820s through the mid-1830s; Dwight Moody's big tent evangelism between 1870 and 1920; and the contemporary Christian Right, which to an unprecedented extent has embedded itself within party politics.

Discovering the Voluntary System: And the Rise and Fall of Evangelical Activism

In 1826, Connecticut evangelist Lyman Beecher was called to the pulpit of the Hanover Street Church in Boston. His appointment was, in effect, a declaration of war on the city's religious establishment. For half a century, Boston Congregationalism had been drifting from the fiery tenets of revealed religion toward more liberal and permissive sentiments that emphasized good works over the deep faith of the spiritually reborn. This drift had powerful political implications. It affected the control of important public institutions like Harvard College and its faculty appointments. It influenced the control of congregations and their extensive landholdings. It shaped public morality, determining the legality of forms of recreation and entertainment, as well as the strictness with which the Sabbath was observed.

Conflict over these issues was rooted in a deeper feeling among religious activists like Beecher that nothing less than the future of the republic itself was at stake. "If we do fail in our great experiment of self-government," Beecher would declare a decade later,

> Our destruction will be as signal as the birthright abandoned, the mercies abused, and the provocation offered to beneficent Heaven. The descent of desolation will correspond with the past elevation. No punishments of Heaven are so severe as those for mercies abused; and no instrumentality employed in their infliction is so dreadful as the wrath of man. No spasms are like the spasms of expiring liberty, and no wailings such as her convulsions extort. It took Rome three hundred years to die; and our death, if we perish, will be as much more terrific as our intelligence and free institutions have given to us more bone, and sinew, and vitality. May God hide me from the day when the dying agonies of my country shall begin! O, thou beloved land! bound together by the ties of brotherhood and common interest and perils, live forever—one and undivided! (1835, 44–45)

For Beecher and his fellow activists, the future of the republic depended not only on the vitality of religious communities, but also on their capacity to shape public values by creating or controlling civic institutions. For them, the religious struggle was also a political and cultural one.

By the time of Beecher's call to Hanover Street, Massachusetts was already deeply split between evangelical Trinitarian and rationalist Unitarian factions. The Trinitarians, who drew their support from farmers and, in the cities, from artisans and laborers, were becoming alarmed by the decline of public and private morality and the destruction of traditional forms of community and economic life. The Unitarians, who enjoyed the patronage of the educated business and professional elites and those elements of the middle classes that shared their values, took a more laissez faire attitude toward the emerging urban and industrial order. Because these differences in outlook and interests not only crosscut the population, but also the commonwealth's congregations, conflict between the factions played out both at the ballot box and in battles for control of local parishes.

"When I came to Boston," Beecher would write many years later, "evangelical people had no political influence there, and in civil affairs those who joined them had but little chance. All offices were in the hands of Unitarians—perhaps a Baptist occasionally; hence, as young men came in from the town, there was a constant stream of proselytes to them" (1866, II: 107). To counteract this, Beecher began forming a cadre of young activists, telling one,

> "The whole influence of Unitarianism a poisonous bribery." I said, "What do you think of that?" "I think it must be stopped, or we shall be stopped." "My opinion is, we can stop it. There must be ten men in our Church—you one—that can assemble in a confidential meeting, and make such arrangements as will do it." I named twelve to bring to me. He did. I explained to them, and said, "You may exert a power that shall be felt throughout the United States. There is a set of smoking loafers who have been in the habit of attending primary meetings, and having it all their own way. Our people don't go. The cause of God is abandoned just here—the cause of souls. They come streaming into this city from all directions to be perverted. Now organize a society. Go to primary meetings; go to this and that man, and persuade them to go and do up the business." (1866, II: 107–8)

This group, the Hanover Association of Young Men, began meeting monthly and, under Beecher's guidance, formed "committees on various important matters relating to state of city and things needing to be done." They launched an attack on lotteries, energetically lobbied the legislature, and got a law passed banning them. They then moved on to more general moral reform projects, writing letters to the newspapers, agitating for the enforcement of the blue laws on Sunday work and recreation, and keeping an eye on such problematic groups as "the colored population," the Irish, and sailors (Beecher 1866, I: 146). Beecher's efforts were dramatically successful and alarmed some of his contemporaries.

Unitarian leader William Ellery Channing, writing anonymously in the *Christian Examiner* in 1829, warned against the power of voluntary associations in language that suggested that he had Beecher and his allies in mind. Conceding that associations could do many good things, he nevertheless feared that

> a few are able to excite in the mass strong and bitter passions, and by these, to obtain an immense ascendancy. Through such an Association, widely spread, yet closely connected by party feeling, a few leaders can send their voices and spirit far and wide, and, where great funds are accumulated, can league a host of instruments, and by menace and appeals to interest, can silence opposition. Accordingly, we fear that in this country, an influence is growing up through widely spread Societies, altogether at war with the spirit of our institutions, and which, unless jealously watched, will, will gradually but surely encroach on freedom of thought, of speech, and of the press. It is very striking to observe, how, by such combinations, the very means of encouraging a free action of men's minds, may be turned against it. . . . We are persuaded that by an artful multiplication of societies, devoted apparently to different objects, but all swayed by the same leaders, and all intended to bear against a hated party, as cruel a persecution may be carried on in a free country as in a despotism. (1829, 114–15)

"We say not that all great Associations *must* be thus abused," Channing continued. "We know that some are useful. We know, too, that there are cases, in which it is important that public opinion should be condensed, or act in a mass. We feel, however, that the danger of great Associations is increased by the very fact, that they are sometimes useful. They are perilous instruments. They ought to be suspected. They are a kind of irregular government created within our Constitutional government" (1829, 114).

Sensitive to such criticisms, Beecher evidently encouraged his activists to keep their sectarian ties under wraps. Writing of their victory over the lotteries, Beecher crowed: "Nobody ever knew where that movement came from. They never knew what hit 'em" (Beecher 1866, II: 108). Recounting their success in vanquishing the liquor dealers, he gloated: "They never knew where *that* came from either." This seems to have been a strategic decision based on his understanding that success in the political arena required a capacity to form alliances beyond the boundaries of his denomination.

The tension between the sectarian motive to galvanize and mobilize a narrow base of disciplined followers to strengthen and build the identity and influence of a particular religious community, and the civic motive to form ecumenical alliances across sectarian lines to achieve secular ends is a recurrent one in the history of evangelical political engagement. Beecher seems to have tried to have it both ways: publicly, his activism served broad civic purposes; privately, it demonstrated how the faithful could influence public opinion and legislation. Arguing for the efficacy of his voluntary system, Beecher wrote,

> They say ministers have lost their influence. The fact is, that they have gained. By voluntary efforts, societies, missions, and revivals, they exert a deeper influence than ever they could by queues, and shoe-buckles, and cocked hats, and gold-headed canes.... The great aim of the Christian Church in relation to the present life is not only to renew the individual man, but also to reform human society. That it may do this needs full and free scope. The Protestantism of the Old World is still fettered by the union of the Church with the State. Only in the United States of America has the experiment been tried of apply Christianity directly to man and to society without the intervention of the state. (1866, I: 253)

To what extent did forming ecumenical coalitions for the sake of civic effectiveness risk displacement of spiritual goals? Beecher and his allies would have argued that education, health, and public order—all secular goods—were necessary preconditions to making people receptive to God's Word (on this, see Hall 2005). They would have further insisted, as good Calvinists in the Edwardsian tradition, that the work of salvation could only be done by God—the most churches could do was to help prepare believers for God's grace.[2] But these arguments were not universally accepted, even in Congregationalist circles: Beecher's opponents suggested that his emphasis on secular reform represented an abandonment of the Calvinist belief in salvation through faith alone and an embrace of the Arminian doctrine of works.

Nonetheless, for the quarter century between 1815 and 1840, there seems to have been enough consensus among the major evangelical factions for Beecher and other leaders to form an evangelical united front of voluntary associations that were amazingly successful, both in rechurching Americans through their revivals and transforming the moral basis of public discourse (Foster 1960). But it is far from clear whether the success of secular voluntary associations like temperance groups translated into religious gains. In *Democracy in America*, de Tocqueville cited the temperance movement as a prime example of the remarkable power of voluntary associations:

> The first time I heard in the United States that a hundred thousand men had bound themselves publicly to abstain from spirituous liquors, it appeared to me more like a joke than a serious engagement, and I did not at once perceive why these temperate citizens did not content themselves with drinking water by their own firesides. I at last understood that these hundred thousand Americans, alarmed by the progress of drunkenness

around them, had made up their minds to patronize temperance. They acted in just the same way as a man of high rank who should dress very plainly in order to inspire the humbler orders with a contempt of luxury. It is probable that if these hundred thousand men had lived in France, each of them would singly have memorialized the government to watch the public houses all over the kingdom. (1835/1945, II: 118)

Neither in this passage, nor in any of his observations on voluntary associations, did he mention the role of churches in driving their formation. This suggests that though religion may have played a major role in the proliferation of voluntary associations, the associations themselves did not—contrary to Beecher's expectations—produce a revival of religion.

Finally, in surveying this early episode in religious activism, we have to assess whether Beecher's efforts can be classified as liberal or conservative, politically and religiously. Theologically, Beecher was a pillar of the New Haven Theology, which elaborated Jonathan Edwards's ideas far beyond their Calvinist roots. He was, accordingly, considered a liberal by Congregationalists and Presbyterians of his own time.[3] The most theologically conservative of these, the Old School Presbyterians, actually tried Beecher for heresy and, in 1837, purged those sympathetic to his ideas from the church's General Assembly (Ahlstrom 1972, 466–68). Politically, Beecher and his associates are harder to label.

Although the inclusive and nondenominational thrust of his revivalism, as well as his openness to the role of women in the church and his opposition to slavery, would certainly place him among the political progressives of his time, his social agenda, particularly his anti-Catholicism, sabbatarianism, and prohibitionist stands, generally places him among the conservatives. However, even some of those stances are not entirely conservative. Much of the support for prohibition came from women, who in many states were prohibited from owning property and had no way to protect themselves and their children from alcoholic husbands squandering the family earnings on drink. Certainly, his political methods, which in their disciplined manipulativeness and mean-spiritedness resonate disturbingly with those of today's Christian Conservatives, seem far from liberal in spirit.

The years between 1837, when the evangelical united front was shattered over theological differences between liberal and conservative Presbyterians, and the economic crisis of the 1870s, which forced Protestants to begin engaging the challenges of an urbanizing America, have been called a sectarian heyday (Ahlstrom 1972, 472). The split between Old School and New School Presbyterians and Congregationalists was only one of many fissures in the national Protestant community. As the slavery crisis deepened in the 1840s, Baptists, Methodists, and Presbyterians formally and amidst some discord split. Lutheran and Reformed churches separated over issues of language and evangelical methods. New sects emerged, including the Seventh Day Adventists, the Disciples of Christ, the Mormons, and others.

The fierceness of disagreements between these sects was painfully evident both during and after the Civil War, as Christians, individually and institutionally, rushed to offer their services to the Union. The liberal Protestants, led by Unitarians and Congregationalists, established the United States Sanitary Commission, a government-chartered nonprofit organization "charged with the duty of methodizing and reducing to practical service the already active but undirected benevolence of people toward the army." They focused their efforts on "the prevention of sickness and suffering among the troops" and the "wisest method which the people at large could use towards the comfort, security, and health of the army" (Brockett 1863, 35–36).

The Sanitary Commission's professionalism and emphasis on scientific rather than sentimental approaches to the relief of suffering brought it into conflict with the United States Christian Commission. The Christian Commission's primary purpose was to act as a clearinghouse for religious activities within the armed forces. It was grounded in the more theologically conservative and sectarian factions of evangelical Protestantism. "From the beginning," its chronicler wrote, "the army was recognized as a field for evangelical effort" (Moss 1869, 81). The commission's object, as stated in its 1863 *Plan of Operations*, was to "promote the spiritual and temporal welfare of the brave men who now are in arms to put down a wicked rebellion" (111).

More practically, the Sanitary Commission viewed the Christian Commission as a competitor in its fundraising efforts. Because both groups depended on the fundraising activities of clergy and women volunteers, they inevitably came into conflict. In the fall of 1862, the Cincinnati branch of the Christian Commission, with the apparent support of the St. Louis and Indianapolis branches, directly challenged the Sanitary Commission's policies of centralized financial administration and nationally coordinated distribution of goods and services. The westerners, doubtless more sympathetic to the more theologically conservative variants of evangelical Protestantism, desired more individualized, personal, and charitable approaches to relief activities. The central office successfully crushed this mutiny, but not without leaving an enduring legacy of ill feeling between the civic and sectarian factions.

These Civil War–era tensions within the Protestant community profoundly shaped the involvement of religious activists in Reconstruction and in the reform of urban charities in the 1880s and 1890s. Determined to create northern-style civil societies in the South, the radical Republicans, working through the military and the Freedman's Bureau (or, as it was officially known, the Bureau of Freedmen, Refugees, and Abandoned Lands), was established to distribute rations and medical supplies, establish schools, and aid benevolent societies in setting up schools and churches, administering confiscated lands, and levying justice in all cases concerning freedmen. The government proposed to economically empower the freedmen by redistributing to them property confiscated from ex-Confederates and, using revenues derived from these lands, to make available to private voluntary agencies buildings, transportation, and protection to whom it entrusted the task of training and educating the freedmen. This open invitation to religious and other voluntary agencies to take on this monumental task inevitably sparked conflicts between the civic and sectarian Protestant factions.

Early in 1865, two of the major freedmen's societies, the New York National Freedmen's Relief Association and the American Union Commission, together with elements from New York's Women's Central Relief Association, a branch of the United States Sanitary Commission, consolidated themselves as the American Freedmen's and Union Commission (New York National Freedmen's Relief Commission 1866, 14). This brought together the eastern elite liberal Protestant—primarily Unitarian and Congregationalist—elements that had been closely allied with the Sanitary Commission. It was led by such men as Yale professor Leonard Bacon, the "pope" of New England Congregationalism; Francis Shaw, the New York Unitarian philanthropist and reformer, as well as the father of the Union Army hero Robert Gould Shaw and charity organization leader Josephine Shaw Lowell; and Bostonian Edward Hooper, a lawyer and financier who would soon be elected treasurer of Harvard.

Despite their pleas for cooperation between the rival freedmen's societies and for a Christian but unsectarian emphasis in their education and relief efforts, the associations that had been closely tied to the Christian Commission—the American Missionary Association, the Methodists' Freedmen's Aid Society, the Baptists' Home Mission Society, and the Quakers' Friends' Association for the Aid and Elevation of the Freedman—resisted consolidation efforts. As one Methodist minister put it, "Methodist hands should have handled Methodist funds, and been appropriated to pay Methodist teachers, to found Methodist schools, and carry on a work for which the denomination should have due credit" (quoted in Swint 1967, 13).

Whereas the sectarians looked to the church as the central institution of reconstruction, the civic Protestants looked to the schoolhouse. "What method will best promote the cause of popular education and pure religion in the South?" asked an *American Freedman* editorial addressing Christian philanthropists.

The necessity of both is almost universally recognized. Neither can take the place of the other. Education unsanctified by religion issues in infidelity and anarchy. Religion unenlightened by education begets superstition and despotism. The schoolhouse without the church produces China; the church without the schoolhouse, Italy; the church *and* the schoolhouse, Republican America.

How to combine these two is an important problem. There are two possible solutions. The religious denominations may undertake the double work. They may plant the parochial school by the side of the church; they may teach at once the rules of arithmetic and the lessons of the catechism, the laws of grammar and the doctrines of theology. Such a system gives parochial schools. On the other hand, the various religious denominations may assume as their peculiar province the work of religious instruction. To that they may confine themselves, while the whole community unites in a common effort for the education of the masses, not only in secular knowledge, but in those precepts of morality and teachings of Christian religion in which all agree. This system is the common school. It is the almost universal system of Protestant Republicanism.

The education of the South, especially of the Freedmen is a truly religious work; none the less so because it is undenominational. Cousin rightly says, "The less we desire our schools to be ecclesiastical, the more they ought to be Christian." Called to this work not only by the claims of country and of humanity, but also by the voice of God, recognizing it as His work, entering upon it in humble trust on Him, aiming by it to render the subjects of our education better fitted to be not only citizens of the Republic but children of our Father in heaven, we desire the more that our schools may be truly Christian because they are unecclesiastical. For this purpose we aim to commission only teachers possessing the spirit of true religion, by which we do not mean persons of any particular doctrinal views, but such as are attracted to the work, not by curiosity, or love of adventure, or its compensation, but by a genuine spirit of love for God and man; for this purpose our schools are opened with such general religious exercises as our experience in the North proves it practicable for all Christians to unite in; for this purpose in all the schools instruction is afforded in the fundamental duties of the Christian religion as inculcated in the command, "Thou shalt love the Lord thy God with all thy heart and soul and strength, and thy neighbor as thyself"; no less for this purpose do we jealously maintain their unsectarian character, not allowing the peculiar tenets of any particular denomination to be taught in the schools (1866, 94–96).

The civic Protestant efforts to promote cooperation failed, as did the whole reconstruction effort, as federal aid was pared away and resurgent white terrorist groups drove Gideonites of both persuasions out of the South. The legacy was a deepening split between the two major evangelical factions that would profoundly affect their approaches to the challenges urbanization in the North.

Dwight Moody and Big Tent Evangelism

It is hard to imagine that anything short of a national catastrophe could have overcome the deep division among Protestant evangelicals following the Civil War. The Panic of 1873 and the four-year depression that followed was such a catastrophe: 18,000 businesses failed; unemployment soared to an estimated 14 percent; wage cuts and deteriorating working conditions sparked strikes and massive civil disorders. Compounding the crisis were major shifts in American social and religious demography: between 1850 and 1880, the number of foreign born in the United States doubled; the majority of the immigrants were Roman Catholics who, as they became citizens, supported the corrupt political machines that increasingly dominated urban politics.

As the crisis deepened following the Panic of 1873, Protestant America, whatever its internal disagreements, shared a growing sense of being besieged by the forces of "rum, Romanism, and rebellion."[4] This perception of a common threat would become the basis for a new set of alliances and coalitions that would reunite the Protestant factions and give rise to their resurgence as an effective political force.

Initially, the Protestant factions responded to the crisis on the basis of their theological dispositions and their experience during the war and reconstruction. The civic Protestants used statistical surveys to frame problems and empanelled commissions of experts to address them. They were less concerned with relieving individual suffering than with ascertaining the worthiness of relief recipients, believing that indiscriminate and sentimental charity were major causes of poverty. The sectarians, in contrast, embraced the rescue mission model of poor relief, offering religious services as a precondition for dispensing food and shelter and, more broadly, in spiritual regeneration through revivalism as the key to the prevention of poverty and the redemption of those who had fallen into it.

A sense of how profoundly these approaches differed is suggested by a 1874 report, "Pauperism in New York," presented to the American Social Science Association's Conference of Public Charities. The initial response of the wealthy to the depression, the report stated, was generous, compassionate—and indiscriminate. It also threatened, in the writer's view, to create a permanent class of paupers.

Despite warnings of the experienced, soup kitchens and free lodgings were opened, by public and private means, with the utmost liberality, in various portions of New York last winter, and enormous sums were contributed by private citizens for these popular benefactions. Before the winter was over, however, most of those engaged in them regretted, without doubt, that they had ever taken part in these kindly but mistaken charities. The reports of competent observers show their effects. The announcement of the intended opening of these and kindred charities immediately called into the city the floating vagrants, beggars, and paupers, who wander form village to village throughout the state. The streets of New York became thronged with this ragged, needy crowd; they filled all the station-houses and lodging places provided by private charity, and overflowed into the island almshouses. Street begging, to the point of importunity, became a custom. Ladies were robbed, even on their own doorsteps, by these mendicants. Petty offenses, such as thieving and drunkenness, increased (American Social Science Association 1874, 18–19).

In the emerging debate between the civic and sectarian evangelicals, a man like Dwight Lyman Moody would, on the face of it, certainly have sided with the sectarians. Born in rural western Massachusetts in 1837, Moody moved to Boston as a teenager to work in his uncle's shoe store. As a condition of employment, his uncle made him agree to regularly attend a local Congregational church and its Sunday school. "The Bible was not a familiar book to the new student," his biographer wrote (Moody 1900, 39). "I can truly say," recalled his teacher, "that I have seen few persons whose minds were spiritually darker than was his when he came into my Sunday-school class."

Moody's agnosticism gave way to an emotional conversion experience. "I remember the morning on which I came out of my room after I had first trusted Christ," Moody recalled. "I thought the old sun shone a good deal brighter than it ever had before—I thought that it was just smiling upon me; and as I walked out upon Boston Common and heard the birds singing in the trees I thought they were all singing a song to me. . . . It seemed to me that I was in love with all creation" (1900, 42).

Moody moved to Chicago in the fall of 1856, where he became an active member of the Plymouth Congregational Church. He began teaching young people and, using business methods (such as issuing stock) to promote it, soon was in charge of the largest Sunday school in the city. In 1860, he decided to give himself full time to Christian work. He became involved with the YMCA, which in these early years was a nondenominational Protestant missionary enterprise. With the outbreak of the Civil War, his YMCA connection led to deep involvement with the United States Christian Commission, which the YMCA's had played a central part in organizing. At the end of the war, on his return to Chicago, Moody became head of the city's YMCA and began a lay ministry in the

Illinois Street Church, an independent nondenominational congregation he had organized.

Moody's approach to his religious work was unusual in an era of intense sectarianism. He not only eschewed proselytizing for any one denomination, he was willing to reach out to any Christian—even to Catholics. Early in his career, when his Sunday school students were harassed by "the lower class of the Roman Catholic element," Moody paid a call on Bishop James Duggan. "Your zeal and devotion are most commendable in behalf of these people," declared the bishop, "and all you need to make you a great power for good is to come within the fold of the true church." "Whatever advantage that would give me among your people," Moody replied, "would be offset by the fact that I could no longer work among the Protestants." Moody asked the bishop if he would be allowed to pray with Protestants if he became a Roman Catholic. "Yes," the bishop replied, "you could pray with Protestants as much as ever." "Would you," Moody asked, "pray with a Protestant?" After the bishop replied that he would and the two knelt where they had been standing in the hall. The result was a cessation of all further annoyance from the Roman Catholic element in the city, and a lifelong friendship between the two men (Moody 1900, 71).

Moody's use of the intensely personal and emotional missionary and revivalist methods of the sectarians and aggressive business methods of financing and promotion framed a broadly civic ecumenical spirit that enabled him to transcend the divisions that were tearing the country and its cities apart during and after the war. This would prove to be an astonishingly powerful combination. Moody preached to more than 100 million people in his evangelistic campaigns (Christianity Today 2008).

Moody's 1878 New Haven, Connecticut, revival illustrates the effectiveness of this strategy (Dastin 1975). On the face of it, New Haven seemed an unpromising place for a religious revival. Yale's theological department was a nursery for the critical biblical scholarship that would be anathema to evangelicals who avowed scriptural inerrancy. In the college, the pioneer political economist (and Episcopal priest) William Graham Sumner had begun teaching immensely popular courses in political economy using the "irreligious" writings of Herbert Spencer (and, at the same time, introducing his students to the unscriptural evolutionary theories of Charles Darwin). In the sciences, the archaeologist Othniel Marsh was already deeply engaged in unearthing and displaying the fossil record that substantiated Darwin's challenge to scriptural accounts of Creation. Surely, the wise men of Yale would have spurned this poorly educated and uncredentialed midwestern former shoe salesman turned itinerant revivalist, as would the college-educated clergy of the Congregational and Episcopal congregations that dominated the religious life of the city's Protestants.

In fact, Moody was welcomed to the city by a broadly representative committee of clergy chaired by Yale's president, the eminent moral philosopher Noah Porter. His revival was bankrolled by an interdenominational committee composed of New Haven's wealthiest and most prominent businessmen and philanthropists. Their generous contributions made possible the erection of a huge tabernacle where, over the course of three months, tens of thousands of men and women flocked to worship.

Not only was the revival an astounding success, whether measured in terms of the number of people who came to worship or the number of congregations that endorsed it, it also led to a long and close relationship between Moody and Yale. He would send two of his sons to the college. The muscular Christian student leaders of Dwight Hall, Yale's YMCA and the platform for university social service, would for a generation make regular pilgrimages to Moody's home in Northfield, Massachusetts, to hone their piety and make the acquaintance of evangelical leaders from throughout the world. And the city's wealthiest businessman, president of the New Haven Clock Company and father of legendary Yale football coach Walter Camp, would become the lead donor to and lifelong senior trustee of Moody's Northfield Academy.

One of the reasons for Moody's success in drawing together the warring Protestant tribes is suggested by a religious census of the city undertaken after his 1879 visit (Collins 1886).[5] The census was conducted by a young clergyman, John Collins, who may have been in Moody's employ. It showed that nearly half of the city's church going population was non-Protestant.

Although Collins conducted his census in 1880, he did not present his findings publicly until 1886, when Moody convened his first Convention of Christian Workers of the United States and Canada—the first of the legendary Northfield conferences—launched to provide training for Christian leaders. Collins was first managing director of the International Christian Workers Association and went on to found the Boys' Clubs of America (Yale University 1922, 200).

If New Haven's business and religious leaders were willing to transcend their differences and embrace Moody's nondenominational revival on the basis of their impression that Protestantism was threatened by rum, Romanism, and rebellion, Collins's census both lent substance to their fears and offered them a way of countering the threat. This resolution was a new kind of big tent evangelicalism that fostered unsectarian cooperation and, at the same time, remobilized Protestants as a political force against vice, crime, and the other evils associated with urban life. But the big tent evangelicals did more than pursue a restrictive and controlling conservative social agenda. They also understood that poor urban populations, especially the young, needed alternatives to the wicked temptations of the city streets if they were to be redeemed. This became the cornerstone of the social gospel, both as a theological stance and as a set of urban institutions. The YMCA, in which Moody was a major figure, took the lead in offering recreational and educational activities to young people, regardless of religious affiliation, in the hope that these would be a portal to more serious religious commitments.

Although historians of the Progressive movement have minimized or ignored the role of religion in the political and institutional response to urban industrialism, the fact is that, especially on the local level, it probably did more to transform the moral agenda that assured progressivism's success than any number of muckraking articles by crusading journalists. One measure of this is the sales of social gospel tracts like Charles Sheldon's *In His Steps—What Would Jesus Do*? First published in 1896, the book has sold more than 30 million copies and ranks as the ninth best-selling book of all time.

The novel tells the tale of a midwestern congregation's dramatic encounter with poverty that poses for every member the question, what would Jesus do? As members of the congregation ponder this question, both individually and collectively, while examining their lives and occupations in the light of Scripture, each is transformed and, taken together, transform their community. The railroad executive provides a cafeteria so his workers will not have to eat lunch in saloons—then resigns his position because he could not stomach the company's violations of the interstate commerce law. The gorgeous choir singer gives up her comfortable church job to sing at revival meetings in the slums. The editor of the daily newspaper stops running advertisements for liquor and tobacco, ends coverage of morally questionable entertainment, and no longer will publish a Sunday edition. He then dramatically transformed the paper's editorial policy. "The editor of the News," he wrote,

> has always advocated the principles of the great political party at present in power, and has heretofore discussed all political questions from the standpoint of expediency, or of belief in the party as opposed to other political organizations. Hereafter, to be perfectly honest with all our readers, the editor will present and discuss all political questions from the standpoint of right and wrong. In other words, the first question asked in this office about any political question will not be, "Is it in the interests of our party?" or, "Is it according to the principles laid down by our party in its platform?" but the question first asked will be, "Is this measure in accordance with the spirit and teachings of Jesus as the author of the greatest standard of life known to men?" That is, to be perfectly plain, the moral side of every political question will be considered its most important side, and the ground will be distinctly taken that nations as well as individuals are under the same law to do all things to the glory of God as the first rule of action. (Sheldon 1896, 68)

The news became a crusader for municipal reform. The college president plunges into Christian political activism. "I confess with some shame," he told the minister,

> that I have purposely avoided the responsibility that I owe to this city personally. I understand that our city officials are a corrupt, unprincipled set of men, controlled in large part by the whiskey element and thoroughly selfish so far as the affairs of city government are concerned. Yet all these years I, with nearly every teacher in the college, have been satisfied to let other men run the municipality and have lived in a little world of my own, out of touch and sympathy with the real world of the people. 'What would Jesus do?' I have even tried to avoid an honest answer. I can no longer do so. My plain duty is to take a personal part in this coming election, go to the primaries, throw the weight of my influence, whatever it is, toward the nomination and election of good men, and plunge into the very depths of the entire horrible whirlpool of deceit, bribery, political trickery and saloonism as it exists in Raymond today. (Sheldon 1896, 89–90)

He was as good as his word, assuming leadership of the forces of reform in the city.

Maxwell, the minister, "watched with growing wonder the results of that simple Promise"—to do as Jesus would do—"as it was being obeyed in these various lives. Those results were already being felt all over the city. Who," he asked himself, "could measure their influence at the end of a year?" The result was, as the ensuing chapters suggest, revolutionary:

> The whole country had watched the progress of the pledge as it had become history in so many lives. . . . Already there had begun a volunteer movement in many churches throughout the country, acting on their own desire to walk closer in the steps of Jesus. The Christian Endeavor Society had, with enthusiasm, in many churches taken the pledge to do as Jesus would do, and the result was already marked in a deeper spiritual life and a power in church influence that was like a new birth for the members. (Sheldon 1896, 173)

The movement spread across denominational lines and beyond the churches into faith-based charities like the settlement houses. At the end of the book, the protagonist, Reverend Henry Maxwell, was invited to a Chicago settlement house to discuss what he had started.

> There were invited into the Settlement Hall, meeting for that night out of work, wretched creatures who had lost faith in God and man, anarchists and infidels, free-thinkers and no-thinkers. The representation of all the city's worst, most hopeless, most dangerous, depraved elements faced

Henry Maxwell and the other disciples when the meeting began. And still the Holy Spirit moved over the great, selfish, pleasure-loving, sin-stained city, and it lay in God's hand, not knowing all that awaited it. Every man and woman at the meeting that night had seen the Settlement motto over the door blazing through the transparency set up by the divinity student: "What would Jesus do?" (Sheldon 1896, 222)

A graduate of Phillips Andover (1879) and Brown University (1883), Sheldon, author of *In His Steps*, is a good example both of the pervasiveness of Moody's big tent evangelicalism and the extent to which his scripturally based activism linked the social gospel to politics and social reform (1925). As Sydney Ahlstrom remarked, "[Sheldon] became a major apostle not only of the Social Gospel but of the broader liberal movement as well" (1972, 776–77).

The social gospel, as Ahlstrom noted, "was anything but new." Its "powerfully rooted" Puritan convictions called on the church to shape, and if need be, remake society. "The second Great Awakening and the Evangelical United Front had intensified this tendency. Antebellum revivalism, in fact, was pervaded by concern for social reform and, beyond that, with a hope for a sanctified citizenry that would make this republic a model for the whole world" (1972, 787). Ahlstrom called attention to the variety of programmatic and political directions in which the social gospel could direct the energies of its adherents. Henry Ward Beecher, son of Lyman and his successor as one of America's most celebrated preachers, made "freedom to speak out on social issues a condition of his accepting the call to Plymouth Church in 1847" (787). In the course of his pastorate he held forth on a wide variety of political issues, including slavery, poverty, and labor relations. Although his outlook was conservative (for example, he blamed the poor for their poverty), "the social orientation which Beecher established at Plymouth Church enabled his successor, Lyman Abbott, to defend quite different economic views from the pulpit and to become the virtual chaplain of Theodore Roosevelt's Progressivism" (Ahlstrom 1972, 788). This change in outlook did not, Ahlstrom observed, require "any basic departure from Beecher's form of what was known as the New Theology: despite the conservativeness of many of Beecher's positions on particular issues, his basic position on the transformative role of the church in public life was identical to that of his Progressive successor.

Although the call to emulate Jesus did not produce the revolution Sheldon predicted in his novel, it seems fair to say that the political mobilization of the evangelicals in a context that enabled them to form effective alliances across denominational and political lines undoubtedly played an important role in the success of progressivism. By 1912, Progressivism had come to entirely dominate national political life. This civic phase in the evolution of evangelical Protestantism was, however, drawing to a close.

Many factors contributed to the disintegration of evangelical unity in the early twentieth century. Some were intrinsically religious, such as the death of charismatic unifying leaders like Moody, the institutionalization of religious communities into bureaucratized denominations, intensifying conflicts over reconciling belief in scriptural inerrancy (a basic tenet of evangelicalism) with science, particularly Darwinism, and the inherently sectarian tendencies of the religious marketplace, in which numbers of adherents and donations counted for more than less quantifiable contributions to the general good of country and community. Others were extrinsic, including a revival of political nativism in response to the continuing influx of immigrants, racism sparked by the migration of southern blacks to northern cities, and deepening concern among social conservatives about growing secularism and immorality in public life.[6] Although the liberal elements in the evangelical coalition of the pre–World War I years shared many of the racist and nativist convictions of their conservative brethren, these became increasingly difficult to sustain with the liberals growing involvement in practical reform politics. There were political issues—such as prohibition—on which there was consensus across the evangelical spectrum. There were others—such as the rights of organized labor and the teaching of evolution—on which accommodation became increasingly difficult.[7]

Certainly, the most serious source of disagreement—and the one that shaped the religious landscape for the rest of the century and into the current one—was between the fundamentalists and the modernists. The fundamentalist split from the evangelical mainstream did not occur because of any dramatic event. Rather, its emergence was a gradual process of conservative dismay with the erosion of old beliefs in biblical inerrancy, the virgin birth, Jesus's atonement for our sins, Christ's bodily resurrection, and the historicity of Christ's miracles. Challenged by critical biblical scholarship and by science, particularly Darwinism, theological conservatives grew increasingly unhappy with the influence, particularly in the seminaries and universities, of churchmen who went too far in accommodating their beliefs to these modern ideas. Beginning in 1876, a mixed group of Presbyterian, Baptist, and Episcopal clergy began holding annual conferences for Bible study and fellowship. But the lines of battle between conservatives and modernists would begin to be clearly drawn in 1894, when church liberals demanded revisions in the Westminster Confession, the credo of orthodox Calvinism. The modernists' efforts mobilized the conservatives who, in 1910, decisively affirmed the five points of faith regarded as fundamental to Christian orthodoxy.

The conservative Presbyterian counterrevolution had broad appeal to leaders in other denominations who shared their unhappiness with theological modernism and the increasingly secular character of American life. Through the 1920s, struggles for control unfolded in all of the major Protestant denominations. Ultimately, fundamentalism was less likely to be associated with particular denominations than it was to act as a rallying point for conservative clergy, seminaries, and growing numbers of freestanding congregations.[8]

"Because they loved their denominations—often unduly—and wished to preserve them from liberal inroads," wrote Sydney Ahlstrom of the beginnings of fundamentalism, "their resort was not in new schemes of scriptural interpretation but in shoring up old schemes; not in new doctrines, but in official confessions and the writings of their own church fathers" (1972, 812–13). His observation calls attention to the fact that, though fundamentalism was a theological perspective shared by a number of faith communities, it was weakened organizationally by its sectarianism, which prevented it from building effective coalitions among the like-minded in either religion or politics.

Although the fundamentalists in the aggregate commanded large numbers of adherents, they were weakened by sectarian fragmentation and weak organizational bases. Some came from denominations, like the Presbyterians, that had embraced modern denominational structures, but others, like the Southern Baptists and Pentecostals, came from groups that were no more than loose confederations of congregations, with no central authority. Many fundamentalist churches were independent congregations. Numbers of adherents meant little in terms of public influence if they could be forged neither into strong denominational bodies nor effectively build alliances within and beyond the religious world. Rather than drawing together at the end of World War I, as Ahlstrom noted, the peace merely assured conservative Christians that "theological and ecclesiastical warfare would be resumed with even greater vehemence" (1972, 816).

Conventional wisdom often characterizes the political stance of religious conservatives after the mid-1920s as a withdrawal "to rural and small-town America" and into "a rigidly patriarchal and puritanical subculture of their own" (Ehrenreich, Hess, and Jacobs, quoted in Wuthnow 1988, 134). In fact, although they had set aside expectations of being able to redeem the major denominations or impose their moral views on the nation as a whole, conservative evangelicals remained politically potent in states and localities, particularly in the South and Midwest, where their numbers enabled them to dominate public life without having to form coalitions and alliances with other groups. They succeeded in getting antievolution laws debated by legislatures in fifteen states—though only Arkansas and Mississippi ended up enacting them. Under pressure from the fundamentalists, many states remained "dry" after the passage of the Twenty-Second Amendment in 1933, and many more permitted towns and counties the power to forbid the sale of alcoholic beverages. Sale of birth control devices was forbidden in most states. By 1930, they had also succeeded in imposing censorship on the movie industry.

The conservatives' early and effective use of new technologies like radio, which enabled them to reach out to mass audiences, suggests that fundamentalists and other religious conservatives had not entirely forsaken their ambitions. Though their antimodernism and anti-intellectualism stood them in good stead during the 1920s, when political conservatism was ascendant, their quarrelsome factionalism ultimately prevented them from becoming a national political force after the 1930s (Abrams 2001; Fore 2007; Hangen 2001; Hoover and Wagner 1997).

The Rise of the Contemporary Christian Right

It is important to recognize that the rise of the Christian Right has roots in the 1940s. America's assumption of leadership of the "free world" during and after World War II would both transform the major political concerns of American religion and alter the relation of religious groups to one another. Positions on foreign and military policy, and on such domestic issues as civil rights and federal government power, took the place of conflicts between liberal modernism and fundamentalism and their social agendas. Recognizing the need for conservative evangelicals to overcome their pervasive disunity in order to begin to counter the liberal denomination's ability to speak with a unified voice—through the Federal (later the National) Council of Churches—on major public issues, the conservatives began organizing their own umbrella organizations. The first, Carl McIntire's American Council of Christian Churches, organized in 1941, explicitly excluded adherents or affiliates of the major ecumenical bodies—the World Council of Churches, the National Council of Churches, and the World Evangelical Fellowship—from membership. In response, a group of conservatives who wanted a less divisive fellowship organized the National Association of Evangelicals (NAE) the following year.

The leaders identified with the NAE set about creating a network of new organizations that would help give evangelical Protestantism a genuinely national identity. These included the National Religious Broadcasters Association (1944), the Evangelical Foreign Missions Association (1945), the Commission on War Relief (1944), Youth for Christ (1944), and a host of other entities that began to tie together the scattered nodes of evangelic commitment and rally them to unified action. These groups were tied to a variety of educational institutions, some old, the

Wheaton College (1860) and the Moody Bible Institute (1886), and some new, like Fuller Theological Seminary (1947). These organization-building and networking activities, combined with the energetic and widely publicized international "crusades" led by Billy Graham, brought neo-evangelicalism to the forefront of public attention. Graham's charisma, his political moderation, and his willingness to overlook the theological disagreements that had for so long factionalized evangelicals brought him support from both conservative and mainline Protestants.

To say that Graham and the evangelicals he represented were politically moderate requires some qualification. Because the cold war had silenced some of the most outspoken liberal Protestants—wiping out in a stroke what remained of the Christian socialist and social gospel enclaves—Graham's outspoken anticommunism, which would have seemed extreme in the 1940s, became part of the national consensus, both within and beyond the world of religion by the 1950s. His anticommunism brought him close to politicians like Richard Nixon, whom he supported against Roman Catholic John F. Kennedy in the election of 1960. On the other hand, Graham's position on civil rights was well ahead of the views of his followers and, indeed, most of the American public. As early as 1952 he had desegregated his revivals, declaring that there was no scriptural basis for segregation. He supported school desegregation and claimed Martin Luther King as a friend. Like Beecher and Moody, he could simultaneously hold conservative and progressive views.

Graham and the NAE only represented one element, albeit an increasingly powerful one, in the still factious evangelical world. The more extreme elements, which shared many of the neo-evangelicals' theological views, but differed with them politically, became active and nationally prominent. The Christian Crusade, organized by Texas evangelist Billy James Hargis, a leading religious broadcaster and a close ally of Senator Joseph McCarthy (for whom he wrote speeches), General Edwin Walker (a leader of the John Birch Society), and Barry Goldwater, was typical of the more extreme organizations. The California-based, Christian Anti-Communist Crusade, organized by Australian evangelist Fred Schwartz, warranted major media coverage in the early 1960s for its "mass meeting anti-Communism" that attracted thousands to rallies throughout the country ("Crusader Schwartz," *Time*, February 9, 1952).[9]

The theological and political moderation and capacity for coalition-building that made Graham and the neo-evangelicals so effective inevitably brought them into conflict with more conservative and doctrinaire leaders like the Reverend Bob Jones. Although Jones backed his early revivals, when Graham sought broad ecumenical (and interracial) support for his 1957 New York crusade, Jones denounced him for consorting with groups that had not embraced the five points of faith deemed essential to orthodoxy by fundamentalists (Turner 1997, 179–83). This split had less to do with doctrinal differences than political ones, particularly over matters of race. By 1957, the civil rights struggle was fast becoming the central issue in American public life. Only three years earlier, the U.S. Supreme Court in Brown v. Board of Education, 347 U.S. 483 (1954), had declared racial segregation unconstitutional and ordered the integration of the nation's public schools. The following year, Rosa Parks initiated the Montgomery bus boycott. In 1957, the year Jones and Graham split, President Eisenhower sent federal troops into Little Rock, Arkansas, to compel the integration of the city's public schools. Politically conservative southerners, backed by the region's white religious leaders, initiated massive resistance, closing down public school systems rather than integrate them, and creating a segregated infrastructure of private nonprofit, often religious, schools to educate the white youth.

Resistance to integration would be the bellwether for a broader political mobilization by conservative Christians that would eventually mature into the Christian Right of the 1980s. Not only would it finally convince conservatives of the necessity for alliance-building as a precondition for political effectiveness, it would also help them overcome their deep-seated hostility to the use of nonprofit organizations to achieve their ends. Not only had conservative evangelicals been doctrinally resistant to using secular voluntary associations (preferring to pursue collective goals through the government or through their congregations), outside the Northeast and the upper Midwest, state corporation and charities laws placed many legal barriers in the way of establishing charitable entities and, in some cases, prohibited them entirely (see Zollmann 1924; Hall 2007).[10] As Lyman Beecher had discovered a century and a half earlier, secular voluntary associations—or nonprofit organizations, as we call them today—could be very powerful and persuasive instruments in the hands of the faithful. They would become essential to the grassroots mobilizations that would make the Christian Right a driving force in the conservative revolution of the late twentieth century.

As discussed earlier (see volume 1, chapters 2 and 11, as well as the introductions to both volumes), the most recent chapter of civic evangelism—the Christian Right—arose in the wake of two precipitating events. These are the legal cases that threatened the economic well being of important institutions in the evangelical subculture, particularly Christian schools and broadcasting media, and the social changes of the 1960s, the sexual revolution and the movements for racial and sexual equality, that threatened the assumptions of religious traditionalists. Although reining in judicial activism by law and by replacing liberal jurists with conservative ones remained a top priority for religious conservatives, in the short term stopping the juggernaut of secularism depended on political engagement. This not only meant getting Christian voters to the polls, but getting Christian candidates on the ballot, creating organizations that could lobby and advocate for Christian positions, and turning the evangelicals' already considerable media power to political purposes.

The political mobilization of religious conservatives was driven by a number of forces. One was the Republican Party's southern strategy, which sought to channel southern whites' resentment at integration and black political enfranchisement by enlisting them in the GOP. Although the architects of the strategy did not make explicit reference to mobilizing religious constituencies, they were well aware of the growing discontent of evangelical Christians with the Democratic Party.

From the beginning of his administration, President Richard Nixon signaled his friendliness to the evangelicals by inviting Billy Graham to give the invocation at his inauguration and by initiating Sunday worship services in the White House (Christian Century 1994). Although not wearing his beliefs on his sleeve, as some of his successors would, Nixon gave public expressions of religion a degree of prominence unparalleled in the twentieth century and, in doing so, welcomed the Christian right into the Republican party. In 2006, reflecting on his role as a strategist in the Nixon administration, Kevin Phillips wrote,

Four decades ago, the new GOP coalition seemed certain to enjoy a major infusion of conservative northern Catholics and southern Protestants. This troubled me not at all. I agreed with the predominating Republican argument at the time that "secular" liberals, by badly misjudging the depth and importance of religion in the United States, had given conservatives a powerful and legitimate electoral opportunity.

When religion was trod upon in the 1960s and thereafter by secular advocates determined to push Christianity out of the public square, the move unleashed an evangelical, fundamentalist and Pentecostal counterreformation, with strong theocratic pressures becoming visible in the Republican national coalition and its leadership ("How the G.O.P. Became God's Own Party," April 2, 2006, B3).

Jimmy Carter's popularity among evangelicals temporarily stalled plans to refashion the Republican coalition. Carter the first self-identified evangelical to be elected to the presidency exemplified the breadth and diversity of the political expressions of Protestant evangelicalism. Though born again and freely using religious rhetoric in his public pronouncements, he backed desegregation and other causes not embraced by the Christian conservatives. Even before Carter's 1976 election, conservative strategists and organizers were looking ahead to 1980 for possible alliances between evangelicals and the Republican Party.

Chief among these was the conservative activist Paul Weyrich, a protégé of the Colorado beer tycoon Joseph Coors. Coors named him to head the Heritage Foundation, a think tank established to "formulate and promote conservative public policies based on the principles of free enterprise, limited government, individual freedom, traditional American values, and a strong national defense." With the intention of recruiting Christians to the conservative cause, Weyrich brought to the foundation Christian Voice, a conservative organization that promoted grassroots political action, including voter registration drives, rating candidates and office holders for morality, and teaching political organizing techniques.

In 1978, the success of Christian Voice led to a struggle for control between those who opposed broad alliances and those who favored them. Its founder, Robert Grant, claimed that, led by men like Weyrich, a nonobservant Jew, and three Catholics (Terry Dolan, Richard Viguerie, and Howard Phillips), the Religious Right was a sham. Weyrich, Dolan, Viguerie, and Phillips left the Christian Voice and recruited televangelist Jerry Falwell to found the Moral Majority. Using political action committees and its outsized media presence, the organization played an important role as an enthusiastic backer of Ronald Reagan's presidential candidacy. The organization, promoting an agenda that included outlawing abortion, opposing homosexuality, promoting family values, and censoring media promoting so-called antifamily agendas, mobilized Protestants and conservative and traditionalist groups to the cause of conservative revolution.

As the end of Reagan's second term approached, the Reverend Pat Robertson, another successful televangelist, wanting to secure the Christian conservative's influence in the Republican Party, launched a campaign for the 1988 presidential nomination. Although the effort failed, he used his campaign machinery to create a new Christian mobilization organization, the Christian Coalition. Hoping to "take over the Republican Party from the bottom up," Robertson worked closely with other religious activist groups, including James Dobson's Family Research Council, Phyllis Schlafly's Eagle Forum, and Focus on the Family. Led by Ralph Reed, the coalition flourished during the Clinton years and took credit for playing a prominent role in the Republican sweep of the congressional elections of 1994. Because of its electioneering activities, the coalition lost its tax-exempt status in 1998 and, saddled with huge tax penalties, declined in influence. However, organizations such as the National Association of Evangelicals and the Ethics & Religious Liberty Commission of the Southern Baptists have flourished in recent years. The difference is these groups have explicit and strong denominational ties rather than functioning as broad-based political entities committed to mobilizing the traditionalist alliance.

Although rooted in older theological divisions between fundamentalists and liberals and more recent political conflicts over civil rights, the

Christian Right in the last years of the twentieth century assumed a number of distinctive features. First, a group of ultraconservative clergy, grouped under the label Reconstructionists (see chapter 6, this volume) began in the 1960s to articulate a radical vision of biblical government and intensive activism by the faithful. Unlike most of the leaders of the Christian Right, who have been political activists in a conventional sense, the Reconstructionists' primary impact has been in the grassroots, among individual believers and freestanding congregations.

If the Reconstructionists represent a new variety of hardcore theologically grounded sectarianism, the activities of Richard John Neuhaus and his followers epitomized efforts to reach across the divisions among Christians. Raised as a Lutheran social activist, Neuhaus converted to Catholicism after the Supreme Court's abortion decision. His Center for Religion and Society, based in the right-wing Rockford Institute, promoted a conservative ecumenical dialogue focused particularly on Protestant evangelicals. Neuhaus played a major role in legitimating and strengthening political ties between conservative Catholics and Protestants.

Perhaps more significantly, like the earlier episodes of evangelical unity, the current one's most enduring influence may not be on politics, but on the hearts and minds of Americans. Between 1790 and 1840, the perfectionism of the evangelicals not only led Americans to embrace social reform as a major form of political activism, but the voluntary association—rather than the political party—as an important instrument of social and political influence. Between 1870 and 1920, inclusive big tent evangelicalism like Dwight Moody's helped create the moral climate and forged the religious and political alliances that produced the social gospel, the belief that the godly and materially privileged and, ultimately, the government had an affirmative obligation to promote social and economic justice. This deep values change, a sharp departure from laissez faire liberalism, helped give rise to the progressive and liberal political movements that dominated public life in America for much of the twentieth century.

There is reason to believe that today's Christian Right may have a similarly enduring impact. The debate over welfare reform in the 1980s and 1990s was framed not by age-old concerns about welfare fraud and the culture of poverty, but by a deeper shift in values. Liberal social welfare policies had sought to alleviate poverty by changing the conditions under which the poor lived: housing projects were built, education and job training programs sought to prepare the poor for the workforce, and government monies underwrote programs of aid to the needy. The war on poverty, despite billions of dollars spent, seemed to have no impact on the persistence of poverty. Marvin Olasky (1992) and other conservative evangelicals have argued that society be changed from the inside out rather than from the outside in. The development of charitable choice and other faith-based initiatives are a direct outgrowth of this view.

Yet today's Christian Right must grapple with internal tensions; some of which deal with big tent issues, such as how closely can evangelical Christians ally themselves with Mormon candidates, and others involve disputes over policy issues, such whether Christian stewardship requires strong support for environmentalism. After several decades of focusing on issues that unified broad sectors of religious conservatives, most notably opposition to abortion and gay rights, evangelicals now face concerns that have a much greater chance of fracturing their coalition and no commanding figure comparable to Lyman Beecher or a Dwight Moody has emerged to help them bridge these divisions.

Conclusion

Is the current prominence of the Christian Right an anomaly—a departure from the Tocquevillian model in which religion exercises but little influence upon the laws and upon the details of public opinion? Or is it a stage of the historical process in which religious groups, struggling to negotiate the tension between sectarian purity and the compromises necessary for public influence in market democracies, are approaching the apogee of doctrinal compromise for the sake of worldly power?

The history of evangelical Protestant political activism surveyed in this paper suggests that the latter is true. Beginning with Lyman Beecher and the evangelical united front of the pre–Civil War decades, through Dwight Moody's remarkable unification of factious Protestants into an evangelical big tent between 1870 and 1920, and finally, with the rise of the contemporary Christian Right, we have seen evangelicals overcome their sectarian impulses to build the broad coalitions and alliances necessary for political effectiveness. Typically, such united fronts have been followed by a descent into sectarianism and political impotence.[11] Whether this will occur to the contemporary Christian Right is as yet unclear.

Richard Neibuhr, writing in the heat of the struggle between the fundamentalists and the modernists in the late 1920s, argued that the relation between faith and worldly engagement was inherently unstable.

> No ideal can be incorporated without the loss of some of its ideal character. When liberty gains a constitution, liberty is compromised; when fraternity elects officers, fraternity yields some of its ideal qualities of brotherhood to the necessities of government. As the gospel of Christ is especially subject to this sacrifice of character in the interest of organic embodiment; for the very essence of Christianity lies in the tension that it

presupposes or creates between the worlds of nature and spirit. . . . Organize its ethics—as organize them you must whenever two or three are
gathered in the name of Christ—and the free spirit of forgiving love becomes a new law, requiring interpretation, commentary, and all the machinery of justice—just the sort of impersonal relationship that the gospel
denies and combats. Place this society in the world, and strenuous as may
be its efforts to transcend or to sublimate its mundane life, it will yet be
unable to escape all taint of conspiracy and connivance with the worldly
interests it despises. Yet, on the other hand, Christian ethics will not permit a world-fleeing asceticism, which seeks purity at the cost of service.
(1929, 4–5)

The history of evangelical political activism since the early nineteenth
century bears this out. Inevitably, the religious activisms have failed to
endure, defeated either by their inability to compromise or by compromises that fatally impaired their spiritual missions. But to say that the
Christian Right and its activist predecessors failed as enduring movements is not to say that they failed to have enduring influence. Despite
their failures, successive waves evangelical political activism, perhaps
more than any other single force in American history, have profoundly
shaped the public values that frame law, legislation, and policy and
determine our conceptions of who we are and our obligations to one
another.

Notes

1. The core tenets of evangelical Protestantism, as adopted at the 1846 conference of the World Evangelical Alliance, are: "The Divine inspiration, authority, and sufficiency of the Holy Scripture; the right and duty of private
   judgment in the interpretation of the Holy Scripture; the unity of the God-
   head and the Trinity of Persons therein; the utter depravity of human nature in consequence of the fall; the Incarnation of the Son of God, His work
   of atonement for sinners, and his mediatorial intercession and reign; the
   justification of the sinner by faith alone; the work of the Holy Spirit in the
   conversion and sanctification of the sinner; the immortality of the soul, the
   resurrection of the body, the judgment of the world by Jesus Christ, with
   the eternal blessedness of the righteous and the eternal punishment of the
   wicked; the Divine institution of the Christian ministry, and the obligation
   and perpetuity of the ordinances of Baptism and the Lord's Supper" (Burton 1909).
2. This doctrine of preparation, evident in the writings of Edwards's grand-
   son (and Beecher's mentor), Yale president Timothy Dwight, was a crucial
   theological innovation. Until the mid-eighteenth century, most orthodox
   Calvinists regarded poverty, sickness, and catastrophe as providential expressions of God's will and, on that basis, strenuously opposed schemes
   for human betterment. Edwards never claimed that his highly emotional-

ized evangelical preaching actually saved sinners; rather, it led them to obey God's commands and prepared them for the possibility that God would save them. Post-Edwardsian Calvinists such as Dwight extended this notion of preparation to include a variety of social and political reforms.

3. The innovations of Dwight and the other New Haven theologians blurred the distinctions between Calvinism, which preached justification by faith alone, and Arminism, which preached good works as a basis for salvation, that had loomed so large during the colonial period. For New Divinity adherents, as the post-Edwardsians called themselves, good works carried out on a large scale—the "business of doing good"—prepared sinners for the reception of God's grace. As Dwight put it, "whatever is to be done, except the work of sanctification, which man cannot do, is to be done by man as the instrument of his Maker. Man is to *plant, and water;* and then, and then only, is warranted either to hope, or to pray, that *God will give the increase*" (1821, IV: 407).

4. This memorable phrase was uttered by Congressman Samuel Burchard in an address to the Republican National Committee on the eve of the election of 1884. Republican James G. Blaine was expected to win the election. Outrage at Burchard's bigoted remark delivered the election to his Democratic opponent, Grover Cleveland. Burchard's views were typical of America's Protestants in the last quarter of the nineteenth century. *Rum* refers to the alleged drunkenness of Irish Catholics; *Romanism* to their subjection to the Papacy; and *Rebellion* both to their sympathy for the Confederacy during the Civil War and their opposition to Reconstructionist policies in the years following.

5. I am indebted to Jon Butler, whose superb essay "Protestant Success in the New American City" called my attention to the importance of statistics gathering for certain Protestant groups after 1880 (Butler 1997).

6. Conservative evangelicals were particularly disturbed by the increasingly secularized and, in their view, immoral character of public life. On the one hand, compulsory school attendance laws and standardized curricula were exposing their children to ideas like evolution and secular interpretations of history that challenged their religious world view. The social experience of school itself, in particular the development of a youth culture in which the athletics, automobiles, and dating played growing roles, reshaped girl's conceptions of their roles and subverted parental authority. Outside of school, the impact of popular magazines and movies glamorized what religious conservatives regarded as immoral behavior. These trends, as well as the response of community religious leaders to them, are discussed in detail in the Lynds's classic study *Middletown* (Lynd and Lynd 1929).

7. According to Ahlstrom, disagreement over the recommendations of the Interchurch World Movement's study of the 1919 steel strike, which was extremely critical of business, prompted the withdrawal of Presbyterians and Baptists from what had promised to be the most ambitious ecumenical effort since the evangelical united front of the early nineteenth century. The movement, launched in 1919 in the heat of postwar triumphalism, was the consummate expression of big tent evangelicalism. Promising the "largest

voluntary offering in history," which would "unite all the benevolent and missionary agencies of American Protestantism in a single campaign for money, men, and spiritual revival," the campaign ended a spectacular failure because conservative denominations bailed out of the effort (Ahlstrom 1972, 896–99; see also Meyer 1988, 1–25; Olds 1923).

8. The term *denomination* is commonly used as a descriptor for any group of religious adherents or congregations subscribing to a common body of beliefs and practices. Historically, it has a far more specific meaning, denoting religious congregations associated by agreement as part of a larger body. The provisions of such agreements allocate authority, financial responsibilities, and elect church leaders. There is enormous variety in denominational structures. Some, like the Roman Catholic Church, are hierarchical and authoritarian. Others, like the United Church of Christ, are egalitarian and democratic. What they have in common is their corporate formalization of interrelationships between congregations. National denominational structures only begin to emerge in the United States in the 1820s, with the establishment of the Protestant Episcopal Church and the efforts of the hierarchy to discipline independent-minded Roman Catholic congregations (Dexter 1880; Coalter, Mulder, and Weeks 1992; Dolan 1992). Most of the support for the Protestant fundamentalism came from nondenominational clergy and churches.

9. http://www.time.com/time/printout/0,8816,938304,00.html (accessed February 21, 2007).

10. The opposition of religious conservatives to nonprofit organizations was a product of geography rather than of belief. Conservatives were concentrated geographically in states where Jeffersonians and Jacksonians—both outspoken opponents of private corporations—had been dominant historically. This deep-rooted suspicion of nonprofits was reinforced over time by pre–Civil War abolitionists, who spread their message through such associations, and by Reconstruction era Gideonites who used them to reeducate the conquered south and educate free blacks. By the mid-twentieth century, support for the civil rights movement by northern grant makers kindled an all-out congressional assault on "foundations and other tax-exempt entities" (Hall 1992, 290).

11. Even before George W. Bush's election, central figures in the alliance between the GOP and the Christian Right were forcefully expressing their dissatisfaction with the compromises Republican congressional leaders were willing to make to enact their legislative agenda. Fragmentation of the religious right has deepened since that time (David Grann, "Robespierre of the Right," *New Republic*, October 27 1997, 20–24).

References

Abrams, Douglas C. 2001. *Selling the Old Time Religion: American Fundamentalists and Mass Culture, 1920–1940*. Athens: University of Georgia.

Ahlstrom, Sidney. E. 1972. *A Religious History of the American People*. New Haven, Conn.: Yale University Press.

American Social Science Association. 1874. "Pauperism in the City of New York: A Report from the Department of Social Economy." In *Conference of Public Charities held at New York, May 20 and 22, 1874*. Cambridge, Mass.: American Social Science Association.

Beecher, Lyman. 1835. *A Plea for the West*. Cincinnati, Ohio: Truman & Smith.

Beecher, Charles. 1866. *Autobiography, Correspondence, etc., of Lyman Beecher, D.D.* New York: Harper & Brothers.

Brockett, Louis P. 1863. *Philanthropic Results of the War in America: Collected from Official and Other Sources*. New York: Wynkoop, Halenbeck, & Thomas.

Burton, Edwin. 1909. "The Evangelical Alliance." In *The Catholic Encyclopedia*. New York: Robert Appleton. Available at: http://www.newadvent.org/cathen/05641a.htm (accessed February 11, 2008).

Butler, Jon. 1997. "Protestant Success in the American City, 1870–1920: The Anxious Secrets of Rev. Walter Laidlaw, Ph.D." In *New Directions in American Religious History*, edited by Harry S. Stout and Darryl G. Hart. New York: Oxford University Press.

Channing, William E. 1829. "Art. V.–1. Fourth Annual Report to the American Unitarian Association." *Christian Examiner and General Review* 7(1)(September): 105–41.

Christian Century. 1994. "Richard Nixon and American Religion." *Christian Century* 111(16)(May 11): 488–89.

Christianity Today. 2008. "Dwight L. Moody: Revivalist with a Common Touch." *Christian History and Biography*. Available at: http://www.christianitytoday.com/history/special/131christians/moody.html (accessed July 14, 2008).

Coalter, Milton J., John M. Mulder, and Louis B. Weeks. 1992. *The Organizational Revolution: Presbyterians and American Denominationalism*. Louisville, Ky.: Westminster John Knox Press.

Collins, John C. 1886. "Religious Statistics." In *Proceedings of the First Convention of Christian Workers in the United States and Canada*. Chicago.

Dastin, Barry L. 1975. "Dwight L. Moody Comes to New Haven." *Journal of the New Haven Colony Historical Society* 23(2)(Spring): 3–57.

de Tocqueville, Alexis. 1945. *Democracy in America*. New York: Alfred A. Knopf.

Dexter, Henry M. 1880. *Congregationalism of the Last Three Hundred Years as Seen in its Literature*. New York: Harper & Brothers.

Dolan, Jay P. 1992. *The American Catholic Experience*. South Bend, Ind.: University of Notre Dame Press.

Dwight, Timothy. 1821. *Travels in New England and New York*. New Haven, Conn.: S. Converse.

Ehrenreich, Barbara, Hess, Elizabeth, and Jacobs, Gloria. 1986. "Unbuckling the Bible Belt." *Mother Jones* (July/August) 11(5): 46.

Finke, Roger, and Rodney Stark. 1992. *The Churching of America: Winners and Losers in our Religious Economy*. New Brunswick, N.J.: Rutgers University Press.

Fore, William F. 2007. "The Unknown History of Televangelism." *Religion-on-line.org*, Available at: http://www.religion-on-line.org/showarticle.asp?title=3369 (accessed March 25, 2007).

Foster, Charles. 1960. *An Errand of Mercy: The Evangelical United Front, 1790–1837*. Chapel Hill: University of North Carolina Press.

Hall, Peter D. 1992. *Inventing the Nonprofit Sector and Other Essays on Philanthropy,*

Voluntarism, and Nonprofit Organizations. Baltimore, Md.: Johns Hopkins University Press.

———. 2005. "The Civic Engagement Tradition." In *Taking Faith Seriously*, edited by Mary Jo Bane, Brent Coffin, and Richard Higgins. Cambridge, Mass.: Harvard University Press.

———. 2007. "A Historical Overview of Philanthropy, Voluntary Associations, and Nonprofit Organizations in the United States, 1600–2000." In *The Nonprofit Sector: A Research Handbook*, 2nd ed., edited by Walter W. Powell and Richard Steinberg. New Haven, Conn.: Yale University Press.

Hangen, Tona J. 2001. *Redeeming the Dial: Radio, Religion, and Popular Culture in America*. Chapel Hill: University of North Carolina Press.

Hoover, Stewart M., and Douglas K. Wagner. 1997. "History and Policy in American Broadcast Treatment of Religion." *Media, Culture, & Society* 19(1)(January): 7–27.

Lynd, Robert S., and Helen M. Lynd. 1929. *Middletown: A Study in American Culture*. New York: Harcourt Brace.

Meyer, Donald. 1988. *The Protestant Search for Political Realism, 1919–1941*. Middletown, Mass.: Wesleyan University Press.

Moody, William R. 1900. *The Life of D. L. Moody*. New York: Fleming B. Revell.

Moss, Lemeul. 1869. *Annals of the United States Christian Commission*. Philadelphia, Pa.: J. B. Lippincott .

Neibuhr, H. Richard. 1929. *The Social Sources of Denominationalism*. New York: Henry Holt.

Olasky, Marvin. 1992. *The Tragedy of American Compassion*. Washington, D.C.: Regnery Publishing.

Olds, Marshall. 1923. *Analysis of the Interchurch World Movement Report on the Steel Strike*. New York: G. P. Putnam's Sons.

Swint, Henry L. 1967. *The Northern Teacher in the South, 1862–1870*. New York: Octagon Books.

Sheldon, Charles M. 1896. *In His Steps: What Would Jesus Do?* Chicago: Chicago Advance.

———. 1925. *Charles M. Sheldon: His Life Story*. New York: George H. Doran.

Turner, Daniel L. 1997. *Standing Without Apology: The History of Bob Jones University*. Greenville, S.C.: Bob Jones University Press.

United States Sanitary Commission. 1861. "An Address to the Secretary of War, May 18, 1861." In *History of the United States Sanitary Commission, Being a General Report of Its Work during the Rebellion*, edited by C. J. Stillé. Philadelphia, Pa.: J. B. Lippincott.

Wuthnow, Robert. 1988. *The Restructuring of American Religion: Society and Faith since World War II*. Princeton, N.J.: Princeton University Press.

Yale University. 1922. *Eighth General Catalogue of the Yale Divinity School*. centennial issue. New Haven, Conn.: Yale University.

Zollmann, Carl. 1924. *American Law of Charities*. Milwaukee, Wis.: Bruce Publishing Company.

Chapter 9

Moral Values and Political Parties: Cycles of Conflict and Accommodation

KIMBERLY H. CONGER

THE CHRISTIAN Right has become a leading factor in Republican Party politics in the United States over the past twenty-five years. Although many scholars and pundits have focused on the movement in national politics, the Christian Right has been active and effective at the state level as well. The movement has a presence in nearly every state, and in many states exerts significant influence on the Republican Party through grassroots mobilization and party personnel. Contrary to popular accounts, however, the movement rarely takes over a party wholesale. The influence of the Christian Right in Republican politics ebbs and flows based on how useful the movement is in achieving the party's election imperative. The relationship among the movement and state parties demonstrates cycles of conflict and accommodation, similar to the fluctuations that any party faction experiences as a normal part of their political life.

At the most basic level, fluctuations in Christian Right influence in state Republican parties is based on the character of the parties. Whatever their other goals and roles in society, political parties exist to win elections. This is the motivation behind the vast majority of the behavior of both the party as an organization and of the people within it. Thus, whatever it takes to win any given election is what will shape the party's needs at that time. This election imperative drives two related phenomena that help us to understand more clearly the patterns of conflict and accommodation between the party and the movement: the actual fluctuations in Christian Right influence in state Republican Party politics based on the state's policy environment and internal party coalition, and the degree to which Christian Right activists have been integrated into the party.

Previous research on the Christian Right and its relationship with the Republican Party demonstrates both the power and perseverance of the movement over time (Cromartie 2001; Diamond 1998; Martin 1996; Oldfield 1996). It illustrates the ways in which the movement has found greater success at the state level than the national (Green, Rozell, and Wilcox 2000, 2003, 2006; Rozell and Wilcox 1995, 1997). Further, it shows that the movement behaves differently in each state in which it seeks influence over Republican politics (Conger and Green 2002; Moen 1992; Persinos 1994; Rozell and Wilcox 1996; Wilcox 1996/2006). The overarching message of this research is that, though the movement has been largely successful in becoming a player in state politics and state Republican parties, it has not had great success in implementing its policy goals. Interestingly, very little work has concentrated on the obvious fluctuations in Christian Right influence over time or tried to offer comparative explanations for movement influence. The state case studies covered in previous work on the movement and state Republican parties do provide some explanations of conflict and accommodation over time, but only for the states regularly examined. I offer a more comprehensive, generalizable approach to the cycles of conflict and accommodation across the states and provide some preliminary evidence for my explanation.

In this chapter, I discuss in greater detail how this process of conflict and accommodation between the Christian Right and the Republican Party takes place, and argue that the fortunes of the Christian Right in Republican Party politics are based on a state's fluctuating public policy environment and the ideological makeup of each party's political coalition. Based on previous research on the movement and party politics, and on national survey research and interviews with more than 100 political observers across the country, I offer a preliminary explanation of how the election imperative drives the relationship among the Christian Right and state Republican parties.

The Process of Influence

The Christian Right has its roots in national politics in the late 1970s and 1980s, but has had noticeable effect at the state level as well. This focus grew out of a realization in the late 1980s that national activity was not particularly successful for the movement (Wilcox 1996/2006; Watson 1997). Although Ronald Reagan was a convinced conservative, his commitment to the causes and issues of the Christian Right was little more than lip service. As activists began to realize how little policy change had been produced by their national activity, the televangelist Pat Robertson decided to run for the Republican presidential nomination against then Vice President George H. W. Bush in 1988. Robertson was unsuccessful, but his campaign was remarkably successful in mobilizing grassroots Christian conservatives into politics, and particularly Republican Party politics (Green and Guth 1988; Green, Rozell, and Wilcox 2001). After the campaign, Robertson formed the Christian Coalition, a national organization made up almost entirely of existing state-level Christian Right organizations (Watson 1997). Further, Robertson encouraged his supporters to take their fight to the states, to run for state and local offices, and to seek leadership positions within each state's Republican Party (Lee May, "Robertson Exhorts Followers to Run for Local Offices," *Los Angeles Times*, March 7, 1988; Thomas Edsall, "Robertson Urges Christian Activists to Take Over GOP State Parties," *Washington Post*, September 10, 1995). This strategy made particular sense in that many of the issues of concern to the Christian Right—abortion, education, and public morality—are inherently state and local concerns.

Thus began the Christian Right's engagement with Republican state party politics. The movement and its activists sought openings in the system and ways that the party could be influenced. In some states, the movement sought to take over the party wholesale, rarely with complete success. In others, the simple presence of large numbers of evangelicals, the main constituency for the Christian Right movement, proved the basis for movement activity. As changes in the subculture made it more acceptable and even praiseworthy to pursue politics as a means of societal change, more and more evangelicals became mobilized. The revitalization of Republican Party organizations in the South was one of the clearest cases of a broad base of evangelicals forming the motivation for the movement to be involved in Republican Party politics. Many scholars and observers credit the movement with this change (Oldfield 1996; Menendez 1996; Moen 1992). Although the South's movement into the Republican camp was gradual, starting most notably with voting in presidential elections, by the mid-1990s, Republicans were elected to all levels of state office in most parts of the South. Not insignificantly, Republican Party organizations at the both the local and state levels experienced influxes of grassroots support around the same time. As Christian Right activists discovered that Republican Party organizations were useful to the movement, they became more involved and built stronger parties (Green and Guth 1988; Green, Rozell, and Wilcox 2000, 2001, 2003, 2006; Moen 1996)

The movement's influence in state Republican politics overlaps with national politics in other ways as well. Most notably, national elections have a real impact on state level organizations' ability to mobilize grassroots support (Green, Rozell, and Wilcox 2006). Particularly in battleground states, where media coverage and political advertising continue throughout the election cycle, the Christian Right can capitalize on their supporters regard—or distaste—for national candidates. This was clearly the case in Ohio in 2004, where the state's battleground identity enhanced the movement's ability to draw supporters and activists into the campaign to define marriage (Green 2006). National issues, or at least issues that are not unique to any individual state, also play a significant role in the Christian Right's ability to affect state-level Republican politics through the national religious media. Christian Radio in particular has an impact on the political issues that evangelicals find important (Diamond 1998). Commentators like James Dobson, Phyllis Schlafly, and Charles Colson can have a great impact not only on the policy opinions of their listeners, but even more generally on the kinds of issues they are most concerned about. These national-level influences are significant because they form the backdrop for the efforts that state-level activists and organizers are engaged in to try to mobilize Christian Right supporters. In many cases, these issues are translated through the lens of state and local politics, but their origins are in the larger Christian Right social movement.

In some states, however, specific catalytic events provoked the Christian Right to seek influence in the state's Republican Party. Local issues, such as textbook adoption and city zoning ordinances, spurred many early activists (Martin 1996). On issues like these, concerned individuals built a movement to try to change public school policies, particularly in literature classes and in science and biology classes. Later activists were catalyzed by the Clinton administration, whose policies brought to the fore issues such as gays in the military and universal health coverage that would pay for abortions. In each case, movement activists saw state Republican parties as the most effective way to gain access to state policy making. Control of or influence in the party gives the movement access to a wide variety of elected and appointed officials with whom activists would otherwise have to build individual relationships. The party gives the movement more return for its efforts, and the Christian Right has sought to take advantage of that throughout the country.

One of the most potent ways that movement activists demonstrate the importance of Christian Right issue positions is by flexing the muscles of their grassroots support. Over the last decade, there has been a shift in religious voting patterns, suggesting a new coalition of more conservative religious believers from a variety of faith backgrounds (see volume 1, chapter 4). These religious traditionalists are socially conservative and vote Republican, giving the Christian Right credibility in an environment of electoral imperatives. In some cases, these traditionalists, and evangelical voters in general, can provide the margin of victory for Republican candidates (Rozell and Wilcox 1995), giving the movement even more power, particularly within states that have become perpetual presidential battlegrounds, such as Ohio and Missouri.

This search for openings in the party continues today and helps us examine the cycles of conflict and cooperation between the movement and the party. Republican parties respond to the movement's desire to use the party as a vehicle for their political goals in a variety of ways. In some cases, the party welcomed the Christian Right as a coalition member because of the resources the movement brought to electoral politics—particularly grassroots mobilization. In many cases, however, the advent of the Christian Right in party politics caused significant conflict within the party. Generally speaking, weaker state parties were more likely to welcome the movement, and stronger ones were more likely to try to rebuff the movement's advances. As political context changes over time, the movement's ability to influence and the party's ability to repel the movement both change as well, forming cycles. The movement's quest for party influence alters the party whatever the outcome, as strong and weak parties alike respond to the changes the movement brings.

Data and Methods

The data I use to provide evidence for the role of the election imperative in the cycles of conflict and accommodation between the Christian Right and state Republican parties come from a variety of sources. I use quantitative data that I and others collected to gauge the level of influence enjoyed by the Christian Right in the Republican politics of each state. To measure this influence systematically, I conducted two political observers' studies in 2001 and 2005. In each study, more than 1,400 people were contacted by e-mail, fax, postal mail, and telephone and asked to respond to approximately twenty questions about the Christian Right in their states' politics, their states' Republican parties, and the relationship between the two. Those contacted were state Republican and Democratic party leaders, leaders of religiously conservative political groups, members of both the political and religious media, political consultants of various partisan loyalties, and academic observers. In 2001, the survey elicited a 28 percent response rate, and in 2005, a 35 percent response rate (for more information, see Conger 2009). I examined the level to which Christian Right activists were involved and assimilated in the Republican Party using a 2004 survey of Christian Right activists (Green, Conger, and Guth 2006).

My argument is primarily based on the more than 100 interviews I conducted in twelve states with state Republican and Democratic Party leaders, leaders of Christian Right political groups, members of both the political and religious media, political consultants of various partisan loyalties, and academic observers. Participants discussed the Republican Party, the Christian Right, and the ways in which these two entities interacted within their state. They also discussed the general political context in which the relationship occurred. In all cases, the interview samples relied on the snowball method with significant observers identified in each state. Because there is no set universe for political observers of the Christian Right, this is the most valid way to ensure full coverage of the topic. Republicans, Democrats, media, and Christian Right activists are all represented in the sample. In all cases, other publicly available data was used to verify and validate much of the interview participants' recollections and observations (for more on the sample and interview data collection, see Conger and McGraw 2008). In addition to these interviews, I rely on publicly available information to bolster my analysis of the Christian Right in state politics, primarily news media and scholarly accounts of activists' activities and strategies. Thus, though my conclusions are preliminary, they rest on a broad base of empirical evidence.

The states discussed in some detail in this chapter—Arizona, Georgia, Indiana, Massachusetts, Minnesota, and Missouri—were chosen primarily for the range of Christian Right influence and underlying political context they exhibit, and for the vividness of the accounts of Christian Right strategy provided both by those I interviewed and from public sources. My goal is to use the differences among the states to demonstrate the ways that state policy environment and Republican Party coalitions affect the cycles of conflict and accommodation we can observe in state politics all over the country.

Conflict and Accommodation

No single explanation can capture the movement's experience across the states. In a few states, the Christian Right has had little support and no presence in state politics. In these states, mainly in the Northeast, there are few evangelicals for the movement to mobilize and most have political systems that make it difficult for insurgent groups to wield influence. In some states, however, the movement has revitalized Republican politics and gained significant and long-term access to state party decision-making. In others, the movement has met with strong and coordinated opposition wherever it looked within the party, but has turned to other avenues of political influence, primarily the state legislature. In most states, however, the movement has achieved a moderate level of influence through a variety of means, and we can observe how the fortunes of the Christian Right have ebbed and flowed over the past twenty years. In these states, the movement has at times caused conflict, but has consistently made peace with the party and remains part of its base coalition. Observers frequently point to the process by which Christian Right activists have been assimilated into the party as a factor influencing conflict and accommodation within the party. Most important, the movement's success fluctuates depending on the policy environment in the state and the coalition of actors and ideas that make up the Republican Party in the state. If these factors are arrayed in the movement's favor, making them useful to the party's election needs, accommodation between the movement and party is likely. On the other hand, if the policy environment and party coalitions are not receptive to Christian Right issues, conflict is the usual result. Frequently, these environments and coalitions ebb and flow over time, sometimes providing the movement with openings into the party, sometimes not. This gives the relationship among the Christian Right and state Republican parties its cyclical characteristics.

Table 9.1 shows the influence of the Christian Right in state Republican parties for three periods—1994, 2000, and 2004. For 1994 and 2000, the levels of influence for each state are measured as an average of respondents' perceptions of the number of members of Christian Right organizations and the number of members sympathetic to movement on each state's Republican committee (see Conger and Green 2000; Persinos 1994). For 2004, the levels of influence are measured as respondents' perception of the number of state Republican committee members sympathetic to movement alone, perceptions of organizational membership were not elicited (see Conger 2009). Influence is operationalized in all three periods as the percentage of each state's Republican Party committee that are members or supporters of the Christian Right as perceived by the respondents in the surveys used to construct these measures. Each state is ranked in each of the years as high, moderate, or low influence. As I use the terms, high influence means that more than 50 percent of the state's Republican Party committee were supporters of the Christian Right; moderate influence means that 25 to 49 percent were; and low influence means that fewer than 25 percent were. These cut points can certainly be debated, but they are helpful because they are linked to the movement's voting capacities on the state committees. For example, with 50 percent or more of the committee identified as Christian Right supporters, it is likely that the movement's policy agendas will be pursued by the state party. Thus the movement would have high influence.[1]

Another way to look at this measureof Christian influence over time is to observe how it has fluctuated between 1994 and 2004. Figure 9.1 demonstrates that significant change in the ten years between 1994 and 2004. The x-axis represents the Christian Right's influence in a state for 1994, and the sections in each bar demonstrate the number of those states in 2004 that had a high, moderate or low level of Christian Right

Table 9.1   Christian Right Influence in State Republican Parties

State	1994	2000	2004	State	1994	2000	2004
AL	H	H	H	MT	M	H	H
AK	H	H	H	NE	M	M	H
AZ	H	M	H	NV	M	M	M
AR	M	H	H	NH	L	M	L
CA	H	M	M	NJ	L	L	L
CO	L	H	H	NM	L	M	H
CT	L	L	L	NY	L	L	L
DE	L	M	M	NC	H	M	H
FL	H	M	M	ND	L	M	M
GA	H	M	H	OH	M	M	M
HI	H	M	M	OK	H	H	H
ID	H	H	H	OR	H	H	H
IL	L	M	M	PA	M	M	H
IN	L	M	M	RI	L	L	L
IA	H	H	H	SC	H	H	H
KS	M	M	H	SD	L	H	M
KY	M	M	H	TN	L	M	H
LA	H	M	H	TX	H	H	H
ME	M	M	M	UT	M	M	H
MD	L	M	M	VT	L	L	M
MA	L	L	M	VA	H	H	M
MI	M	H	H	WA	H	M	M
MN	H	H	H	WV	L	H	M
MS	M	H	H	WI	L	M	M
MO	L	H	M	WY	L	M	M
				Total	1994	2000	2004
				H	18	18	25
				M	12	15	20
				L	20	7	5

Trend Summary:
48 percent increased between 1994 and 2004.
8 percent decreased between 1994 and 2004.
18 percent increased and decreased between 1994 and 2004.

Source: Author's compilation based on Persinos 1994, Conger and Green 2002, and Political Observer Study 2004
Note: H: High Influence (More than 50 percent of State Republican Committee); M: Moderate Influence (25 percent to 49 percent of State Republican Committee); L: Little Influence (Less than 25 percent of State Republican Committee).

influence. The y-axis is the count of the number of states in each category for 2004. What is clear from figure 9.1 is that of the states that were low influence in 2004, some stayed low significance, but many increased over time. Most moved up to moderate influence, but a few moved into the high influence category. For those states that exhibited a moderate

Figure 9.1   Change in Christian Right Influence from 1994 to 2004

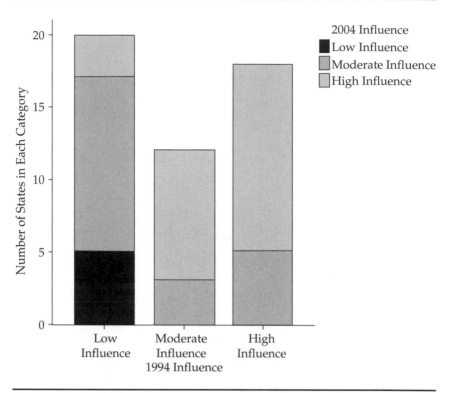

Source: Author's compilation based on Persinos 1994 and Political Observer Study 2004.

level in 1994, none decreased to low influence, a few stayed the same and quite a few increased to high influence. For those states with high influence in 1994, none moved to low influence and only a few decreased to moderate influence. Most of these continued to exhibit high influence in 2004. This suggests that though the general trend among the states is upward, the influence the Christian Right has in states certainly fluctuates over time.

As table 9.1 and figure 9.1 demonstrate, the perception of influence of the Christian Right movement in state Republican parties does fluctuate, with thirty-four states recording differing levels of influence across the three periods, and nine recording both increases and decreases. Although it is clear from the summary counts of the influence levels that the movement has gained influence across the board over the decade of data, variation from period to period as to which states exhibit significant influence and which do not is considerable. These variations are based on the states, not the movement across the states, which exhibits an upward trend not visible in each state individually. The results demonstrate that the influence of the Christian Right has demonstrably increased overall across the country but varies over time within each state. This variance can be linked to the idea of cycles of conflict and accommodation between the movement and the state parties. The idea is further strengthened by the presence of most northeastern states in the bottom 20 percent of states in all three periods, which suggests that the influence does not fluctuate in states where the movement's policy goals have little appeal (Conger and Green 2002; Oldfield 1996; Wilcox 1996/2006).

Although table 9.1 reveals that the influence of the Christian Right in state Republican parties is indeed fluctuating, the data cannot tell us the reasons for such variation. For this, we must turn to qualitative assessments based on the interview and public data described earlier. Practically, the qualitative approach is necessary because no systematic measures of the dynamics underlying the influence fluctuations exist. Substantively, this makes sense because each state's politics and context differ to such a significant degree that idiographic explanations may best capture reality. Note Peter Hall's discussion of how the context affects the outcome of evangelical activism (chapter 8, this volume). Although he is discussing how similar beliefs are translated into different politics and different strategies depending on the time period, the idea lends credence to my claim that the movement behaves differently depending on its state context. Using qualitative data, we can begin to identify regularities in the political contexts of states that help to account for the cycles of conflict and accommodation that exist. I focus on the state's policy environment and the makeup of the Republican parties' coalition as a first step toward generalizing across the states.

A state's policy environment consists of the underlying conservatism or liberalism of the population and the issues that are important to voters. Some of these issues are perennial and specific to the state; others are linked to larger national trends or new events or circumstances in a state. The Christian Right movement is a product of the state in which it operates, so its relationship with the Republican Party will be influenced by the important issues current in the states' politics.

In one election cycle, taxes may be the dominant issue, whereas stem cell research may be more important in the next. This changing policy environment is a driving force behind the cycles of conflict and accommodation between the Christian Right and the Republican Party. Parties have always faced these disputes as new issues and larger political conflicts have given greater power to new leaders and new factions within the party. The Christian Right seems to be the dominant party player when the movement's primary issues are most important. As economic issues become more important, however, the movement tends to recede from the spotlight because other—primarily business—interests are better able to steer the party toward success. These changes highlight the fact that the movement is primarily reactive to the political environment in which it operates. Although it seems logical that, as political actors, these state movements affect the larger political environment, the bulk of the movement's influence is based on state political and social characteristics over which it has no control.

This process of policy environment change creating opportunities for the Christian Right or its opponents is noted by many of the activists and observers I interviewed. The interviews suggest that the Christian Right benefits from being in the right place at the right time. Many Christian Right activists pointed to the growing importance of stem cell research well before the 2000 election made it a major issue, and others described the necessity of preparing for a battle on gay marriage long before the issue became highly salient in the 2004 elections. These examples demonstrate the degree to which activists are aware of the political contexts in which they operate, and particularly how they are able to translate issues and ideas that are current at the national level to the unique context of their individual states.

In Arizona, a state where the Christian Right has a moderate level of influence and faces a libertarian policy environment, Republican Party activists point to the role of the repeal of sodomy laws in the mid-1990s as the point where same-sex marriage became an issue in Arizona politics. One observer noted that, for many years, the Christian Right was able to convince legislators to reaffirm the sodomy ban each time it came up for review. But over time, as public opinion changed, the movement lost its majority on the issue and this presaged the current discussions about same-sex marriage.

In Indiana, a conservative state where Christian Right influence has been only moderate, the movement has had significant success in passing symbolic legislation because the state's Democrats are also relatively conservative. One observer noted that "Democrats are pretty conservative in Indiana. . . . [Most national people] really marvel at the moderateness of Democrats in Indiana." Other observers point to the fact that the legislation passed protecting the public display of the Ten Commandments was written and sponsored by a Democrat.

Massachusetts is an example of a dramatic change in the influence of the Christian Right. Until late 2003, the Christian Right had had a marginal influence throughout the Northeast, particularly in states like Massachusetts with strong traditions of secular and Democratic politics. But the policy environment in the state changed dramatically in November 2003, when the state Supreme Court ruled that the state's constitution prohibited officials from denying marriage licenses to same-sex couples. Although observers in other states had suggested that the issue would become an important one in the future, no one was sure from which state the challenge would issue. The Massachusetts Supreme Court gave the state six months to rewrite state law in line with its decision; the legislature failed to do so, and a proposed constitutional amendment that banned same-sex marriage but permitted civil unions subsequently failed to receive enough support to pass. Same-sex marriages have been taking place in the state since mid-2004. Another constitutional amendment campaign was launched by the Massachusetts Family Institute in 2004. With help from the national Family Research Council, the group was able to collect the required number of signatures to place the amendment before the constitutional convention.[2]

A second constitutional convention vote in 2007 defeated the movement's attempt to place the amendment before voters for a referendum. By state law, a similar amendment cannot appear on the ballot until 2012. Nevertheless, it is clear is that same-sex marriage galvanized the Christian Right in a state in which the movement had had no previous profile. The Massachusetts Family Institute is a chapter of the national Family Research Council, and was started with its help. But the organization seems to have taken on a life of its own as conservatives and Christian Right supporters in the state feel threatened enough to act, even in small numbers. The policy environment in Massachusetts changed significantly, almost overnight. That it did is dramatic proof for one common pattern in the data: the policy environment changes the way that the movement and party interact. In Massachusetts, Christian Right issues suddenly became highly important and visible, and thus the Republican Party needed to account for this by accommodating a group that had largely caused conflict within its ranks in the past.

Similarly, in Georgia the Christian Right has faced a changing policy environment outside the Republican Party. Although movement activists helped rebuild the party in Georgia through grassroots mobilizing (Bullock 2006), after 1994 achieving larger Christian Right policy goals became more difficult. Conservative candidates frequently received Republican nominations for state offices, but were defeated by Democrats in general elections. Many observers believe these developments were the product of the racial divide in the state. As more African American voters became mobilized into the Democratic Party in response to the conservative goals of Republican candidates, the gains in voting power brought by the Christian Right to the Republicans were equaled in the Democratic Party (Bullock and Smith 2000). The movement's ability to mobilize new voters thus ceased to make a difference to Republican electoral fortunes, and therefore more moderate, non–Christian Right candidates were nominated and elected in the late 1990s and early 2000s. Observers noted the frustration movement activists felt as they were forced to moderate their goals to accommodate this changing state policy context. This ebb and flow within a single state demonstrates the cyclical nature of Christian Right influence based on the state's political environment.

The role of the policy environment has been less dramatic but no less important in other states. In Minnesota, a polarized state with a fairly liberal policy environment, Republicans followed national trends in the early 1990s, nominating a committed Christian Right supporter, Alan Quist, for governor. The state party organization opposed Quist, but he won the nomination through the Republican caucus system. The party was consequently forced to deal with his candidacy and supporters throughout the election (Gilbert and Peterson 1997). Observers noted that Christian Right activists became involved in party politics in response to Quist's candidacy, particularly at the local levels. Following his candidacy, movement supporters gained positions of power in the party for ten years.

Economic issues came to the fore significantly in the later 1990s when voters chose Jesse Ventura, an independent, as governor. The Christian Right began to lose power in the Republican Party in Minnesota at this point because party activists perceived that voters were not responding to the movement's issues. Observers pointed to this period as a time of redefining the party's image away from Christian Right issues. Other Republican entities in the state, such as the legislative caucuses, distanced themselves from the Republican Party organization to present a more moderate face. Consequently, a more socially moderate and economically conservative portion of the party coalition advanced in the early 2000s. As values voters began to focus again on social issues as the national and state economy slowed down, Republicans nominated and elected Tim Pawlenty, a man with a long history as a Christian Right supporter, as governor (Gilbert 2006). Minnesota's experience demonstrates how the policy environment surrounding the Christian Right and Republican Party, and how voters react to that environment, significantly affects the relationship between party and movement both positively and negatively in the same state over time.

The policy environment, then, can affect the distribution of influence among the interest factions that make up the Republican Party. In many states, the party contains both big and small business conservatives who are more concerned with economic than with social issues. These individuals tend to be less socially conservative than the Christian Right, and see the movement as a threat to the party's ability to attract supporters across the wide spectrum of other conservatives. Further, many parties, particularly in the West, have libertarian factions that are completely opposed to the kind of social control necessary to implement many of the Christian Right movement's policy goals. In many cases, the conflict or accommodation between the movement and the party were described as directly related to the relative power of coalition partners in Republican politics over time. A Republican Party's internal coalition depends both on the spectrum of voters' opinions within a state and the experience of various coalition members' success in turning out those voters. The Christian Right was generally a newcomer to the party coalition mix in the 1980s, but has since established itself as a legitimate member in nearly every state. Conflict still occurs, however, and the movement must determine how best to create influence in party organizations in which the majority of members are hostile to it.

Becoming a majority partner in a Republican Party coalition can of course make accommodation within the party much easier. In Missouri, the Christian Right is considered the dominant partner inside the party. This has given it significant intraparty power and credibility in navigating disagreements, particularly with business conservatives. For example, significant controversy has recently emerged in the state over the medical and business potential of stem cell research. Republican Governor Matt Blunt supported a bill that would allow somatic nuclear transfer, a form of human stem cell research, to be practiced in the state. Approval of this research would likely mean millions of dollars in profits for the state's growing biotechnology industry (Matthew Franck and Jo Mannies, "GOP Hopes to Avoid Party Rift in Session Anti-Abortion Measure Will Be Focus of Work," *St. Louis Post-Dispatch*, September 6, 2005). It is strongly opposed by the Christian Right faction of the party as a form of human cloning, and several activists discussed the likelihood of Governor Blunt losing conservative support if he signed the bill. As one pro-life activist remarked, "there was an expectation that when the Republicans were elected, that a lot of these issues would be taken care of. They are not being taken care of" (Jo Mannies, "Catholics will Lobby for Stem-Cell Ban," *St. Louis Post-Dispatch*, April 1, 2005, C1). Although the issue was eventually put to the people in a popular referendum in 2006, its passage only presaged more controversy in the party, as factions supporting stem cell research pointed to the fact that the Christian Right opposition is a minority opinion in the state. The movement remains in solid control of the state Republican party, but it is clear that the policy environment of the state is putting pressure on the coalition within the party. Future assessments may show this as a turning point in the party's accommodation of the Christian Right within its ranks.

The Republican Party coalition in Arizona demonstrates how the Christian Right navigates its attempts at influence in a hostile coalition environment. The party is made up of traditional business conservatives, a strong libertarian faction, and social conservatives made up of both Christian Right and Mormon factions. The Christian Right, though successful in filling local party committees in some areas of the state, is largely left out of Republican Party organizational considerations. Observers suggest that the Christian Right has been marginalized because the state party organization is both weak and dominated by business conservatives. Even though the large numbers of evangelical and Mormon voters in the state make socially conservative issues important in many election contests, observers believe that the presence of a strong libertarian faction in the party and in the electorate have made it almost impossible for the movement to exert significant power within the party. Even with one of their own winning the gubernatorial nomination in 2004—Len Munsil was the former director of the Christian Right–affiliated Center for Arizona Policy—most observers believe that the nomination was a gesture to keep movement voters in the party rather than a real accommodation by the Republican Party organization. Munsil's campaign accounts for the survey-based perceptions of high levels of Christian Right influence in Arizona's Republican Party shown in table 9.1. The qualitative data, however, presents a more complex story. It suggests that the dominant group within the party structure can shape the movement's ability to influence party politics and that the affiliations of candidates are not necessarily a decisive indicator of Christian Right influence in the state party.

These processes of conflict and accommodation cause fluctuations in the ability of the Christian Right to exert influence in the Republican Party at the state level. A state's policy environment makes it easy or difficult for the movement to pursue its goals; sometimes both over a number of years as the political opportunities wax and wane and wax again. Even so, a larger dynamic is observable in the data. Over time, Christian Right activists have been assimilated into the Republican Party organization both in the states and at the national level. This has changed both the activists and the party to the extent that both the party and movement are distinctly different—some would say stronger—because of the integration of Christian Right activists.

Assimilated Activists and a More Conservative Party

As any political activist becomes more familiar with an organization over time, they come to understand the rules of the game and begin to feel that they are part of the organization (Rothenberg 1992; Verba, Schlozman, and Brady 1995). In this way, political organizations perpetuate themselves and train new leaders. This same process has helped to transform many Christian Right activists into party regulars; people who have moved up within the party organization and now hold positions of authority. The process is familiar to those who study social movements. Steven Brint and Seth Abrutyn in chapter 4 of this volume describe the importance of grassroots activists in connecting the larger movement and its organizations to the average citizen in the pews. These connections allow the movement to integrate itself with the larger nonpolitical evangelical community and provide fertile ground for new activist recruitment.

Growing involvement in party politics has moderated the tactics and rhetoric of Christian Right activists, if not their policy goals (see chapter 7, this volume). Many begin to act as if their Republican identities are more important than their Christian Right commitments. As one can imagine, this transformation has significant implications for both the Christian Right movement and the Republican Party. It has made the movement more pragmatic and the state parties more conservative. This process has occurred over time, and it has been noted by scholars (Adams 1997; Moen 1992, 1994) and political professionals alike.

In state Republican parties all over the country, Christian Right activists were mobilized into the party for a variety of reasons, particularly with Pat Robertson's run for president, again demonstrating that national efforts are translated into state politics and used to mobilize activists. In most states, Robertson activists were seen by state parties as a new grassroots resource on which to draw, and movement supporters began to wield influence in the party by their involvement in day-to-day party functions like voter identification and fundraising. This process continued through the early 1990s, reaching a peak between 1992 and 1994, as Christian Right activists were motivated by the actions of the early Clinton administration to seek a change in power in Washington. As these activists became more involved in party politics, they tended to moderate their more radical stances, at least outwardly (Rozell and Wilcox 1996/2006; Rozell 1997). Substantial evidence indicates that participation in the party taught Christian Right activists the logic of compromise in the pursuit of long-term goals, something clearly missing from many earlier attempts to change public policy (Conger and McGraw 2008; Hertzke 1993; Moen 1992; Rozell and Wilcox 1996). In this way, the integration of Christian Right activists into the Republican Party has been an important process in the evolution and development for the group as a whole. As Clyde Wilcox demonstrates in this volume, the movement and party have coevolved, changing both the party and the activists themselves (see chapter 11).

A 2004 survey of Christian Right activists (Green, Conger, and Guth 2006) offers evidence on the degree of integration that currently exists. Of the 612 respondents to the survey, 110 (18 percent), served in party leadership positions, and 136 (22 percent) had done so in the past. These groups overlap to some extent, but it seems likely that at least 25 percent of the respondents have been or are currently part of the leadership structure of the Republican Party in their states. We can reasonably assume that the same proportion of the general population of Christian Right activists is involved in Republican politics. This suggests a significant portion of movement activists are successful in achieving leadership positions within the Republican Party.

The qualitative evidence on the integration of Christian Right activists into the Republican Party is much broader than the existing quantitative evidence. Virtually from the beginning of the Christian Right's contemporary forays into party politics, scholars and journalists have noted the differences between newly minted activists and those who have been involved in politics, especially party politics, for a longer time (Dodson 1990; Wilcox 2003). One observer noted the increasing sophistication of veteran political actors: "You've got the religious conservative protestant evangelical who is politically active and becoming more sophisticated politically over time. You see those folks a lot in positions of leadership; they're elected officials, party leaders, that sort of thing."

Further, a generational difference seems to divide older and younger activists in terms of strategy and goals. Activists mobilized at earlier times in the movement's history exhibit more amateur true-believer behavior, whereas those mobilized later tend to more resemble political professionals (Penning and Smidt 2002; Quebedeaux 1974, 1983; see also chapter 11, this volume). Finally, in almost every case, as activists move into positions of authority within the Republican Party, the ways in which they talk about the movement and its goals changes. In interviews, they are much more likely to use the language of family and traditional conservative values than that of religious beliefs and moral values, mirrors the earlier findings of Nathaniel Klemp and Stephen Macedo (see chapter 7, this volume). Christian Right activists have become much more sensitive to the requirements of public discourse and are consistently observable using different language when talking to outsiders to the movement. Like Klemp and Macedo, I believe this is evidence of the growing sophistication of movement activists, not necessarily evidence of duplicity. The actions of the activists as they evolve in politics demonstrate this as well (Conger and McGraw 2008).

Many political observers believe that it is the experience of party politics and its attendant necessity of compromise and political expediency that transform movement activists into regular party participants. One Christian Right activist explained it this way: "At least through the Robertson era I had that stigma as one of those far-right-wing kooks, but now some things have evolved and a lot of us I guess are being more perceived as . . . they know we're [conservative on the] issues but at least we can talk to and work with. And to me, that's not a bad deal." Another noted, "What I've seen in the fifteen years or so . . . is the ones that have stayed in have become more sophisticated as to expectations of working with the moderate wing of the party."

These statements suggest that movement activists are changed by their involvement in the Republican Party. As they are assimilated into its ranks, they become more knowledgeable about the political process and are able to shift their strategies to be more effective in the political arena. Most activists claim not to have changed their policy opinions, but only their tactics and rhetoric (Shields 2007). Many explain the process as learning that politics are not an all-or-nothing enterprise, but one of small changes over time. Much of the assimilation into the party and its norms comes about as movement activists learn more about the political process. Several activists pointed out that, to be successful in promoting their policy positions, they had to learn the internal structure of the party and how best to operate within it. One noted, "Our community has assimilated into the process. A number of our people began by starting Christian Coalition chapters, and serving as their leaders and then ran for [public] office" (Bullock 2006, 78). Further, activists are learning to talk about politics and policy very differently. Macedo and Klemp discuss a two-tier rhetorical system in which religious reasoning holds internally, but public reasoning is portrayed to those outside the movement (see chapter 7, this volume). It is clear that this emphasis on public reason is change that has occurred as activists have learned how to be more effective within state politics.

It is also clear that the generational change within the movement has made it easier for younger activists to become part of the Republican Party leadership structure. Among those I interviewed, there is a significant difference between the goals and strategies of the younger, newer activists and those of older activists who had been involved in politics and the Republican Party for some time (see also Penning and Smidt 2002). Most of the younger activists were very conscious of public perceptions of the movement—that the Christian Right is seen by many as too conservative, too strident, and too powerful. Many took great pains to demonstrate their Republican or traditional conservative bona fides. When asked specifically about the movement and its impact on their own issues and behavior, most agreed with many of the movement's goals, but not its tactics. They were to a person pro-life, against gay marriage, and pro-moral values in public life. But they were also much more likely to cite incremental goals as opposed to proposing sweeping changes in society and politics.

Many older activists expressed the view that any apparent acceptance of abortion, even if rare and regulated, would help to maintain Roe v. Wade, 410 U.S. 113 (1973). One remarked to a colleague, "Well, I just can't be in favor of [regulating abortion clinics] because that will be the state's legitimizing the abortion practice." Younger activists, however, seemed to be much more comfortable with incremental change and limited goals, voicing the opinion that the all-or-nothing strategy has had little impact. On this issue, one activist said, "Look, there's a way. We're sort of the next generation; let's actually try to advance the ball. Let's stay on the ground, but do it in a wise manner."

Most strikingly, many younger activists were somewhat disinclined to see themselves as part of the Christian Right movement. They were uncomfortable with the label and found it pejorative. They were more inclined to think of themselves as evangelical Republicans than as members of a movement. This may signal a larger shift in the movement, away from Christian Right affiliation and toward Republican identification and greater pragmatism in tactics. The party itself is changing as well as business conservatives learn to work with social conservatives. This may explain part of the identity shift among some younger activists.

Clearly some of these changes have been the result of the movement's focus on state politics as movement activists spend more time seeking policy change in the most effective ways they can through the Republican Party. The party's need to win elections has also rubbed off on many parts of the movement both within and outside the party. These changes have had an impact on the movement, sometimes leading to a division between those willing to work within party politics and those who find purity of purpose more important than incremental change.

The Republican Party is certainly different today than it was in 1980, and probably stronger for its interaction with the Christian Right. Almost to a person, Republican leaders not affiliated with the Christian Right point to the role the movement has played in revitalizing grassroots politics in the party. This is true in terms of state and local party organizations, of the large numbers of volunteers who have become involved in political campaigns, and of those who have run for office themselves, particularly for local school boards (Deckman 2004). Most speak with high regard for the movement's ability to provide new grassroots energy for the party, even if their own ideological leanings do not mesh with those of the movement. This influx of volunteers at all levels has had an impact not only on the party's strategy, but also on its policy program. State parties in which the Christian Right plays a significant role have moved to the right over the past twenty years, at least on issues close to the movement (Adams 1997). It is very rare to find a party that does not endorse a pro-life position or oppose stem cell research. Although some longtime Republican activists are uncomfortable with these positions, many see them as inevitable as the party seeks to solidify its relationship with what has become the backbone of their voter base—rural, small town, and suburban evangelicals.

The Democrats and Moral Values Voters

The phenomenon of the moral values voter, identified in the aftermath of the 2004 election, is significant as much for its impact on Democrats as for its explanation of the Bush victory. Increasingly, the Democrats have been described as having a "God problem" (Bolce and DeMaio 2002; Smith 2006). The party is seen as, at best, being uncomfortable with religion, and, at worst, hostile to it. This perception can be a problem in a country where more than 80 percent of the population believes in God. The Democratic Party has a much higher proportion of secular adherents than the Republican Party does. Nevertheless, a decided majority of Democrats hold religious beliefs (Layman 2001). The way they approach religion and its relationship to politics may differ from religious Republicans, however, as Wayne Baker and Connie Boudens describe elsewhere in this volume (see chapter 3). They demonstrate that an individual's orientation toward secular-rationalist values has a bigger impact on voting behavior than their religious affiliation. This makes sense, particularly in light of John Green's findings (see volume 1, chapter 4); people with secular commitments are drawn to the Democratic Party, and those with traditional-religious commitments are drawn to the Republicans.

This image of a godless Democratic Party has been reinforced by the statements of the several of the party's recent presidential candidates. Most glaringly, Howard Dean described the Book of Job as part of the New Testament (cited in Jodi Wilgoren, "The 2004 Campaign: The Vermont Governor; Dean Narrowing His Separation of Church and Stump," *New York Times*, January 4, 2004, 1:12). The Democratic Party's God problem was further brought into high relief during the 2004 election with the controversy concerning John Kerry's Catholic faith and his vocal support for abortion rights. Some Catholic bishops stated publicly that Kerry should be denied communion, and Kerry had difficulty shaking the impression that his faith was less than heartfelt.

These issues resonated at the state level as well. One Democratic state leader, for example, said that the party clearly had lost religious voters in the 2004 election because the party's gubernatorial candidate simply was not credible on religious issues. When asked about faith, the candidate responded with an inconsequential story from childhood that demonstrated no real understanding of or resonance with the question. The Democratic leader I interviewed believed that religious voters on both sides of the partisan divide were uncomfortable with such a contrived and unreflective answer.

Although the Democratic National Committee hired religious liaisons for the 2004 campaign in many states to help with the presidential race, these individuals were widely seen as having no real impact on the tenor of political debate in the states. State level Democratic leaders seem to be divided, however, on the impact of a religion gap in their state's politics. In Colorado, Margaret Atencio, a party vice chairwoman, said that Democrats should stop using the separation of church and state as a litmus test: "We can't ask people to make a choice between religion and us" (Chris Frates, "Democrats Seek Better Balance of Religion, Politics," *Denver Post*, August 29, 2005, B5). But other Democratic Party leaders I interviewed were insistent in believing that the Democratic Party's lack of a religious base is a positive because it gives the party a way to distinguish itself from the Republican Party and to appeal to the religiously moderate mainstream.

Although controversy persists in the Democratic Party about the role of religion, in a number of states conservative Democrats with unimpeachable religious credentials, such as Heath Shuler of North Carolina and Brad Ellsworth of Indiana, have made inroads into Republican hegemony over religious voters. These candidates have shown particular appeal in the Midwest. They tend to be pro-life Democrats, generally Catholic, who are able to combine, in a convincing way, a conservative social agenda with more progressive fiscal attitudes. An organization called Democrats for Life has been gaining supporters and starting state-level chapters over the past several years. These chapters have been initiated, in many cases, by these new types of religiously aware Democrats. That many state Democratic parties are encouraging a conversation about social issues, particularly abortion, suggests that the party is trying to address its perceived God problem.

Clearly, this issue has also become important for Democrats on the national stage. After the 2004 election, many Democratic leaders became alarmed and sought the advice of conservative and liberal religious leaders alike (David Kirkpatrick, "Some Democrats Believe the Party Should Get Religion," *New York Times*, November 17, 2004, A20; Adam Smith, "Democrats Get Religion," *St. Petersburg Times*, May 29, 2005, 1P). Most of those consulted stressed the importance of softening the party's pro-choice position and focusing on how the Democrats' traditional issues of equality, opportunity, education, and health care can be framed as faith issues. To this end, Democrats in the U.S. House of Representatives formed the House Democrats' Faith Working Group. In addition, the national Democratic Party, under Howard Dean's direction, began to reach out to pro-life voters by buying airtime on Christian radio stations to explain the deep moral convictions of party members (Daniel Burke, "Helping Democrats Bridge the 'God Gap,'" *Washington Post*, October 21, 2006, B9).

The 2006 congressional elections demonstrated the degree to which the party has taken seriously its perceived disadvantage on faith issues. In races all over the country, the head of the Democratic Congressional Campaign Committee, Rahm Emanuel of Illinois, recruited candidates he believed could win. In many cases, these were conservative, even pro-life, Democrats (Naftali Bendavid, "The House that Rahm Built," *Chicago Tribune*, November 12, 2006). Religious themes and language were used by Democratic congressional candidates all over the country, and the tactics seemed to work. The Democrats won back the majority in both the House and Senate, and exit polls indicate that conservative Catholics voted less Republican in 2006. The so-called God Gap was significantly smaller in 2006 than in previous elections (Thomas Fitzgerald, "The 'God Gap' Lessened in the Last Election," *Philadelphia Enquirer*, November 26, 2006).

The race for the 2008 Democratic presidential nomination demonstrates the continuing salience of religious issues and religious voters for the Democratic Party. Democratic candidates went out of their way to demonstrate their religious credentials. Barack Obama spoke at Rick Warren's Saddleback Church during a global AIDS conference, and Hillary Clinton openly discussed how much she prays. This increased attention to religion shows clearly that the Democratic Party has the same motivation as all parties; they need votes to win elections. Democrats now believe that they have an opportunity to win the votes of moderately religious Americans who in the past have not felt confident of the Democrats' commitment to moral values rooted in religious traditions.

Many observers, both Republican and Democrat, question the motivation of a revived conversation among Democrats about religious issues and wonder how long it will last. It is easy to suspect that the renewed interest is temporary and strategic. Yet it is equally clear that the sentiment at the state level is real. In many cases, state Democratic parties have had to change after years of facing losses over religious issues and culminating in the disappointing 2004 election.

Conclusion

I have examined the relationship between the Christian Right and the Republican Party at the state level. To understand their interconnections fully, I have discussed the cycles of conflict and accommodation that characterize the relationship, observing particularly the process by which the Christian Right seeks influence within a state's Republican Party. Over time, it is clear that the movement and party have learned to work together and that movement activists and party strategy are both changed by the contact.

The Christian Right is a significant force in the Republican parties of many states. Over the past twenty-five years, the movement has made inroads into the party as activists have acceded to positions of leadership and learned the rules of the party game. But the relationship among the movement and state Republican parties fluctuates based on the political realities of a state's context. The imperative to win elections at both the state and national level makes the movement more or less attractive to the party depending on the policy environment. Internal party coalitions also have an impact on the cycles of conflict and accommodations evident within the relationship. Overall, however, it is clear that the Christian Right and the Republican Party have significantly influenced each other's behavior and strategy. The contemporary Christian Right, with its more practical activists, is a direct outgrowth of the movement's concentration on success in party politics. The contemporary Republican Party, with its coherent ideological focus and its core of conservative Christian grassroots supporters, is just as clearly a product of its interactions with the Christian Right.

One important impact of the Christian Right has been to change the issue discussion in the Democratic Party and to increase the appeal of candidates who can discuss their religious beliefs openly and sincerely. Although Democrats have an antagonistic relationship with the Christian Right, they have become much more welcoming to candidates who are comfortable expressing religious beliefs.

Notes

1. These cut points for differences in influence are in some ways arbitrary. But instead of implying a false precision by reporting the numerical values for each state's Republican Central committee, it seems more accurate to report a more generalized ordinal variable. Even though this can mask a slight change moving a state from one category to another, this measure is based on observers' perceptions and thus should be interpreted broadly.
2. See http://www.voteonmarriage.org.

References

Adams, Greg D. 1997. "Abortion: Evidence of an Issue Evolution." *American Journal of Political Science* 41(4): 718–37.

Bolce, Louis, and Gerald De Maio. 2002. "Our Secularist Democratic Party." *The Public Interest* 149(1): 3–20.

Bullock, Charles S. III. 2006. "The Influence of Christian Conservatives in the Empire State of the South." In *Representing God at the Statehouse: Religion and Politics in the American States*, edited by Edward L. Clearly and Allen D. Hertzke. Lanham, Md.: Rowman & Littlefield.

Bullock, Charles S. III, and Mark C. Smith. 2000. "Georgia: The Christian Right Meets Its Match." In *Prayers in the Precincts: The Christian Right in the 1998 Elections*, edited by John C. Green, Mark J. Rozell, and Clyde Wilcox. Washington, D.C.: Georgetown University Press.

Cromartie, Michael. 2001. "Religious Conservatives in American Politics 1980–2000: An Assessment." *Witherspoon Fellowship Lectures*. Washington, D.C.: Family Research Council.

Conger, Kimberly H. 2009. "A Matter of Context: Christian Right Influence in State Politics." *State Politics and Policy Quarterly*. (forthcoming).

Conger, Kimberly H., and John C. Green. 2002. "The Christian Right in the States: 2000." *Campaigns and Elections* 23(1): 58–65.

Conger, Kimberly H., and Bryan T. McGraw. 2008. "Religious Conservatives and the Requirements of Citizenship: Political Autonomy." *Perspectives on Politics* 6(2): 253–66.

Deckman, Melissa M. 2004. *School Board Battles: The Christian Right in Local Politics*. Washington, D.C.: Georgetown University Press.

Diamond, Sara. 1998. *Not by Politics Alone: the Enduring Influence of the Christian Right*. New York: Guilford Press.

Dodson, Debra L. 1990. "Socialization of Party Activists: National Convention Delegates, 1972–1981." *American Journal of Political Science* 34(4): 1119–41.

Gilbert, Christopher P. 2006. "Minnesota: Battleground Politics in a New Setting." In *The Values Campaign? The Christian Right in the 2004 Elections*, edited by John C. Green, Mark J. Rozell, and Clyde Wilcox. Washington, D.C.: Georgetown University Press.

Gilbert, Christopher P., and David A. M. Peterson. 1997. "Minnesota: Onward Quistian Soldiers? Christian Conservatives Confront Their Limitations." In *God at the Grassroots, 1996*, edited by Mark J. Rozell and Clyde Wilcox. Lanham, Md.: Rowman & Littlefield.

Green, John C. 2006. "Ohio: The Bible and the Buckeye State." In *The Values Campaign: The Christian Right and the 2004 Election*, edited by John C. Green, Mark J. Rozell, and Clyde Wilcox. Washington, D.C.: Georgetown University Press.

Green, John C., and James L. Guth. 1988. "The Christian Right in the Republican Party: The Case of Pat Robertson's Supporters." *Journal of Politics* 50(1): 150–65.

Green, John C., Kimberly H. Conger, and James L. Guth. 2006. "Agents of Value: Christian Right Activists in 2004." In John C. Green, Mark J. Rozell, and Clyde Wilcox, eds. *The Values Campaign: The Christian Right and the 2004 Election*, edited by John C. Green, Mark J. Rozell, and Clyde Wilcox. Washington, D.C.: Georgetown University Press.

Green, John C., Mark J. Rozell, and Clyde Wilcox. 2000. *Prayers in the Precincts: The Christian Right in the 1998 Elections*. Washington, D.C.: Georgetown University Press.

———. 2001. "Social Movements and Party Politics: The Case of the Christian Right." *Journal for the Scientific Study of Religion* 40(3): 413–26.

———. 2003. *The Christian Right in American Politics: Marching to the Millennium*. Washington, D.C.: Georgetown University Press.

———. 2006. *The Values Campaign? The Christian Right and the 2004 Elections*. Washington, D.C.: Georgetown University Press.

Hertzke, Allen D. 1993. *Echoes of Discontent: Jesse Jackson, Pat Robertson, and the Resurgence of Populism*. Washington, D.C.: CQ Press.

Layman, Geoffrey. 2001. *The Great Divide: Religious and Cultural Conflict in American Party Politics*. New York: Columbia University Press.

Martin, William. 1996. *With God on Our Side: The Rise of the Religious Right in America*. New York: Broadway Books.

Menendez, Albert J. 1996. *Evangelicals at the Ballot Box*. Amherst, N.Y.: Prometheus Books.

Moen, Matthew C. 1992. *The Transformation of the Christian Right*. Tuscaloosa: University of Alabama Press.

———. 1994. "From Revolution to Evolution: The Changing Nature of the Christian Right." *Sociology of Religion* 55(3): 345–57.

———. 1996. "The Evolving Politics of the Christian Right." *PS: Political Science and Politics* 29(3): 461–64.

Oldfield, Duane Murray. 1996. *The Right and the Righteous: The Christian Right Confronts the Republican Party*. Lanham, Md.: Rowman & Littlefield.

Penning, James M., and Corwin E. Smidt. 2002. *Evangelicalism: The Next Generation*. Grand Rapids, Mich.: Baker Academic.

Persinos, John F. 1994. "Has the Christian Right Taken Over the Republican Party?" *Campaigns and Elections* 15(9)(September): 20–24.

Quebedeaux, Richard. 1974. *The Young Evangelicals: Revolution in Orthodoxy*. New York: Harper & Row.

———. 1983. *The New Charismatics II*. New York: Harper & Row.

Rothenberg, Lawrence S. 1992. *Linking Citizens to Government: Interest Group Politics at Common Cause*. Cambridge: Cambridge University Press.

Rozell, Mark J. 1997. "Growing Up Politically: The New Politics of the New Christian Right." In *Sojourners in the Wilderness: The Christian Right in Comparative Perspective*, edited by Corwin E. Smidt and James M. Penning. Lanham, Md.: Rowman & Littlefield.

Rozell, Mark J., and Clyde Wilcox. 1995. *God at the Grass Roots: The Christian Right in the 1994 Elections*. Lanham, Md.: Rowman & Littlefield.

———. 1996. *Second Coming: The New Christian Right in Virginia Politics*. Baltimore, Md.: The Johns Hopkins University Press.

———. 1997. *God at the Grass Roots, 1996: The Christian Right in the American Elections*. Lanham, Md.: Rowman & Littlefield.

Shields, Jon A. 2007. "Between Passion and Deliberation: The Christian Right and Democratic Ideals." *Political Science Quarterly* 122(1): 89–113.

Smith, Gregory A. 2006. "Do the Democrats Have a God Problem? How Public Perceptions May Spell Trouble for the Party." *Pew Forum on Religion and Public Life Survey Report*. Washington, D.C.: Pew Research Center. http://pew forum.org/docs/index.php?DocID=148.

Verba, Sidney, Kay Lehman Schlozman, and Henry E. Brady. 1995. *Voice and Equality: Civic Voluntarism in American Politics*. Cambridge, Mass.: Harvard University Press.

Watson, Justin. 1997. *The Christian Coalition: Dreams of Restoration, Demands for Recognition*. New York: St. Martin's Press.

Wilcox, Clyde. 1996/2006. *Onward Christian Soldiers? The Religious Right in American Politics*. Boulder, Colo.: Westview Press.

———. 2003. "The Christian Right and Democratic Virtues." Marburg, Germany: European Consortium for Political Research.

Chapter 10

Politics as the Construction of Relations: Religious Identity and Political Expression

D. MICHAEL LINDSAY

ISTORICALLY, AMERICAN evangelicalism has been a protesting movement, one committed to reform on selective moral issues (Marsden 2006; Young 2002). As such, the evangelical movement has often been more defined by political issues than theological concerns. Indeed, Gabriel Almond, Scott Appleby, and Emmanuel Sivan have suggested that the evangelical movement's theological diversity is held together by political coalitions (2003). As a social movement that includes diverse perspectives, evangelicals' *public theology*—theological reflection focused on public concerns—has existed mainly to birth and buttress particular political and social positions. No doubt this springs from the movement's lineage as part of the larger family of Protestant Christianity. The curious development involves the relatively recent alliance of this reforming movement with conservative politics.[1] This was certainly not the case in previous generations (see chapter 4, this volume).

If the seeds were sown in the 1960s and 1970s for the alliance between evangelicals and conservative politics, their labor began bearing fruit in the 1980s (for historical background, see the introduction). To learn more about these developments, I conducted semistructured, in-person interviews with 360 evangelical leaders, selected because they either self-identify as evangelical or affirm three characteristics that distinguish evangelicals. These include believing in the Bible as authoritative for every aspect of one's life, having a personal relationship with God through Jesus Christ (which typically entails a born-again experience), and endorsing an activist approach to faith—one that motivates the adherent to various forms of religious outreach. The leaders represented the following six arenas: government-politics; arts-entertainment-media; religion; the nonprofit-social sector; higher education; and business-corporate life. Elsewhere, I have detailed the methodology employed and the social and religious profile of informants in the study (Lindsay 2007), but the number of high-ranking informants within the political realm is noteworthy. Interviews with two former presidents of the United States, as well as four dozen cabinet secretaries and senior White House staffers from the last five administrations (from 1976 through 2006), provide useful data for examining the ways that elites have drawn on religious elements of the evangelical movement for political expression.[2]

I argue that the contemporary evangelical movement—which some have referred to as being based on strong religion (Almond, Appleby, and Sivan 2003)—has two elements that make it particularly well suited for political mobilization. These include convictions and sensibilities that give rise to boundaries constructed for political gain and populist strategies of action.[3] With some exceptions, leaders within the movement have forged ties with political conservatives. I conclude with a discussion of how this development has produced some important differences of opinion within the movement and how these differences signal the possibility of significant fractures within evangelicalism's future.

Constructing Boundaries

Politics entails the construction of relations, and that typically involves forming alliances and identifying opponents. The anthropologist Mary Douglas has shown how symbolic lines and boundaries can bring order into experience, and especially in the political sphere, boundaries can make action efficient by adjudicating among competing demands (1970). I found that evangelicalism's *elastic orthodoxy* makes it particularly well suited to construct and maintain symbolic and social boundaries.[4] Their elastic orthodoxy entails adherents' holding a core set of shared religious convictions without those convictions being so firm that they are unable to form alliances with people who do not share them. As the sociologist Christian Smith has shown, the strength of evangelicals' religious convictions actually enables them to interact with people outside that tradition (Smith et al. 1998). He argued that a subcultural theory of religious vitality explains how rising religious pluralism in the United States has actually strengthened, not weakened, the evangelical movement. I found this tension between deeply held belief and engagement with wider society has provided strategic political advantage for evangelicals. It enabled them to establish boundaries that built alliances around shared opponents, both real and ideological.

Nathaniel Klemp and Stephen Macedo explore the two-tiered rhetoric of conservative Protestants, arguing that their religious convictions are firm, but that their rhetoric is strategic (chapter 7, this volume). My research affirms this line of thought. Evangelicals' core religious beliefs about God, the Bible, heaven, and hell are relatively similar today to what evangelicals espoused fifty years ago. Their orthodoxy has not changed. However, as evangelicals have become more prominent in American politics, they have come to recognize that alliances can be built with groups that do not always agree with their religious beliefs. Using particular rhetorical strategies—both inside and outside the movement—they have been able to cooperate with other groups for shared political advantage.[5]

Evangelical commitment to orthodoxy—a set of fundamental beliefs—keeps the movement cohesive; the elasticity of that orthodoxy, however, enables them to build political bridges. This, in essence, is what differentiates evangelicals from fundamentalists. Whereas evangelicals and fundamentalists share many of the same beliefs, the two differ in how they act upon these shared convictions: fundamentalists separate from pluralistic society, whereas evangelicals engage it. The utility of their elastic orthodoxy is evident in how evangelicals have constructed relations with their political opponents and established political allies.

Opponents

The philosopher Eric Hoffer (1951/2002) argued that social movements may not need a god, but that they must have a devil. Successful movements galvanize around joint opposition to some force or individual; if only for rhetorical purposes, social movements require a nemesis as a rallying point. According to several observers from within the movement, American evangelicalism has a history of opposing particular devils (Tony Campolo, interview, March 3, 2006).[6] Evangelicals in the 1920s opposed Darwinian evolution, just as many of them, especially in the North, had opposed slavery in the nineteenth century. As these social issues bedeviled evangelicals, patriotic sentiment percolated throughout the movement (Martin 1996). From the 1930s to the 1960s, communism was the object of evangelical opposition; to the extent that evangelicals discussed political issues from the pulpit, they expressed grave concern about the spread of communism around the world and its occasional appearance within this country. Evangelicals rallied around the American flag and a sense of American uniqueness as a distinctively Christian nation;[7] this was particularly the case among the Youth for Christ leadership cohort of the 1940s.[8] Such elements within evangelicalism allowed movement leaders to define their political opponents as unpatriotic or ashamed of being an American (for an extensive treatment, see Rosin 2007).

In the 1980s, groups like the Moral Majority thrived because they were able to articulate a discourse of opposition that resonated with many social conservatives (Harding 2001; Martin 1996). Leaders such as Jerry Falwell drew on the movement's elastic orthodoxy as a way of drawing sharp boundaries between evangelical coreligionists and those outside the movement. Just as opposition to godless communism rallied evangelicals in the 1950s and 1960s, secular humanism became the common enemy of the 1970s and 1980s. The term, popularized by an American pastor who established a retreat center in the Swiss Alps, was a catch-all phrase for ideological impulses that evangelicals believed were contributing to the creep of secularization in American society.[9] In an ironic twist, the first U.S. president to be charged by evangelical leaders with endorsing secular humanism, Jimmy Carter, was a born-again Christian (Lindsay 2007).

As people who hold the Bible in special regard, evangelicals often cite Scripture as justification for their opposition to certain groups or ideas. The Bible is replete with allusions to enemies or opposing forces. Indeed, the figure of a serpent or Satan can be found throughout the biblical text, including several episodes that appear in the accounts of Jesus's life. Some of the evangelicals I interviewed acknowledged the conflicting admonitions about enemies that appear in the Bible. At one point, Jesus instructs his disciples to love their enemies, but elsewhere declares harsh judgment on those who oppose his disciples. The epistle to the Ephesians speaks of a fight "not against flesh and blood, but against the rulers, against the authorities, against the powers of this dark world and against the spiritual forces of evil" (6:12).

As Rhys Williams documents in this volume, warring rhetoric buttresses the evangelical tendency to draw sharp boundaries between allies and adversaries (see chapter 5). This, in turn, strengthens the movement's elastic orthodoxy. For example, Larry Norman, the professional golfer, described the filmmaker Michael Moore as "Satan incarnate" (Larry Nelson, interview, July 6, 2004). Others referenced what has been called the culture wars, which pits conservatives against liberals, not just in politics, but also on myriad social issues (Hunter 1991).[10] Not surprisingly, most conservative evangelical leaders agreed with the sentiment expressed by Don Hodel, a cabinet secretary under Reagan, "At the national level, there are almost no Democrats who are people of faith in a born-again sense. . . . If you are an evangelical Christian and want to live your faith, I don't think there's room for you in the Democratic Party. It's unfortunate. . . . Not all Republicans are conservative Christians, not by a long shot, but . . . I don't know [how] Christian politicians can be Democrats" (Interview, October 4, 2004). The boundaries in the culture wars, for most conservative evangelicals I studied, are drawn along party lines. However, informants see their faith as one part of a wider matrix of opposing forces. As one governmental leader put it, "It isn't just the Christian piece; it's also. . . the black and conservative piece. . . . It's also the pro-life piece amongst a constellation of pro-choice people. There's a lot in that stew" (Kay James, interview, September 14, 2004). Dozens referred to the public square as a battle for hostile territory, but the struggle with political adversaries does not intimidate them. As one leader said, "Big deal! So what? That's what we're here for" (Don Eberly, interview, July 15, 2004).

Conservative evangelicals have also learned not to acknowledge mistakes to their political adversaries. They learned this lesson from Jimmy Carter's presidency. Multiple leaders spoke disapprovingly of the image of President Carter sitting on the floor of the Oval Office listening to complaints of congressional leaders over his administration before the national address that came to be known as his malaise speech in July 1979. For Carter, being willing to admit mistakes embodies the Christian ideal of humility, but for other evangelicals, it is a sign of weakness that can be exploited by political adversaries. The day following President George W. Bush's second inauguration, I asked Karen Hughes, the president's close advisor, to name the biggest mistake they had made during his first term: "Biggest mistake, oh gosh, I'm sure we made a lot of mistakes. . . . It's hard to talk about that because it has policy ramifications for the president. . . . He struggles with this question, too, because . . . right now if he says them, it has ramifications [in Washington and] around the world" (Interview, January 21, 2005).

The construction and maintenance of boundaries by evangelicals in the political realm reflect larger trends whereby evangelicals differentiate between us and them. For decades, evangelical movement leaders have produced and disseminated a narrative that presents the group as being somewhat persecuted as a religious minority. The irony of course, is that evangelicals have founded groups like the Moral Majority even as they promulgate a discourse that says their opinions are not valued by society. It is this perception of being marginalized by the cultural elite that causes movement leaders to use this rhetorical distancing mechanism. This language within the movement creates a perception among evangelicals that they are an embattled group, yet, as Christian Smith pointed out, they are not so countercultural as to be removed from the respective layers of community—local, national, and global—of which they are a part (1998). In the aggregate, this embattled rhetoric contributes to a sense of exclusion felt by many evangelicals.

This is one area, though, where the opinions of movement leaders like the late Jerry Falwell and James Dobson differed from evangelical political and cultural elites. Indeed, most evangelical public leaders I interviewed—those evangelicals who head mainstream political, business, and cultural institutions—say their secular peers are "not antagonistic toward Christianity. They're apathetic toward Christianity . . . they just don't want to deal with it. . . . They don't care" (David McFadzean, interview, September 27, 2004). One informant referred to this notion of feeling embattled as a "manufactured thing" that is felt more often by evangelicals in "middle America" than by evangelicals working directly in centers of elite cultural production (Don Holt, interview October 7, 2004). Nevertheless, the rhetoric has provided a rallying cry for many evangelicals in drawing sharp boundaries against their political opponents.

Allies

Along with identifying political adversaries, evangelicals have built significant bonds with important allies. Chief among these are fellow religious conservatives who actively practice their faith, including Roman Catholics, Mormons, Jews, and Muslims. The pro-life movement began with Roman Catholics in the early 1970s, but prominent evangelical physician, C. Everett Koop, was an early ally. Koop met Dr. Harold O. J. Brown, an evangelical theologian and ethicist, at a Christian men's conference in 1975. Later that year, they joined Billy Graham and Francis Schaeffer in forming the Christian Action Council, a group focused on lobbying Congress for legislation that would remove some of the allowances permitted by Roe v. Wade, 410 U.S. 113 (1973) (see also chapter 6, this volume). In 1977, Koop, Schaeffer, and Schaeffer's son Franky produced a five-segment film series and companion book titled *Whatever Happened to the Human Race?* Koop and Schaeffer traveled the nation, promoting their film and spurring the faithful to action. Soon after, what began as a Roman Catholic concern became a passionate issue for evangelicals as well. This reveals the durability of American evangelicalism; its elastic orthodoxy maintains a degree of cohesion yet is not so inflexible that the movement cannot change with the times. Indeed, the abortion debate became one of the primary issues around which evangelicals drew upon their bridge-building religious sensibilities. They joined common cause with other groups for a larger purpose—namely, safeguarding the sanctity of life.

Gradually, this single issue of shared conviction expanded. With the Moral Majority's formation in 1979, evangelicals found an outlet through which they could campaign on other issues such as suppressing the homosexual movement and advancing their vision for family life. It is on these pillars that evangelicals further cemented alliances with other religious conservatives, thus producing what John Green has called the traditionalist alliance. Francis Schaeffer argued that many groups shared evangelicals' convictions regarding human sexuality and the family; working together, he suggested, these groups would be more successful politically than they would working alone. Building on this notion, which Schaeffer called co-belligerency, the evangelical leaders reached out to Jews, Catholics, Mormons, and even secularists to participate in the political aims they sought[11] (for a discussion of relations within the traditionalist alliance during the early 2000s, see chapter 4, volume 1).

The elastic orthodoxy of modern American evangelicalism enables the movement to modify its outreach strategies to different constituencies. Whereas the pro-life movement has been the principal domain of the evangelical-Catholic rapprochement, it is shared ideas about American civic life—such as infusing religious expression into the public schools—that have galvanized synergy between evangelicals and Mormons, and the primary context for this dialogue and cooperation has been the Republican Party. As a result, evangelicals and Mormons have stressed joint political aims in their outreach efforts toward the other, whereas evangelicals and Catholics have focused on shared theological convictions.

Evangelicals have also drawn on their elastic orthodoxy in building alliances with conservative Jews and conservative Muslims. In some instances, these cobelligerents have worked together to fight the encroachment of secularism in the public sphere through activism on matters like homosexuality while maintaining theological differences. Principally, however, their joint efforts have involved matters of religious freedom and concern over persecution of religious minorities—for example, the successful passage of the International Religious Freedom Act of 1998 and the Victims of Trafficking and Protection Act of 2000 (Hertzke 2004).

Evangelical institutions and initiatives have supported these political alliances, some of which are evangelical para-church organizations.[12] However, since the 1970s, evangelicals have founded and donated funds to support a considerable number of politically oriented initiatives, even though they are not explicitly evangelical or religious groups. These include the Council for National Policy, the Arlington Group, the Christian Coalition, and the Family Research Council. Also, groups like Focus on the Family have established political action committees, such as Focus on the Family Action, and Christian media, such as talk radio and magazines, have expanded the reach of evangelicals and their political allies.

A few initiatives have supported the agenda of evangelical progressives, such as a journal called *The Post-American*, which eventually was renamed *Sojourners*. Figures like Ron Sider and Jim Wallis began to call on their fellow evangelicals to mobilize for social action through documents like the "Chicago Declaration of Evangelical Social Concern," which was first distributed in 1973. In it they stated, "We must attack the materialism of our culture. . . . Before God and a billion hungry neighbors, we must rethink our values regarding our present standard of living and promote a more just acquisition and distribution of the world's resources."[13] Most evangelicals did not share the sentiments of Wallis and Sider, but groups such as Evangelicals for Social Action (founded in 1978) and Call to Renewal (1995) provided institutional bases for evangelicals who disagreed with the Republican agenda. They are, however, beginning to make inroads within mainstream evangelical circles, as evidenced by the National Association of Evangelicals' call for more social action directed at alleviating poverty and environmental degradation.

Some political leaders admitted to me, usually off the record, that they curried favor with leaders of the evangelical movement for political gain. These politicians admitted that they attended evangelical gatherings to tap into the wide network of informal alliances evangelicals have built over the years. Representative Tony Hall (D-OH) told me that he first attended the National Prayer Breakfast, "because I was a politician: I would be seen." He thought, "Maybe this would be a good thing for my career if I were to be seen with godly people" (Interview, February 4, 2005). Over time, he said, the political advantages of attending receded in his decision to be part of the annual event as his personal faith became more important to him. However, he admitted that many politicians in Washington, himself included, engage in fellowship with people of faith at times for political purposes.

The process of building political alliances has been done mostly by governmental leaders and those who lead large evangelical institutions, but not megachurch pastors. It is not uncommon for notable ministers like Bill Hybels or Rick Warren to meet with politicians or to speak at various political gatherings organized by evangelicals. But these pastors devote little time to maintaining the informal networks that have served as the skeleton enabling evangelicals to flex their political muscle. I identified three dozen organizations that have been critical to building evangelical political alliances,[14] and only one of them—Rick Warren's P.E.A.C.E. Plan—is headed by a pastor.

Today, conservative evangelicals use their political alliances as a way of maintaining close relations with politicians they support. For several years, they have convened weekly meetings with congressional leaders and Republican officials to discuss public policy and specific strategies. These strictly closed-door meetings include the Values Action Team[15] and the Arlington Group,[16] both of which are attended by prominent senators and representatives from the White House. Groups like these have existed for quite some time, but the prominence of conservative evangelicals in Washington has pushed these strategy-shaping meetings into the public limelight (Karen Tumulty and Matthew Cooper, "What

Does Bush Owe the Religious Right?" *Time*, January 30, 2005; Alan Cooperman, "Opponents of Gay Marriage Divided; At Issue Is Scope of an Amendment," *Washington Post*, November 29, 2003).

Strategy sessions, however, are not the principal source of cohesion behind evangelicals' alliance building. Instead, their political power resides in the informal relational substructure of personal friendships and mutual involvement outside the political sphere. Serving on the boards of evangelical nonprofit organizations and personal ties with leaders and their families have generated bonds of loyalty and mutual commitment that have been fundamental to evangelicals' political expression in contemporary American politics. Movement leaders like Charles Colson have mentored senior governmental leaders such as Michael Gerson, one of George W. Bush's chief lieutenants during his first term. Colson gave Gerson his first job out of college and later helped him move into politics working for Senator Daniel Coats. These kinds of long-term relationships between evangelical and Republican leaders have amplified the evangelical movement's influence in politics. As John Padgett and Christopher Ansell demonstrated, deep relational ties among powerful actors can be critical to achieving certain objectives (1993), and I found the interpersonal networks among evangelicals that honeycomb Washington today have been fundamental to evangelicalism's advance. These networks point to the various boundaries that evangelicals have drawn between allies and opponents and the mechanisms that have maintained those forms of social differentiation (for an analysis of relations in contemporary conservative politics, see chapter 4, this volume).

Evangelical Populism

The historian Nathan Hatch identified five elements of the "democratization of American Christianity" that occurred along with the development of Jeffersonian and Jacksonian democracy during the early years of the Republic (1989). These elements still characterize the populism of contemporary American evangelicalism. First, evangelicalism prefers large-scale forms of religious expression, yet elicits that by individual appeals. In belief and practice, evangelicals focus on the individual's soul and in the necessity of personal conversion. However, they often rely on mass rallies and revival meetings as the context in which appeals for conversion are made. Second, evangelicals value the incorporation of popular ditties and indigenous folk music in their services; this practice requires them to stay current on popular culture and seek creative ways to mimic mainstream cultural goods and trends. Third, iconoclastic individuals often provide leadership for the movement. These outspoken—sometimes reactionary—leaders effectively capture media attention and build coalitions of followers because of their opposition to the establishment. Fourth, the evangelical movement's populism depends, in part, on the impression that evangelicals are not part of the establishment. This was not always the case. Evangelicals in 1900 were influential in every sphere of American public life, but in the decades following, they lost that power (Marsden 2006). This sense of loss and the desire to regain it animates contemporary evangelicalism. As one CEO told me, "We lost the universities. We lost the cities and thought centers. We lost the media" (Paul Klaassen, interview, July 15, 2004). To the extent that evangelicals have sought to "take over America," as some critics charge, it has largely involved a hope to enact significant social change through mobilized political action. As part of that, movement leaders engage rhetorical dichotomies that distinguish between traditional believers (who are "good") and secular activists (who are "bad"). Finally, evangelicalism's populism, like that which Hatch describes, favors simplicity and pragmatism instead of doctrinal complexity or rhetorical flourish. This is the domain of the PowerPoint sermon and the affect-oriented praise chorus.

Evangelicalism's populism contributes greatly to its significant size and expanding reach. As others have noted, these populist sensibilities have enabled evangelicalism to become the fastest growing religious movement in the world (Jenkins 2002; Martin 1990). These five attributes—individualistic, contemporary, iconoclastic, antielitist, and pragmatic—have given the movement and its adherents energy and a sense of urgency. In religious terms, this energy translates into a drive to talk to others about faith, using all resources at their disposal and making use of whatever time they have. This theme emerged hundreds of times as I conducted interviews. One representative example was the name plaque that sat on the desk of Clayton Brown, a successful executive in Chicago. The back side of the name plate was inscribed with the phrase "Perhaps Today." I asked Brown why he would have that statement facing him as he sat at his desk, and he replied, "That reminds me the Lord might come any minute, especially today" (Interview, October 8, 2004). The statement kept the imperative to act on his faith at the forefront of Brown's mind throughout the day. In political terms, this sense of urgency translates into a desire to get something done, which is more easily accomplished in a democratic society like ours where mobilized constituents can vote candidates into office.

Political Mobilization

Connected to evangelicalism's focus on individual salvation is a push for moral reform. Moral activism motivates adherents to become involved in the political process. Others have shown that the enclave mentality of American evangelicals from the 1930s until the 1970s was an anomaly (Marsden 2006; Young 2002; Smith 2000). As Alexis de Toc-queville noted, organized religion provided the institutional means through which active citizenship was cultivated during Jacksonian democracy, and evangelical churches and voluntary associations led the way (1834/2000). A convinced religious viewpoint can give rise to polit-ical fervor. In recent decades, evangelicals have drawn on their faith in mobilizing for political action. Peter Wehner, a senior White House offi-cial, elaborated on the nexus between evangelicalism and political mobi-lization: "As Christians, we are called to advance certain principles—justice and mercy, goodness and righteousness, human dignity, human decency. . . . And politics is one of the realms in which you can do that. . . . People have legitimate moral concerns, and politics is a way to express them . . . a way to make a difference, to help improve human lives" (Interview, August 4, 2004).

Of course, not all observers think that justice and mercy is what evan-gelicals have advanced. Indeed, the invocation of one's personal faith in crafting public policy is disconcerting to many (Linker 2006; Kaplan 2004). To these detractors, evangelical activism threatens the social order that sustains liberal democracy. For them, living in a free, pluralistic so-ciety demands that religion remain in the personal sphere; it is what en-sures the flourishing of liberal society. The evangelical leaders I inter-viewed claim to not impose religion on others, but neither do they deny that religion plays a role in their objectives and strategies. Former presi-dential speechwriter Michael Gerson told me that for believers like him, the evangelical faith is where "you get your moral passion furnished, your depth of commitment because you think it's true and right" (Inter-view, March 17, 2005). For Gerson and others, the idea of divorcing one's religious identity from civic participation is not a requirement of liberal democracy; it is instead a denial of "what it means for me to be who I am." Faith plays such a salient role in these leaders' lives that they cannot conceive of active citizenship apart from their moral convictions, which are shaped by their evangelical commitments.

Leaders within the evangelical movement have tapped their tradi-tion's populism to produce energy and momentum around political is-sues and particular candidates. One of the most important but often overlooked examples from recent history is the massive Washington for Jesus rally that was held in the run-up to the 1980 presidential cam-paign. Five hundred thousand adherents assembled on the National Mall. Through media initiatives, mailing lists, and personal outreach, movement leaders gathered the crowd on April 29, the anniversary of the date the settlers first landed at Jamestown in 1607. The event linked evangelical fervor with patriotic sentiment and showed that evangeli-cals' political muscle was more organized than it had ever been (Wilcox 1996). The event also solidified the political importance of certain movement leaders like Pat Robertson within conservative politics, and organizers were convinced of the event's significance. Bill Bright, founder of Campus Crusade for Christ and another rally organizer, called the event "the single most important day in the history of the United States since the Declaration of Independence" (Clarkson 1997, 108). More than one movement leader told me that they believed this precipitated Ronald Reagan's election. Of course, subsequent research has shown that evangelical leaders vigorously supported Reagan's candidacy, but more rank-and-file adherents cast their ballots for Carter (Woodberry and Smith 1998; Manza and Brooks 1997; Woodberry and Brink 1996). The tide would turn by 1984, at which time rank-and-file members followed movement leaders in backing Reagan and moving squarely inside the Republican fold. But the Washington for Jesus rally was a signal event.

The sociologist Robert Michels argued that organization necessitates oligarchic governance; a small group must lead all organized bodies, even those advancing populist or democratic ideals (1962). This principle, which Michels called the iron law of oligarchy, means that power inevitably will be held in the hands of relatively few people. Even as the evangelical movement has drawn on its populist attributes for political expression, an elite of conservative evangelicals—funders like Richard DeVos and spokespersons like Richard Land—have served as nodes of information and introduction between networks of important evangelicals and powerful Republicans. Indeed, Michels predicted that populist-oriented groups, such as large crowds or mass rallies, are easier to dominate than smaller gatherings. Crowds are less cohesive, so it is easier for a small group to gain control. Perhaps this has been to evangelicals' political advantage.[17] As movement leaders encouraged evangelicals to become more involved in the political process, a rising number of evangelical millionaires were entering the public stage and seeking to deploy their financial resources for the kinds of social change they favored (Lindsay 2007; O'Connor 2001).[18]

The collaboration among like-minded political, business, and cultural elites and leaders within the evangelical movement precipitated an organizing moment—the point at which well-resourced actors began to work together intentionally for conservative political objectives. Conservative leanings have been part of modern American evangelicalism for decades, but the constitution of overlapping networks of resourced leaders who were organized behind a particular political agenda occurred in the latter years of Jimmy Carter's presidency. The Washington for Jesus rally was the first sign of their ability to mobilize for political action. Reagan's sweep of the evangelical vote in 1984, and the loyalty these voters gave to George H. W. Bush in 1988 and during his term in office, cemented the alliance for many within the evangelical fold.[19]

"Triumphalistic Majoritarianism"

Evangelicalism's populism causes some movement leaders to claim that they represent the majority view on selective issues. This is the rhetorical flourish that gave rise to Jerry Falwell's justification in founding of the Moral Majority in 1979. Movement leaders like Tim and Beverly La-Haye, Ralph Reed, Jay Sekulow, Donald Wildmon, Janet Parshall, John Hagee, and Adrian Rogers joined Falwell's campaign, and as Susan Friend Harding showed, their mastery of a discourse that resonated with followers contributed greatly to evangelicalism's rising influence within conservative U.S. politics (2001).

Voting, like all cultural phenomena, has a distinctly expressive dimension within a pluralistic democracy (Peterson 1979; Fiorina 1976). People enact certain cultural rituals as a way of expressing norms and beliefs that they hold dear. Casting a ballot for a particular candidate can become an expressive symbol, that is, a way of affirming individual-level values in the larger public square. By identifying with the candidate in a fundamental way—as might happen if religious identity is salient for both a candidate and a voter—voting for the candidate can become an implicit vote for oneself.[20] This is especially relevant for religious traditions like evangelicalism in which religious identity is chosen by the adherent, not ascribed to him or her by birth or tradition. Evangelicals—unlike Roman Catholics, Jews, and mainline Protestants—believe the individual must take ownership of his faith by freely choosing it. That is why evangelicals' religious identity is so salient for them. Hence, evangelical religious identity can be a powerful force in electoral voting. Candidates such as Jimmy Carter and George W. Bush have been able to capitalize on the expressive power of evangelical religious identity as greater attention has been paid to the religious identities of presidential contenders.

Tapping into the expressive component of presidential politics is how voters' evangelical faith has been brought to bear on U.S. political life between 1976 and 2006.[21] As one leading Republican told me, "getting our people into power is something that we [evangelicals] like. . . . It's sort of like, well now the world can see that we're equal with them." Indeed, evangelicals' rising influence in politics is a source of great pride among most of the conservative evangelical leaders I interviewed.[22] Part of this is because they feel far less influential in fields like higher education, the arts, and media.

Cosmopolitans and Populists

And a cohort of evangelical leaders—whom I call cosmopolitan evangelicals—are bothered by their fellow believers who relish in political triumph at the expense of intellectual and artistic respectability (for more on differences in style among evangelical leaders, see chapters 5, 9, and 11). Robert Seiple, who once headed the evangelical organization World Vision and later served as the first ambassador-at-large for International Religious Freedom, referred to this majoritarian-inspired rhetoric of political activism as a "triumphal expression of the sunburst of American evangelicalism" (Interview, November 2, 2004). The evangelical historian Mark Noll wrote about the same subject in the conservative journal *First Things*. Here he warned against confusing the "dignity bestowed by popularity with the status earned by insight" (2001).

The distaste some informants expressed over the rhetoric espoused by Falwell and company points to a larger division within the leadership of American evangelicalism. Evangelical populism dominates the movement's subculture; here, leaders can mobilize millions for collective action. But the movement's cosmopolitan figures—like many in this study—convey a more nuanced approach to achieving their goals, goals that they share with their more populist brothers and sisters. They are less interested in running the country by the triumph of a majority, and instead present their faith as advocating Christian civility in a healthy, pluralistic public square—one voice among many (Skillen 2004; Mouw 1992). Cosmopolitan evangelicals lead mainstream social institutions— they are artists and professors, business executives and governmental leaders. They are less oriented toward the internal community of evangelicals and more toward wider society.

As the sociologist Randall Collins has shown, cosmopolitanism is often correlated with social power because is essentially entails the ability to maintain a wide network of acquaintances so that an array of people can be called upon when conflicts arise or favors are needed (1975). Robert Merton's category of cosmopolitan (1957; Merton, Fiske, and Curtis 1946), like that of Kwame Anthony Appiah's (2006), relies on ongoing interaction and persuasive influence on constituents outside one's local circle of influence. The cosmopolitan evangelicals that I interviewed resist the bombast and rhetorical hype of populist evangelicalism. Personal taste and disposition are surely factors that condition the extent to which these cosmopolitan evangelicals sought to differentiate themselves (Bourdieu 1977, 1984). Yet, the more important factor involves the range of social networks of which they are a part and the access they have to powerful institutions. The social worlds they inhabit are populated with key leaders of our society; as one informant described it, this is "move-the-dial Christianity" (Al Sikes, interview, July 14, 2004). Political leaders George W. Bush and Jimmy Carter may benefit from the support of populist evangelicals, but they are not one of them. Neither attended Christian colleges and neither have spent much time working within the evangelical subculture. In fact, both come from well-to-do families; Carter, though portrayed as a peanut farmer, came from a local elite family.[23] Their personal backgrounds, educational and professional experiences, and orientations to public life are shaped by cosmopolitan sensibilities.

It is a mistake, therefore, to conflate evangelical influence with evangelical populism. Some—I would argue most—prominent evangelicals in American politics are of this cosmopolitan variety. Of course, populist leaders are among those most identified with the evangelical movement. That is not surprising, for whatever influence they wield and attention they enjoy comes from their position within the subculture. Without their respective institutional bases within evangelicalism, they would have little clout. Individuals like Franklin Graham and Joel Osteen are prominent media figures who represent, at least in part, evangelicalism to wider society, yet they are only part of the movement's leadership structure in American politics.

Sometimes tensions flare between these two groups, and populist leaders clash with their cosmopolitan coreligionists. The late Adrian Rogers, for instance, rebuked Jimmy Carter as a secular humanist. In a particularly charged meeting, then House Majority Leader Dick Armey clashed with James Dobson, resulting in a campaign by Dobson to oust Armey from his leadership post. Armey later told me, "That was simply, in my estimation, because I failed to kiss his ring" (Interview, February 3, 2005). Over the years, there have been sustained internal conflicts between populist and cosmopolitan evangelicals in Washington, but on the most part the two groups have worked together to secure greater political influence for the movement and its priorities. Some, however, question the wisdom in identifying evangelicalism with conservative politics, and even more raise suspicions about the propriety of pursuing evangelical goals through political means.

Differences of Opinion

The alliance between American evangelicalism and the Republican Party is surprising in some ways. For example, Christian Smith (2000) showed that 68 percent of theologically conservative Protestants do not identify with the Christian Right, and nearly 35 percent think critiques of the Christian Right are legitimate. Although there are historical, theological, and social reasons why evangelicals have joined in common cause with political conservatives, a surprising number of countervailing forces can be found within the evangelical movement. In 1999, as many were leading the charge for President Clinton's impeachment, for example, several influential evangelical leaders—Tony Campolo, Gordon McDonald, and Bill Hybels, to name a few—huddled with the president in spiritual solidarity.

Today, Jim Wallis regularly advises leaders of the Democratic Party on how to connect with evangelical voters, and Tony Campolo spoke to a meeting of every Democrat in the U.S. Senate at the request of Hillary Rodham Clinton. Rick Warren befriended then-Senator Barack Obama and invited him and Senator Sam Brownback to speak at the 2006 World AIDS Day conference his church hosted in southern California. Richard Cizik, chief lobbyist of the National Association of Evangelicals, persuaded eighty-six evangelical leaders in early 2006 to sign the Evangelical Climate Initiative, a statement about the urgency of fighting global warming. And, after losing the 2004 presidential race, Democrats founded strategy groups, support networks, and mobilization campaigns to connect better with the evangelical public. Common Good Strategies and the Democratic Faith Working Group on Capitol Hill are among these. A number of observers, however, say that Democrats' initiatives are "making the same mistakes that the folks on the Right made" (Robert Seiple, interview, November 2, 2004). Namely, they are attaching religious labels to partisan activities in ways that strike some as disingenuous.

Beyond differences between the evangelical Left and the evangelical Right, I found two kinds of arguments against evangelical involvement in politics altogether. The first deals with pragmatic concerns. Leaders who raised these kinds of objections have either become disenchanted with politics for one reason or another, or they believe politics and religion largely should not mix. The second set of objections deal with theological concerns; informants who raise these issues worry that active political engagement is inimical to faithful Christian practice. Curiously, every leader who raised the latter point was active in politics at the time. Such objections, therefore, do not fully dissuade even those who raise them.

Pragmatic Objections

Several of the architects of the nascent Christian Right have abjured in recent years. In fact, as early as 1985, leaders within the Moral Majority were increasingly uneasy about the alliance between religion and conservative politics. Cal Thomas resigned from his position as vice president of the organization to pursue a new career as a columnist. In his opinion, the marriage between evangelical faith and the Republican agenda is "doomed to futility" (Interview, June 23, 2005). Thomas and the evangelical pastor Ed Dobson wrote *Blinded by Might: Why the Religious Right Can't Save America* around this theme (1996). In it, they asked, "How can you [evangelicals] impose a morality on people that you can't impose on yourself?" Citing rampant materialism, sexual promiscuity, and evangelical hubris, Thomas and Dobson (not to be confused with Focus on the Family's James Dobson) renounced their involvement with conservative politics. Charles Colson, an official in the Nixon administration who served prison time because of his involvement in the Watergate scandal, has since become a significant leader within the evangelical movement, founding Prison Fellowship Ministries and the Wilberforce Forum. He reflected on his experience in the White House and offered the following warning to fellow evangelicals: "When I served under President Nixon, one of my jobs was to work special interest groups, including religious leaders. We would invite them to the White House, wine and dine them, take them on cruises about the presidential yacht. . . . Ironically, few were more easily impressed than religious leaders. The very people who should have been immune to the worldly pomp seemed most vulnerable" (Colson 1994, 11).

David Kuo was active in conservative politics for quite some time, and when I interviewed him in 2003 was serving as deputy director of the White House Office of Faith-Based and Community Initiatives. He spoke at length about various evangelical leaders and ministries that sought to curry favor with politicians and their staffs. "They genuflect to the title, not the person, and you have to remember that or else your feelings will be hurt," he told me. "They'll be inviting you to lunch one day, and then you change jobs and they won't return your phone calls" (Interview, October 28, 2003). Speaking off the record, he alluded to some disappointment with the ways in which lower ranking officials in the Bush administration sometimes mocked evangelical leaders who came to visit the White House. Kuo subsequently wrote about this (2006), acknowledging that some of his former colleagues called evangelicals "nuts" and "crazies." Kuo's book, *Tempting Faith: An Inside Story of Political Seduction*, was released shortly before the November elections in 2006, and in it he admonished fellow evangelicals to "fast" from political action for at least two years and redirect the energies toward the poor and toward "loving our neighbors." Kuo did not advocate that evangelicals abandon politics, but he believes, as a practical matter, that politics can have a corrupting influence.

Several leaders also feel that politics and religion should remain separate spheres. Don Eberly has served in several senior posts under recent Republican administrations as well as in the Congress. Endorsing a viewpoint that can be traced back to Saint Augustine, Eberly said, "We should do a far better job of separating out redemptive functions, which are functions of the church, and other functions, which are mostly social or governmental. I don't think the state serves a redemptive function" (Interview, July 15, 2004). Similar sentiments were expressed by other evangelicals who have been active in politics, many of whom referred to the separation of church and state. President Carter told me, "I was very careful not to mix church and state. . . . President Nixon had regular religious services in the White House. I thought that was outside my purview as an elected public official. . . . My father inculcated my belief in the strict separation of church and state, of politics and religion" (Interview, November 16, 2004). This did not mean that Carter kept his faith entirely private while serving in office. In fact, he is the most evangelistic—that is, one who speaks openly about his faith—president of the modern era. On multiple occasions, Carter shared his evangelical faith with foreign heads of state. However, he did it while away from Washington—distance which, in his mind, loosened some of the strictures surrounding church-state separation—and only at the invitation of the other person. He spoke candidly about his beliefs with European and Asian heads of state, and as Gary Smith noted (2006), it is usually in foreign affairs that a president shows his true philosophical commitments. Domestically, the presidency is more encumbered by political considerations, but abroad the president has much greater latitude to act.[24] With regards to expressing his own faith, Carter felt much more at ease while traveling than at home. Carter and other leaders I interviewed sought ways to engage their faith in politics but remained wary of linking the two spheres too closely.

Religious Objections

A number of evangelicals in government also raised concerns about identifying their faith with partisan activities on theological grounds. These fall into three categories. The first addresses the impossibility of politics achieving spiritual outcomes. According to this line of thought, it is inappropriate—some even said sinful—to use politics for religious aims. Brady Anderson, the former USAID administrator, said, "Too many Christians believe that somehow God's kingdom is going to be imposed in a political way" (Interview, March 27, 2004). The implication is that fellow evangelicals in their political zeal may be trying to do just that. Michael Cromartie, a longtime Washington insider who heads the Evangelical Studies Project at the Ethics and Public Policy Center, asked, "What do these people think they are doing? They're missing the very point of the gospel—why Jesus came and what he calls us to do. The Kingdom of God is not going to arrive on Air Force One" (Interview, July 22, 2003).

Others spoke about the incommensurability of Christian virtues and political success. They implied that an evangelical could advance one or the other, but rarely both. When Karen Hughes, an active member of her Presbyterian church, was considering the offer to join George W. Bush in Washington, she deliberated at length. She told me:

I think all Christians struggle about involvement in the political process because on the one hand Christ said, "My kingdom is not of this world," and on the other, it's clear that he believes that it's important for those in authority to be people of faith. . . . I think there's always that tension there, and I worried about what getting involved in the political process at the national level would mean [for my faith]. I remember praying a lot for a clear signal . . . and I don't know that I ever felt like . . . this is what I definitely need to do. (Interview, January 21, 2005)

Along these same lines, former U.S. representative and under secretary for Homeland Security Asa Hutchison related, "I've often thought that the Christian faith is almost inconsistent with politics because the essence of politics is promotion, getting ahead, advancement. How can you be a politician if you don't talk about your successes in life? . . . But that's really not consistent with the scriptural [admonition for] humility and modesty" (Interview, December 10, 2004). Finally, evangelical leaders raised concerns that politics can overtake a person's faith. Political success can cause one to lose, in one person's words, "the sense that history is driven by God, that you do the best you can, but at the end you hold lightly to the things of the world."

The rub for evangelicals who espouse these theological concerns is that theirs is a faith that makes claims on all areas of one's life. According to evangelical ideals, faith is not just a part of their life; it is constitutive of every aspect of their lives—their families, their jobs, their avocations. The comprehensive nature of the evangelical faith compels evangelicals in government to bring their faith to bear on policy positions and political activities. Multiple times these leaders acknowledged that they fall short of their ideals, and a few discussed how their actions betrayed their faith. But for most, compartmentalizing their faith would be a mistake. Glenn Hubbard, who once chaired the White House Council of Economic Advisors, said, "If you believe that faith is important in your own life, how could you then say it's not related to the other things that I do? I can't imagine how you could do that" (Interview, August 23, 2004).

Conclusion

American evangelicalism has succeeded in the political realm because the movement's rhetoric and beliefs encourage adherents to construct boundaries and to employ populist strategies for wider influence. Through various alliances over the last fifty years, evangelicals—for the most part—have joined in common cause with theological, social, and political conservatives. The movement's elastic orthodoxy and historic connection with populist religious traditions have furthered evangelicals' political expression. Movement leaders have mobilized large crowds and have harnessed their resources in support of particular candidates and policies. This has produced a discourse within the movement that celebrates the triumph of the majority, which is surprising because even by the most generous counts, evangelicals do not constitute a majority in this country (Hackett and Lindsay 2008).

Evangelicals' political success and the strategies they have employed reveal significant fractures within the movement, several of which I have surveyed here. These include the differences between populist evangelicalism, with its popularity and bombast, and cosmopolitan evangelicalism, with its alternative sources of power and differential degree of influence. Not all evangelical leaders support Republican candidates, and today the evangelical Left is following some of the tactics pioneered by the evangelical Right nearly thirty years ago. Some evangelicals in government are bothered by contemporary developments, expressing disbelief that politics can achieve religious objectives or disillusionment with how little their political gains have accomplished. Others raise more fundamental concerns about the propriety of faith in the political process.

It remains to be seen what will be the legacy of evangelicals' political gains from the last thirty years. De Tocqueville observed nearly two centuries ago that Americans can channel their religious commitments in service to the common good. Such could be the case again as engaged citizens tap additional resources to meet collective challenges and opportunities. By the same token, recent developments could mark the triumph of just another group and its narrow interests. History will be the judge. The rise of evangelicalism, however, can teach us much about the ways that entrepreneurial leaders can draw on the internal strengths of a movement to secure legitimacy and wider influence. In a democracy where political relations are constructed for mobilization, religious groups once located on the social periphery can make significant advancements in a relatively short span of time. Evangelicals have capitalized on the advantages afforded them and become a central firmament within the constellation of American political power.

Notes

1.   Indeed, in other contexts, such as Great Britain, evangelicals are often at the other end of the political spectrum, advocating liberal and sometimes socialist political positions.

2.   Over the course of my research, I approached 431 possible informants for an interview. I completed 360 interviews; in more formal quantitative analyses, this would indicate an 84 percent response rate. Although the re-

search methodology employed was not based on a random sample, I did examine whether the informants who completed interviews differed in any meaningful way from those who refused to participate in the study or who agreed to participate but whose interview was not able to be completed by the project's end. No meaningful differences could be found in terms of region of the country, race, sex, age, sector of influence, political affiliation, or current position held.

3. I use the term *convictions* to include norms, reasoning, and ideology—matters of belief. I use the term *sensibilities* to refer to matters of religious practice—routines, demeanor, perceptions, and way of life.

4. Here I use Lamont and Molnar's definitions: symbolic boundaries as "conceptual distinctions made by social actors to categorize objects, people, practices, and even time and space;" which is distinct from social boundaries, defined as "objectified forms of social differences manifested in unequal access to and unequal distribution of resources (material and nonmaterial) and social opportunities" (2002, 168).

5. For example, the recent rhetoric surrounding the cultural commission—taken from the Genesis passage where humans are instructed to be fruitful, to multiply, and to care for the earth (1:28)—within the evangelical movement has justified their engagement with wider society. This rhetorical strategy has encouraged evangelical activism in a variety of domains, including politics, and has compelled evangelicals to work with others as a Christian mandate. Grounding the rhetoric in a biblical exhortation (Genesis in this case) gives the mandate even greater weight.

6. In this interview, Campolo related a story of the evangelical historian Mark Noll making a similar argument to President Bill Clinton when the president asked Campolo to arrange a meeting so he could learn why American evangelicals were opposing him and other Democrats in the 1990s. James Morone noted evangelicals' demonization of particular sides in cultural debates has occurred throughout American history (2003). Rhys Williams explores how evangelicals have created a moral other in their discourse about secular elites (chapter 5, this volume).

7. Of course, it should be noted that not all evangelicals shared these sentiments then, and certainly do not today. Black evangelicals, for example, do not long for a return to colonial or antebellum America, and few of them think of this era of American history as particularly Christian (see Emerson and Smith 2000).

8. This patriotism is part of why William Randolph Hearst liked the group and eventually telegrammed the editors at his newspapers to "puff Graham," an act that catapulted Billy Graham to celebrity status in mid-century America.

9. The American pastor Francis Schaeffer founded L'Abri Fellowship as a quasi-commune for Christian students in 1955. L'Abri, which means *the shelter*, was established as a place where students could contemplate existential questions in an intellectually and spiritually "safe place," as well as practice Christian living in community. Schaeffer's thinking was influenced by Reformed theologians, including Cornelius Van Til and G. Gre-

sham Machen. See Ingersoll in this volume for more on Schaeffer's influence, particularly on Reconstructionist theology.

10. Not all informants felt this way, especially those who lived on the West coast. Guy Anthony, a technology executive in Silicon Valley, captured the sentiment of several dozen leaders I met: "I think evangelicalism is becoming militant to the point of losing its effectiveness. . . . The whole 'culture wars' deal . . . it's not even clear to me who the enemy is" (Guy Anthony, interview, May 19, 2004).

11. Of course, some fundamentalist leaders, such as the Reverend Bob Jones, completely disagreed with welcoming these co-belligerents to the evangelical-dominated coalition.

12. From the Greek *para*, para-church organizations work alongside existing church structures to provide specialized services such as evangelistic outreach, international relief and development, or social justice. One of the oldest Protestant examples is a group formed out of the Anglican tradition, the Society for Promoting Christian Knowledge, which was founded in 1698 by Thomas Bray to encourage Christian education.

13. http://www.esa-online.org.

14. In my larger work, I identified 142 sources of evangelical cohesion over the last three decades in different sectors of American public life (Lindsay 2007). These include explicitly evangelical parachurch groups, events, and initiatives as well as secular entities that have been particularly conducive for evangelical leaders' involvement. Within the political domain, these include the following: Democratic Faith Working Group, Moral Majority, Christian Coalition, Center for Christian Statesmanship, Heritage Foundation, National Prayer Breakfast, White House Public Liaison Office, Washington for Jesus event, Free Congress Foundation, Wilberforce Forum, Common Good Strategies, Arlington Group, Values Action Team, Office of Faith-Based and Community Initiatives, Institute for Global Engagement, Sojourners, Legacy, Council for National Policy, The Fellowship, American Studies Program of the Council for Christian Colleges and Universities, Pew Forum on Religion and Public Life, Christian Embassy, White House Christian Fellowship, Family Research Council, Ethics and Public Policy Center, Focus on the Family Action, International Justice Mission, PEACE Plan, Evangelicals for Social Action, C.S. Lewis Institute, Renaissance Weekend, Religious Roundtable, The Clapham Institute, Evangelicals and Catholics Together, Center for Public Justice, and American Family Association.

15. The Values Action Team includes representatives from Focus on the Family, the Family Research Council, the Eagle Forum, the Traditional Values Coalition, and Concerned Women for America, among others. Insiders report these Thursday gatherings, which began in 1998, discuss issues like Supreme Court nominees, policies on the family, and the execution of a pro-life agenda (see Schroedel and Corbin 2002).

16. Named for its original meeting spot in northern Virginia, the Arlington Group is composed of roughly seventy-five members who meet regularly for off the record brainstorming sessions on conservative policies and media messages. With Paul Weyrich as the main convener of the Arlington

Group, breakfasts that the Arlington Group sponsors for lawmakers are often called Weyrich breakfasts inside the Washington Beltway.

17. In no way do I mean to imply that evangelicals are "rubes" or "dupes" and are, therefore, easier to control. In fact, my research has shown quite the opposite, as evangelicals have demonstrated intelligence and cosmopolitan sensibilities in multiple domains (Lindsay 2007). However, I am persuaded that the movement's populist roots in American history and democratic impulses today have made it particularly well suited to be organized for political action. Rising levels of wealth, education, and access to media enabled a cadre of evangelical leaders in the late 1970s and 1980s to capitalize upon their resources for strategic advantage. The dynamic between their overall theological and social conservatism matched well with the political and economic conservatism of Ronald Reagan and other Republican leaders.

18. Examples of wealthy evangelical donors funding support for particular social policies include Richard DeVos, cofounder of Amway, and Howard Ahmanson of the Home Savings bank fortune.

19. White evangelicals were Bush's strongest supporters going into the 1988 election. As economic struggles plagued the waning months of his campaign, Bush's candidacy appealed to evangelicals on social issues. Mainline Protestants, a tradition that included Bush himself, were growing increasingly critical of the sagging economy; evangelicals, on the other hand, were more approving. Even through the spring of 1992, evangelicals stood with Bush. Data from National Survey of Religion and Politics conducted at the University of Akron that year showed that 43 percent of evangelicals gave a high evaluation of Bush's job in office, compared to only 38 percent of mainline Protestants and only 35 percent of Roman Catholics.

20. Of course, other identity markers—such as gender and race—have been documented as expressive symbols in presidential politics as well (Schuessler 2000; Ellison and London 1992). Shared ideology, however, can be particularly salient in politics (Bawn 1999; Bohmann 1990; Wattier 1983).

21. That, in my estimation, is why so many evangelicals voted for George W. Bush. According to the Pew Research Center, Bush received 72 percent of the votes from evangelicals in 2000, and 78 percent in 2004. Evangelicals voted for this president as a way of validating their own faith perspective and as a way of legitimating their opinion. As Frank Parkin suggested, social movements entail expressive action that is guided by a particular moral outlook, an outlook that concerns the way things ought to be (1968). This, I conclude, has been fundamental to explaining why and how evangelicals have become more engaged in American politics. They are increasingly concerned with using their own agency to set the world, from their perspective, as it ought to be.

22. Some expressed concern, as will be explored in the next section.

23. I thank G. William Domhoff for drawing this connection for me.

24. Gary Smith made this point by noting the salience of human rights in Carter's foreign policy and the ways in which faith compelled him to act in the Panama Canal treaties and the Camp David Accords, among other diplomatic efforts while in office (2006).

References

Almond, Gabriel A., R. Scott Appleby, and Emmanuel Sivan. 2003. *Strong Religion: The Rise of Fundamentalisms Around the World*. Chicago: University of Chicago Press.

Appiah, Kwame Anthony. 2006. *Cosmopolitanism: Ethics in a World of Strangers*. New York: W. W. Norton.

Bawn, Kathleen. 1999. "Constructing 'Us': Ideology, Coalition Politics, and False Consciousness." *American Journal of Political Science* 43(2): 303–34.

Bohmann, James F. 1990. "Communication, Ideology, and Democratic Theory." *American Political Science Review* 84(1): 93–109.

Bourdieu, Pierre. 1977. *Reproduction in Education, Society, and Culture*, translated by Richard Nice. Beverly Hills, Calif.: Sage Publications.

———. 1984. *Distinction: A Social Critique of the Judgment of Taste*, translated by Richard Nice. Cambridge, Mass.: Harvard University Press.

Clarkson, Frederick. 1997. *Eternal Hostility: The Struggle Between Theocracy and Democracy*. Monroe, Maine: Common Courage Press.

Collins, Randall. 1975. *Conflict Sociology: Toward an Explanatory Science*. New York: Academic Press.

Colson, Charles. 1994. "Christians in Politics: Being Salt or Being Suckers." *Rutherford Newsletter*. March 1994. Published by the Rutherford Institute.

de Tocqueville, Alexis. 1834/2000. *Democracy in America*, translated and annotated by Stephen D. Grant. Indianapolis, Ind.: Hackett Publishing.

Douglas, Mary. 1970. *Natural Symbols: Explorations in Cosmology*. London: Barrie & Rockliff the Cresset.

Ellison, Christopher G., and Bruce London. 1992. "The Social and Political Participation of Black Americans: Compensatory and Ethnic Community Perspectives Revisited." *Social Forces* 70(3): 681–701.

Emerson, Michael O., and Christian Smith, 2000. *Divided by Faith: Evangelical Religion and the Problem of Race in America*. New York: Oxford University Press

Fiorina, Morris P. 1976. "The Voting Decision: Instrumental and Expressive Aspects." *The Journal of Politics* 38(2): 390–413.

Hackett, Conrad, and D. Michael Lindsay. 2008. "Measuring Evangelicalism: Consequences of Different Operationalization Strategies." *Journal for the Scientific Study of Religion* 47(3): 499–514.

Harding, Susan Friend. 2001. *The Book of Jerry Falwell: Fundamentalist Language and Politics*. Princeton, N.J.: Princeton University Press.

Hatch, Nathan. 1989. *The Democratization of American Christianity*. New Haven, Conn.: Yale University Press.

Hertzke, Allen D. 2004. *Freeing God's Children: The Unlikely Alliance for Global Human Rights*. Lanham, Md.: Rowman & Littlefield.

Hoffer, Eric. 1951/2002. *The True Believer: Thoughts on the Nature of Mass Movements*. New York: Harper Perennial Modern Classics.

Hunter, James Davison. 1991. *Culture Wars: The Struggle to Define America*. New York: Basic Books.

Jenkins, Philip. 2002. *The Next Christendom: The Coming of Global Christianity*. New York: Oxford University Press.

Kaplan, Esther. 2004. *With God on Their Side*. New York: The New Press.

Kuo, David. 2006. *Tempting Faith: An Inside Story of Political Seduction*. New York: Free Press.

Lamont, Michèle, and Virag Molnar. 2002. "The Study of Boundaries in the Social Sciences." *Annual Review of Sociology* 28(2002): 167–95.

Lindsay, D. Michael. 2007. *Faith in the Halls of Power: How Evangelicals Joined the American Elite*. New York: Oxford University Press.

Linker, Damon. 2006. *The Theocons: Secular America under Siege*. New York: Doubleday.

Manza, Jeff, and Clem Brooks. 1997. "The Religious Factor in U.S. Presidential Elections, 1960–1992." *American Journal of Sociology* 103(1): 38–81.

Marsden, George. 2006. *Fundamentalism and American Culture*, 2nd ed. New York: Oxford University Press.

Martin, David. 1990. *Tongues of Fire: The Explosion of Protestantism in Latin America*. Oxford: Blackwell.

Martin, William C. 1996. *With God on Our Side: The Rise of the Religious Right in America*. New York: Broadway Books.

Merton, Robert K. 1957. *Social Theory and Social Structure*. Glencoe, Ill.: Free Press.

Merton, Robert King, with Marjorie Fiske and Alberta Curtis, 1946. *Mass Persuasion: The Social Psychology of a War Bond Drive*. New York: Harper and Brothers.

Michels, Robert. 1962. Political *Parties: A Sociological Study of the Oligarchical Tendencies of Modern Democracy*, translated by Eden and Cedar Paul. New York: Free Press.

Morone, James A. 2003. *Hellfire Nation: The Politics of Sin in American History*. New Haven, Conn.: Yale University Press.

Mouw, Richard. 1992. *Uncommon Decency: Christian Civility in an Uncivilized World*. Downers Grove, Ill.: InterVarsity Press.

Noll, Mark A. 2001. "Minding the Evangelical Mind." *First Things*, January 2001. Available at: http://www.firstthings.com/article.php3?id_article=2121 (accessed March 31, 2009).

O'Connor, Alice. 2001. *Poverty Knowledge: Social Science, Social Policy, and the Poor in Twentieth-Century U.S. History*. Princeton, N.J.: Princeton University Press.

Padgett, John F., and Christopher K. Ansell. 1993. "Robust Action and the Rise of the Medici, 1400–1434." *American Journal of Sociology* 98(6): 1259–319.

Parkin, Frank. 1968. *Middle Class Radicalism: The Social Bases of the British Campaign for Nuclear Disarmament*. Manchester, U.K.: Manchester University Press.

Peterson, Richard A. 1979. "Revitalizing the Culture Concept." *Annual Review of Sociology* 5(1): 137–66.

Rosin, Hanna. 2007. *God's Harvard: A Christian College on a Mission to Save America*. New York: HarcourtBrace.

Schroedel, Jean Reith, and Tanya Corbin. 2002. "Gender Relations and Institutional Conflicts Over Mifepristone." *Women & Politics* 24(1): 35–60.

Schuessler, Alexander A. 2000. *A Logic of Expressive Choice*. Princeton, N.J.: Princeton University Press.

Skillen, James W. 2004. *In Pursuit of Justice: Christian-Democratic Explorations*. Lanham, Md.: Rowman & Littlefield.

Smith, Christian. 2000. *Christian America: What Evangelicals Really Want*. Berkeley: University of California Press.

Smith, Christian, with Michael Emerson, Sally Gallagher, Paul Kennedy, and

David Sikkink. 1998. *American Evangelicalism: Embattled and Thriving*. Chicago: University of Chicago Press.

Smith, Gary Scott. 2006. *Faith and the Presidency: From George Washington to George W. Bush*. New York: Oxford University Press.

Wattier, Mark J. 1983. "Ideological Voting in 1980 Republican Presidential Primaries." *The Journal of Politics* 45: 1016–26.

Wilcox, Clyde. 1996. *Onward Christian Soldiers: The Religious Right in American Politics*. Boulder, Colo.: Westview Press.

Woodberry, Robert D., and Paul Brink. 1996. "Evangelicals and Politics: Surveying a Contemporary Mason-Dixon Line." Presentation at Annual Meeting of American Sociological Association, New York (August 1996).

Woodberry, Robert D., and Christian S. Smith. 1998. "Fundamentalism Et Al: Conservative Protestants in America." *Annual Review of Sociology* 24(1996): 25–56.

Young, Michael P. 2002. "Confessional Protest: The Religious Birth of U.S. National Social Movements." *American Sociological Review* 67(5): 660–88.

Chapter 11

Of Movements and Metaphors: The Coevolution of the Christian Right and the GOP

CLYDE WILCOX

O N MAY 3, 2007, competing Republican presidential candidates were asked to raise their hands if they did not believe in evolution. Three candidates—Senator Sam Brownback, former governor Mike Huckabee, and Representative Tom Tacredo—raised their hands. In a later debate on June 5, Huckabee, an ordained Baptist minister, defended his position by quoting the first verse of Genesis—"In the beginning, God created the heavens and the Earth." But he also objected to the question. "It's interesting that that question would even be asked of somebody running for president. I'm not planning on writing the curriculum for an eighth-grade science book. I'm asking for the opportunity to be president of the United States."

This exchange in a presidential debate would have been inconceivable three decades earlier, but the rise of the Christian Right and its active involvement in GOP politics has made discussions of faith and theology commonplace in primary election politics. The relationship between the Christian Right and the Republican Party has been debated, with different positions sometimes coming from the same individual. Senator John McCain, who had in 2000 denounced Christian Right leaders as "agents of intolerance" intoned in 2006 that "I believe that the Christian Right has a major role to play in the Republican Party. . . . I believe they have a right to be a part of our party" (*Meet the Press*, April 2, 2006).

But others have suggested that the Christian Right is not merely one voice in the GOP, but the dominant voice. In March 2005, former U.S. senator and ambassador to the UN John Danforth, an ordained Episcopal minister, argued in an op-ed piece in the *New York Times* that the Christian Right had taken over his party. "By a series of recent initiatives, Republicans have transformed our party into the political arm of conservative Christians. . . . The problem is not with people or churches that are politically active. It is with a party that has gone so far in adopting a sectarian agenda that it has become the political extension of a religious movement" (John C. Danforth, 2005. "In the Name of Politics." *The New York Times*, March 30, 2005). Danforth mentioned a series of issues which he believes the Christian Right has pushed the GOP to extreme positions, including abortion, stem cell research, and the debate over Terry Schiavo.

Scholars have also differed in their descriptions of the relationship between the Christian Right and the GOP. Accounts generally fall into two broad theoretical camps emphasizing different aspects of the formation and mobilization of the Christian Right, and these can be summarized by two very different metaphors. The first depicts the Christian Right as a barbarian army invading the citadel of Republican Party politics, overrunning moderates, and taking control. The second account views Christian Right organizations as agents of the Republican Party, smooth talking evangelical voters into giving the party their votes, their volunteer hours, and their campaign contributions.

The first metaphor implies that the Christian Right began as an independent social movement external to the Republican Party. The movement chose to focus its efforts on electing public officials who shared their policy agenda, and chose the Republican Party as its vehicle in these electoral efforts. The movement's activists—often unskilled in the niceties of democratic politics—invaded the Republican Party and sought to take over its infrastructure to advance its aims. The second metaphor suggests that GOP factions identified white evangelical voters as a potential coalition partner who could be wooed to create a partisan majority. Christian Right organizations were formed to entice evangelical voters into politics and win their allegiance to the GOP, using primarily symbolic promises rather than concrete policy payoffs. Thus the Christian Right groups were always partisan organizations, following partisan goals.

Both accounts center on creation stories—accounts of how and why Christian Right groups were formed, of which resources were mobilized and how they were mobilized. Yet the Christian Right has worked within the Republican Party for nearly thirty years, and the relationship has certainly evolved over time. Regardless of the original impetus to form the groups, they have changed the Republican Party and been changed by their interactions with it. After describing the major competing narratives about the Christian Right and the GOP, I offer a third account that uses the metaphor of coevolution of party and movement.

The Christian Right as Social Movement: The "Barbarian Horde" Invades

The Christian Right has often been depicted as a social movement that sought to gain influence in and even take over the Republican Party. Christian conservatives were portrayed as an invading army seeking to redeem America, which chose partisan politics as its primary route. Book and article titles that mention "God's warriors," "Christian soldiers," "an army that meets on Sunday," and "an invisible army" became so common that many have been repeatedly recycled (Buell and Sigelman 1985; Green 1996; Guth et al. 1996; Wilcox 1992; Wilcox and Larson 2006; Wilcox, Linzey, and Jelen 1991; Wilcox and Robinson 2007b).[1] This language echoes that used by many Christian conservative activists, who often quote from biblical sources that speak of putting on the armor of God (see Ephesians 6:11). But the metaphor is more commonly used by party moderates, who have spoken of invasions, of Nazis in jackboots, and of fanatical activists marching to divine orders (Rozell and Wilcox 1996a).

Building the Movement Army

The metaphor of Christian Right as invading army is consistent with many theoretical accounts of social movement mobilization. These accounts argue that Christian fundamentalists and evangelicals mobilized in much the same way as earlier social movement activists, such as the civil rights movement, using religious and secular resources. Evangelical and fundamentalist Christians had various grievances against society and government policy. Religious leaders built common identities within this previously divided community, and used available resources to construct organizations that could mobilize activists, pressure parties, and lobby government officials. Because the media was markedly more hostile to the Christian Right than to feminists, environmentalists, and other contemporary social movement activists, evangelicals focused their efforts on winning elections rather than persuading the American people, and chose the most conservative party—the GOP—as their vehicle. But the ultimate goal was to change policies, not to elect Republicans.

Scholarly accounts of social movements typically start with grievances. In the case of the Christian Right, these are variously described as the growing secularization of society as embodied in public schools and mass media, the rise of the feminist movement and the legalization of abortion, and the rise of the gay and lesbian rights movement (Moen

1989; Oldfield 1996; Reed 1994; Wald, Owen, and Hill 1989). Other accounts focus on concerns over government regulation of religious schools and broadcasting. Evangelicals perceived that their lifestyle was under attack (Lorentzen 1980; Wilcox 1992), and that it was increasingly difficult to raise their children to share their values (Bates 1993). Some felt that social changes endangered America's special covenant with God (Lienesch 1993; Reed 1996; Wilcox, Linzey, and Jelen 1991).

Social movement activists helped build interpretive frames and social identities to unite evangelicals, much as the labor, civil rights, and feminist movements had done (Salisbury 1969; Snow et al. 1986; Wald, Silverman, and Fridy 2005). Early movement leaders such as Pat Robertson and Jerry Falwell mobilized existing resources to subsidize collective action costs. Falwell's status within the Baptist Bible Fellowship, and the resources of his television ministry allowed him to quickly assemble a national organization for the Moral Majority, at least on paper (Guth 1983; Liebman 1983). Robertson's television ministry and business empire were helpful to Christian Voice initially, and then later to his presidential campaign and the launching of the Christian Coalition (Brown, Powell, and Wilcox 1995). These groups sought to build united identities as evangelicals among those previously divided by theology (Wilcox, Rozell, and Gunn 1996), and to build organizations with enough resources to engage society and government at many levels.

Thus the Christian Right as an external army fits well with existing social movement theories (Wald, Silverman, and Fridy 2005). And once the army was assembled, it invaded the GOP, because its leaders came to believe that electoral politics were the only available means to change policy.

The Movement Army Invades the Party

The notion that the Christian Right invaded the Republican Party in the 1980s and 1990s is common lore among old-time GOP moderates and reinforced by documents and statements by Christian Right leaders. The Christian Coalition was put together from the ashes of Pat Robertson's failed presidential campaign—one that challenged the party establishment and mobilized activists who had not previously been Republicans, much less GOP activists.

The Christian Coalition's training manuals—especially the one distributed at the Christian Coalition's first Road to Victory conference, provided detailed instructions on party rules, and how to exploit them to win control of party committees. When asked by a reporter about a *Campaigns & Elections* article from 1994 that suggested that the Christian Right was the dominant force in GOP politics in eighteen states and a substantial force in thirteen others, Robertson replied, "We must complete the job in all 50 states. I'm glad to see all this that they say about 31, but that leaves, my goodness, a lot more. We've got more work to do. Because I like 100 percent, not 60 or 70" (Thomas Edsall, "Robertson Urges Christian Activists to Take Over GOP State Parties," *Washington Post*, September 10, 1995, A1).

Barbarian armies generally invade cities that are vulnerable, and which have resources that are worth exploiting. The Christian Right did not seek to win control of Republican Party committees in every state—instead, they chose states with permeable parties that could credibly contend for power in statewide elections. That is, the movement made strategic decisions concerning where it was worth trying to win control of party committees.

American political parties are porous, and open to outside influence (Rozell and Wilcox 1996a; Schwartz 1990, 2006), but the rules vary from state to state. Open nomination rules in some states made it easier for Christian Right activists to control the nomination process, and to win control of party committees (Green, Guth, and Wilcox 1998; Green, Rozell, and Wilcox 2001). In one county in Virginia, Christian Right activists took over a county GOP committee in a single evening, with plaques prepared in advance thanking the surprised party officers for their years of service (Rozell and Wilcox 1996a). But in states with less open rules, the Christian Right often did not try to win control.

Christian Right efforts to win control of party organizations were more concentrated in southern states in the 1980s and 1990s, because these parties were competitive in statewide elections and therefore worth controlling, and because there were more evangelicals in these states to support the invasion. Moreover, these Republican committees were typically smaller and less well established, because the GOP had only recently become competitive in these states and there was less opposition (Bruce 1995; Bullock and Smith 1997; Guth and Smith 1997; Swisher and Smith 1997).

In other states, such as West Virginia, New York, and California, the Christian Right made less effort to become active in GOP party politics. In West Virginia, the GOP was small and relatively weak, and unlikely to win statewide elections because of its antiunion policies; in New York the party rules were more established, and moderate elites better established, and in California the party was too diverse (Fetzer and Soper 1997; Rausch and Rausch 1997; Spitzer 2000).

The Christian Right as Partisan Mobilization: The Seduction of Evangelicals

The Christian Right can also be conceived as not an external social movement invading the party, but as a set of partisan organizations created to help the GOP woo evangelical voters. Party strategists believed that evangelical votes could transform the GOP into a majority party, and that symbolic positions on a few key issues was all that would be needed to win those votes. In this case, the Christian Right is less a spontaneous mobilization of angry fundamentalists and evangelicals, but instead a calculated mobilization by partisans who seduced evangelical voters with policy promises, many of which remain unfulfilled nearly thirty years later (Mohseni and Wilcox 2007).

The notion that political parties would build social movement organizations to help them mobilize voters is not new, nor is it unique to the United States. Nancy Rosenblum has referred to the associational nexus that surrounds religious parties and secular parties with religious factions—the network of civil society organizations that are bound to the party and aid in its mobilization (2003). The Christian Right can be conceived as part of the nexus of organizations that are created by party elites to help it raise money, win votes, and develop its ideas, along with many other quasi-party organizations.

Republican strategists were clearly involved in the early formation of Christian Right organizations and helped provide critical resources for these efforts. Recognizing a potential cleavage that could divide Democrats and win votes for Republicans, GOP strategists invested resources in evangelical entrepreneurs and created programs to train the evangelical rank and file to be good partisans (Leege et al. 2002).

After a series of small, isolated social movement protests in the late 1970s, GOP strategists planned the formation of the first wave of Christian Right groups. Longtime Republican activist Morton Blackwell described the strategy, calling evangelicals "the greatest tract of virgin timber on the political landscape. . . . We set about quite systematically to identify leaders, to teach them how to become effective, how to organize, how to communicate, how to raise funds, how to use direct-mail technology—skills to make them more effective" (cited in Martin 1996, 191). These activists sought out evangelical leaders such as Falwell, offered direct mail technology to fund his Moral Majority, and provided a variety of other resources including training and connections to party leaders.

Because theological and denominational divisions were strong in the evangelical community in the late 1970s, these strategists sought to create separate organizations to mobilize different religious constituencies. The Moral Majority was established to mobilize independent fundamentalists, Religious Roundtable was set up to appeal to the Southern Baptists, and Christian Voice was focused on mobilizing Pentecostals (Martin 1996). This strategy fit well with the short-term goal of electing a Republican president in 1980, but was less suitable for building a lasting social movement.

The role of partisan activists in mobilizing the Christian Coalition is even more substantial. The Republican National Senatorial Committee provided seed money to form the Christian Coalition, which hired long-time Republican operative Ralph Reed to direct its operations. President Bush in 1992 helped mount fundraising events for the coalition, which had pledged to use the money to identify and mobilize voters on his behalf. Many of the other top Christian Coalition leaders of the early 1990s—including Chuck Cunningham, D. J. Gribbon, and Guy Rodgers—had backgrounds in partisan mobilization and returned to these careers when the Christian Coalition faltered.

From the start, the Christian Coalition focused its energy on voter identification and mobilization in districts where Republican candidates were in close races. The organization's training manuals focused on identifying potential Republican voters, and its original contacting questions included candidate preference in 1992. Its voter guides were tailored to highlight and in some cases manufacture policy difference between Republican and Democratic candidates in elections that would lead evangelicals to favor GOP candidates. The distribution of the guides was targeted to swing districts. Thus the central efforts of the Christian Coalition were dictated by the electoral needs of the GOP.

Robertson publicly proclaimed the coalition's goal of defeating influential Democrats, and of helping the Republicans gain control of Congress by 1994 and the presidency by 2000. Although he sometimes remembered to couch his language to fit the nonpartisan requirements for a tax-exempt charity, he frequently forgot these niceties in his enthusiasm for his cause. Robertson told Miles O'Brien in a CNN interview on August 15, 1996, "so far, we have been more or less nonpartisan, but I think, rather clearly—Republican."

The Christian Coalition collapsed in the late 1990s, and Republican Party activists sought to duplicate the group's activities within the party. In 2004, the Bush administration sought to replicate the voter mobilizations of the Christian Coalition in house by acquiring the membership lists of conservative congregations and mailing carefully targeted communications (Wilcox and Robinson 2007a, 2007c). The Republican National Committee mailed pieces to select voters in West Virginia that extensively borrowed from earlier mailings by Christian Right organizations. Republican activists created ad hoc groups such as *Let Freedom Ring*, which distributed videos to churches in Ohio, Pennsylvania, and West Virginia touting Bush's personal faith, along with promises that any pastor who showed the video in church and who followed the guidelines would be defended in court from any IRS challenge.

To paraphrase Voltaire, when the Christian Coalition ceased to exist, it was necessary for the Republican Party to reinvent it. Nearly all of the activities that the Christian Coalition conducted on behalf of George H. W. Bush in 1992 occurred again in 2004 on behalf of George W. Bush, but they were done by the party, and not by an organization that was partially created by the party. The GOP cut back on its outsourcing of evangelical mobilization in 2004.

The Christian Right as GOP Faction

The narrative of the Christian Right as partisan mobilization fits well with theories of party competition, party factions, and partisan coalitions. In the United States, with large umbrella parties that combine multiple factions, strategists are constantly exploring for crosscutting and wedge issues that can divide the opposition and win intraparty and interparty elections. Evangelicals were identified as a likely target for GOP mobilization for a variety of reasons, including geography, issue positions, and infrastructure (Leege et al. 2002).

Conservative activists saw evangelicals as natural allies not only in interparty battles but for intraparty disputes as well. Paul Weyrich, Morton Blackwell, and others who sparked the formation of the Christian Right groups of the late 1970s believed that evangelical voters would help in their efforts to create a more conservative Republican party. But not all Republicans welcomed evangelicals to the table. The first "invasion" was welcomed by conservatives and opposed by moderates, including the business community.

But over time, the business community provided financial support for voter mobilization efforts and may have ultimately benefited the most from the incursion of the movement. Some theorists have suggested that business interests seek to build relatively low-cost coalitions that do not threaten their ability to win particularistic benefits (Bailey 2004). In this regard, the Christian Right was ultimately a very attractive coalition partner for business groups—Christian Right organizations have typically supported a wide array of cuts in taxes and regulations affecting businesses, and Christian Right groups have generally settled for symbolic victories that do not impose lifestyle costs on socially liberal business executives.

Thus the Christian Right may have been formed with the help of social conservatives, and then been supported by business moderates. Conservative GOP activists who were initially eager to help form the Moral Majority did not perhaps expect how easily a group like the Christian Coalition might be formed, or how easily it could be persuaded to place opposition to gasoline taxes and national health care at the top of its agenda. They did not expect the movement to settle so quickly for symbolic assurances rather than concrete victories.

Indeed, by many standards the courtship of evangelicals by the GOP has been nearly costless, for there have been few occasions where the party has been forced to deliver substantial policy concessions in exchange for votes. John Danforth's op-ed cited earlier suggested that the GOP had adopted Christian Right positions on a number of key issues. But on every one of these issues, the Christian Right has ultimately lost. The special bill for Terry Schiavo allowed her parents access to federal courts but gave them no legal basis to win an appeal, and did not apply to any similar case. Meanwhile, the GOP-controlled Congress was cutting funds to the national health care program that kept Schiavo alive. Christian conservatives limited the use of national funds for stem cell research, but this created opportunities for states and private industry to jump to the forefront of such research. Even in Danforth's home state, voters approved a measure to allow state funding of stem cell research, and elected a Democrat who favored that policy over an incumbent Republican who opposed it. And the national constitutional amendment to bar same-sex marriages was stalled, with no serious effort by George Bush or congressional Republicans to push it through, even when they had the majority in both chambers from 2005 to 2006.

Meanwhile, other elements of the GOP coalition enjoyed considerable success over the past several years. Businesses have repeatedly enjoyed both broad and narrow reductions in taxes and regulation. They have benefited from an explosion in earmarked contracts as well. Neoconservatives have directed key elements of foreign policy. The Christian Right has had far less influence on party priorities.

Social Movement or Partisan Mobilization?

These two creation narratives portray a very different relationship between the party and movement. In the first, the Christian Right is an invading army, defeating party moderates in internal battles and winning control of the party, which they use as a tool in policy battles. Over time, the Christian Right has won many party primaries and gradually the center of gravity of the party has swung to the right (Adams 1997), as Christian conservatives entered the party and some moderates left.

In the second, evangelicals are wooed by partisan actors who promise policy change on issues such as abortion, gay rights, and prayer in schools. But, like many partisan groups, evangelicals have no effective exit strategy, and thus little leverage in actual bargaining. The symbolic courtship has been especially intense in the past two presidential elections because voters have been relatively polarized and candidates have assumed that mobilization of the base was important, but the Christian Right has had few concrete victories in policy even when the GOP controlled national government.

The two narratives tell different stories, and are captured by different metaphors, but they are not entirely contradictory. The Christian Right of the 1970s was formed with the help of Republican operatives but also with many resources that were indigenous to the evangelical community. The first wave of activists had a distinctive policy agenda, and fought with party moderates while supporting Reagan's economic and foreign policies. The second wave, in the 1990s, was also a distinctive faction within the party, and although movement organizations sought to teach them the art of compromise, they continued to pressure the party to adopt more conservative social policies.

Clearly the Christian Right was not merely partisan mobilization, because surveys of donors to presidential candidates in 1988 showed that party moderates and conservatives were openly hostile to the Christian Right, and surveys of state party delegations in the 1990s frequently showed two polarized factions with large divisions on issues (Brown, Powell, Wilcox 1995; Rozell and Wilcox 1996b). This hostility was most evident in states that chose candidates through convention and caucuses, both because this nomination method afforded the Christian Right more power and because it forced moderates and evangelicals to interact personally.

Yet it is also evident that partisan strategists helped provide resources to some Christian Right groups, and shape the mobilization. GOP strategists believed that creating Christian Right groups could help them win elections, even if it caused friction within the party. And, over time, party activists sought to change the nature of evangelical mobilization, from an initially unpolished and controversial Moral Majority through the more domesticated Christian Coalition into eventually a party-based micro-targeted mobilization of evangelical voters. They sought to train Christian Right activists to be pragmatic and to compromise on issues, with the hope that they would settle for minor policy payoffs.

The Coevolution of the Christian Right and the GOP

A third metaphor may in the end be preferable to either that of the invading army or that of the party-organized seducer—a metaphor of coevolution. Over thirty years, the engagement between Christian conservatives and Republican regulars can be conceived as interactive and as changing both groups. The Christian Right of the 1990s was shaped by Republican operatives, but the GOP was different in 1990 than it had been in 1978 because of the incursion of evangelicals, and the Christian Right of the 1990s was also very different than it had been a decade earlier. The interaction between the Christian Right and the GOP changed both over the course of the past twenty-five years, and neither of the dominant metaphors of the creation of the movement is useful in understanding those changes.

Some studies have used evolutionary concepts to describe social movements, and a few have even referred to this body of research as a paradigm (Young 1988). But in fact there have been very few efforts to formalize and test theoretical predictions (Hannan, Carroll, and Polos 2003). Thus far, ecological models of social movements are probably better thought of as metaphors than as theories (Gaziano 1996), but they can provide insights into the relationship between parties and social movement organizations (Witko 2009).

Here I explore the metaphor of coevolution of the Christian Right and the GOP. In biology, species coevolve when they exert mutual influence on the reproductive success of the members of the paired species. This sometimes manifests as an arms races between predator and prey, such as the evolution of thorns on acacia trees and of long tongues by giraffes to circumvent those thorns, or various appendages on predatory insects that lead other insect species to develop armor. But coevolution can be cooperative as well, as when species of flowers evolve particular enticements that affect the reproductive success of various moth species that might help fertilize them. Species coevolve when their interactions affect the ability of individuals to pass along their genes—that is, the interaction between the two species helps some individuals at the expense of others.

It is probably most useful to depict the Republican Party and the Christian Right as overlapping subspecies with diverse population characteristics, in which some members are advantaged and others disadvantaged by the evolutionary interaction with the other subspecies. In this case, we are interested in the way that interactions between the Christian Right and the GOP have altered the ability of various members of the populations to reproduce themselves culturally. The incursion of evangelicals into the Republican Party makes it easier for some kinds of partisans to win elections and to write their preferences into law. And the active collaboration of Republican activists gave advantages to some Christian conservative leaders, groups, and ideologies in the competition with other evangelicals for members and activists.[2]

The Christian Right and the Evolution of the Republican Party

Within American political parties, factions compete for funds and votes, and also to determine the candidates who will represent the parties and the platforms on which those candidates. In the late 1970s and early 1980s, the natural ecology of the Republican Party was altered by the influx of first fundamentalist Christians, then by Pentecostal Christians and neo-evangelicals in the early 1990s. In some places, there were multiple and sometimes overlapping waves of mobilization, as in Virginia when Jerry Falwell mobilized independent Baptists in the early 1980s,

Michael Farris mobilized homeschool advocates in 1993, and then Oliver North mobilized charismatic Christians in 1994, two overlapping groups with somewhat different characteristics and issue agendas (Rozell and Wilcox 1996b).

Evolution is generally believed to happen most quickly in isolated, small populations (Gould 1989), and the impact of the Christian Right was most substantial in states where the party was relatively small, and where party rules allowed for easy penetration by social movements. Christian conservative activists seized control of party committees in the early 1990s in many states, and continue to exert influence (Hertzke 1993). They soon represented significant portions of delegates in state party conventions, and among primary election voters (Green, Rozell, and Wilcox 2001).

In these states, the Christian Right made available to GOP candidates and factions a new resource stream of dedicated evangelical activists and voters. Studies of Christian Right activists showed them to be long-time Republicans, many of whom had done little other than vote in past elections. Contrary to stereotypes, they were generally well educated and affluent, and were primarily distinctive in their orthodox religious views and the centrality of those beliefs to their political worldview. Many took extreme positions on political issues, and were uninterested in compromise with those inside or outside the party (Wilcox 1992; Wilcox, Linzey, and Jelen 1991).

In many of these states, Christian Right support was enough to enable extreme candidates to win nominations. Many of these candidates had little political experience, and were unable or unwilling to appeal to moderate voters. In most cases, these candidates lost in the general election, sometimes badly (Appleton and Francis 1997; Gilbert and Peterson 1995; Rozell and Wilcox 1996a). In some cases, these candidates hurt the rest of the GOP ticket.

The second wave of Christian Right mobilization with groups such as the Christian Coalition sought a more pragmatic strategy, and offered candidates special training in how to frame their issue positions in ways that could win evangelical votes without losing those of suburban moderates. The Christian Coalition also sought to channel evangelical activists into directional rather than positional politics—that is, to work and vote for GOP candidates who were at least somewhat more conservative than their Democratic opponents, even if their policy positions were far from ideal. Christian Coalition voter guides frequently exaggerated the real differences between the two parties' candidates by carefully choosing issues and ascribing positions to incumbents based on votes.[3] This favored candidates who were bilingual in their ability to use faith language in addressing evangelicals, but secular language in speaking with business groups, and who would focus their campaigns on unifying themes such as tax cuts rather than on abortion (Green, Rozell, and Wilcox 2003). Evangelical voters mobilized by the Christian Right frequently helped push this new type of Republican candidate to victory in close races. Over time, the impact of evangelicals on intra-party nominations moved the overall position of the party to the right on issues such as abortion (Adams 1997).

If the primary element of evolution is the gene, then the primary unit of cultural evolution might be the mime, the idea element. The ideas that the Republican Party came to stand for changed over time as the Christian Right fought to control party platforms. The movement surged into the GOP in the 1980 nominating process, and ended the longtime support in the platform for the ERA while inserting a pro-life plank. In 1996, the movement triumphed over more moderate elements in resisting a plank that would have called for tolerance of Republicans with divergent views on abortion. But the impact of the movement is probably even more significant on state party platforms in states such as Texas, where the platform devotes considerable space to movement agenda items (Wilcox and Robinson 2007b).

As Christian conservatives came to constitute an increasing share of party activists and primary election voters, potential candidates made strategic decisions in positioning themselves on the issue of abortion (Carmines and Woods 2002; Layman and Carsey 1998). GOP candidates increasingly found it vital to appeal in some way to evangelicals. Mean-while, social liberals flooded into the Democratic Party. This made it eas-ier for GOP candidates to appeal to evangelicals, stressing directional rather than positional cues. The social liberalism of Democratic candi-dates made it easier for Republican candidates to draw a stark contrast to their opponent.

This favored candidates who were more comfortable using religious language openly, and in sending subtle religious signals. George W. Bush had great advantages over his father in this regard, speaking pub-licly of his faith and also sending more narrow-cast signals in phrases such as the "wonder working power" of private charity, which had more religious resonance than his father's "a thousand points of light" (Wilcox and Robinson 2007a). Regular "God talk" by GOP candidates helped them send these signals over the previous decade, although De-mocrats have now begun to contest that language.

Perhaps the most important impact of the evangelical influx into the GOP was to transform it in Congress and many state legislatures from a perpetual opposition party to a governing party. Ironically, this may have served to strengthen the business wing of the party, as state and national party leaders rushed to build strong connections between busi-ness lobbyists and committee chairs to cement their new majority status (Berry and Wilcox 2007).

The Republican Party and the Evolution of the Christian Right

If the Christian Right helped to mold the GOP, the GOP surely sought to shape the evolution of the Christian Right as well. It is possible that without active GOP support, many of the most visible Christian Right organizations would not have formed. Although Jerry Falwell had made some halting steps onto the national stage before he was recruited by GOP strategists, he was dubious whether evangelicals could be mobilized into electoral politics. Without the promise of outside resources, the Moral Majority, and the Christian Coalition after it, might never have formed.

In the first wave of mobilization of the movement in the 1980s, Republican strategists sought short-term electoral gains by creating separate organizations to mobilize specific theological and denominational niches. This worked well in the 1980 and 1984 presidential elections, but it was less useful to an effort to build a cooperative social movement. Among the first wave of organizations, the Moral Majority was preeminent because of Falwell's unique resources and because fundamentalism provides theological resources that are easier to politicize than does evangelicalism and Pentecostalism (Jelen 1991). Many of the other first-wave organizations faded soon after the 1980 election.

But the visibility of the Moral Majority was a decided mixed blessing for the GOP. Falwell quickly became one of the most unpopular men in America, and state chapters of the Moral Majority frequently attracted attention for colorful actions—the Maryland chapter, for example, made a major push against what they deemed pornographic sugar cookies being sold in Ocean City. In many areas, support from the Moral Majority was a net negative in the campaign as Democrats mobilized moderates who feared fundamentalist extremism, frequently morphing GOP candidate's faces into that of Jerry Falwell in television ads.

When Ralph Reed and other GOP operatives planned the Christian Coalition, they sought to avoid the religious particularism that had plagued the 1980s groups. They sought to draw conservative Catholics, Pentecostals, fundamentalists, and evangelicals, and even, for a time, African Americans. This was a longer term strategy, consistent with Robertson's announced goal of a GOP congressional majority within six years and a conservative GOP president by 2000. Robertson clearly wanted to build a large grassroots organization. At the Road to Victory conference in 1991, he said, "I have big goals. . . . There are 175,000 precincts in America. The Precincts are where politics gets done, where the people live. . . . I want to see, by the end of this decade, ten keen, active members of the Christian Coalition in every single precinct in America, that's 175,000 activists" (Thomas B. Edsall, 1995. "Robertson Urges Christian Activists to Take Over GOP State Parties." *The Washington Post*, September 10, 1995, A24).[4]

In the Christian Right ecology of the 1990s, the Christian Coalition was the largest and most visible organization, and most clearly linked to the GOP and to partisan goals. The coalition worked to elect moderate Republicans in general elections, and argued for a seat at the table of compromise. Focus on the Family was the coalition's main competition, but it built on existing networks of state organizations and specialized tactically in lobbying state legislatures.[5] Focus was less pragmatic than the coalition, and more prone to stake extreme positions on issues. Its one-time affiliate, Family Research Council, found its niche in producing research reports that became the staple of the movement. Concerned Women for America continued, distinctive in the crusading themes in its rhetoric and in its focus on appealing to women. In addition, several organizations found smaller niches on particular issues, or pairs of issues. Citizens for Excellence in Education specialized in ideologically extreme appeals based on issues affecting schools. Traditional Values Coalition centered on sexuality in the media. As new issues arose, various groups sought to carve out financial support on these issues, or new groups were formed to mobilize concerned citizens.[6]

Republican operatives sought to advantage the Christian Coalition within the 1990s Christian Right. They channeled donors, facilitated ties with party officials, and frequently brought media attention to Ralph Reed. They especially channeled resources to the help finance the group's large voter identification and voter guide projects. The reliance on large donations was ultimately part of the downfall of the Christian Coalition, however, for the IRS eventually decided that its voter guides violated tax law.[7]

The effort to build the Christian Coalition was in many ways a studied reaction to the failures of the Moral Majority. The controversial televangelist Pat Robertson was pushed to the background, signing fundraising letters and giving occasional speeches but leaving the practical political work to seasoned professionals. GOP activists from other organizations were chosen to lead state and local chapters instead of local pastors, and the organization's message was centrally controlled. Ralph Reed was a more soothing voice than Jerry Falwell, Pat Robertson, or James Dobson of Focus on the Family.

Without large contributions by GOP activists to the Christian Coalition, it seems likely that Focus on the Family, with its more combative leader James Dobson, would have been the leading voice of the movement. With Focus at its head, the Christian Right might have demanded greater policy concessions in exchange for voter mobilization than the Christian Coalition did. It might have focused its energies in internal party battles instead of rallying behind moderate Republicans in battleground states. And it might have focused its energies on somewhat different issues than the Christian Coalition.

Thus the maturation of the Christian Right can be seen as a result of

Republican resources designed to influence the evolution of the movement—to create a domesticated and ecumenical version of the Moral
Majority. If the movement changed from one of amateur purists into
pragmatic professionals, this was at least partly because GOP activists
wanted to mold the movement into something that was easier to negotiate with and less threatening to moderate voters.

The more recent effort to move evangelical mobilization within the
GOP infrastructure, using carefully targeted communications, will have
important consequences if successful. First, direct mail, e-mail, and phone
mobilization carry less risk of countermobilization because moderate
voters are less likely to see the messages used to mobilize the movement. This might be especially important in elections where persuading
moderate voters is critical to victory. Second, if party candidates can mobilize evangelical voters directly, then movement organizations will
have less bargaining power in party coalitions because they will not be
responsible for delivering votes.

The greater religious ecumenical coalition in the Christian Right of
the 1990s was also aided and partially directed by Republican strategists, who sought to build a more powerful movement that would unite
"people of faith" rather than merely Bible Baptist Fellowship members.
This dialogue within conservative evangelicalism was helped along by
the growth of nondenominational megachurches, but in the 1990s GOP
resources clearly aided ecumenical groups, whereas in the late 1970s
they had flown to more particularistic organizations.

Some have argued that the involvement with the GOP changed
Christian Right activists over time—that involvement in Republican
politics has increased the democratic virtues of Christian conservatives,
leading them to be more tolerant and accommodating toward their political opponents. Christian Right training sessions frequently emphasized the role of mutual respect in the political process, and especially
the norms of civility. Moreover, operating in the Republican ecology
may have exposed Christian conservatives to differing viewpoints,
which may have led them to greater understanding of diverse viewpoints through intragroup deliberation (Shields 2007). Although survey
research does not consistently show that political involvement leads social movement activists toward greater tolerance (Dodson 1990; Wilcox
2003), it may well be true that Republican involvement helped those
who were more pragmatic have greater voice within in the movement.

The Evolution of Evangelical Politics

The relationship between the Christian Right and the GOP may have
helped shape the broader contours of evangelical politics in the United
States. The Christian Right represents only one element of evangelical

politics, which are complex and multifaceted. Liberal white evangelical groups supported George McGovern and are evident in organizations such as the Sojourners (Wallis 1996). African American evangelicals share a general moral conservatism with their white counterparts, but have distinctive views on economic issues and civil rights (Emerson and Smith 2000; Harris 1999). In many parts of the country, evangelicals once worked closely with mainline Protestants, who have a greater focus on social justice issues (Djupe and Gilbert 2003). It is therefore useful to take a step back and consider how the Republican Party has influenced the evolution of the broader evangelical political voice.

Although evangelicals have always been focused on personal piety and especially the control of sexuality, the religious community is broad, diverse, and energetic, and includes activists with issue concerns beyond abortion and gay marriage. In recent years, evangelicals have pressed for international policies to oppose genocide and the spread of AIDS, and to combat international poverty (Hertzke 2004). Evangelical groups have opposed global warming, and the torture of suspected terrorists. These issues have divided the community, but evangelicals are not unanimous on any issues, not even abortion or even same-sex marriage.

Republican support for the Christian Right, and for the Christian Coalition and similar electoral groups, gave reproductive advantage to one set of voices in the evangelical community. Groups that sought to mobilize evangelicals into GOP electoral politics had more resources than other groups, and were able to spread their ideas more effectively. Absent political resources to one set of groups in the community, evangelicalism might have years ago developed the richer and more diverse agenda that it is now beginning to articulate.

Moreover, the partisan edge to the political mobilization of evangelicals has centered on fear and even hatred of political enemies, because these emotions are useful in stimulating voter turnout. Direct mail solicitations from Moral Majority, Focus on the Family, and Christian Coalition warned of the evils of liberals, feminists, and environmentalists. Fundraising appeals warned that liberals would soon ban Christians from wearing religious jewelry, and would ban the Bible as hate speech. Movement groups pronounced with some considerable alliteration that the gay rights movement sought to "promote pedophiles as prophets of the New World Order" (Frank V. York and Robert H. Knight, "Homosexual Behavior and Pedophilia." Available at: http://us2000.org/cfmc/Pedophilia.pdf).

This type of polarized message is ideal for partisan mobilization, but it is less useful for religious proselytizing. Moral Majority leader Cal Thomas warned that the movement had been "blinded by might," drawn to the dichotomous worldview of Democratic evil and Republican virtue instead of the inclusive message of the gospel (Thomas and Dobson 2000). The additional resources of the Republican Party enabled the Christian Right of the 1970s to triumph over other, more moderate, and less angry voices in the community.[8]

Thus the partisan nature of the GOP involvement with evangelicals has advantaged those in the community who see the world as more deeply divided, who see their political enemies as more dangerous, and who fear liberals. If the Christian Right had not defined the evangelical voice in the 1970s, evangelicals might be working in more diverse coalitions and using less divisive rhetoric. That is, Republican intervention gave the Christian Right a reproductive advantage over other evangelical voices.

One interesting development in evangelical politics has grown out of Republican efforts to create a broader activist and electoral coalition, as well as the opportunities that partisan politics create for crosscutting conversations. Young and well-educated evangelicals are now engaged in serious theological conversations with Catholics—something that would have been unheard-of before the Christian Right was mobilized (Robinson 2008). The membership and leadership of the Moral Majority was hostile to Catholics (Wilcox 1989), but the Christian Coalition and Republican leaders encouraged Catholics and evangelicals to cooperate politically (Bendyna et al. 2001, 2000).

In these conversations, Catholics are acknowledging the importance of biblical sources in understanding God's will, and evangelicals are finding great depth in the long theological tradition of the Catholic Church. Evangelicals are finding their positions challenged on issues such as social welfare, immigration, and the death penalty, and refer to themselves as being "in the listening boat" on issues where they are under conviction.

In evolutionary theory, sometimes catastrophic events open up broad ecological niches. Impacts and eruptions can disrupt ecosystems, allowing new species to quickly evolve. At other times, more secular changes can occur in an environment, such as the glacier that divided the flycatchers in the United States into two separate avian subspecies.

Today much of the leadership of the Christian Right is aging and less active. Jerry Falwell has died, and Pat Robertson and James Dobson have health problems, and are all less active politically. Moreover, their extreme rhetoric makes them less attractive voices for younger evangelicals.

Meanwhile, a new generation of evangelical leaders is taking the stage, one that was heralded by scholars decades ago as having a new vision (Hunter 1987; Penning and Smidt 2002; Quebedeaux 1974, 1983). And the religious organization of evangelicalism is changing, with the relative power of fundamentalists giving way to nondenominational and theologically eclectic megachurches. Many young evangelical leaders see the United States not as a battleground, but as a mission ground, and are more willing to enter into conversations with those with whom they disagree.

It is possible to imagine, therefore, that a more complex and nuanced evangelical voice will arise in the next decade, despite GOP efforts to advantage certain voices in the community. It will probably be a conservative voice, especially on social issues, but it is likely that different members of the evangelical population will be able to draw on different sets of resources, and at least compete with the Christian Right.

Conclusion: Taking Stock of the Evolutionary Metaphor

These three metaphors have very different implications for understanding evangelical political mobilization. Perhaps more important, they suggest different sets of questions for political scientists and sociologists who study religious mobilization in politics, and also different sets of questions about the democratic effects of the Christian Right.

The first metaphor of the Christian Right as barbarian invaders of the GOP assumes that the Christian Right is a social movement that has made a tactical decision to work within the GOP. In this view, the Christian Right is very much like the labor, civil rights, feminist, and antiwar movements that influenced the development of the Democratic Party in the twentieth century. The metaphor invites us to focus attention on whether the Christian Right has won control of state and local party organizations, and the influence of the movement on the priorities of Republicans in government. It invites us to balance the democratic effects of increased participation by a disenfranchised minority which is noted for intolerance and extreme political views.

The second metaphor, of the Christian Right as partisan seduction, suggests that the movement is different from those earlier social movements because partisan actors played a significant role in recruiting movement leaders and forming movement organizations. This metaphor invites us to focus on the promises made to evangelical voters, and the nature of appeals by party elites. It also invites us to consider the democratic effects of creating a majority Republican coalition by primarily symbolic promises to evangelicals, and to consider what the party has actually given to evangelicals in terms of concrete policy.

These are all important questions, but they have been extensively explored over the past twenty years. Moreover, deciding between these two competing stories requires us to read a great deal into a limited set of facts—the NRSC startup grant to the Christian Coalition, the recruitment of Jerry Falwell by GOP conservative activists, and activities by the movement in local and state political parties.

The evolutionary metaphor frees us from needing to decide if the Christian Right is an external force seeking to influence the party, or a partisan mobilization aimed to helping the party win elections. By thinking of the Republican Party and Christian conservatives as related subspecies, we can focus on how the two have influenced each other over more than a quarter century of interaction. It focuses our attention on how the relationship has changed both the GOP and the Christian Right over time, and how it has influenced evangelical's political voices. Thus the relationship between the Republican Party and the movement is different in 2008 than it was in 1978, because both the Republican Party and the Christian Right have changed as a result of their mutual interactions.

Evolution occurs when a particular set of genes confers reproductive advantages on certain elements of the population. The Republican Party has conferred certain advantages on some Christian Right groups, and in the process helped produce a movement that has been helpful to the party in close elections. By channeling resources to the Christian Coalition in the late 1980s, GOP activists helped elevate the group at the expense of more radical and uncompromising organizations. In turn, the Christian Coalition was less threatening to moderate voters, and willing to concentrate its resources in races where moderate Republicans were running.

Similarly, the Christian Right has helped certain types of candidates and platform planks defeat other types of candidates and ideas within the Republican Party. There is little doubt that the party's congressional delegation is a much different one than when the Christian Right began. The Republican Party caucuses in Iowa in 1980 were won by George W. Bush, who defeated Ronald Reagan among party activists. In 2008, Mike Huckabee beat George Romney in a contest that centered on religious identity.

The Republican Party's cultivation of the Christian Right has also altered the broader ecology of evangelical politics, giving additional resources to one set of voices and seeking to quiet others. Groups closest to the GOP have sought to quiet the National Association of Evangelicals on issues such as global warming and torture, for example, and to keep evangelicals focused on issues that help the GOP in elections. Meanwhile, voices that have sought to reach compromise on these issues by adopting policies that might reduce the number of abortions without outlawing the procedure have subsisted on many fewer resources.

It is also worth noting that the coevolution of the Christian Right and the Republican Party has influenced the evolution of the Democratic Party as well. The visible presence of Jerry Falwell and Pat Robertson made it attractive for the Democratic Party to run advertisements in many parts of the country linking them to GOP candidates. This inevitably attracted more secular activists to the Democratic Party, which in turned pushed more observant Christians to the Republicans. In the 2000 and 2004 presidential elections, Democratic candidates found it difficult to speak authentically about their faith, although both Bush and Kerry were personally religious men.

In the past few years, however, Democratic groups have spent much time, effort, and money on efforts to reframe some of their key agenda as based in moral and religious values in an effort to win votes of religiously motivated moderates. Indeed, issues such as support for health care for the poor, for laws protecting the environment, for progressive taxation, and other key Democratic issues were originally motivated by faith concerns among progressive Catholics and mainline Protestants; the party's incoherent message on those values is a more recent result of the coevolution of the Christian Right and the GOP. Today candidates in both parties are anxious to establish their religious credentials early in the campaign, and to decide on an approach to discussing issues of faith.

In the 2008 campaign, Barack Obama worked hard on an outreach to moderate evangelicals, and was successful in some states, especially among the young. Obama's invitation to Rick Warren to deliver the inaugural invocation met with strong opposition from cultural liberals, who focused especially on Warren's endorsement of a California proposition that eliminated same-sex marriage in that state. Democratic efforts to woo younger evangelicals may well alter the resources available to social moderates in the party, and at the same time engagement with Democrats may affect the agenda of evangelicals.

Perhaps the most substantial impact of the coevolution of the Christian Right and the GOP has been an escalation of faith-based language and symbols in electoral campaigns. Yet the elevation of religious talk in national elections has not been accompanied with a richer dialogue on moral issues, because it is advantageous for parties to simplify issues and to build resentment. It may well be that the coevolution of the Republican Party and the Christian Right has served to hinder the kind of cultural deliberative conversation that evangelicals must engage in to convince the culture on any of the issues in their agenda.

Notes

1. Thanks to John Green for his suggestions on titles for my work over the years.
2. There is a certain irony in the use of an evolutionary metaphor to describe changes in a social movement that throughout the twentieth century has consistently opposed the teaching of evolution in the public schools. Those

within the movement would willingly talk of changes in the movement in terms of "maturation," however, and argue that today's Christian Right is more sophisticated than that of the 1970s. And scholars have written of this maturation, using at times even the language of evolution (see Moen 1989, 1994; Rozell and Wilcox 1996a).

3. In general, Christian Coalition voter guides were reasonably accurate in portraying ideology of incumbents, but on occasion they used votes such as for the Washington, D.C., city budget to assign to a Democratic candidate a position supporting taxpayer funded abortions. Republicans who voted for the city budget did not earn the same designation.

4. The ambitiousness of this goal is disguised by Robertson's poor math. Ten activists in 175,000 precincts translates to 1,750,000.

5. Focus on the Family is a larger radio and publication ministry, which became more politically active in the 1990s. It began to affiliate with state chapters during this period, often jointly with Family Research Council.

6. Most interesting in the Christian Right is the continued success of CWA, which was far eclipsed by first the Moral Majority and then Christian Coalition and Focus on the Family in the media spotlight, but which has survived and prospered throughout the era. The organizational base of CWA in local prayer groups kept its costs low, and its more diverse financial base kept it out of direct competition with other organizations. Although CWA has worked at times with other organizations, it is primarily steered its own path within the movement.

7. The group's voter guides were thinly disguised partisan instruments, but they would have been fully legal as independent expenditures by a PAC. But PACs must raise their funds through small contributions from many people, and the Christian Coalition chose to forgo the building of a PAC because it was easier to line up a few big donors. Once the legal problems of the organization became evident, direct mail and telemarketing revenues began to plummet.

8. Secular and liberal opponents of the Christian Right frequently use similarly scary images to raise money from those who oppose the Christian Right.

References

Adams, Greg D. 1997. "Abortion: Evidence of an Issue Evolution." *American Journal of Political Science* 41(3): 718–37.

Appleton, Andrew M., and Daniel Francis. 1997. "Washington: Mobilizing for Victory." In *God at the Grassroots 1996: The Christian Right in the 1996 Elections*, edited by Mark J. Rozell and Clyde Wilcox. Lanham, Md.: Rowman & Littlefield.

Bailey, Michael. 2004. "The (Sometimes Surprising) Consequences of Societally Unrepresentative Contributors on Legislative Responsiveness." *Business and Politic* 6(3): 1087.

Bates, Stephen. 1993. *Battleground: One Mother's Crusade, the Religious Right, and the Struggle for Control of Our Classrooms*. New York: Poseidon Press.

Bendyna, Mary, John C. Green, Mark J. Rozell, and Clyde Wilcox. 2000.

"Catholics and the Christian Right: A View from Four States." *Journal for the Scientific Study of Religion* 39(3): 321–32.

———. 2001. "Uneasy Alliance: Conservative Catholics and the Christian Right." *Sociology of Religion* 62(1): 51–64.

Berry, Jeffrey M., and Clyde Wilcox. 2007. *The Interest Group Society*. New York: Pearson Longman.

Brown, Clifford W., Lynda W. Powell, and Clyde Wilcox. 1995. *Serious Money: Fundraising and Contributing in Presidential Nomination Campaigns*. New York: Cambridge University Press.

Bruce, John M. 1995. "Texas: The Emergence of the Christian Right." In *God at the Grassroots: The Christian Right in the 1994 Elections*, edited by Mark J. Rozell and Clyde Wilcox. Lanham, Md.: Rowman & Littlefield.

Buell, Emmett, and Lee Sigelman. 1985. "An Army that Meets Every Sunday? Popular Support for the Moral Majority in 1980." *Social Science Quarterly* 66(4): 426–34.

Bullock, Charles S. III, and Mark S. Smith. 1997. "Georgia: Purists, Pragmatists, and Electoral Outcomes." In *God at the Grassroots, 1996: The Christian Right in the 1996 Elections*, edited by Mark J. Rozell and Clyde Wilcox. Lanham, Md.: Rowman & Littlefield.

Carmines, Edward G., and James Woods. 2002. "The Role of Party Activists in the Evolution of the Abortion Issue." *Political Behavior* 24(4): 361–77.

Djupe, Paul A., and Christopher P. Gilbert. 2003. *The Prophetic Pulpit: Clergy, Churches, and Communities in American Politics*. Lanham, Md.: Rowman & Littlefield.

Dodson, Debra L. 1990. "Socialization of Party Activists: National Convention Delegates, 1972–81." *American Journal of Political Science* 34(4): 1119–141.

Emerson, Michael O., and Christian Smith. 2000. *Divided by Faith: Evangelical Religion and the Problem of Race in America*. New York: Oxford University Press.

Fetzer, Joel, and J. Christopher Soper. 1997. "California: Between a Rock and a Hard Place." In *God at the Grassroots 1996: The Christian Right in the 1996 Elections*, edited by Mark J. Rozell and Clyde Wilcox. Lanham, Md.: Rowman & Littlefield.

Gaziano, Emanuel. 1996. "Ecological Metaphors as Scientific Boundary Work: Innovation and Authority in Interwar Sociology and Biology." *The American Journal of Sociology* 101(4): 874–907.

Gilbert, Christopher P., and David A. Peterson. 1995. "Minnesota: Christians and Quistians in the GOP." In *God at the Grassroots: The Christian Right in the 1994 Elections*, edited by Mark J. Rozell and Clyde Wilcox. Lanham, Md.: Rowman & Littlefield.

Gould, Stephen Jay. 1989. *Wonderful Life: The Burgess Shale and the Nature of History*. New York: W. W. Norton.

Green, John C. 1996. "A Look at the "Invisible Army": Pat Robertson's 1988 Activist Corps." In *Religion and the Culture Wars: Dispatches from the Front*, edited by John C. Green, James L. Guth, Corwin E. Smidt, and Lyman A. Kellstedt. Lanham, Md.: Rowman & Littlefield.

Green, John C., James L. Guth, and Clyde Wilcox. 1998. "Less than Conquerors: The Christian Right in State Republican Parties." In *Social Movements and*

American Political Institutions, edited by Anne N. Costain and Andrew S. Mc-Farland. Lanham, Md.: Rowman & Littlefield.

Green, John C., Mark J. Rozell, and Clyde Wilcox. 2001. "Social Movements and Party Politics: The Case of the Christian Right." *Journal for the Scientific Study of Religion* 40(3): 413–26.

———. 2003. "The Christian Right's Long March." In *The Christian Right in American Elections: Marching to the Millennium*, edited by John C. Green, Mark J. Rozell, and Clyde Wilcox. Washington, D.C.: Georgetown University Press.

Guth, James L. 1983. "The New Christian Right." In *The New Christian Right: Mobilization and Legitimation*, edited by Robert C. Liebman and Robert Wuthnow. New York: Aldine Publishing.

Guth, James L., and Oran P. Smith. 1997. "South Carolina Christian Right: Just Part of the Family Now?" In *God at the Grassroots 1996: The Christian Right in the 1996 Elections*, edited by Mark J. Rozell and Clyde Wilcox. Lanham, Md.: Rowman & Littlefield.

Guth, James L., John C. Green, Lyman A. Kellstedt, and Corwin E. Smidt. 1996. "Onward Christian Soldiers: Religious Activist Groups in American Politics." In *Religion and the Culture Wars: Dispatches from the Front*, edited by John C. Green, James L. Guth, Lyman A. Kellstedt, and Corwin E. Smidt. Lanham, Md.: Rowman & Littlefield.

Hannan, Michael T., Glenn R. Carroll, and Laszlo Polos. 2003. "The Organizational Niche." *Sociological Theory* 21(4): 309–40.

Harris, Fredrick C. 1999. *Something Within: Religion in African-American Political Activism*. New York: Oxford University Press.

Hertzke, Allen D. 1993. *Echoes of Discontent: Jesse Jackson, Pat Robertson, and the Resurgence of Populism*. Washington, D.C.: CQ Press.

———. 2004. *Freeing God's Children: The Unlikely Alliance for Global Human Rights*. Lanham, Md.: Rowman & Littlefield.

Hunter, James Davison. 1987. *Evangelicalism: The Coming Generation*. Chicago: University of Chicago Press.

Jelen, Ted G. 1991. *The Political Mobilization of Religious Beliefs*. New York: Praeger.

Layman, Geoffrey, and Tom Carsey. 1998. "Why Do Party Activists Convert? An Analysis of Individual-Level Change on the Abortion Issue." *Political Research Quarterly* 51(3): 723–40.

Leege, David C., Kenneth D. Wald, Brian S. Krueger, and Paul D. Mueller. 2002. *The Politics of Cultural Differences: Social Change and Voter Mobilization Strategies in the Post-New Deal Period*. Princeton, N.J.: Princeton University Press.

Liebman, Robert C. 1983. "Mobilizing the Moral Majority." In *The New Christian Right: Mobilization and Legitimation*, edited by Robert C. Liebman and Robert Wuthnow. New York: Aldine Publishing.

Lienesch, Michael. 1993. *Redeeming America: Piety and Politics in the New Christian Right*. Chapel Hill: University of North Carolina Press.

Lorentzen, Louise. 1980. "Evangelical Life Style Concerns Expressed as Political Action." *Sociological Analysis* 41(1): 144–54.

Martin, William. 1996. *With God on Our Side: The Rise of the Religious Right in America*. New York: Broadway Books.

Moen, Matthew C. 1989. *The Christian Right and Congress*. Tuscaloosa: University of Alabama Press.

————. 1994. "From Revolution to Evolution: The Changing Nature of the Christian Right." *Sociology of Religion* 55(3): 345–57.

Mohseni, Payam, and Clyde Wilcox. 2007. "Religion and Political Parties." In *Handbook of Religion & Politics*, edited by Jeffrey Haynes. London: Routledge.

Oldfield, Duane M. 1996. *The Right and the Righteous: The Christian Right Confronts the Republican Party.* Lanham, Md.: Rowman & Littlefield.

Penning, James M., and Corwin E. Smidt. 2002. *Evangelicalism : the next generation.* Grand Rapids, Mich.: Baker Academic.

Quebedeaux, Richard. 1974. *The Young Evangelicals; Revolution in Orthodoxy.* New York: Harper & Row.

————. 1983. *The New Charismatics II.* San Francisco: Harper & Row.

Rausch, John David Jr., and Mary S. Rausch. 1997. "West Virginia: In Search of the Christian Right." In *God at the Grassroots 1996: The Christian Right in the 1996 Elections*, edited by Mark J. Rozell and Clyde Wilcox. Lanham, Md.: Rowman & Littlefield.

Reed, Ralph E. 1994. *Politically Incorrect: The Emerging Faith Factor in American Politics.* Dallas, Tex.: Word Books Pub Group.

————. 1996. *Active Faith: How Christians Are Changing the Soul of American Politics.* New York: Free Press.

Robinson, Carin. 2008. "Doctrine, Discussion and Disagreement: Evangelical and Catholics Together in American Politics." Ph.D. diss., Georgetown University.

Rosenblum, Nancy L. 2003. "Religious Parties, Religious Political Identity, and the Cold Shoulder of Liberal Democratic Thought." *Ethical Theory and Moral Practice* 6(1): 25–53.

Rozell, Mark J., and Clyde Wilcox. 1996a. *Second Coming: The New Christian Right in Virginia Politics.* Baltimore, Md.: Johns Hopkins University Press.

————. 1996b. "Second Coming: The Strategies of the New Christian Right." *Political Science Quarterly* 111(2): 271–94.

Salisbury, Robert H. 1969. "An Exchange Theory of Interest Groups." *Midwest Journal of Political Science* 13(1): 1–32.

Schwartz, Mildred A. 1990. *The Party Network: The Robust Organization of Illinois Republicans.* Madison: University of Wisconsin Press.

————. 2006. *Party Movements in the United States and Canada: Strategies of Persistence.* Lanham, Md.: Rowman & Littlefield.

Shields, Jon A. 2007. "Between Passion and Deliberation: The Christian Right and Democratic Ideals." *Political Science Quarterly* 12(1): 89–113.

Snow, David A., E. Burke Rochford Jr., Steven K. Worden, and Robert D. Benford. 1986. "Frame Alignment Processes, Micromobilization, and Movement Participation." *American Sociological Review* 51(4): 464–81.

Spitzer, Robert J. 2000. "New York, New York: Start Spreadin' the News." In *Prayers in the Precincts: The Christian Right in the 1998 Elections*, edited by John C. Green, Mark J. Rozell, and Clyde Wilcox. Washington, D.C.: Georgetown University Press.

Swisher, Ray, and Christian Smith. 1997. "North Carolina: Jesse's Last Stand? The Christian Right in the Elections." In *God at the Grassroots 1996: The Christian Right in the 1996 Elections*, edited by Mark J. Rozell and Clyde Wilcox. Lanham, Md.: Rowman & Littlefield.

Thomas, Cal, and Ed Dobson. 2000. *Blinded by Might: Why the Religious Right Can't Save America*. Grand Rapids, Mich.: Zondervan Publishing.

Wald, Kenneth D., Dennis E. Owen, and Samuel S. Hill Jr. 1989. "Evangelical Politics and Status Issues." *Journal for the Scientific Study of Religion* 28(1): 1–16.

Wald, Kenneth D., Adam L. Silverman, and Kevin Fridy. 2005. "Making Sense of Religion in Political Life." *Annual Review of Political Science* 8(2005): 121–43.

Wallis, Jim. 1996. *Who Speaks for God? A New Politics of Compassion, Community, and Civility*. New York: Delacorte Press.

Wilcox, Clyde. 1989. "Evangelicals and the Moral Majority." *Journal for the Scientific Study of Religion* 28(4): 400–14.

———. 1992. *God's Warriors: The Christian Right in Twentieth Century America*. Baltimore, Md.: Johns Hopkins University Press.

———. 2003. "The Christian Right and Democratic Virtues." Marburg, Germany: European Consortium for Political Research.

Wilcox, Clyde, and Carin Larson. 2006. *Onward Christian Soldiers: The Christian Right in American Politics*, 3rd ed. Boulder, Colo.: Westview Press.

Wilcox, Clyde, and Carin Robinson. 2007a. "The Faith of George W. Bush: The Personal, Practical, and Political." In *Religion and American Presidents*, edited by Mark J. Rozell and Gleaves Whitney. New York: Palgrave McMillan.

———. 2007b. *Onward Christian Soldiers: The Christian Right in American Politics*, 3rd ed. Boulder, Colo.: Westview Press.

———. 2007c. "Prayers, Parties, and Preachers: The Evolving Nature of Political and Religious Mobilization." In *Religion and Political Mobilization in the United States*, edited by Matthew J. Wilson. Washington, D.C.: Georgetown University Press.

Wilcox, Clyde, Sharon Linzey, and Ted G. Jelen. 1991. "Reluctant Warriors: Premillennialism and Politics in the Moral Majority." *Journal for the Scientific Study of Religion* 30(3): 245–58.

Wilcox, Clyde, Mark J. Rozell, and Roland Gunn. 1996. "Religious Coalitions in the New Christian Right." *Social Science Quarterly* 77(3): 543–59.

Witko, Christopher. 2009. "The Ecology of Party-Organized Interest Relationships." *Polity* 41(2): 211-34.

Young, Ruth C. 1988. "Is Population Ecology a Useful Paradigm for the Study of Organizations?" *The American Journal of Sociology* 94(1): 1–24.

Index

Boldface numbers refer to figures and tables